The Other '68ers

The Other '68ers

*Student Protest and Christian Democracy
in West Germany*

ANNA VON DER GOLTZ

OXFORD
UNIVERSITY PRESS

OXFORD
UNIVERSITY PRESS

Great Clarendon Street, Oxford, OX2 6DP,
United Kingdom

Oxford University Press is a department of the University of Oxford.
It furthers the University's objective of excellence in research, scholarship,
and education by publishing worldwide. Oxford is a registered trade mark of
Oxford University Press in the UK and in certain other countries

First Edition published in 2021

Impression: 1

Published in the United States of America by Oxford University Press
198 Madison Avenue, New York, NY 10016, United States of America

British Library Cataloguing in Publication Data
Data available

Library of Congress Control Number: 2021934763

ISBN 978–0–19–884952–0

DOI: 10.1093/oso/9780198849520.001.0001

Printed and bound by
CPI Group (UK) Ltd, Croydon, CR0 4YY

To Nico and Jasper

Acknowledgements

This book, my second, took a lot longer to research and write than my first. I originally conceptualized the idea for *The Other '68ers* and began the research in 2008, while still a Prize Fellow at Magdalen College, Oxford. I was then side-tracked by other projects and life events, among them a move to the United States. Along the way, I received support from numerous institutions and individuals. It is a pleasure to finally be able to express my gratitude here.

The Fellows of Magdalen College provided funds and an intellectual home in the project's very early stages. While in Oxford, I benefited immeasurably from collaborating with my colleagues on the oral history project that became *Europe's 1968: Voices of Revolt* (Oxford University Press, 2013). It certainly distracted me from thinking about the centre-right, but this would have been a very different—and, I'm convinced, a much less interesting—book if I had not learned a great deal about doing oral history and the 1960s in Europe from my interlocutors. In particular, I want to thank Robert Gildea, James Mark, Anette Warring, John Davis, and Juliane Fürst for intellectual stimulation and their friendship.

In 2008, I had the good fortune to meet Bernd Weisbrod at a conference, who then invited me to be a postdoctoral visiting fellow at the Graduate School on 'Generations in Modern History' at the University of Göttingen. His and the group's nuanced take on generational histories has influenced my thinking on the topic in lasting ways. I have benefited immensely from his spirited and constructive critique and from participating in the workshops and conferences that different members of the Graduate School organized over the years. I am extremely grateful to all its members, not least to Uffa Jensen, who helped to organize my stay.

An Early Career Fellowship from the Leverhulme Trust brought me to the History Faculty at the University of Cambridge and to Wolfson College, for the better part of 2011. There, I profited, in particular, from the productive exchanges in Richard J. Evans's weekly workshop on German history and from the discussions in the Modern European History Seminar.

Since taking up my post at Georgetown University in 2012, a semester of Junior Faculty Leave, several Summer Academic Grants, a grant for a manuscript workshop from the Mortara Center, and continuous research support from the BMW Center for German and European Studies (CGES) and the School of Foreign Service (SFS) helped to facilitate steady progress on the book. Faculty and staff in CGES, SFS, and the History Department have all provided a wonderful home base. A Kluge Fellowship from the Library of Congress allowed me to start drafting the first chapters while looking out over the US Supreme Court.

I am grateful to the many colleagues in Germany, Britain, and the United States, who invited me to present my arguments in various research seminars over the years: the fellows at the German Historical Institutes in London and Washington, D.C., Alexander Sedlmaier in Bangor, Paul Betts (then) at Sussex, Dieter Gosewinkel at the WZB, Paul Nolte in Berlin, Andreas Rödder in Mainz, Frank Bösch and Martin Sabrow in Potsdam, Nick Stargardt in Oxford, the organizers of *Der Kreis* in Berkeley, especially Elena Kempf, Jim Brophy in Delaware, Jennifer Allen at Yale, and, last but not least, my colleagues in Georgetown's History Faculty Seminar. Critical feedback on numerous conference presentations further helped me to develop and refine my arguments.

Various colleagues read my original book proposal and drafts of this manuscript or related articles I published, and their feedback has been invaluable in bringing this book to completion: Martin Conway, Mario Daniels, Michael David-Fox, David Collins, Jim Collins, Michael Kazin, Richard Kuisel, Eric Langenbacher, Jamie Martin, Aviel Roshwald, Jordan Sand, Lu Seegers, Eva-Maria Silies, Quinn Slobodian, Bernd Weisbrod, Judith Tucker, and Thomas Zimmer. Several anonymous reviewers also offered criticism that was always helpful and deeply appreciated.

At Georgetown, I have taught various courses on the 1960s and learned a lot from the many lively conversations with my terrific students. Special thanks to the undergraduate freshmen in my proseminar on '1968 in Europe' and to the graduates in 'The 1960s in Transnational Perspective', a seminar I happily co-taught with Michael Kazin.

Several Georgetown graduate students in the MA program in German and European Studies and in the History PhD program helped with bits of research, translations, and copy editing. My sincere thanks to Robert Mevissen, Rebecca Payne, Hannah Morris, Ricky Bordelon, Alexander Finn Macartney, Alistair Somerville, Thom Loyd, Juliet Kelso, and Brent McDonnell for all their work.

Oral history interviews are one major group of sources for this study, and I am extremely grateful to the former centre-right activists who took time out of their often busy schedules to talk to me about their political lives. Many of them also kindly shared documents in their possession. Even if they do not agree with all of its analysis, I could not have written this book without their help.

It has been a great experience to work with Oxford University Press again. Thanks to Cathryn Steele, Stephanie Ireland, Katie Bishop, and Thomas Deva for shepherding the manuscript through peer review and production.

Family and friends on both sides of the Atlantic have provided much needed emotional and logistical support, not least by housing, feeding, and entertaining me while doing archival work and interviews. A special shout-out to Henrike Heick, Sandra Jasper, Sarah Jastram, Kim Klehmet, and Birgitta Ashoff. My adopted 'DC family' has helped me to feel at home in a city that I hardly knew before moving to the United States and reminds me almost daily that there are even more enjoyable things in life than writing books. I am particularly grateful to Ben Mahler for his help with some of the illustrations.

This study owes some of its inspiration to my actual family, probably in more ways than they are aware. I have often thought that my interest in the subject of *The Other '68ers* must have been piqued early on, when observing some of the family dynamics on display in my grandparents' house in Essen, a building erected on the visible remnants of a Nazi-era anti-aircraft position on grounds owned by the Krupp dynasty. My mother, Heide, always seemed to stand out in these surroundings. At the age of eighteen, she had left the Catholic Church that meant so much to her father, who had consistently voted for the Christian Democrats since the war. The first one in her family to attend university, she moved to Freiburg to study English and Geography in the late 1960s, eventually becoming a public school teacher in Bremen. Later on, she worked in education in a local museum of ethnology and natural history. She never married and raised me by herself in a culturally left-wing, urban milieu where everybody rode their bike, even when it rained. At our annual Christmas Day gathering in Essen, I not only noticed how different she was from her parents in almost every respect but would often also see her spar with her brother-in-law. Like my mother, he had been born in 1948, and he later married her younger sister. Like my mother, he had been a first-generation student, and they both often shared stories about growing up in fairly chaotic conditions in postwar West Germany. However, in most other ways, they were quite different, including in their politics—although neither one of them was overtly political and both had an argumentative streak. He had studied law in Marburg, joined a fraternity, pursued a thriving career in the insurance industry, made his home in a Cologne suburb with my aunt and my two cousins, and played golf in his spare time. I always found it intriguing that he and my mother had been born in the same year and both been students in the 1960s and yet fashioned such different personas and lives. The annual scenes in Essen no doubt sparked my interest in postwar generational dynamics, but they also must have made me intuitively sceptical of overly deterministic histories of generation.

After her retirement, my mother transcribed many of the interviews on which parts of this book are based. In the process, we had numerous enlightening conversations about how she had experienced the years around 1968. It is one of my great regrets that I did not complete this book during her lifetime. She died in 2017—far too early at merely sixty-eight. I miss her every day.

Luckily, I still have wonderful family members in my life: among them my aunt Gaby, my mother-in-law Gisi, and Christoph and Sofia, my brother- and sister-in-law. They have all been tremendously supportive, especially in the past few years.

This book is dedicated to the two people closest to me: my husband, Nico, and my son, Jasper, who was born in 2015. Nico has been an enthusiastic and patient supporter of this work from the very beginning. Jasper remains unimpressed, because the book is shorter than the first volume of Harry Potter. Both fill my life with love and daily laughter. Writing this as I am, in the midst of a global pandemic that has brought life as we knew it to a near standstill, it is difficult to imagine what the future holds. But I am immensely grateful for every day that the three of us get to spend together.

Anna von der Goltz

Washington, D.C.,
July 2020

Contents

Abbreviations

ACDP	Archiv für Christlich-Demokratische Politik
ACSP	Archiv für Christlich-Soziale Politik
ADS	Aktionskomitee Demokratischer Studenten (Action Committee of Democratic Students)
AHR	American Historical Review
AI	Amnesty International
AdsD	Archiv der sozialen Demokratie
APO	Außerparlamentarische Opposition (Extraparliamentary Opposition)
ArchAPO	Archiv APO und soziale Bewegungen
ARD	Arbeitsgemeinschaft der öffentlich-rechtlichen Rundfunkanstalten der Bundesrepublik Deutschland (Germany's premier public television station)
AUSS	Aktionszentrum Unabhängiger und Sozialistischer Schüler (Action Centre of Independent and Socialist Pupils)
BAK	Bundesarchiv, Koblenz
BfV	Bundesamt für Verfassungsschutz (Federal Office for the Protection of the Constitution)
BFW	Bund Freiheit der Wissenschaft (Association for the Protection of Academic Freedom)
BRD	Bundesrepublik Deutschland (Federal Republic of Germany)
BSU	Bonner Studentenunion (Bonn Student Union)
CDU	Christlich Demokratische Union (Christian Democratic Union)
CIA	Central Intelligence Agency
CSU	Christlich Soziale Union (Christian Social Union)
DKP	Deutsche Kommunistische Partei (German Communist Party)
DM	Demokratische Mitte (Democratic Centre)
Dpa	Deutsche Presseagentur (German Press Agency)
DSU	Deutsche Studentenunion (German Student Union)
EDS	European Democrat Students
epd	Evangelischer Pressedienst
EZA	Evangelisches Zentral Archiv
FAZ	Frankfurter Allgemeine Zeitung
FCS	Federation of Conservative Students (United Kingdom)
FDJ	Freie Deutsche Jugend (Free German Youth)
FDP	Freie Demokratische Partei (Free Democratic Party)
FLN	Front de Libération Nationale (National Liberation Front, Algeria)
FRG	Federal Republic of Germany
FU	Freie Universität Berlin (Free University Berlin)
GDR	German Democratic Republic

GN	Göttinger Nachrichten
GSC	German Subject Collection
HIA	Hoover Institution Library and Archives
HIS	Hamburger Institut für Sozialforschung
ICCS	International Union of Christian Democrat and Conservative Students
IfZ	Institut für Zeitgeschichte
ISC	International Student Conference
JU	Junge Union (Young Union)
Jusos	Jungsozialisten (Young Socialists)
KSU	Kölner Studentenunion (Cologne Student Union)
LAB	Landesarchiv Berlin
LSD	Liberaldemokratischer Hochschulbund (Liberal Democratic Higher Education Association)
MSB Spartakus	Marxistischer Studentenbund Spartakus (Marxist Student Association Spartakus)
MSU	Münchener Studentenunion (Munich Student Union)
NHB	Nationaldemokratischer Hochschulbund (National Democratic Higher Education League)
NATO	North Atlantic Treaty Organisation
NofU	Notgemeinschaft für eine Freie Universität (Emergency Community for a Free University)
NPD	Nationaldemokratische Partei (National Democratic Party)
NVA	Nationale Volksarmee (National People's Army, East Germany)
POW	Prisoner of war
RAF	Rote Armee Fraktion (Red Army Faction)
RBB	Rundfunk Berlin-Brandenburg
RCDS	Ring Christlich-Demokratischer Studenten (Association of Christian Democratic Students)
SA	Sturmabteilung (Nazi stormtroopers)
SD	Sicherheitsdienst (Nazi Security Service)
SDS	Sozalistischer Deutscher Studentenbund (Socialist German Student League)
SHB	Sozialdemokratischer Hochschulbund (Social Democratic Higher Education League)
SLH	Sozialliberaler Hochschulbund (Social-Liberal Higher Education League)
SPD	Sozialdemokratische Partei Deutschlands (Social Democratic Party of Germany)
SS	Schutzstaffel (Nazi paramilitary organization that oversaw the Holocaust)
SZ	Süddeutsche Zeitung
taz	die tageszeitung
TU	Technische Universität Berlin (Technical University of Berlin)
UP	Unidad Popular (Chile)
UN	United Nations

VDS	Vereinigte Deutsche Studentenschaften (Association of German Students)
VfZ	Vierteljahrshefte für Zeitgeschichte
VKS	Verband Kritischer Schüler (Association of Critical Pupils)
YAF	Young Americans for Freedom
ZDF	Zweites Deutsches Fernsehen (Germany's second public television network)

List of Illustrations

Introduction

In May 1988, a group of people, all of whom had been student activists in West Germany around 1968, came together to reminisce about what the revolt of those years meant to them in retrospect. Twenty years after the events, '1968' had become a symbolic shorthand for a major moment of political and cultural upheaval, one that was commemorated around the globe in the late 1980s.[1] The former activists, most of them in their forties or early fifties, got together at an educational institution in Bad Godesberg, a wealthy neighbourhood in the capital Bonn, to relive their personal experiences with the student movement and to take stock of the ways in which it had transformed West German society. During the conference, Josef Heichrich ('Jupp') Darchinger, one of the most famous political photographers of the Federal Republic, documented the proceedings and took cheerful group photographs.[2] Moreover, the gathering generated considerable media interest. West Germany's prime television newscasts showed clips from the day, and most of the major daily and weekly papers featured reports about the meeting. A few months later, the ZDF, one of the country's public service television channels, showed a widely viewed documentary about the political trajectories of some of those who had attended, sparking another wave of extensive public commentary about this particular group of former activists.[3]

The heightened media interest was because those who met in Bonn in 1988 were unusual '68ers—a term that had become common to describe social actors who had been young activists around 1968 and still embodied the spirit of these years.[4] Contrary to the '68er archetypes featured in most of the commemorative

---

[1] Timothy S. Brown, 1968. Transnational and Global Perspectives, Version: 1.0, in: Docupedia-Zeitgeschichte, 11.06.2012, URL: http://docupedia.de/zg/1968?oldid=84582 (accessed on 10 April 2014).

[2] As part of its vast Jupp Darchinger photographic collection, the Archiv der sozialen Demokratie (AdsD) holds dozens of negatives of photographs he took on the day. One of his group photographs was published on the cover of *RCDS Magazin* no. 5 (1988); on Darchinger's career, see 'Das Auge von Bonn', *Der Spiegel*, 46 (1997), 52–3.

[3] ZDF, Bonn direkt, 15 May 1988; Gunter Hofmann, 'Nach links Flagge zeigen', *Die Zeit*, 21 (20 May 1988); Oliver Tolmein, 'Die "alternativen 68er Sieger" treffen sich', *tageszeitung* (17 May 1988), 5; Helmut Lölhöffel, 'Unaufhaltsamer Aufstieg der Alternativ-68er', *Frankfurter Rundschau* (17 May 1988); Heiko Gebhardt, 'Wir waren Demokraten', *Stern* (19 May 1988); also Martin Stallmann, *Die Erfindung von '1968': Der studentische Protest im bundesdeutschen Fernsehen 1977–1998* (Göttingen, 2017), 142. Heinz Hemming/Werner A. Perger, *Die anderen 68er: Dutschkes Gegenspieler und was aus ihnen wurde*, Dokumentation, BRD 1988, 43', first shown on ZDF, 4 August 1988, 10.15 p.m.

[4] June Edmunds and Bryan S. Turner, *Generations, Culture and Society* (Buckingham and Philadelphia, PA, 2002), 15–16.

The Other '68ers: Student Protest and Christian Democracy in West Germany. Anna von der Goltz, Oxford University Press (2021). © Anna von der Goltz. DOI: 10.1093/oso/9780198849520.003.0001

reports about the student movement that had begun to appear in the run-up to the twentieth anniversary, they had not been involved in the Socialist German Student League (*Sozialistischer Deutscher Studentenbund*, SDS), the radical left-wing group that had been at the forefront of protest in the late 1960s. Nor had they lived in the infamous Kommune 1, one of the Federal Republic's first experiments with communal living, whose inhabitants were household names.[5] Instead, they were Christian Democrats—and prominent ones at that.

Between the mid-1960s and late 1970s, all those who later gathered in Bonn had been politically active in the Association of Christian Democratic Students (*Ring Christlich-Demokratischer Studenten*, RCDS), a national political student group founded in 1951 that was closely affiliated with the two Christian Democratic sister parties, the Christian Democratic Union (CDU) and the Bavarian Christian Social Union (CSU).[6] They had thus been active at a time when the radical Left had questioned the very foundations of the Federal Republic of Germany (FRG) and defied the 'establishment' in highly visible and provocative ways. They had one more thing in common: since 1968, many of them had successfully entered the political institutions of the Federal Republic, particularly those in the hands of the Christian Democrats, who had returned to power in 1982. The television documentary about them included an interview with Chancellor Helmut Kohl, in which he praised these particular '68ers for having carried fresh ideas into his own party.[7]

At this point, many of those who gathered in Bonn indeed held high-ranking posts in the CDU/CSU, in the capital's political bureaucracy, or in one of the state capitals. They were men—for almost all those in attendance were male—like Wulf Schönbohm (b. 1941), who headed the CDU's powerful policy and planning division; Peter Radunski (b. 1939), who was the party's number three and chief campaign strategist; Peter Gauweiler (b. 1949), who was Secretary of State in the State Interior Ministry in Bavaria; Horst Teltschik (b. 1940), who was a key aide to the Chancellor and his 'clandestine Foreign Minister'; and Friedbert Pflüger (b. 1955), who was a few years younger than the others but already served as press secretary to Federal President Richard von Weizsäcker.[8] The television documentary named them 'Dutschke's adversaries' to highlight the fact that, as students, some of them had gone face to face with Rudi Dutschke, the iconic

[5] Detlef Siegfried, 'Stars der Revolte: Die Kommune 1', in *Medien und Imagepolitik im 20. Jahrhundert: Deutschland, Europa, USA*, edited by Daniela Münkel and Lu Seegers (Frankfurt am Main, 2008), 229–45.

[6] RCDS members were not automatically members of the CDU/CSU and the group was nominally independent, but it had a close relationship to the Christian Democrats, received some party funding, and was generally thought of as the CDU/CSU's student arm. For an organizational overview written by a former RCDS national chair, see Johannes Weberling, *Für Freiheit und Menschenrechte: Der Ring Christlich-Demokratischer Studenten (RCDS), 1945–1986* (Düsseldorf, 1990).

[7] Hemming/Perger, *Die anderen 68er.*

[8] Andreas Wirsching, *Abschied vom Provisorium: Geschichte der Bundesrepublik Deutschland 1982–1990*, vol. 6 (Munich, 2006), 182.

Illustration 0.1 Group photograph of the self-described 'Alternative '68ers', Bonn, May 1988.

(J.H. Darchinger/Friedrich-Ebert-Stiftung)

figurehead of SDS. The group photographs taken in Bonn showed them lined up under a banner that said simply 'The alternative '68ers'.[9]

In a speech he gave at the conference and in interviews with the press, Schönbohm, who had been national chair of RCDS at the height of the student revolt in 1967/68, justified why they had the right to claim 1968 for themselves. 'Whether left-wingers or conservatives, we all had the feeling at the time that something had to happen. That the dreadful social paralysis of the end of the 1960s had to come to an end. That through commitment it was possible to change something.'[10] 'But we were completely isolated inside the universities', he went on, 'because we were the only political student group that rejected the revolutionary-socialist utopia of SDS. [. . .] We wanted reform and not a revolution', he declared.[11] Since then, the left-wing student movement had realized none of its actual political goals, including the system's revolutionary transformation, he opined. Instead, its effects had been mostly cultural.

[9] The name was a nod to the term 'alternative' that they had used to demarcate themselves from the Left since the 1960s—and one that was also popular on the Left in the 1970s.

[10] Quoted in 'Die 68er der CDU', *Zeit Magazin*, 33 (12 August 1988), 10.

[11] *Schönbohm Private Papers*, 'Die alternativen "68er" – was bleibt von der APO-Zeit?', MS (15 May 1988).

Schönbohm had clearly done his research. The notion that the revolt had set a cultural revolution in motion, transforming authoritarian and patriarchal societies into ones with flatter hierarchies, greater pluralism of lifestyles, and more participation from below, had begun to dominate western commemorations of 1968 in the 1980s—and it has had remarkable staying power.[12] The balance sheet of the centre-right was directly reversed, Schönbohm suggested. 'In our case it is the other way around: we achieved a lot politically, but little culturally.' Invoking a famous quotation by Dutschke, he declared gleefully that they had been particularly successful at 'marching through the institutions' of the Bonn Republic and were now 'well-established'. Their former opponents, on the other hand, were in crisis, he contended: out of power in Bonn and overtaken by the *Zeitgeist*. 'All the glamour is gone', Schönbohm, who had often felt on the margins around 1968, concluded with belated satisfaction.[13] A few months later, a multi-page spread on the '68ers of the CDU' in the weekly *Die Zeit* featured the bearded former RCDS chair in a leather jacket and introduced him to the paper's mostly left-liberal readers as 'the Lenin of the CDU'.[14]

What are we to make of these retrospective political claims and generational (self-)representations that suggest that centre-right students had played major roles around 1968 and been deeply affected by these years? Was this mere political posturing at a time of Christian Democratic hegemony? A brazen attempt to appropriate one of the key moments of the Left and to reinterpret democratic agency in the history of the Federal Republic? An invention of tradition with no grounds in lived reality? This book is an attempt to engage with these questions. However, it is also much more than that. This is a history of 1968 and its afterlives told from a new perspective.

The Other '68ers sheds light on a neglected aspect of one of the major moments of Germany's late twentieth century. At the core of this study are young activists from RCDS and from groups affiliated with the German Student Union (*Deutsche Studentenunion*, DSU), a centre-right umbrella group founded on campuses across the country in 1967/68. As such, it is a book about a political minority, albeit a vocal one. Even at this moment of political upheaval, only a small minority of students (around 5 per cent) was politically active. Even fewer were members of student groups of the centre-right. There were approximately 300,000 students at West German universities in the second half of the 1960s, and only about 2,300 of them were members of RCDS—less than 1 per cent of the student population.[15]

---

[12] 'Wir 68er waren alle ganz anders', interview with Tilman Fichter and Wulf Schönbohm, conducted by Werner A. Perger, *Deutsches Allgemeines Sonntagsblatt*, 10 April 1988; Kristin Ross, *May '68 and its Afterlives* (Chicago, IL, 2002); Silja Behre, *Bewegte Erinnerung: Deutungskämpfe um '1968' in deutsch-französischer Perspektive* (Tübingen, 2016).

[13] *Schönbohm Private Papers*, 'Die alternativen "68er" – was bleibt von der APO-Zeit?', MS (15 May 1988).

[14] 'Die 68er der CDU', *Zeit Magazin*, 33 (12 August 1988), 10.

[15] René Ahlberg, 'Die politische Konzeption des Sozialistischen Deutschen Studentenbundes', Beilage zur Wochenzeitung *Das Parlament* B20/68 (15 May 1968), 3–4; Konrad Jarausch, *Deutsche Studenten 1800–1970* (Frankfurt am Main, 1984), 232.

Much the same can be said of their main opponents, however. The strength of the student Left should not be overestimated either, in spite of the importance much of the scholarship has accorded to them. SDS may have come to symbolize student protest around 1968, but, prior to 1967, it was only the third largest political student group in West Germany. Before June of that year, SDS had merely around 1,200 members. Even at the height of its popularity in 1967/8, the membership of SDS never exceeded 2,500, meaning that fewer than 1 per cent of West German students belonged to the radical group.[16] In terms of membership, then, RCDS and SDS were approximately the same size around 1968. Despite this, we know hardly anything about the former's role during these years.

This is not an organizational history of RCDS and like-minded groups. It is a broader cultural history of politics around 1968. Its subjects are centre-right activists—their ideas, experiences, and memories. The book examines both what they did around 1968 and what they later thought they had done in those years. It interweaves individual voices with the archival record; it combines elements of a 'collective biography' of a group of people, who dedicated much of their lives to politics, with an in-depth study of the ideas and repertoires of centre-right students in the 1960s, 1970s, and beyond.[17] In line with much of the recent literature, it thus adopts an extended periodization of 1968. While eschewing fixed chronological markers, '1968' here denotes roughly the period between the mid-1960s and the late 1970s, when centre-right activists engaged most closely, indeed often obsessively, with the student Left.[18] Similarly, it does not use a fixed age bracket—e.g. the cohort born between 1938 and 1948 that is often used to establish who counts as a '68er[19]—to determine who the other '68ers were. It studies activists who played notable roles in centre-right groups during the extended 1968 moment, with a special focus on those who later claimed that these years had meant something to them.[20]

---

[16] Ahlberg, 'politische Konzeption'; Andrea Wienhaus, *Bildungswege zu '1968': Eine Kollektivbiografie des Sozialistischen Deutschen Studentenbundes* (Bielefeld, 2014).

[17] Paul Sturges, 'Collective biography in the 1980s', *Biography* 6, 4 (1983), 316–32; for Germany, Dorothee Wierling, *Geboren im Jahr Eins: Der Jahrgang 1949 in der DDR. Versuch einer Kollektivbiographie* (Berlin, 2002); Catherine Epstein, *The Last Revolutionaries: German Communists and Their Century* (Cambridge, MA, 2003).

[18] This is similar to Timothy Brown's periodization, who defines 1968 as lasting from 1962–78. Timothy S. Brown, *West Germany and the Global Sixties: The Antiauthoritarian Revolt, 1962–1978* (New York, 2013). In French historiography, the notion of the '"68 years" lasting from the end of the Algerian war until François Mitterand's election is similarly influential. See Philippe Artières and Michelle Zancarini-Forunel (eds.), *68: Une Histoire Collective (1962–1981)* (Paris, 2008).

[19] Heinz Bude, *Das Altern einer Generation: Die Jahrgänge 1938 bis 1948* (Frankfurt, 1997); Christina von Hodenberg, *Das andere Achtundsechzig: Gesellschaftsgeschichte einer Revolte* (Munich, 2018).

[20] Those interviewed for this book, like those who later defined themselves publicly as '68ers of the centre-right—were born between 1937 and 1955 and thus included several different micro-cohorts. On the role of micro-cohorts in social movements, see Nancy Whittier, 'Political Generations, Micro-Cohorts and the Transformation of Social Movements', *American Sociological Review*, 62 (1997), 760–78.

This book asks a number of simple but important questions about these individuals and this period: what was it like to experience 1968 on the other side of the political spectrum in West Germany? Did centre-right activists share the New Left critique of advanced industrial society and German authoritarianism, and how did they relate to activists of the Left and to the broader student movement? What were their views of the older generation, whom young New Leftists often condemned for their association with the Nazi past and what they regarded as their failure to build a truly democratic society after 1945? How did these young activists respond to the broader social and cultural transformations of this dynamic decade? How did they view West Germany's—and their own—place in the wider world at a time when activists' political imaginations were increasingly global? What was their relationship to the CDU/CSU, and what role have they played in (West) German politics since 1968? And in what ways have they shaped the memory wars that continue to wage about this period in German history?

1968 and Histories of the Federal Republic

The years around 1968 are among the most closely examined periods in Germany's twentieth century. In 2018, the fiftieth anniversary demonstrated once again that public and scholarly interest in the protest movements of this era remains high. A wave of new publications appeared, and numerous public commemorations were held. As in previous years, however, the focus was predominantly on the role of the Left.[21] Historical research on 1968 began in earnest in the 1990s, and we now have a vast international literature on the subject, one that has examined the revolt through a number of different frameworks, ranging from political and social histories that have placed 1968 in broader temporal and societal contexts, to histories of gender, cultural histories, histories of emotions, and transnational and global histories.[22] The scholarship has extended beyond a

[21] Heinz Bude, *Adorno für Ruinenkinder: Eine Geschichte von 1968* (Munich, 2018); Wolfgang Kraushaar, *Die blinden Flecken der 68er Bewegung* (Stuttgart, 2018). Earlier examples of otherwise exhaustive monographs on 1968 that do not touch on centre-right activists are Brown, *West Germany and the Global Sixties*; and Gerd-Rainer Horn, *The Spirit of '68: Rebellion in Western Europe and North America, 1956–1976* (Oxford, 2007). However, one major recent contribution to the literature explicitly includes 'other' experiences of 1968. It shifts the focus to universities beyond the two capitals of the revolt, Frankfurt and West Berlin, looks at older people's attitudes toward the student movement, and discusses the role of (left-wing) women. von Hodenberg, *Das andere Achtundsechzig*.

[22] Christina von Hodenberg and Detlef Siegfried (eds.), *Wo '1968' liegt: Reform und Revolte in der Geschichte der Bundesrepublik* (Göttingen, 2006); Axel Schildt, Detlef Siegfried, and Karl-Christian Lammers (eds.), *Dynamische Zeiten: Die 60er Jahre in den beiden deutschen Gesellschaften* (Hamburg, 2000); Kristina Schulz, *Der lange Atem der Provokation: Die Frauenbewegung in der Bundesrepublik und in Frankreich 1968–1976* (Frankfurt and New York, 2002); Ute Kätzel, *Die 68erinnen: Porträt einer rebellischen Frauengeneration* (Berlin, 2002); Joachim Scharloth, *1968: Eine Kommunikationsgeschichte* (Munich, 2011); Joachim Häberlen, *The Emotional Politics of the Alternative Left: West Germany*

sole focus on students and the dynamics of protest, with responses by other social actors and the state taking centre stage in more recent studies of these years.[23]

The first way in which this book contributes to this rich literature is by redirecting our historical gaze to take in the spectrum of political diversity characterizing the West German student experience of 1968. In doing so, it shifts attention back to the student movement and the political conflicts of these years. It thus returns to familiar territory. However, it examines a history that we think we already understand fully from a perspective to which we are unaccustomed, thereby opening up new vistas. Whereas we have fine-grained analyses of the West German (student) Left around 1968, including collective portraits and individual biographies of some of its protagonists, there have been very few studies of activists of the right.[24] The few exceptions that exist to date are intellectual histories that trace the reinvigoration and realignment of West German conservative thought through its leading thinkers' opposition to 1968. These works have shown that the student revolt sparked a flurry of activity among conservative intellectuals, including the founding of a number of influential new publications, such as Caspar von Schrenck-Notzing's *Criticón* and Klaus Motschmann's *Konservativ heute*, as well as of influential conferences and discussion circles.[25] For the most part, existing studies focus on political figures who

1968–1984 (Cambridge, 2018); Norbert Frei, *1968: Jugendrevolte und globaler Protest* (Munich, 2008); Martin Klimke, *The Other Alliance: Student Protest in West Germany and the United States in the Global Sixties* (Princeton, NJ, 2009); Quinn Slobodian, *Foreign Front: Third World Politics in Sixties West Germany* (Durham, NC, 2012); Macartney, Alexander Finn, *War in the Postwar: Japan and West Germany Protest the Vietnam War and the Global Strategy of Imperialism* (PhD dissertation, Georgetown University, 2019).

[23] Knud Andresen, *Gebremste Radikalisierung: Die IG Metall und ihre Jugend 1968 bis in die 1980er Jahre* (Göttingen, 2016); Klaus Weinhauer, *Schutzpolizei in der Bundesrepublik: Zwischen Bürgerkrieg und Innerer Sicherheit: Die turbulenten sechziger Jahre* (Paderborn, 2003); Karrin Hanshew, *Terror and Democracy in West Germany* (New York, 2012); Richard Vinen, *The Long '68: Radical Protest and Its Enemies* (London, 2018).

[24] Belinda Davis, *The Internal Life of Politics: Extraparliamentary Opposition in West Germany, 1962–1983* (Cambridge, forthcoming); Aribert Reimann, *Dieter Kunzelmann: Avantgardist, Protestler, Radikaler* (Göttingen, 2009); Michaela Karl, *Rudi Dutschke: Revolutionär ohne Revolution* (Frankfurt am Main, 2003). A few German language studies and edited collections have begun to examine the right, though rarely in ways that put activists at the centre. See e.g. Massimiliano Livi, Daniel Schmidt and Michael Sturm (eds.), *Die 70er Jahre als schwarzes Jahrzehnt: Politisierungs- und Mobilisierungsprozesse zwischen rechter Mitte und extremer Rechter in Italien und der Bundesrepublik 1967–1982* (Bielefeld, 2010); Manuel Seitenbecher, 'Die Reform als Revolution in verträglicher Dosis: Der Ring Christlich-Demokratischer Studenten (RCDS) während der 68er-Jahre an der FU Berlin', *Zeitschrift für Geschichtswissenschaft* 6 (2010), 505–26; Olaf Bartz, Konservative Studenten und die Studentenbewegung: Die 'Kölner Studenten-Union', in: *Westfälische Forschung*, 48 (1998), 241–56; and, most importantly, Nikolai Wehrs, *Der Protest der Professoren: Der 'Bund der Freiheit der Wissenschaft' in den 1970er Jahren* (Göttingen, 2014), a study of conservative academics around 1968. On the contrary, there is a very robust literature on US conservative movements, in the 1960s and beyond, and this book takes important cues from some of these works. An early example was David Farber and Jeff Roche (eds.), *The Conservative Sixties* (New York, 2003). A French example, though not focused on students, is François Audigier, *Histoire Du SAC: La Part D'ombre Du Gaullisme* (Paris, 2003).

[25] Jerry Z. Muller, 'German Neoconservatism and the History of the Bonn Republic, 1968 to 1985', *German Politics and Society*, 18, 1 (2000), 1–32; Axel Schildt, '"Die Kräfte der Gegenreform sind auf

turned right in the wake of 1968—liberal intellectuals who became liberal-conservatives because they rejected the 'excesses' of the student movement or more clearly reactionary figures, who began to embrace a radicalized and explicitly anti-liberal conservatism during these years. Some recent works have also dealt with political opposition to the 1968 Left on the far right and traced the intellectual roots of the present-day European radical Right all the way back to the 1960s when its fierce opposition to egalitarianism and multiculturalism began to take shape.[26]

This book tells a different story: not just one of conservative resistance and reaction, but also one of participation, engagement, and interaction. It focuses on young activists of the centre-right, who were often closely involved in the student movement. Their views represented a significant portion of the student body of the late 1960s, and, especially during the early Kohl era, they were far more politically influential than the radical Right. The protagonists of this book were a part of 1968. They participated in many of the key protest events and embraced some of the characteristic practices of these years and, in more than one instance, were swept along by the anti-authoritarian spirit that animated the broader revolt. These other '68ers, as they are called here, reacted to the Left but without necessarily championing a reactionary politics, especially in the early phase of student unrest.

Second, by foregrounding the role of centre-right students around 1968, this book joins recent works that have revisited the extraordinary role that Christian Democracy played in the history of postwar Europe.[27] It would indeed be difficult to overstate the influence of Christian Democrats in the continent's history after 1945, especially in the Federal Republic. Apart from the Social-Liberal interlude between

breiter Front angetreten". Zur konservativen Tendenzwende in den Siebzigerjahren', *Archiv für Sozialgeschichte*, 44 (2004), 449–7; Stefan Winckler, Felix Dirsch, and Hartmuth Becker (eds.), *Die 68er und ihre Gegner: Der Widerstand gegen die Kulturrevolution*, (Graz and Stuttgart, 2004); Riccardo Bavaj, 'Turning "Liberal Critics" into "Liberal-Conservatives": Kurt Sontheimer and the Re-Coding of the Political Culture in the Wake of the Student Revolt of "1968"', *German Politics and Society*, 27, 1 (2009), 39–59; Dominik Geppert and Jens Hacke (eds.), *Streit um den Staat: Intellektuelle Debatten in der Bundesrepublik 1960–1980* (Göttingen, 2008); for a French example of this approach, see Serge Audier, *La pensée anti-68: Essai sur les origines d'une restauration intellectuelle* (Paris, 2009).

[26] For France and Italy, Tamir Bar-On, *Where Have All the Fascists Gone?* (Ashgate, 2007); Andrea Mammone, *Transnational Neofascism in France and Italy* (New York and Cambridge, 2015); for Germany, Quinn Slobodian, 'Germany's 1968 and Its Enemies', *AHR*, 123, 3, (2018), 749–52; Volker Weiß has recently cautioned against the tendency to write the history of the right as a simple reaction to 1968. He emphasizes that (West) Germany's 'New Right' had much deeper roots in German history. Volker Weiß, *Die autoritäre Revolte: Die Neue Rechte und der Untergang des Abendlandes* (Stuttgart, 2017), 28 and 37.

[27] Tom Buchanan and Martin Conway (eds.), *Political Catholicism in Europe 1918–1965* (Oxford, 1996); Frank Bösch, *Die Adenauer-CDU: Gründung, Aufstieg und Krise einer Erfolgspartei 1945–1969* (Stuttgart, 2001); Wolfram Kaiser, *Christian Democracy and the Origins of European Union* (Cambridge, 2007); Frank Bösch, 'Die Krise als Chance. Die Neuformierung der Christdemokraten in den siebziger Jahren', in *Das Ende der Zuversicht? Die siebziger Jahre als Geschichte*, edited by Konrad Jarausch (Göttingen, 2008), 296–309; Martina Steber, *Die Hüter der Begriffe: Politische Sprachen des Konservativen in Großbritannien und der Bundesrepublik Deutschland 1945–1980* (Berlin, 2017); James Chappel, *Catholic Modern: The Challenge of Totalitarianism and the Remaking of the Church* (Cambridge, MA, 2018), 182–226.

1969 and 1982, the CDU/CSU governed the 'old' Federal Republic throughout its entire existence. Nevertheless, historians of the postwar have often focused their attention on groups or movements that were more flamboyant, not least the left-wing radicals of the 1960s. Rather than viewing Christian Democracy as a straight-forward restoration of traditional conservatism, however, newer works treat it as a remarkably flexible ideological formation, a dynamic and evolving phenomenon that shared more common ground with the Left than once assumed.[28] This book builds on these insights. It sheds fresh light on how West Germany's centre-right dealt with the crisis of hegemony and political identity it experienced in the wake of 1968, how it coped with generational change in its ranks, how it transformed and modernized after losing power at the national level for the first time in 1969, and how it managed to re-emerge so successfully in the 1980s. This study thus helps us to understand why the age of Christian Democracy was interrupted but never really ended in the Federal Republic—at least until now.[29]

Third, by revisiting the idea that 1968 represented a watershed of sorts, *The Other '68ers* contributes to recent attempts to historicize the 'old' Federal Republic—a distinct entity that, like its neighbour to the east, the German Democratic Republic (GDR), ceased to exist with the end of the Cold War.[30] Until recently, the years around 1968 were often interpreted as the 'second founding' of the Federal Republic, as the moment when an authoritarian society shed its illiberal tendencies and filled an imposed democratic order with life.[31] As the political scientist and left-wing public intellectual Claus Leggewie put it in 1987: 'The symbolic number '68 symbolizes a potentiated 1949, the antifascist

---

[28] Martin Conway, 'The Age of Christian Democracy', in *European Christian Democracy: Historical Legacies and Comparative Perspectives*, edited by Thomas Kselman and Joseph A. Buttigieg (Notre Dame, IN, 2003), 43–67; Marco Duranti, *The Conservative Human Rights Revolution: European Identity, Transnational Politics, and the Origins of the European Convention* (Oxford, 2017), 375.

[29] Conway, 'The Age of Christian Democracy'; Franz Walter and Frank Bösch, 'Das Ende des christdemokratischen Zeitalters? Zur Zukunft eines Erfolgsmodells', in *Die CDU nach Kohl*, edited by Tobias Dürr and Rüdiger Soldt (Frankfurt am Main, 1998), 46–58.

[30] Frank Biess and Astrid Eckert, 'Why Do We Need New Narratives for the History of the Federal Republic?', *Central European History*, 52, 1 (2019), 1–18; Frank Bösch (ed.), *A History Shared and Divided: East and West Germany since the 1970s* (New York, 2018); Sonja Levsen and Cornelius Torp (eds.), *Wo liegt die Bundesrepublik? Vergleichende Perspektiven auf die westdeutsche Geschichte* (Göttingen, 2016); Frank Bajohr, Anselm Doering-Manteuffel, Claudia Kemper, and Detlef Siegfried (eds.), *Mehr als eine Erzählung: Zeitgeschichtliche Perspektiven auf die Bundesrepublik* (Göttingen, 2016).

[31] Franz-Werner Kersting, Jürgen Reulecke, and Hans-Ulrich Thamer (eds.), *Die zweite Gründung der Bundesrepublik: Generationswechsel und intellektuelle Wortergreifungen 1955 bis 1975* (Stuttgart, 2010); Clemens Albrecht, Günter C. Behrmann, and Michael Bock (eds.), *Die intellektuelle Gründung der Bundesrepublik: Eine Wirkungsgeschichte der Frankfurter Schule* (Frankfurt am Main, 1999); Matthias Frese, Julia Paulus, and Karl Teppe (eds.), *Demokratisierung und gesellschaftlicher Aufbruch: Die sechziger Jahre als Wendezeit der Bundesrepublik* (Paderborn, 2003).

re-establishment of the Federal Republic. The quasi-democracy released its children.'[32]

How exactly this post-fascist state turned into a stable liberal democracy in the space of just a few decades has been one of the guiding questions of most of the scholarship produced over the last thirty years. That the history of West Germany represented a remarkable democratic 'success story'—a kind of *Sonderweg* in reverse—was the premise of many of the works produced from the 1980s into the 2000s. In this period, historians published a growing number of surveys and came up with a variety of closely related paradigms to describe the process of social and political transformation the Federal Republic underwent, be it 'liberal-ization', 'Westernization', or 'recivilization'.[33] Many of the most influential works, however, downplayed the importance of 1968 in explaining the FRG's transform-ation. They saw the events of these years at best as 'surface froth' produced by structural shifts underneath and pointed out that the protests involved only a tiny left-wing minority.[34] This study, by contrast, reasserts that political activism in 1968 mattered. The close involvement of the centre-right in this age of protest, which the book details, suggests that it was a broader and more consequential moment than much of this literature has allowed.

At the same time, recent works have been right to be sceptical of the 'success narrative', pointing out the normative assumptions that underpinned this inter-pretation and all the ways in which many of united Germany's most pressing problems had their roots in the Cold War-era FRG.[35] By emphasizing that the student movement mattered, this study does not seek to reify 1968 as the birth-place of authentic West German democracy. Rather, it takes its cues from more critical recent works by treating the process of West Germany's liberalization and democratization not as a linear evolution, but as a far more winding and heavily contested one—and as one that was not just optimistic and forward-looking but

---

[32] Claus Leggewie, *Der Geist steht rechts: Ausflüge in die Denkfabriken der Wende* (Berlin, 1987), 214.

[33] Manfred Görtemaker, *Geschichte der Bundesrepublik Deutschland: Von der Gründung bis zur Gegenwart* (Frankfurt, 2004); Edgar Wolfrum, *Die geglückte Demokratie: Geschichte der Bundesrepublik und ihren Anfängen* (Stuttgart, 2006); Ulrich Herbert (ed.), *Wandlungsprozesse in Westdeutschland: Belastung, Integration, Liberalisierung 1945–1980* (Göttingen, 2002); Anselm Doering-Manteuffel, *Wie westlich sind die Deutschen: Amerikanisierung und Westernisierung im 20. Jahrhundert* (Göttingen, 1999); Axel Schildt, *Ankunft im Westen. Ein Essay zur Erfolgsgeschichte der Bundesrepublik* (Frankfurt, 1999); Heinrich August Winkler, *Der lange Weg nach Westen*, vol. 2: *Deutsche Geschichte vom 'Dritten Reich' bis zur Wiedervereinigung* (Munich, 2000); Konrad H. Jarausch, *After Hitler: Recivilizing Germans, 1945–1955* (New York, 2006).

[34] Similarly, many influential European surveys are sceptical of the idea that the Western 1968 mattered. See e. g. Tony Judt, *Postwar: A History of Europe Since 1945* (New York, 2005), 390–421; Mark Mazower, *Dark Continent: Europe's Twentieth Century* (London, 1998), 322–4.

[35] Eckart Conze, *Die Suche nach Sicherheit: Eine Geschichte der Bundesrepublik von 1949 bis in die Gegenwart* (Munich, 2009); Eckert and Biess, 'Why Do We Need New Narratives'.

driven by persistent fears about the fragility of democracy in Germany.[36] As we shall see, liberal and illiberal impulses were often present simultaneously—on both ends of the political spectrum. Such an approach allows us to comprehend much more fully, and in a much more nuanced way, exactly how this watershed moment transformed West German society. 1968 was far from a smooth transition to cultural democratization. West Germany only became a stable democratic order as a result of fierce public disputes in which the stakes were high.[37] The struggle over what democracy meant and how to guard it did not just play out in the realm of intellectual debate. It was an everyday lived experience for many, including the protagonists of this book, who saw their own biographies as being intimately connected to the fate of West German democracy.

The Other '68ers and Histories of Generation

The book does not just provide a new historical perspective on Germany's 1968 and on the political culture of the Federal Republic. It also offers a larger contribution to, and implicit critique of, broader ways in which some historians have written contemporary German history. Its biggest conceptual contribution lies in rethinking how to write a history of generation, which has been one of the most influential approaches to twentieth-century German history in the past two decades.

Germany has been referred to as the 'country of generations', because the many social and political ruptures in its history made the experiences and mentalities of different age cohorts diverge more starkly than in countries with more continuous political traditions.[38] Historians have been drawn to generation to explain the impact of political ruptures on individuals and to chart change over time.[39] This

---

[36] Frank Biess, *Republik der Angst: Eine andere Geschichte der Bundesrepublik* (Hamburg, 2019); Christian Schletter, *Grabgesang der Demokratie: Die Debatten über das Scheitern der bundesdeutschen Demokratie von 1965 bis 1985* (Göttingen, 2015).

[37] Dirk A. Moses, *German Intellectuals and the Nazi Past* (Cambridge, 2006); Jens Hacke, *Philosophie der Bürgerlichkeit: Die liberalkonservative Begründung der Bundesrepublik* (Göttingen, 2006); Geppert and Hacke, *Streit um den Staat*; Frank Biess, 'Thinking after Hitler: The new intellectual history of the Federal Republic of Germany', *History and Theory*, 51 (2012), 221–45.

[38] Heinz Bude, 'Die 50er Jahre im Spiegel der Flakhelfer- und der 68er-Generation', in *Generationalität und Lebensgeschichte im 20. Jahrhundert*, edited by Jürgen Reulecke and Elisabeth Müller-Luckner (Munich, 2003), 145.

[39] Mark Roseman (ed.), *Generations in Conflict* (Cambridge, 1995); Ulrich Herbert, *Best: Biographische Studien über Radikalismus, Weltanschauung und Vernunft, 1903–1989* (Bonn, 1996); Ulrich Herbert, 'Drei politische Generationen im 20. Jahrhundert', in Reulecke and Müller-Luckner, *Generationalität*, 95–115; Michael Wildt, *Generation of the Unbound: The Leadership Corps of the Reich Security Main Office* (Jerusalem, 2002); Mary Fulbrook, *Dissonant Lives: Generations and Violence Through the German Dictatorships* (Oxford, 2011); Hans Ulrich Wehler, *Deutsche Gesellschaftsgeschichte*, vol. 5: *Bundesrepublik und DDR 1949–1990* (Munich, 2008); Thomas A. Kohut, *A German Generation: An Experiential History of the Twentieth Century* (New Haven, CT, 2012); Ulrike Jureit and Michael Wildt (eds.), *Generationen: Zur Relevanz eines wissenschaftlichen*

trope is intellectually seductive. It allows us to discuss big structural developments in conjunction with the ways in which individual actors were shaped by and effected events. It helps historians craft neat periodizations and compelling narratives explaining not only how the character of Germany changed multiple times throughout the twentieth century 'but also the very character of people themselves', as Mary Fulbrook eloquently phrased it in her book *Dissonant Lives*.[40]

One downside of this approach, however, is that it often tends to generalize the experiences and features of a particular subset of a cohort and to portray them as the universal characteristics of all those who were the same age. To put it simply, in many generational histories one uniform generation succeeds another. This leaves little room for understanding diversity, and often division, within generational cohorts.[41] In histories of 1968 this tendency has been particularly pronounced—and lately arguably buttressed by the global and transnational turn; the '68ers appear as the first 'global generation', a worldwide community of young activists with near-uniform ideas and traits.[42]

Histories of 1968 in the Federal Republic have not just tended to portray the '68ers as a uniform collective. They have focused, in particular, on intergenerational conflict—be it on the '68ers' critique of their parents for their conduct during the Nazi years, or on the frequently contentious relationship between the '68ers and the so-called '45ers, an influential generation of intellectuals who lived through Germany's wartime defeat as young adults and felt that they had a special stake in the stability of the new state.[43] This book, by contrast, focuses first and foremost on *intra*generational debates and clashes. We are accustomed to viewing the years around 1968 as a period of heightened political contestation, of spirited intellectual debates, and heated confrontations between individuals with different political views and philosophies. The key argument here is that this contestation also played out among the young and even among students. *The Other '68ers*

Grundbegriffs (Hamburg, 2005) see also Holger Nehring, '"Generation" as Political Argument in the West European Protest Movements in the 1960s', in *Generations in Twentieth-Century Europe*, edited by Stephen Lovell (Basingstoke, 2007), 57–78.

[40] Fulbrook, *Dissonant Lives*, 2; for a persuasive critique of the trope of generational change in histories of twentieth-century Germany, Ulrike Jureit, 'Generation, Generationalität, Generationenforschung, Version: 2.0', in: *Docupedia-Zeitgeschichte*, 03.08.2017, http://dx.doi.org/10.14765/zzf.dok.2.1117.v2

[41] This is not just an issue in German history writing. See e.g. Chinese historian Wang Zheng's critique of studies that have focused one-sidedly on Mao's 'Red Guard Generation' at the expense of those who were critical of this project of social transformation. Abosede George, Clive Glaser, Margaret D. Jacobs, Chitra Joshi, Emily Marker, Alexandra Walsham, Wang Zheng, and Bernd Weisbrod, 'AHR Conversation: Each Generation Writes Its Own History of Generations', *AHR*, 123, 5 (2018), 1507–8.

[42] Beate Fietze, '1968 als Symbol der ersten globalen Generation', *Berliner Journal für Soziologie*, 3 (1997), 365–86; Edmunds and Turner, *Generations, Culture and Society*.

[43] Christina von Hodenberg, *Konsens und Krise: Eine Geschichte der westdeutschen Medienöffentlichkeit, 1945 bis 1973* (Göttingen, 2006); Moses, *German Intellectuals*; Wehrs, *Der Protest der Professoren;* for reflections on these and other ways of analysing generation around 1968, see Anna von der Goltz (ed.), *Talkin' 'Bout My Generation: Conflicts of 'Generation Building' and Europe's '1968'* (Göttingen, 2011).

asserts that political conflict was indeed key in 1968—but not just among activists on the Left and their older antagonists in the media and other positions of authority, but also among student activists of a similar age.

In shifting our gaze toward political conflicts among the '68ers, this book—like most other histories of generation—takes important cues from Karl Mannheim's sociology of knowledge. Mannheim, a German sociologist, was born in Budapest in 1893 and experienced the tumultuous first few decades of Europe's twentieth century as a young man. Writing in 1928, at a time when youth was a particularly salient political category, he came up with a more nuanced and constructivist understanding of generations to critique the notion of naturally recurring generational cycles that had been common until then. His ideas have structured most generational histories since.[44] Mannheim's theory of generations sought to explain how '[e]arly impressions tend to coalesce into a natural view of the world'. Members of a generation were 'unwittingly determined' by the natural world view that they acquired in youth, he argued. Mannheim distinguished between what he termed 'generation location' (put simply, the mere fact of having been born or educated in a particular region at a particular time), 'actual generation', and 'generation unit':

> Youth experiencing the same concrete historical problems may be said to be part of the same actual generation; while those groups within the same actual generation which work up the material of their common experiences in different specific ways, constitute separate generation units.[45]

Most historians of modern Germany who have examined generations have dealt with what Mannheim would have called 'generation units'. They have focused on particular (and often quite small) communities whose members not only shared a set of age-specific experiences, but who also drew very similar conclusions from these and conceived of themselves as members of a generational collective.[46] However, such treatments frequently overlook that Mannheim's model provided for the formation of multiple generation units within any one context. '[W]ithin any generation there can exist a number of differentiated,

---

[44] Herbert, 'Drei politische Generationen'; Gabriele Rosenthal, 'Zur interaktionellen Konstitution von Generationen: Generationenabfolgen in Familien von 1890 bis 1970 in Deutschland', in *Generationen-Beziehungen, Austausch und Tradierung*, edited by Jürgen Mansel, Gabriele Rosenthal, and Angelika Tölke (Opladen, 1997), 57–73. On the history of the concept, see Ohad Parnes, Ulrike Vedder, and Stefan Willer (eds.), *Das Konzept der Generation: Eine Wissenschafts- und Kulturgeschichte* (Frankfurt, 2008).

[45] Karl Mannheim, 'The Problem of Generations', in idem, *Essays on the Sociology of Knowledge*, edited by Paul Kecskemeti (London, 1952), 276–322, here 304.

[46] Herbert, *Best*; Wildt, *Generation of the Unbound*; Kohut, *A German Generation*; Christoph Cornelißen (ed.), *Geschichtswissenschaft im Geist der Demokratie: Wolfgang J. Mommsen und seine Generation* (Berlin, 2010).

antagonistic generation units', he theorized. These were 'oriented toward each other', but 'only in the sense of fighting one another'.[47] Rather than being marked by a 'unitary Zeitgeist', each era was therefore defined by 'mutually antagonistic impulses'.[48] This insight has rarely been reflected in German histories of generation, which have overwhelmingly treated them as homogeneous entities.[49] Although the period around 1968 is often described as one of unchecked left-wing hegemony, this dualism between different groups of activists—or 'generation units' in Mannheim's terminology—was, in fact, a defining feature of West German student politics at this time, as this book argues. In focusing on intra-generational relations among different kinds of '68ers, this study thus takes important cues from a commonly overlooked aspect of Mannheim's conceptualization of generation, but it does not use it as a theoretical corset. Newer works on generation have done much to historicize the very assumptions on which Mannheim's theory was based and have shown that his model privileged young, bourgeois, politicized, male intellectuals, who often outlined eloquently how major political caesuras had affected them—making it tempting for historians to adopt the stories they told as scholarly interpretations.[50] They established that Mannheim defined what constituted a generation in very specific—and ultimately quite narrow—terms. The experiences of more 'silent' actors, or social experiences that were not strictly speaking political, often do not fit as neatly into his categories.[51] Building on these insights, *The Other '68ers* therefore does not just focus on those who were very vocal about what they had done during the years of the student movement—such as the men who met in Bonn in May 1988. Instead, the analysis also includes centre-right activists who had played important roles around 1968 but have been more hesitant in giving their experiences generational form, notably women activists and Christian Democratic 'renegades'.

These recent works on generation have also pointed out that Mannheim's concept was a product of its time in that it relied on interwar ideas of developmental psychology. According to the sociologist, identities were indelibly stamped by (political) experiences individuals acquired around the age of seventeen. The

---

[47]   Mannheim, 'The Problem of Generations', 306–7.

[48]   Mannheim, 'The Problem of Generations', 318.

[49]   The only comparable approach by a historian of Germany is A. Dirk Moses's influential study of the '45ers, which focuses on the antagonism between two key West German intellectuals, the sociologists Jürgen Habermas and Wilhelm Hennis. It is primarily an intellectual history, however, and closely focused on these two individuals and their postwar body of thought. Moses, *German Intellectuals*.

[50]   Charles Tilly, *Stories, Identities and Political Change* (Oxford, 2002), x.

[51]   Jürgen Zinnecker, '"Das Problem der Generationen": Überlegungen zu Karl Mannheims kanonischem Text', in Reulecke and Müller-Luckner, *Generationalität*, 33–58; Eva-Maria Silies, *Liebe, Lust und Last: Die Pille als weibliche Generationserfahrung in der Bundesrepublik 1960–1980* (Göttingen, 2010); Christina Benninghaus, 'Das Geschlecht der Generation. Zum Zusammenhang von Generationalität und Männlichkeit um 1930', in: Jureit and Wildt, *Generationen*, 127–58; for a specific critique of the limitations of generational histories of 1968, see Maud Anne Bracke, 'One-dimensional conflict? Recent scholarship on 1968 and the limitations of the generation concept', *Journal of Contemporary History*, 47, 3 (2012), 638–46.

impact of earlier (or later) experiences, the fact that identities hardly remain static throughout an individual's life course, or understanding how and why people sustain a sense of belonging to a generational collective over time was of less interest to him. The most theoretically rigorous and innovative works on generation produced in the last few years—many of them by historians of Germany—have done much to deconstruct Mannheim's theory and put it back together in different forms by drawing on insights from neighbouring disciplines to capture a wider range of (generational) experiences than his model allowed. Moreover, these works no longer treat generations simply as objective 'things', as essentialist entities that remain stable throughout the lives of their members and explain everything about individual trajectories. Instead, they treat them as contingent communities bound by affect and imagination that require communication to generate and sustain a sense of belonging over time.[52]

This book builds on these studies in adopting a more constructivist understanding of generation. Rather than simply establishing the other '68ers' historical agency—asserting their role in the history of the Federal Republic, in other words—it also analyses their generational subjectivities and self-fashioning. Why and how their student experiences remained relevant to them in an ever-changing present is one of its main subjects. This book is thus based on the premise that, like all self-conscious generation units, the other '68ers were at once a real and an imagined community, and it tries to disentangle the two realms only as much as possible. This is not to suggest that centre-right activists simply invented a self-serving history of collective action and participation in 1968.[53] As we shall see, the stories they told were always tied to actual experiences in the 1960s and 1970s, different elements of which they chose to accentuate at different times.

[52] Bernd Weisbrod, 'Generation und Generationalität in der Neueren Geschichte', *Aus Politik und Zeitgeschichte* (2005), B8, 3–9; Ulrike Jureit, *Generationenforschung* (Göttingen, 2006); Lovell, *Generations in Twentieth-Century Europe*; Björn Bohnenkamp, Till Manning, and Eva-Maria Silies (eds.), *Generation als Erzählung: Neue Perspektiven auf ein kulturelles Deutungsmuster* (Göttingen, 2009); Lutz Niethammer, 'Die letzte Gemeinschaft: Über die Konstruierbarkeit von Generationen und ihre Grenzen', in *Historische Beiträge zur Generationsforschung*, edited by Bernd Weisbrod (Göttingen, 2009), 13–38; Andreas Petersen, *Radikale Jugend: Die sozialistische Jugendbewegung in der Schweiz 1900–1930: Radikalisierungsanalyse und Generationentheorie* (Zurich, 2001); Beate Fietze, *Historische Generationen: Über einen sozialen Mechanismus kulturellen Wandels und kollektiver Kreativität* (Bielefeld, 2009); the specific German contributions to the historiography of generation are outlined eloquently by Bernd Weisbrod in a 2018 AHR conversation. Abosede George, Clive Glaser, Margaret D. Jacobs, Chitra Joshi, Emily Marker, Alexandra Walsham, Wang Zheng, and Bernd Weisbrod, 'AHR Conversation: Each Generation Writes Its Own History of Generations', *AHR*, 123, 5 (2018), 1505–46; on the dangers of reifying identities, such as generation, and using them uncritically as categories of analysis, see Rogers Brubaker and Frederick Cooper, 'Beyond "Identity"', *Theory and Society*, 29, 1 (2000), 1–47, here 5.
[53] This is in contrast to the thought-provoking study on the afterlives of the French 1968 by Kristin Ross, who treats 'generation' as a political ploy by converts to liberalism that sought to detract from the revolutionary aspirations of the movement. Ross, *1968 and Its Afterlives*. I build on Lutz Niethammer here, who points out that the constructedness of generations as symbolic homes has its limits. Niethammer, 'Die letzte Gemeinschaft'.

In short, *The Other '68ers* does not simply paint a collective portrait of centre-right activists, one that illustrates who they were, what they did in 1968, and how those years shaped them as political actors. It pays equally close attention to how they made sense of their experiences with activism, the stories they told in retrospect (and the ones they preferred not to tell), and how and why what they selected as relevant about these years changed with time. In doing so, it aims for a reflexive use of a notoriously slippery concept, even if it does not escape entirely the ambiguities of generation.

Sources

This book relies on a variety of sources to fulfil its different goals. It uses archival documents from twelve archives in Germany and the United States and from a number of private collections, many of them analysed here for the first time, to establish the contours of centre-right activism around 1968. Pamphlets, speeches, government and party documents, and newspaper and other media reports allow us to track what the other '68ers did in 1968, not least the manifold ways in which they related to the Left at the time. Posters, cartoons, and photographs provide insights into their aesthetic preferences and how they represented themselves to the outside world. Opinion polls and sociological studies from the period help to contextualize the views of students who were politically active. They also allow us to trace how generational interpretations shaped understandings of the student movement from the very beginning.

Given that one of this book's major goals is to understand what activists thought they were doing around 1968, at the time and with hindsight, personal testimonies are among the most important sources of this study. Some of its protagonists, particularly those who went on to pursue high-profile careers in politics, later published autobiographies or memoirs.[54] Others narrated their personal recollections of activism publicly, sometimes repeatedly throughout the decades, usually on the occasion of major anniversaries of 1968. Such testimonies have much to reveal about the meaning centre-right activists ascribed to 1968 and how they fit this period into their overall life story at different moments in time.[55]

This study is not just based on written testimonies, however. It also makes use of more than two dozen oral history interviews with a sample of former centre-right

---

[54] Peter Radunski, *Aus der politischen Kulisse: Mein Beruf zur Politik* (Berlin/Kassel, 2014/15); Friedbert Pflüger, *Ehrenwort: Das System Kohl und der Neubeginn* (Munich, 2000); Horst Teltschik, *329 Tage: Innenansichten der Einigung* (Berlin, 1991); Detlef Stronk, *Berlin in den Achtziger Jahren: Im Brennpunkt der Deutsch-Deutschen Geschichte* (Berlin, 2009). Others had written draft memoirs or autobiographical sketches that they had not published but were willing to share with me.

[55] Volker Depkat, 'Autobiographie und die soziale Konstruktion von Wirklichkeit', *Geschichte und Gesellschaft*, 29, 3 (2003), 441–76; Volker Depkat, *Lebenswenden und Zeitenwenden: Deutsche Politiker und die Erfahrungen des 20. Jahrhundert* (Munich, 2007).

activists. Between 2008 and 2014, I travelled across the old Federal Republic, from Berlin to Bonn and from Munich to Hamburg, to record the memories of former centre-right activists. I first approached those who had been most visible— chairpersons or leading figures in RCDS or the Student Unions—especially those who had been active in the centres of left-wing protest and had therefore been at the forefront of engagement with the student movement; others I identified via snowball technique. When the stories my interviewees told me began to sound familiar, I sought out people whose names I had seen mentioned in documents from the period, but who had spoken less frequently about their roles on the centre-right, particularly women and activists whose political views shifted after 1968.

During the semi-structured interviews that usually lasted between one-and-a-half and three hours, I first allowed people to tell the story they wanted to tell, by inviting them to talk freely about their lives, how they got involved in student activism, and what they remembered about 1968.[56] I then followed up with questions about specific issues they had brought up, things other interviewees had told me or that I had seen in the archives, or about what seemed like inconsistencies in their stories. This technique generated rich information about 1968 and what these years have meant to activists of the centre-right. Like all other sources, however, oral history interviews have to be analysed with care. Interviewing people forty, and sometimes nearly fifty, years after the events meant that they talked about 1968 with great temporal distance and narrated the past through the prism of the present. People 'tell the past as it appears to them'.[57] Their life stories were framed by a host of public representations of the student movement—and therefore by debates about a highly contested era in which they had often intervened themselves.[58] This book addresses this issue by using personal testimonies not so much to document what happened, but primarily to understand how the interviewees articulated subjective experiences of activism around 1968. Nevertheless, the interviews often also produced vivid descriptions of events and revealed crucial pieces of factual information that I then did my best to cross-reference with written sources from the period. In an effort to ensure readability and avoid repetition, the testimonies are used freely throughout the text, but they feature first and foremost as records of perceptions. As much as possible, I have contextualized them with other sources, including personal testimonies by the same people from earlier or later periods.[59]

---

[56] Lynn Abrams, *Oral History Theory*, 2nd ed. (Abingdon, 2016), 124.

[57] Alessandro Portelli, *The Death of Luigi Trastulli and Other Stories: Form and Meaning in Oral History* (Albany, NY, 1991), 52; also Abrams, *Oral History Theory*, 7, 90; *Klatch, A Generation Divided*, 13.

[58] For a discussion of similar methodological issues with autobiographies and memoirs, see Konrad Jarausch, *Broken Lives: How Ordinary Germans Experienced the 20th Century* (Princeton, NJ, 2018).

[59] My methodology here thus differs from the one we adopted in our collectively written book on European activism around 1968. Robert Gildea, James Mark, and Anette Warring (eds.), *Europe's 1968:*

One additional factor 'makes oral history different', as oral history pioneer Alessandro Portelli put it: the historian is intimately involved in creating these sources in the first place.[60] The mere fact of my presence, including the assumptions my interviewees had about who I was, influenced how they told their stories. Many just seemed pleasantly surprised, perhaps even a bit flattered, that a German historian who was based abroad and had been born a decade after 1968 was interested in obscure details about their student days; some assumed that I had sought them out because I was politically sympathetic; others were guarded because I did not seem sympathetic enough.[61] Even if I rarely discuss it explicitly in the chapters of the book, I have done my best to reflect on how these mutual perceptions—what oral historians call intersubjectivity—shaped the narratives.[62]

Interviewing historical actors inevitably means that one learns things that could not have been gleaned from the archival record or published memoirs alone. The interviews took place in a great variety of settings: in people's private homes or in office suites or restaurants. I interviewed one former activist from West Berlin in an opulent private members' club overlooking Berlin's beautiful Gendarmenmarkt. Another, who was still visibly frail and hooked up to a medical device, I interviewed in the courtyard of a Bonn hospital where he had just undergone surgery. These starkly different settings alone—each chosen by the respective interviewee—provided information about these individuals before they even spoke. Beyond producing a narrative account of their political lives, such encounters yielded insights into who the other '68ers had become, how they chose to present themselves, what mattered to them, and how they lived. I may have only recorded what they said, but could not help to take note of small gestures—such as when one of them lit a cigar during the interview or when the wives of male interviewees came into the room to serve refreshments. All of this found its way into my analysis in one way or another.[63]

Voices of Revolt (Oxford, 2013). That book relied overwhelmingly on oral testimonies. Almost all quotations from the interviews in this book are attributed to the interviewees by name. In a very few cases, I have anonymized the interviewees. This was done in cases where providing the interviewee's name would not add much to the interpretation or the personal information conveyed might be embarrassing.

[60] Portelli, *The Death of Luigi Trastulli*, 45–58.

[61] Two instances highlight these differences in perception: one interviewee assumed I had been in RCDS and offered me help in getting this book published through the Konrad Adenauer Foundation, the think tank affiliated with the CDU. Another interviewee told me that his partner had warned him against speaking to me because I wore a high-collared black coat in a photograph shown on my university's web page—the implication being that I looked like a leftie. Regardless of such assumptions, I did my best to build rapport with all my interviewees, as it made for better interviews. For a far more extreme example of dealing with interviewees' assumptions about an interviewer's politics, see Kathleen Blee, 'Evidence, Empathy and Ethics: Lessons from Oral Histories of the Klan', *Journal of American History*, 80, 2 (1993), 596–606; on the importance of building rapport also V.R. Yow, *Recording Oral History* (2005), 157–87.

[62] Abrams, *Oral History Theory*, 62.

[63] On the importance of performance during an interview, see Abrams, *Oral History Theory*, 22 and 151.

The interviewees' very mode of talking about their lives was also instructive. With some exceptions, centre-right activists were less emphatically self-reflexive than activists of the Left for whom self-critique was an important part of the alternative culture they had helped to create. The other '68ers were also much more focused on traditional politics than activists of the Left, whom I had interviewed for a previous project. Left-wing activists often viewed the personal as political and therefore found it quite natural—or even imperative—to talk about their personal lives to a relative stranger.[64] Interviewing former centre-right activists was a very different experience, but it was invaluable in helping me see them as three-dimensional characters whose subjectivity mattered.

Regardless of what some of my interviewees may have tacitly assumed, however, this is not a work of political advocacy. To be sure, the actions of left-wing activists and groups are often analysed here through the prism of how they appeared to their political opponents, meaning that the more extreme aspects of left-wing activism take centre stage. However, this specific perspective should not be read as a verdict on the character of the 1968 Left as a whole. By examining these years from the perspective of the centre-right, this book does not purport to offer a comprehensive analysis of student activism around 1968. What is more, that I chose a methodology long associated with challenging established power dynamics and giving 'a voice to the voiceless'—indeed a methodology pioneered by historians with links to the 1968 Left[65]—does not mean that the goal of this book is to portray activists of the centre-right as objectively powerless or marginalized. On the contrary, many of them arrived at the centre of power quite some time before the '68ers of the Left, and they have done much to shape public memories of the student movement, even if scholars have rarely taken note. Oral histories with '68ers of the centre-right, in combination with a wealth of written sources from the period, allow me to trace what it was like to experience 1968 on the 'other side'. Uncovering this little-known history is the aim of this book.

[64] Gildea, Mark and Warring, *Europe's 1968*; see further Sven Reichardt, *Authentizität und Gemeinschaft: Linksalternatives Leben in den siebziger und frühen achtziger Jahren* (Berlin, 2014), 887; Celia Hughes, *Young Lives on the Left: Sixties Activism and the Liberation of the Self* (Manchester, 2015).

[65] Luisa Passerini, *Autobiography of a Generation: Italy, 1968* (Hanover, 1996). The earliest works of oral history in Germany were also produced by left-wing historians. Lutz Niethammer (ed.), *'Die Jahre weiß man nicht, wo man die heute hinsetzen soll.' Faschismuserfahrungen im Ruhrgebiet* (Berlin/Bonn, 1983); Lutz Niethammer (ed.), *'Hinterher merkt man, daß es richtig war, daß es schiefgegangen ist.' Nachkriegserfahrungen im Ruhrgebiet* (Berlin/Bonn 1983); Lutz Niethammer and Alexander von Plato (eds.), *'Wir kriegen jetzt andere Zeiten': Auf der Suche nach der Erfahrung des Volkes in nachfaschistischen Ländern* (Bonn, 1989); on the history of oral history in Germany, Knud Andresen, Linde Apel, and Kirsten Heinsohn (eds.), *Es gilt das gesprochene Wort: Oral History und Zeitgeschichte heute* (Göttingen, 2015); see further Abrams, *Oral History Theory*, 4–5; 154–6; and Robert Gildea and James Mark, 'Introduction', Gildea, Mark, and Warring, *Europe's 1968*, 9.

Chapter Structure

The structure of this book is partly thematic and partly chronological. The first chapter, *Between Engagement and Enmity*, charts the involvement of centre-right students in some of the key moments and debates around student activism from the mid-1960s until the climactic years of the West German protest movement in 1967/68. It demonstrates that centre-right students were there throughout, and not just as passive observers. Writing them back into the history of 1968, this chapter reveals that student activism in these years was a much broader, more versatile, and, ultimately, more consequential phenomenon than the traditionally narrower focus on left-wing radicals allows.

The second chapter, *Talking About (My) Generation*, engages with several major themes that have long animated research on the West German 1960s: protesters' family backgrounds and wartime childhoods, the meaning of the Nazi past to their activism, and intergenerational relations. Like their student peers on the Left, centre-right activists had been raised in a post-genocidal society. With that in mind, how did they view and engage with Germany's recent history of mass violence? The chapter highlights the centrality of anti-totalitarianism to their thinking. It also shows that, inspired by the '45ers and nudged by social scientists who routinely portrayed student protest as a symptom of generational conflict, they began to think of themselves as a distinct generational community in the late 1960s.

Between Adenauer and Coca-Cola, the third chapter, focuses on the cultural practices of centre-right students to determine to what extent they participated in the broader cultural moment that was 1968. It examines different forms of cultural expression and everyday aesthetics to investigate whether centre-right activists viewed these as political. It also examines their attitudes toward the evident modernization of sexuality in West Germany in this period. Most importantly, it puts women's experiences centre stage. Analysing changing gender roles and centre-right women's attitudes toward the emerging women's movement, it seeks to understand why at least some of them thought that emancipation did not have to equal revolution.

The fourth chapter, entitled *From Berlin to Saigon and Back*, argues that centre-right activists not only disagreed with left-wing students' plans for the Federal Republic's domestic future, but that they also had a distinct internationalist imagination. In spite of an ever-growing literature on the Global 1960s, we know surprisingly little about how centre-right activists conceived of the global. This chapter broadens our view of student internationalism around 1968 by showing that the centre-right also looked beyond the borders of the Federal Republic. The chapter explores three areas on their 'mental map' in detail: the powerful ways in which the Cold War binary structured the centre-right's view of the world; the (Western) European ties of conservative and centre-right student groups; and, finally, their campaigns for human rights in the wake of 1968.

Chapter 5, *Combative Politics*, examines the shift toward a much more confrontational form of campus politics in the wake of the dissolution of SDS in 1969/70, one in which concerns about left-wing violence moved centre stage. It analyses centre-right students' roles in some of the key debates of the 1970s—the controversy surrounding the 'Radicals Decree', the 'Mescalero Affair', and students' alleged support for the terrorism of the RAF. It argues that RCDS was instrumental in making a scandal of left-wing activism at a time when a left-wing coalition governed the country for the first time since the war. Centre-right students contributed much to the febrile climate of the 1970s, this chapter shows, stoking public hysteria and helping to create a climate of distrust that made left-wing dissent politically suspect. Their conduct highlights that the process of political liberalization in the wake of 1968 was not a linear but rather a winding one.

The final chapter, *The (Ir)Resistible Rise of the Other '68ers*, traces how these former student activists became a major public phenomenon after Kohl was elected Chancellor in 1982. It charts the other '68ers' short 'march through the institutions' and assesses their programmatic, strategic, and cultural impact on the CDU/CSU from the 1970s into the 1980s. Second, it analyses the role that commemorations of 1968 and generational claims played in their rise to public prominence. It shows that the other '68ers helped to shape memories of the student movement in important ways and, from the 1980s into the early 2000s, were key players in the memory wars about how exactly 1968 had transformed West German politics and society.

The Conclusion summarizes and expands upon the findings of the book's six chapters. It offers some overarching comments about how this study helps us to rethink the existing scholarship on 1968 and postwar German history more broadly. It also teases out some of the commonalities between activists of the Left and Right to highlight the ways in which the other '68ers and their student opponents on the Left often moved in tandem, even if inadvertently so.

The chapters of this book tell a very specific story—that of the other '68ers. However, in doing so, they address much larger historical and conceptual questions: about the nature of generational belonging; about the ways in which Germans struggled over democracy in the postwar period and came to terms with the Nazi past; about the contested nature of memory; and about the place of 1968 in German history. In short, this book casts a well-known chapter of Germany's twentieth century in a new light.

1

Between Engagement and Enmity

On 29 January 1968 remarkable scenes occurred in the southwestern city of
Freiburg, home to one of West Germany's oldest universities. On this day, the
sociologist Ralf Dahrendorf, one of the key thinkers of postwar German liberalism
and the new rising star of the liberal Free Democratic Party (FDP), held a
spontaneous, open-air debate with SDS activist Rudi Dutschke. Dutschke was a
prominent left-wing radical based in West Berlin, who would only barely survive
an extreme right-wing assassination attempt on him less than three months later.
Sitting atop a vehicle equipped with a loudspeaker, the charismatic SDS figurehead
and the prominent liberal professor laid out their contrasting visions of politics in
the Federal Republic for several hours. Thousands of curious onlookers surrounded them. The left-liberal weekly *Die Zeit* described the unusual scenes thus:

> Rudi Dutschke, the dear enfant terrible of the German bourgeoisie, had come to
> strike fear in the Liberals. Pale-faced, longhaired and wearing a leather jacket—
> exactly how one would describe the cliché of a revolutionary—he was sitting on a
> sound truck, the professor from the FDP beside him. In monotonous staccato,
> the itinerant preacher of the protest chanted his theses about the corruption of
> the establishment, the political impotence of the parties, and the [...] one-track
> specialists of politics. Dahrendorf defended the liberal position of reform within
> the parliamentary system and spoke about the protest's one-track specialists, who
> rebelled for understandable reasons, but, through their radical methods, had
> provided the conservatives the occasion and pretext to block reforms.[1]

This memorable encounter between Dahrendorf and Dutschke has often been
invoked in the scholarship and in commemorative pieces on 1968 because it
involved two of the era's best-known protagonists. Moreover, it reflected what
is generally considered one of the most important frontlines of these years:
Dutschke, the magnetic student rebel who called for revolution, and Dahrendorf,
one of West Germany's chief public intellectuals and a staunch defender of the
country's democratic institutions and parliamentary pluralism, albeit one who
explicitly championed reform of the system.[2] The scene clearly invokes notions of

---

[1] Rolf Zundel, 'Liberale Blume im Knopfloch', *Die Zeit*, 5 (2 February 1968), 3.
[2] A recent major biography of Dahrendorf, for instance, opens with the legendary clash between
these two figures and calls the photographs taken on the day 'iconic'. A section of the photograph of

The Other '68ers: Student Protest and Christian Democracy in West Germany. Anna von der Goltz,
Oxford University Press (2021). © Anna von der Goltz. DOI: 10.1093/oso/9780198849520.003.0002

generational conflict—between Dutschke, the '68er, and Dahrendorf, the '45er—and of 1968 as defined first and foremost by the vehement disagreements and contrasting visions of two clearly delineated generations of prominent West German intellectuals.[3]

Moreover, the numerous pictures taken by some of the leading photographers of the Bonn Republic, who were in town to cover the FDP's annual convention, convey the quirky spirit of these years: Dutschke in his fur-collared leather jacket perched next to a cross-legged, suited Dahrendorf on the roof of a car, surrounded by a huge crowd of listeners as well as cameras and microphones. What could better represent the spontaneity and urgency of political debate during these years and the glare of public attention under which it took place?

Accounts and images of the day that focus on the two most prominent protagonists, however, conceal as much as they reveal about the event in Freiburg—and, as this book hopes to show, about West German student protest and political debate around 1968 more generally. In fact, Dutschke was not the only student leader who took part in the discussion. At least three young centre-right activists were present throughout. What is more, they were instrumental in making the debate happen in the first place—a debate which most commentators interpreted as a win for Dahrendorf and liberal reformism.[4]

A few weeks earlier, Meinhard Ade (b. 1944) and Ignaz Bender (b. 1937), two young Christian Democrats with a history of involvement in student politics in the city, had founded the centre-right student group Democratic Centre [Demokratische Mitte, DM]. The DM was modelled on similar groups in places like Munich and Cologne, and was intended to counter an upsurge in radical left-wing protest activity at Freiburg's renowned Albert Ludwig University. On 29 January, Ade and Bender heard that activists from the extraparliamentary opposition (Außerparlamentarische Opposition, APO), a broad-based protest movement that had organized demonstrations across the country over the previous year, were on their way to storm the FDP convention in an effort to unmask

---

Dahrendorf and Dutschke taken by dpa photographer Fritz Reiss graces the book's cover. See Franziska Meifort, *Ralf Dahrendorf: Eine Biographie* (Munich, 2017), 11, book cover, and 336; see also Ralf Dahrendorf, 'Die Revolution, die nie stattfand', *Die Zeit*, 20 (13 May 1988), available at https://www.zeit.de/1988/20/die-revolution-die-nie-stattfand (accessed on 22 May 2018); Thomas Hauser, 'Revolte ante portas: Als Rudi Dutschke und Ralf Dahrendorf 1968 in Freiburg debattierten', *Badische Zeitung* (26 January 2018), available at https://www.badische-zeitung.de/revolte-ante-portas-als-rudi-dutschke-und-ralf-dahrendorf-1968-in-freiburg-debattierten–148624438.html (accessed on 22 May 2018).

[3] Explaining 1968 as the clash between these two political generations is a common trope. See e.g. Wehler, *Deutsche Gesellschaftsgeschichte 1949–1990*, 310; for a powerful critique of this paradigm, see von Hodenberg, *Das andere Achtundsechzig*, 13–14.

[4] Meifort, *Dahrendorf*, 167–8. Media coverage of the student protests was often highly personalized and heavily focused on Dutschke. Stallmann, *Die Erfindung von '1968'*, 305–52. Dahrendorf was also not the only FDP delegate who took part. His liberal colleague Hermann Oxfort, the chair of the Free Democrats in West Berlin, was there and participated, as was Hildegard Hamm-Brücher, a member of the party board.

the only remaining opposition party in the *Bundestag* as yet another 'establish-ment' club. The two centre-right activists quickly made their way to the city centre, which looked 'like a besieged fortress'.[5]

The left-wing protesters had not simply shown up to stir trouble, however. The FDP's youth organization, the Young Democrats (*Jungdemokraten*) had, in fact, invited SDS chair Karl Dietrich ('K.D.') Wolff and Dutschke to a debate with Dahrendorf during the convention's opening night. However, they had not cleared the invitation with the party leadership. The latter objected and cancelled the debate, but the SDS activists turned up anyway. A small group of Liberal delegates, among them Dahrendorf, then stepped outside to pre-empt a suspected 'go-in'.[6] When the sociologist came out of the municipal hall to meet the pro-testers, the young centre-right activists were there and offered to let him debate Dutschke on top of a former West Berlin taxicab, a Mercedes 180 Diesel. The car belonged to Axel Wormit, a fellow DM activist, who often used it to campaign for a local Christian Democratic candidate. It had one of the party's loudspeaker systems installed on its roof, which is how Dahrendorf and Dutschke obtained their megaphones.[7] The centre-right activists' only condition had been that they would also take part.

Throughout the debate, Ade and Bender stood directly next to Dutschke and Dahrendorf and helped to keep order. Ade, who would later be closely involved in the programmatic renewal of the Christian Democrats in the 1970s and, in the 1980s, serve as a key aide to Federal President Richard von Weizsäcker, also weighed in repeatedly. Rather than siding with Dutschke (b. 1940), who was close to him in age, however, he sided with Dahrendorf (b. 1929), the '45er, who portrayed existing institutions as the best means to affect change.[8]

Both of them were even captured in many of the photographs taken on the day, but because their faces were not as well-known then (nor are they today), they easily get lost in the crowd. The images that would come to form part of the

---

[5] Rolf Zundel, 'Liberale Blume im Knopfloch', *Die Zeit*, 5 (2 February 1968), 3.

[6] 'Linker Lou', *Der Spiegel*, 4 (22 January 1968), 25; Meifort, *Dahrendorf*, 16–7. Bender claimed later—a little hyperbolically—that he had alerted the FDP delegates inside the convention centre to the threat of imminent disruption and thereby saved the Liberals' entire convention. *Ignaz Bender Private Papers*, Ignaz Bender, 'Die Rettung des Freiburger FDP-Parteitags im Januar 1968', *Memoiren*, MS (2014), n.p.; Bender interview; given that Dutschke and Dahrendorf had previously agreed to debate each other, this seems somewhat exaggerated. However, the planned debate between them was supposed to take place in the nearby Paulus Hall and involve several other people. At the very least, then, the centre-right activists' intervention led to the unconventional staging of the debate on top of the vehicle. 'Linker Lou', *Der Spiegel*, 4 (22 January 1968), 25.

[7] Ade interview; Bender interview; Axel Wormit, telephone communication with the author, 12 June 2018; the *FAZ*'s coverage of the debate noted that the vehicle belonged to the RCDS. Günther von Lojewski, 'Die Stunde Dahrendorfs', *Frankfurter Allgemeine Zeitung* (31 January 1968), 4.

[8] Ade interview; also APO-Archiv (ArchAPO), RCDS, 18. Ord. Bundesdelegierten-Versammlung, file 1968, '6. Beschluss der 18. Ord. DV' and 'Beschluss der 18. Ord. DV (60. Antrag)'; and Bender interview.

iconography of 1968 typically zoomed in on Dutschke and Dahrendorf. What is more, the two centre-right activists were often cropped from later reproductions of photographs that originally showed them—such as the famous photograph by Fritz Reiss featured on this book's cover.[9] Their presence and involvement in one of the best-known protest events of the late 1960s—and subsequent erasure from this history—however, hints at an important aspect of these years that is all too often overlooked: the political upheaval around this time was not just characterized by a confrontation between the old and the young or between two different generations of intellectuals. Instead, it involved student activists who were the same age as their activist peers on the Left, but whose political style and ideas about how to remedy the ills of the political system of the Federal Republic differed profoundly.

Illustration 1.1 Socialist student leader Rudi Dutschke and the sociologist Ralf Dahrendorf debate on the roof of a car in Freiburg in January 1968. Pictured to Dahrendorf's right are centre-right activists Meinhard Ade (face partially covered) and Ignaz Bender (shown in profile).
(J.H. Darchinger/Friedrich-Ebert-Stiftung)

[9] Ade was captured in photographs taken on the day more often than Bender. See e.g. the photograph Reiss took for dpa that is used on this book's cover. On the history of this image, see further Jens Kitzler Klaus Riexinger, 'Wer ist "A 1833 Reiss"?', *Badische Zeitung* (8 April 2018), available at http://www.badische-zeitung.de/freiburg/wer-ist-a-1833-reiss-151296978.html (accessed on 22 May 2018). See also Günther Hofmann, 'Nach links Flagge zeigen', *Die Zeit*, 21 (1988), 7, who mentions Ade's presence in the 1968 Reiss photograph.

This chapter charts the involvement of centre-right students in some of the key moments and debates around student activism from the mid-1960s until the climactic years of the protest movement in 1967/68. It traces their early mobilization in the middle of the decade, shows how they rallied increasingly from 1967 onward to formulate a response to the upsurge in left-wing protest activity, and examines their theoretical efforts and relationship with activists of the Left. The final section introduces a group of Christian Democratic 'renegades' whose close engagement with the Left made them rethink their politics in fundamental ways. Looking at some of the key themes and events of these years from the perspective of the centre-right, the chapter demonstrates that centre-right students were there throughout 1968, and not just as passive observers. As we will see, they were an important part of this political moment and engaged with and participated in the student movement in manifold ways. Writing them back into the history of 1968—by quite literally expanding the frame—reveals that political activism in these years was a much broader, more versatile, and, ultimately, more consequential phenomenon than the traditionally narrower focus on left-wing radicals in much of the literature allows.

Centre-Right Students in the Streets

By the time that he helped stage the debate between Dutschke and Dahrendorf in 1968, Ignaz Bender had already been politically active for several years. A Freiburg native, he had been involved in West German student politics throughout the late 1950s and early 1960s, first in Bonn, then in his hometown. He had advocated for greater student representation in university affairs since the early 1960s. As early as 1961, Bender was involved in a strike to protest against the poor quality and excessive pricing of the food served in the Freiburg University cafeteria, one of the first strikes on a West German campus.[10] Bender was also active nationally as a leading member of the Association of German Students (*Vereinigte Deutsche Studentenschaften*, VDS). On 1 July 1965, however, he made national headlines when an event he organized under the auspices of VDS drew approximately 40 per cent of the West German student population into the streets to demand educational reform, the largest student demonstrations the Federal Republic had witnessed to that day.[11] Inspired by the pedagogue Georg Picht's diagnosis of a

---

[10] Ignaz Bender, 'Der Freiburger Mensastreik', *Memoiren*, MS (2014), n.p.; Bender interview. At the time of writing, the unpublished memoirs that Bender had kindly shared with me had not yet appeared in print but were forthcoming as Ignaz Bender, *Erlebtes und Bewegtes—in Hochschule, Europe und der Welt* (Baden-Baden, 2020).

[11] Sigward Lönnendonker and Tilman Fichter, *Hochschule im Umbruch: Teil IV: Die Krise (1964–1967)* (Berlin, 1975), document no. 417, 220; 'Heißer Sommer', *Der Spiegel*, 21 (1965), 76–7. The article includes a photograph of Bender; also 'Die Wecker der Nation', *Semester-Spiegel* [Münster], 12, 80 (1965).

Illustration 1.2 Cover of the student magazine *Semester-Spiegel* (Münster) featuring the student demonstrations of 'Action 1 July' 1965 with organizer Ignaz Bender on the right.
(Semester-Spiegel, Münster)

looming 'education crisis' in the Federal Republic, up to 100,000 students marched in university towns from Kiel to Munich on this day to demand more funding for teaching and scholarship and a merit-based restructuring of the education system.[12]

'Action 1 July—Educational Crisis' illustrated that things had begun to stir within the universities and that West German students were willing to take to the streets en masse for the first time in the postwar period. Even the foreign press,

---

[12] Georg Picht, *Die deutsche Bildungskatastrophe: Analyse und Dokumentation* (Freiburg im Breisgau, 1964); 'Heißer Sommer', *Der Spiegel*, 21 (1965), 77; also 'Deutsche Studenten demonstrieren', *Die Zeit*, 28 (1965), 9; Bender interview.

keeping an ever-watchful eye on the country's democratic potential, took note of West German students' new oppositional stance.[13] As such, these demonstrations have sometimes been interpreted as part and parcel of the anti-establishment radicalism of 1968.[14] However, the fact that it was a Christian Democratic activist who organized them casts 'Action 1 July' in a rather different light, highlighting, as it does, the integral role that the centre-right played in this opening phase of student unrest as well as the breadth of students' unhappiness with the status quo.

It would indeed be something of a stretch to interpret 'Action 1 July' as the stuff of left-wing radicalism. Picht's study, extracts of which had been serialized in the popular conservative weekly *Christ und Welt* and which provided the intellectual backbone of 'Action 1 July', compared the West German education system to those of its Western European neighbours and the United States and found that it lagged far behind. This led Picht to conclude that the Federal Republic's economic competitiveness and international standing were threatened. At stake was nothing less than the 'naked existence of the people', as the editor of *Christ und Welt* put it in his foreword.[15] Picht's findings did not just have unmistakably nationalist overtones; they were also tied to the Cold War logic of having to continuously outdo the Federal Republic's Eastern neighbour, socialist East Germany. His project of educational reform aimed at tapping the full potential of West Germany's workforce was thus perfectly in line with conservative visions for the country's future.[16]

Bender had met Picht at a gathering of a Catholic women's youth group and, alarmed by the grim picture the pedagogue had painted, came up with the idea of a 'propagandistic mass action' to generate momentum for reform.[17] Given that Bender was a Christian Democratic student leader and that the Christian Democrats had governed the Federal Republic continuously since its foundation, first under Chancellor Konrad Adenauer and then under Ludwig Erhard, the plan to stage such protests was a delicate matter. While other Christian Democratic student leaders generally welcomed the calls for better funding for education, they also worried that attacks against their own mother party would backfire. They thus attempted to ensure that the VDS-run event did not have too obvious an anti-government thrust.[18] Their efforts paid off. As Nick Thomas has rightly noted, the

---

[13] 'Protests over Education in Germany', *The Times* (London), 2 July 1965, 10.

[14] Wolfgang Kraushaar, 'Denkmodelle der 68er', *Aus Politik und Zeitgeschichte* B 22–3 (2001).

[15] Giselher Wirsing, 'Einführender Leitartikel aus "Christ und Welt"', in Picht, *Die deutsche Bildungskatastrophe*, 12. Wirsing was a well-known right-wing author in postwar Germany. During the Nazi years, he had worked for the security service of Hitler's SS, the SD.

[16] Philipp Gassert, *Kurt Georg Kiesinger: 1904–1988* (Munich, 2006), 435–8; 'Heißer Sommer', *Der Spiegel*, 21 (1965), 76–7. On the nationalist overtones of Picht's study, see also Wehrs, *Protest der Professoren*, 45.

[17] 'Heißer Sommer', *Der Spiegel*, 21 (1965), 76–7; Bender interview.

[18] ACDP, 4-6-7, 'Rechenschaftsbericht des Bundesvorsitzenden Gert Hammer' [1966], 22–3; ACDP, 4-6-52/3, RCDS leaders Gert Hammer und Wolfgang Weltin, letter to the state- and group chairpersons, 24 May 1965.

'rather genteel and decorous form of the mass meetings' on 1 July 1965 stood 'in stark contrast with the openly confrontational style of protests that were to follow in the coming years'.[19] Bender later stressed that the demonstrations had been meant to issue a wake-up call rather than a fundamental critique of the system. 'That was really not against the state, but rather I wanted to integrate the establishment. [...] That was [...] essentially quite a different event than what came afterwards.'[20]

Bender continued to advocate for educational reform well beyond 1 July 1965. In September of that year, he helped to launch the campaign 'Student auf's Land' [Students to the Countryside], which encouraged pupils from rural areas to attend university, first in the surrounding areas of Freiburg, then in other West German states as well. Picht's book had argued that the tripartite structure of the school system maintained the outdated class structures of the Wilhelmine era and that the system was particularly detrimental to pupils in rural areas where the vast majority did not enrol in higher schools.[21] To address this problem, student activists travelled to small towns and villages, gave short presentations and answered questions about university life in an effort to encourage pupils from rural areas to continue their education. The campaign was quite successful; in Baden-Württemberg alone, students hosted hundreds of such events and the number of applicants to higher schools rose significantly in subsequent years.[22]

Although inspired by Picht's warnings about the need to safeguard West German economic competitiveness, the egalitarian and meritocratic thrust of 'Student auf's Land' appealed to students of varying political affiliation. Bender remembered campaigning alongside K.D. Wolff (b. 1943), who, as national chair of SDS, marched next to Dutschke en route to the FDP convention in Freiburg in January 1968. '"Students to the Countryside" really brought students, from the conservatives to the socialists, under one roof', Bender remembered later.[23] Marching on 1 July 1965 and campaigning for educational reform, then, did not have to be based on a radical opposition to the Christian Democratic government or the political system of the Federal Republic as a whole, and it involved students from across the political spectrum. This set it apart from many of the better-known student protests of 1967 and 1968. These early protests indicated that many students—centre-right activists prominently among them—cared about their future, wanted change, and, along with their student peers on the Left, demanded that their voices be heard.

---

[19]   Thomas, *Protest Movements*, 54–5.   [20]   Bender interview.
[21]   Picht, *Bildungskatastrophe*, 31–5.
[22]   Ignaz Bender, 'Student aufs Land', *Die Zeit*, 13 (25 March 1966); see further Sebastian Brandt, *Universität und Öffentlichkeit: Das Beispiel der Albert-Ludwigs-Universität Freiburg, 1945–1975* (Dr Phil Dissertation, 2014), 127–9.
[23]   Bender interview.

Educational reform was far from the only issue capable of bringing students of both the Left and Right out into the streets in the mid- and late-1960s. Nor did 'Action 1 July' remain the sole occasion when a centre-right activist organized a major protest. Klaus Laepple (b. 1939), a CDU member since 1957 and active in the Cologne chapter of RCDS, even gained national notoriety as the '"Provo" of the CDU'. The nickname was derived from the Dutch countercultural movement that had achieved international fame for throwing smoke bombs at the Dutch royal wedding parade in March 1966.[24] Laepple was the leader of the student council at the University of Cologne, where he organized a student sit-in against major fare increases in Cologne's public transport system in October 1966. Such demonstrations against rising fare prices were an important element of youth protest around this time and related clashes rocked inner cities from Freiburg to Bremen in the late 1960s. But Cologne was the first city in which things came to a head.[25]

On 24 October 1966 pupils and students staged a sit-in on the tram tracks to block traffic in the centre of the city, which culminated in the biggest clashes between protesters and the police that the city had seen since 1945.[26] While the sit-in was peaceful at first, the resulting traffic jams led to chaotic scenes that eventually escalated. *Der Spiegel* described the events, which soon became known as the Cologne 'tram riots', thus:

Until well after midnight, rioting teenagers smashed the windows of the blocked trams, knocked down benches, and lit trashcans, sandboxes, and a ticket machine on fire. For hours parts of the city centre were impassable. The mounted police deployed, shot water cannons and struck with truncheons. Finally, stones were thrown at the uniformed officers; ambulances flashing their emergency lights rushed to the scene.[27]

Laepple was not physically involved in the clashes with the police and would later suggest, in a clear attempt to distance himself from the violent scenes, that these

---

[24] Eva Schmidt-Häuer, 'Der "Provo" von der CDU', *Die Zeit*, 1 (1967), 7; Laepple interview; on the Dutch provos and the media coverage of their movement, see Niek Pas, *Provo! Mediafenomeen 1965–1967* (Amsterdam, 2015).

[25] Alexander Sedlmaier, *Consumption and Violence: Radical Protest in Cold-War West Germany* (Ann Arbor, MI, 2014), 146–67; in a poll of 2,145 West German 15–25-year olds published in early 1968, 63 per cent of respondents stated that they were willing to demonstrate against a fare increase for bus and tram rides. This was a significantly higher number than young people willing to demonstrate against the war in Vietnam (54 per cent) or the expropriation of the Springer publishing house (23 per cent)—key issues of protest around 1968. Bundesarchiv, Koblenz (BAK), N1229, no. 213, Summary of the IFAK/EMNID poll compiled by the Press and Information Office of the Federal Government, 19 February 1968; see also *Der Spiegel*, 8 (1968). I thank Alexander Sedlmaier for first bringing Laepple's role to my attention.

[26] Kurt Holl and Claudia Glunz (eds.), *1968 am Rhein: Satisfaction und ruhender Verkehr* (Cologne, 1998), 44.

[27] 'Mit faulem Obst', *Der Spiegel*, 52 (1966), 58–9.

had been driven by 'dark elements' among the demonstrators, 'who only wanted to agitate'.[28] Nevertheless, as the student leader who had organized the original sit-in, he became the public face of the 'tram riots'. The city-owned transport company decided to sue the 26-year old personally for a substantial 89,392.45 Deutsche Mark in lost income—the equivalent of almost 180,000 Euros today. Several months before the widely publicized West Berlin trial of left-wing communard Fritz Teufel for throwing stones at police on 2 June 1967, it was the Christian Democratic student leader Laepple who was in the dock for challenging state authority.[29]

Reporting from the courtroom in Cologne, the liberal weekly *Die Zeit* cautioned 'it requires fantasy to see the chair of the General Student Council of Cologne University, Klaus Laepple, as a revolutionary, acting as an academic "Provo" for dark, oppositional goals'. He was a rather 'refined revolutionary', a 'smart man in a blazer and with a diplomat's briefcase in his left hand', according to the paper.[30] West German judges seemingly looked beyond his sleek appearance, however. Although the civil case against him was eventually settled out of court, a resulting criminal case went all the way to the Federal Court of Justice, Germany's highest court of criminal and civil jurisdiction. The judges concluded that the traffic blockade had put the tram drivers under psychological 'duress' based on § 240 of the West German criminal code. Laepple thereby entered the annals of West German legal history: the so-called 'Laepple verdict' defined the use of violence by protesters in the broadest possible terms and would serve as a precedent to criminalize peace activists and anti-nuclear campaigners who engaged in sit-ins in the decades to come.[31] Few of them must have been aware that the case for the criminalization of their protests was based on the actions of a young Christian Democrat in 1966.

Laepple saw himself as an advocate for student interests rather than an anti-establishment figure—in his capacity as chair of the student council he had primarily campaigned for improved conditions in student dormitories and other material comforts for young scholars and he would later embark on a high-profile career in the tourism industry. Nonetheless, he recalled that his prolonged dealings with the judiciary and the experience of being subjected to arbitrary displays of state power had begun to raise broader questions in his mind about the vitality of West German democracy and its treatment of minorities.

---

[28] Laepple interview.

[29] Caroline Dostal, *Demonstranten vor Gericht: Ein Beitrag zur Justizgeschichte der Bundesrepublik* (Frankfurt am Main, 2006).

[30] Eva Schmidt-Häuer, 'Der "Provo" von der CDU', *Die Zeit*, 1 (1967), 7.

[31] Richard Schmid, 'Was dürfen Demonstranten? Das Laepple-Urteil des Bundesgerichtshofs: ein Fehlurteil', *Die Zeit*, 38 (1969), 11; Holl and Glunz, *1968 am Rhein*, 72–3; Sedlmaier, *Consumption and Violence*, 148.

And then somewhere, of course, one also receives [...] this feeling: Is everything still right? Is that still appropriate? Is that what we personally have imagined as democracy? Then came these monumental doubts. In other words, [...] how are minorities treated in a society? Because, of course, we were a minority.[32]

No other moment in the years around 1968 raised concerns about arbitrary displays of state power and the Federal Republic's way of handling youthful dissent more than the events of 2 June 1967. On this day, student protests erupted in West Berlin against the visiting Shah of Iran, Mohammad Reza Pahlavi, an autocratic ruler whose repressive regime was sustained by its close military and economic ties to the United States. That evening, a demonstration in front of the city's opera house, where the Shah and his wife Farah Diba were enjoying a production of Mozart's *The Magic Flute*, was met with a particularly brutal response from city police and Iranian pro-Shah demonstrators, including under-cover agents of Iran's SAVAK, the Pahlavi dynasty's intelligence service.[33] Dozens of young anti-Shah demonstrators sustained injuries from blows issued with slats and batons, and 26-year old student Benno Ohnesorg died after being shot in the back of the head by one Karl-Heinz Kurras, a plainclothes West Berlin policeman.[34] Ohnesorg, who had married merely two months earlier and whose pregnant wife also attended the demonstration, was far from a student radical; the banner he carried on the day modestly called for the 'Autonomy of Tehran University'.[35]

Ohnesorg's death was a critical event in the history of the West German student movement. Such was its significance that it has been suggested that the West German '68ers might more accurately be described as the 'generation of June 2nd' or the "67ers', because, to many young activists, this date symbolized the forma-tive experience of state violence that fuelled their own radicalization.[36] As a case in

---

[32] Laepple interview.   [33] Slobodian, *Foreign Front*, 111–17.

[34] In 2009, the belated revelation that Kurras had been an informal collaborator of the East German security service (Stasi) caused a true media storm, suggesting, as it did, that the Stasi had engineered the event that altered the path of the student movement and rocked the Federal Republic in the days, months, and years to come. Unexpected and suggestive as this revelation may have been, however, there is no evidence that Kurras was following orders from the East German regime when he killed Ohnesorg. Moreover, he was far from the only West Berlin policeman who used excessive force on 2 June 1967. Eckart Michels, *Schahbesuch 1967: Fanal für die Studentenbewegung* (Berlin, 2017), 214–17.

[35] Michels, *Schahbesuch 1967*, 189 and 195.

[36] The Hamburg sociology student and former leader of the SHB Jens Litten spoke of the activist 'Generation of June 2nd' as early as 1969. Jens Litten, 'Die Generation des 2. Juni', *Der Spiegel*, 7 (10 February 1969), 36–7; an influential anthology of interviews with former student activists published in 1977, one of the first commemorative publications on the student movement, did much to reify June 2nd as the origin myth of the movement. Peter Mosler, *Was wir wollten, was wir wurden: Studentenrevolte—zehn Jahre danach* (Reinbek near Hamburg, 1977), 29; in a *Der Spiegel* poll con-ducted in 1988, 65 per cent of respondents who had been students in 1967, said they had been influenced decisively or originally politicized by the events of 2 June 1967. Michels, *Schahbesuch 1967*, 8; also Kraushaar, *1968*, 257–9; Frei, *1968*, 118.

point, one of the newly created left-wing terrorist groups of the early 1970s would name itself 'June 2nd Movement' to stress that its own turn towards political violence had been caused by the police brutality of that day.[37] The date of 2 June 1967 was a crystallizing moment during which the system seemed to have revealed its brutally repressive side and its central place in the global system of imperialist oppression. This sparked a major new wave of anti-authoritarian and anti-imperialist mobilization, and, in the minds of young leftists, underscored the need for open resistance at home. SDS membership roughly doubled in the aftermath of 2 June, and polls suggested that around a quarter of all West German students and up to a third of the West Berlin student population had taken to the streets in protest following Ohnesorg's death.[38] Their indignation was fuelled by the fact that much of the West Berlin press and the city's authorities, including the Social Democratic mayor Heinrich Albertz, initially blamed the anti-Shah demonstrators for the death of the student.

Centre-right students were not swayed by the APO's critique of the repressive Shah. Both West Berlin Christian Democrat Jürgen Klemann and Maria-Theresia ('Musch') van Schewick, who was active in the Bonn Student Union, for instance, recalled that they had been supportive of the modernizing US-backed Shah, and that they had been particularly fond of his wife, whom Klemann referred to as the 'pretty Farah Diba'.[39] Nevertheless, the need to respond to the shooting in West Berlin and to the growing outrage among students over police brutality dominated the centre-right's political endeavours at the time. In the summer of 1967, the RCDS national leadership reported '[o]ur work in the past semester naturally bore the mark of the incidents in Berlin, with their climax, 2 June'.[40] Like the SPD, the West Berlin CDU had pointed its finger at the anti-Shah protesters, who, the party argued, had sought to 'undermine the democratic order' and ought to be held responsible for the injuries of a number of policemen.[41] Few centre-right student activists, on the other hand, sided with the police or fully backed the statements of the CDU.[42] On the contrary, many made a point of expressing their 'shock and

---

[37] Bommi Baumann, *How It All Began: The Personal Account of a West German Urban Guerilla* (Vancouver, 2006), 40 and 87.

[38] Wienhaus, *Bildungswege zu '1968'*, 46; on the polling data, see the analysis of a poll of over 3,000 students conducted by Rudolf Wildenmann, 26 April 1968, in BAK, B138/10262.

[39] Klemann interview; van Schewick interview. The SDS, in turn, took to mocking the centre-right's fascination with Farah Diba. In the run-up to student parliamentary elections in Cologne, the SDS led a donkey around campus, bedecked with signs for the centre-right's *Aktion '67* that said 'Farah Dieba (sic) is the most beautiful'. Bartz, 'Konservative Studenten und die Studentenbewegung'.

[40] 'Bericht des Bundesvorstandes über seine Arbeit im SS 1967', in: ArchAPO RCDS, 18. Ord. Bundesdelegierten-Versammlung. Mappe 1968.

[41] 'Erklärung des Geschäftsführenden Landesvorstandes der CDU vom 3. Juni 1967', printed in Siegward Lönnendonker, Tilman Fichter, and Jochen Staadt (eds.), *Hochschule im Umbruch: Teil V: Gewalt und Gegengewalt (1967–1969)* (Berlin, 1983), 180.

[42] The West Berlin RCDS, for instance, criticized the local CDU for its response. See 'Beschluss der Mitgliederversammlung des RCDS vom 5. Juni 1967', in: ArchAPO, Berlin Flugblätter Juni–Juli 1967.

outrage' over the conduct of the police.[43] An article in the Christian Democratic student paper *Civis* went as far as turning the conventional Cold War image of West Berlin as a beacon of the free world on its head and offered a searing indictment of the coverage of Ohnesorg's death in the conservative press and of the callous reactions of ordinary West Berliners. The city, the author Claus Menzel argued,

> has lost its greatest virtue. Because Berliners did not feel outrage when the shooting of Ohnesorg became known, no shame when the political leadership spread false information and denied the dead his last honours, no compassion with the pregnant wife of the student, no alarm over a parliament that accepted without objection what the Senate said. On the contrary: the mourners were offered beatings, the tires of cars adorned with black flags were slashed, passersby who supported the students were called 'communist pigs'.[44]

The date of 2 June never featured as an origin myth in the stories of centre-right activists who sought to make sense of their political trajectories like it did in left-wing storytelling. As Jürgen Klemann of the West Berlin RCDS put it, 'that a person died, naturally of course, did not leave us unaffected, but [...] I did not sense that this was the beginning of a new era. Everything went on as usual.'[45] Nonetheless, the date was a staging post in many interviews conducted for this book. For many, 2 June was used to signal the extent to which centre-right activists were aware of and touched personally by the major milestones of student protest.[46] In retrospect, Klaus Laepple, for one, rejected what he perceived as the excessively 'emotional' response on the part of the student Left in the aftermath of Ohnesorg's death. At the same time, however, he stressed that, upon hearing the news of a student's death at a demonstration, he had immediately interrupted his vacation on the Spanish island of Mallorca to fly back to Cologne to help formulate a response.[47] Wolfgang Bergsdorf (b. 1941), who was then active in student politics in Bonn and who would become one of Chancellor Kohl's closest confidants in the 1970s and 1980s, summed up his reaction as: 'Horror! Horror!'[48] Peter Radunski, who was active in West Berlin student politics at the time and later oversaw all of the CDU's major political campaigns of the late 1970s and 1980s, remembered thinking: 'A student is not supposed to be shot at a demonstration here!'[49] While he recalled having grown more uncomfortable over time

---

[43] Hamburger Institut für Sozialforschung (HIS), Studentenbewegung, studentische Verbände, RCDS, Ulrich Grasser, quoted in *RCDS Notizen* 2 (WS 67/68).
[44] Claus Menzel, 'Das Maul stopfen', *Civis*, 7 (1967), 14–15.   [45] Klemann interview.
[46] On the manifold ways in which 2 June 1967 featured as an origin myth in left-wing commemorations of the student movement, see Behre, *Bewegte Erinnerung*, 76–7; on Ohnesorg as one of 1968's chief martyrs, see Cornils, *Writing the Revolution*, 16–23.
[47] Laepple interview; the vast majority of activists interviewed for this book recalled exactly where they had been when they heard the news of the student's death.
[48] Bergsdorf interview.   [49] Radunski interview.

with the developments set in motion by the events of 2 June, namely the radicalization of parts of the student movement, he had initially reasoned that the
protests against police brutality were a good thing and ultimately beneficial for
West German democracy.[50] Radunski and two Christian Democratic co-authors
argued in a 1968 treatise on the phenomenon of student unrest: 'In this particular
case, the students have demonstrated a basic democratic virtue: resistance against
an abuse of state power. This is an improvement for German democracy [...].'[51]

Radunski and others even participated in the public displays of mourning that
followed Ohnesorg's death. When the East German regime opened the transit
road from the island city of West Berlin to West Germany on 8 June to allow the
student's body to be transported to his native Hanover for burial, several RCDS
activists, along with thousands of other students, escorted the coffin en route to
the East German checkpoint at Dreilinden.[52] RCDS also sent a student representative to Hanover where a memorial service was held for Ohnesorg the next day.[53]
In Bonn, the centre-right-run student council organized a semi-official memorial
service for Ohnesorg at which the liberal political scientist Karl-Dietrich Bracher
condemned the 'police terror' as well as the Springer press's 'smear campaign'
against the demonstrators and warned of a repetition of 1933.[54]

As we can see, then, centre-right activists were closely involved in some of the
key protest events of the mid-1960s. Calls for educational reform, greater representation of student interests, and critiques of state authority and the excessive use
of force could be heard on different sides of the political spectrum at the time.
Demonstrations that called attention to these issues brought otherwise very
different kinds of students out into the streets—and even landed activists of
both the Left and the Right in the country's courtrooms. Rather than simply
guarding the status quo, as one might expect conservatives to do, centre-right
students were remarkably restive in this period. They demanded change and
questioned the authority and conduct of government and state institutions, even
those run by Christian Democrats. This suggests that students across the political
spectrum were initially responding to similar social and political undercurrents in
a society that was on the move. It was only later, when the left-wing student
movement increasingly turned away from generic student issues and became
preoccupied with more general political concerns—notably the US-led war in
Vietnam and the planned emergency laws—that the relationship between activists

---

[50] RCDS leaflet, 14 June 1967 and the invitation to a debate on 26 June 1967 from the RCDS at the
TU Berlin, in: ArchAPO, Berlin FU Allgemein 10.-20.6.1967.
[51] Wulf Schönbohm, Peter Radunski, and Jürgen-Bernd Runge, *Die herausgeforderte Demokratie:
Deutsche Studenten zwischen Reform und Revolution* (Mainz, 1968), 10.
[52] 'Gegen die Polizeimaßnahmen beim Schah-Besuch in der Bundesrepublik', 5 June 1967, *RCDS-
Brief*, 4 (1967), 15; *Colloquium*, 7 (1967), 24; Haberl interview.
[53] See the list of events attended by members of the RCDS federal leadership, ArchAPO, RCDS, file
'18. Ord. Bundesdelegierten-Versammlung. Mappe 1968'.
[54] von Hodenberg, *Das andere Achtundsechzig*, 36–7.

from different sides of the political spectrum began to change, becoming, as we will see, more adversarial over time.

'Be Where the Action Is!'

For all the common ground that existed between Left and Right in the early phase of student unrest, the unprecedented surge in left-wing mobilization across West German universities in the wake of Ohnesorg's death posed a formidable challenge to centre-right students accustomed to holding majorities in most student parliaments for much of the postwar period. It forced them to boost their own efforts, not least in terms of organizing and rallying supporters.

The years around 1968 were an age of acronyms, with numerous established and newly founded political groups vying for students' support. Apart from RCDS, some of the other major groups were the SPD-affiliated *Sozialdemokratischer Hochschulbund* (SHB) and the *Liberaldemokratischer Hochschulbund* (LSD), which was tied to the FDP. SDS, however, was undoubtedly the most prominent actor within the broader student movement from 1966 onward. Founded in 1946 as the official student organization of the SPD, SDS split from its mother party after the Social Democrats had turned away from its Socialist principles and embraced reform capitalism in its Bad Godesberg Programme of 1959. Because the students stuck to their Marxist orientation, the SPD expelled all SDS members from the party in 1961. (The SHB succeeded SDS as the party's new student wing.)

From this point onward, SDS adopted an ever more openly revolutionary stance.[55] Its two competing factions—the traditionalists and anti-authoritarians—primarily disagreed about tactics, but less about the desired outcome of their agitation. The goal of SDS was a radical transformation of the political system of the Federal Republic and the introduction of a form of democracy by councils [*Rätedemokratie*], beginning in West Berlin.[56] While SDS was the leading voice in the student campaign for educational reform in the early and mid-1960s, its struggle for greater student participation became increasingly tied to a much more far-reaching critique of existing political institutions. For the Socialist students, calling for change in university governance served as a springboard to attack capitalist society per se, both at home and abroad.[57] Instead of educational

---

[55] On the early history of the SDS, see Tilman Fichter, *SDS und SPD: Parteilichkeit jenseits der Partei* (Opladen, 1988); Willy Albrecht, *Der Sozialistische Deutsche Studentenbund (SDS). Vom parteikonformen Studentenverband zum Repräsentanten der Neuen Linken* (Bonn, 1994); Tilman Fichter and Siegward Lönnendonker, *Kleine Geschichte des SDS: Der Sozialistische Deutsche Studentenbund von Helmut Schmidt bis Rudi Dutschke* (Bonn, 2008).

[56] 'Ein Gespräch über die Zukunft mit Rudi Dutschke, Bernd Rabehl und Christian Semler', *Kursbuch*, 14 (August 1968), 146–74.

[57] Thomas, *Protest Movements*, 59; Wehrs, *Protest der Professoren*, 53.

reform, the US-led war in Vietnam, the grand coalition's proposed emergency laws, and the disproportionate influence wielded by Axel C. Springer's conservative media empire became the emotive issues of the day in the late 1960s. Although it was only the third largest student group prior to 1967, SDS became synonymous with the broader phenomenon of student unrest, both on campus and in the eyes of the general public.[58] The Socialist students shaped the political debate on—and well beyond—West German university campuses.

This outsized influence meant that student activists of the centre-right had to respond to and increasingly define their own politics with reference to SDS. Their politics, organization, and repertoires became increasingly reactive. From 1967 onward, the need to offer a 'central response to all actions of SDS' governed their political endeavours, as the group's national leadership reported.[59] While SHB and LSD were in a similar position, they responded by edging closer to the goals and tactics of the New Left students. As a result, Christian Democratic students could pride themselves on providing the only true counterweight to the SDS-led student movement. 'The transformation of other political student organizations into satellites of SDS has given RCDS the opportunity and the responsibility to be the sole political opposition to SDS at German universities', pronounced the national leadership of RCDS in early 1968.[60]

In order to put up an effective opposition, Christian Democratic students professionalized their own operations and took countless leaves out of the radical student Left's book: they put more effort into effective and more pointed sloganeering and began to disseminate leaflets centrally to offer a coherent message.[61] RCDS also emulated some of SDS's organizational innovations, including its expansion into the country's secondary schools.[62] When SDS activists helped to set up the national *Action Centre of Independent and Socialist Pupils* (*Aktionszentrum Unabhängiger und Sozialistischer Schüler*, AUSS) in April 1967, for instance, RCDS national chair Wulf Schönbohm attended the founding meeting and recorded his observations in a 12-page document disseminated

---

[58] There were approximately 300,000 students at West German universities in the second half of the 1960s. Prior to 1967, SDS had around 1,200 members (compared to appr. 2,200 and 1,500 for RCDS and SHB, respectively). After June 1967, the number of SDS members rose to approximately 2,500. René Ahlberg, 'Die politische Konzeption des Sozialistischen Deutschen Studentenbundes', Beilage zur Wochenzeitung *Das Parlament* B20/68 (15 May 1968), 3–4; Wienhaus, *Bildungswege zu '1968'*, 46; according to various national polls conducted in 1968, only around 10 per cent of West German students sympathized with SDS and only 15 per cent wanted to overthrow the political system of the Federal Republic. Rohstock, *Von der 'Ordinarienuniversität" zur" Revolutionszentrale'*, 247.

[59] ArchAPO, RCDS, 18. Ord. Bundesdelegierten-Versammlung (1968), 'Vorstellungen des RCDS-Bundesvorstandes über seine Arbeit im SS 1967'.

[60] ArchAPO, RCDS, 18. Ord. Bundesdelegierten-Versammlung (1968), 'Vorstellungen des RCDS-Bundesvorstandes über seine Arbeit im WS 67/68'.

[61] Schönbohm interview.

[62] On the socialist movement of high school students, see Axel Schildt, 'Nachwuchs fuer die Rebellion. Die Schülerbewegung der späten sechziger Jahre', in Reulecke, *Generationalität und Lebensgeschichte im 20. Jahrhundert*, 229–51.

among the RCDS leadership. The centre-right could not afford to 'remain inactive' in the face of such effective left-wing wooing of the country's youth, he argued, and should seek to provide its own platform for politicized pupils.[63] By October 1967, a Christian Democratic pupils' league had been set up in West Berlin and similar local groups emerged across West Germany in the coming months and years. In late 1969, a new national organization for secondary school pupils, the *Association of Critical Pupils* (*Verband Kritischer Schüler*, VKS), was founded, a precursor to the CDU/CSU-affiliated *Schüler Union*, which was set up in the summer of 1972 and exists to this day.[64]

New centre-right groups that sought to mobilize students to stop the socialist revolution in its tracks did not just emerge off campus. As the left-wing student movement picked up steam in the wake of 2 June 1967, members of Catholic fraternities, non-fencing fraternities, and of RCDS founded various independent centre-right umbrella groups at West German universities. These groups' explicit mission was to restore a sense of order and normalcy on campus after a period of growing unrest and to keep the insurgent Left in check, a task they often did vocally and with remarkable success.[65]

Initially operating under different names that often included the word 'action' to express their drive and zest for standing up to the Left—*Aktion '67, Aktion '68, Aktion 20. Konvent*[66]—these new groups emerged across the country on campuses from West Berlin to Aachen and from Kiel to Freiburg. They were most visible and successful in Catholic areas of the country, not least in Munich and Cologne where they won clear majorities in the local student parliaments in 1967 and 1968.[67] It was in these Catholic parts of West Germany that they were able to mobilize students whose natural political home was Christian Democracy and also draw on the organizational resources of the *Cartellverband*, the umbrella organization of Catholic all-male student fraternities, which had over

[63] See Wulf Schönbohm's report about AUSS in ArchAPO, RCDS, 'RCDS-Brief'.

[64] Joseph Stenger, *La Schüler-Union: Etude d'un mouvement politique de jeunes lycéens en République Fédérale allemande de 1972 à 1980* (Frankfurt/M., Bern, 1981); Linde Apel, 'Die Opposition der Opposition. Politische Mobilisierung an Oberschulen jenseits der Protestgeneration', in Livi, Schmidt, and Sturm, *Die 1970er Jahre als schwarzes Jahrzehnt*, 57–72.

[65] Olaf Bartz, 'Konservative Studenten und die Studentenbewegung: Die "Kölner Studenten-Union"', *Westfälische Forschung*, 48 (1998), 241–56.

[66] Wolfgang Bergsdorf, '"Aktion 67" setzt völlig neue Akzente', *Die Welt* (17 July 1967); Universitätsarchiv Bonn, BSU, Aktion 68, Leaflet, 9 January 1968.

[67] The Munich Student Union won an absolute majority in December 1967; the Cologne Student Union won an absolute majority in July 1968; IFZ, ED-0738-1, *Münchener Studentenzeitung*, special election issue 'Die Wahl' (December 1967); Westdeutsche Rektorenkonferenz (ed.), *Übersicht über die Wahlen zur Studentenvertretung im Sommersemester 1968 bzw. Wintersemester 1968/69* (Bonn: Westdeutsche Rektorenkonferenz, 1969). While the major successses of these groups occurred in traditionally Catholic areas of the country, centre-right umbrella groups also received the largest share of votes at universities in some traditionally Protestant, or majority Protestant, cities like Kiel and Frankfurt am Main in 1969.

30,000 members in the mid-1960s—more than ten times that of RCDS (or SDS for that matter).[68]

Late April 1968 was a particularly tumultuous phase of the student movement. SDS icon Rudi Dutschke had been gunned down in West Berlin by right-wing extremist Josef Bachmann less than two weeks prior, and the assassination attempt had been followed by major street riots across West German cities over Easter 1968. In an effort to coordinate their anti-Left efforts during this time, these local centre-right groups joined in a national federation, the German Student Union (*Deutsche Studentenunion*, DSU).[69] It was named after the most successful group of its kind, the Munich Student Union (*Münchener Studentenunion*, MSU), which had caused a small sensation by winning 26 out of 51 seats in the Munich student parliament the previous December and had since become the centre-right model to emulate. Many of the other groups thereafter changed their names to 'Student Union' (*Aktion '68* became the *Bonner Studentenunion*, BSU; *Aktion'67* became the *Kölner Studentenunion*, KSU).[70] At the end of the 1960s, these groups were remarkably successful in student parliamentary elections. In the winter semester of 1968/69, for instance, RCDS and/or DSU gained the largest number of seats at universities in Cologne, Bonn, Frankfurt, Erlangen-Nürnberg, Gießen, Kiel, Mainz, and Regensburg.[71]

Although it was emphatically not affiliated with the Christian Democrats, did not receive party funding, and at times had a tense relationship with a federal RCDS leadership anxious to protect its campus turf, there was extensive overlap between DSU in its early phase and the Association of Christian Democratic Students.[72] Many of the student parliamentary candidates for the local groups were drawn entirely from the ranks of RCDS. In addition, the founding meeting of DSU took place at Schloss Eichholz, a castle owned by the Konrad Adenauer Foundation, a CDU-affiliated think tank.[73] The federal chair of RCDS at the time,

[68] Härdtl interview; Aretz interview; Thomas Großbölting, *Losing Heaven: Religion in Germany since 1945* (New York and Oxford, 2017), 60.

[69] ACDP, 04-006/63/1, DSU Leaflet 'Kleiner Student—was nun?'; a list of local DSU affiliates compiled in 1970 can be found at 'Mitgliedsgruppen 1970', http://dsu-slh.de/Mitgliedsgruppen%201970.pdf (accessed on 2 April 2018).

[70] IFZ, ED-0738-1, *Münchener Studentenzeitung*, special election issue 'Die Wahl' (December 1967).

[71] Westdeutsche Rektorenkonferenz (ed.), *Übersicht über die Ergebnisse der Wahlen zu den Studentenvertretungen* (Bonn, 1968–1984).

[72] Instead funding came from the private sector, the Christian Labour Union, and, after 1969, increasingly from the West German state. BAK, BA138/23260, DSU to Chancellor Kiesinger, 18 April 1969; Kiesinger to DSU 4 June 1969; Bartz, 'Konservative Studenten und die Studentenbewegung'; Aretz interview. The DSU moved further left in the 1970s, changing its name to Sozialliberaler Hochschulbund (SLH) in 1972.

[73] BAK, B165-311, Wulf Carstensen to Heinrich Stutz, letter, 22 April 1968; Hoover Institution Archives (HIA), German Subject Collection (GSC), Box 87, 'Aktion 20. Konvent: Die progressive Alternative', brochure; Lothar Labusch, 'Kritische Sympathie für Christdemokraten', *Kölner Stadt-Anzeiger* (14 May 1968); Stephan Eisel (ed.), *50 Jahre Bildungszentrum Schloss Eichholz: Die Geburtsstätte der Konrad-Adenauer-Stiftung* (Eichholz, 2006).

Uwe-Rainer Simon, attended this meeting alongside his deputy Detlef Stronk, who had already been prominently involved in MSU.[74] Moreover, DSU's first chair was none other than the Cologne-based Christian Democratic student leader Klaus Laepple, who had gained nationwide fame as the 'Provo of the CDU' in the wake of the Cologne tram riots.[75] In short, RCDS and the Student Unions were closely intertwined.

The prominent sociologist Erwin K. Scheuch, who was emerging as one of the most vocal critics of the left-wing student movement among the professoriate, spoke at the founding meeting. There, he urged centre-right activists to take a leaf out of the Left's book by generating the greatest possible visibility for their own campaigns. Consequently, 'Be Where the Action Is!' became the English language motto of an organization that sought to pair its reactive stance with an emphatically modern image.[76] Contrary to RCDS, however, which eventually engaged in a broader political debate with the left-wing student movement, the Student Unions remained quite narrowly focused on bread-and-butter student issues. As Wighard Härdtl, a young Christian Democrat who was also involved in *Aktion 20. Konvent* in West Berlin, put it later: '[The] improving of study conditions, more academic chairs, better facilities, and, of course, an element of participation in decision-making [were central to the group], but [it] was not a revolutionary movement; rather, it [...] was understood as advocacy for the student body.'[77] Instead of overthrowing the political system, they envisaged a reform of the education system, with a focus on tangible improvements in higher education.[78]

A Silent Majority?

In line with their oppositional self-definitions, activists of the centre-right would later claim that, though marginalized in public debate around 1968, they had been representatives of a 'silent majority' of students at the time. In doing so, they appropriated a powerful political label popularized by US President Richard M. Nixon in a speech on the war in Vietnam that he gave on 3 November 1969.[79]

[74] ACDP, 4-6-13-2, 'Report of the RCDS Federal Board About its Activities in the Summer Semester of 1968'; Stronk interview.

[75] Bartz, 'Konservative Studenten und die Studentenbewegung', 246; Eva Schmidt-Häuer, 'Der "Provo" von der CDU', *Die Zeit*, 1 (1967), 7; Laepple interview.

[76] BAK, B165-311, Wulf Carstensen to Heinrich Stutz, letter, 22 April 1968; ACDP, 04-006/63/1, DSU Leaflet 'Kleiner Student—was nun?'.

[77] Härdtl interview.

[78] Deutsche Studentenunion, *Konzepte zur Reform von Gesellschaft, Bildungswesen und Hochschule* (Bonn, 1970), available at http://dsu-slh.de/schriftenreihe%20band%201.pdf (accessed on 2 April 2018); Deutsche Studentenunion, *Überlegungen zu einem Bildungsgesamtplan* (Bonn, 1970), available at http://dsu-slh.de/schriftenreihe%20band%203.pdf (accessed on 2 April 2018).

[79] The following section is based on von der Goltz and Waldschmidt Nelson, 'Introduction: "Silent Majorities" and Conservative Mobilization in the 1960s and 1970s in Transatlantic Perspective'.

The voices of ordinary Americans, Nixon warned, had been drowned out by a vocal, anti-war minority responsible for 'mounting demonstration in the street [sic]' that sought to impose its view on ordinary Americans.[80] The notion of noisy minorities dominating the agenda at the expense of a 'silent majority' of ordinary citizens quickly captured the imagination of conservative groups across Western Europe, which often invoked the label from the late 1960s onward in an explicit attempt to mobilize against a resurgent and highly visible Left. In West Germany, the 'silent majority' entered the political lexicon alongside similar concepts that expressed the idea that regimes of public attention marginalized conservatives and had to be upended to regain political power.[81] 'Do you want to remain part of the "silent majority"?', asked the Heidelberg chapter of RCDS, for instance, in a piece designed to get out the vote in elections to the local student parliament.[82]

As should be clear by now, centre-right activists were hardly silent in the face of increasing left-wing mobilization around 1968, but how accurate was the claim that they represented the majority of West German students? The short answer is that it was mostly wishful thinking. There were approximately 300,000 students at West German universities in the second half of the 1960s. Only about 2,200–2,300 of them were members of RCDS—less than 1 per cent of the student population.[83] Statistics about students' partisan leanings presented a similar picture. In 1967, only 26 per cent of West German students reported that they supported the Christian Democrats (vs 48 per cent who said that they backed the Social Democrats). By 1973/4, student support for the Christian Democrats had sunk to 14 per cent and would not rise again until the mid-1970s.[84] In this sense at least, centre-right claims of representing the majority of students were hyperbolic at best.

Much the same can be said of their main opponents in SDS, however, who did not represent the majority of students either. Before the death of Benno Ohnesorg, SDS had merely around 1,200 members. Even at the height of its popularity in

---

[80] 'Address to the Nation on the War in Vietnam', 3 November 1969. Available at http://www. nixonlibrary.gov/forkids/speechesforkids/silentmajority/silentmajority_transcript.pdf (accessed on 20 May 2013).

[81] von der Goltz and Waldschmidt Nelson, *Inventing the Silent Majority*, particularly the chapter by Martin Geyer, 'Elisabeth Noelle-Neumann's "Spiral of Silence", the Silent Majority, and the Conservative Moment of the 1970s', 251–74.

[82] See the self-description of RCDS in the Heidelberg-based paper Dialog, no. 4, n.d., *ArchAPO*, RCDS, file 'RCDS-Brief'; c.f. von der Goltz, 'A polarized generation?', 195.

[83] René Ahlberg, 'Die politische Konzeption des Sozialistischen Deutschen Studentenbundes', Beilage zur Wochenzeitung *Das Parlament* B20/68 (15 May 1968), 3–4; Jarausch, *Deutsche Studenten*, 232.

[84] See the analysis of a poll of more than 3,000 students conducted by Rudolf Wildenmann, 26 April 1968, BAK, B138/10262; and the comparative analysis of eight different polls conducted by the Federal Ministry of Education and Scholarship, 14 October 1976, BAK, B138/33393; Sozialwissenschaftliches Forschungsinstitut der Konrad-Adenauer Stiftung, *Empirische Daten im Zusammenhang der Diskussion um eine Tendenzwende in der Bundesrepublik* (Sankt Augustin, May 1978). I am grateful to Jeffrey Herf for making the latter source available to me.

1967/8, fewer than 1 per cent of West German students belonged to the radical left-wing group.[85] What is more, opinion polls—imperfect though they no doubt were as an unbiased measure of collective attitudes[86]—consistently suggested that the vast majority of students did not support the revolutionary politics of SDS. A poll of over 3,000 students conducted in early 1968 showed that nearly three quarters favoured demonstrations as a means of political expression, that just over a third had taken part in a demonstration by then, and that half thought that there were good reasons to criticize the political system of the Federal Republic.[87] These numbers are often cited in the literature to underline the strength of the left-wing student movement and the political homogeneity of this cohort.[88] But these figures should not be read as clear-cut evidence of left-wing political preferences. As we have seen, centre-right students also took to the streets and debated the shortcomings of West German democracy. According to various national polls conducted in 1968, only around 10 per cent of West German students actually sympathized with the revolutionary goals of SDS.[89] Only 27 per cent of students said that they agreed with SDS figurehead Rudi Dutschke; 26 per cent reported being indifferent towards him, and 44 per cent stated that they rejected the radical student leader.[90]

The same survey showed that 50 per cent of students broadly agreed with the policies of Christian Democratic Chancellor Kurt Georg Kiesinger. A few months earlier, 36 per cent of students had named postwar conservative Chancellor Konrad Adenauer as their greatest role model in another poll.[91] Even among

---

[85] Ahlberg, 'Die politische Konzeption des Sozialistischen Deutschen Studentenbundes'; Wienhaus, *Bildungswege zu '1968'*, 46.

[86] For critical insights into the difficulties associated with using contemporary statistics and polling data, see Anja Kruke, *Demoskopie in der Bundesrepublik Deutschland: Meinungsforschung, Parteien und Medien 1949–1990* (Düsseldorf, 2007); Rüdiger Graf and Kim Christian Priemel, 'Zeitgeschichte in der Welt der Sozialwissenschaften. Legitimität und Originalität einer Disziplin', *VfZ*, 59, 4 (2011), 479–508; Bernhard Dietz, Christopher Neumaier, and Andreas Rödder (eds.), *Gab es den Wertewandel? Neue Forschungen zum gesellschaftlich-kulturellen Wandel seit den 1960er Jahren* (Munich, 2014). I build on Detlef Siegfried's work here, who argued that these sources should of course be used with care, but that they nevertheless provide the best measure that we have of broad patterns of opinion and changes to them over time. Detlef Siegfried, *1968: Protest, Revolte, Gegenkultur* (Ditzingen, 2018), 19–20.

[87] See the analysis of a poll of over 3,000 students conducted by Rudolf Wildenmann, 26 April 1968, BAK, B138/10262; *Der Spiegel*, 8 (19 February 1968), 40; Klaus Allerbeck, *Soziologie radikaler Studentenbewegungen: Eine vergleichende Untersuchung in der Bundesrepublik Deutschland und den Vereinigten Staaten* (Munich and Vienna, 1973), 50.

[88] Götz Aly, *Unser Kampf. 1968—Ein irritierter Blick zurück* (Frankfurt/Main, 2008), 81.

[89] Rohstock, *Von der 'Ordinarientuniversität" zur" Revolutionszentrale'*, 247.

[90] See the report on a poll of over 2,000 pupils and students aged between 15 and 25, conducted by the EMNID institute, compiled by the Federal Government's Press and Information Office, 19 February 1968, BAK, N1229/213; results summarized in *Der Spiegel*, 8 (19 February 1968), 40.

[91] *Der Spiegel*, 26 (1967), 28. Only the physicist and philosopher Carl Friedrich von Weizsäcker scored higher than Adenauer, with 42 per cent. See also BAK, ZSG 132/1363 and ZSG 132/1363 II, which include additional data and commentary on this poll.

See the report on a poll of over 2,000 pupils and students aged between 15 and 25, conducted by the EMNID institute, compiled by the Federal Government's Press and Information Office, 19 February

students in West Berlin—often held up as the capital of student revolt—the radical left-wing communard Fritz Teufel was as unpopular as the staunchly conservative chair of the local Christian Democrats, Franz Amrehn.[92] Student opinion, then, was clearly spread across a much greater political spectrum than the focus on the radical Left would suggest. As the influential news magazine *Der Spiegel* concluded in mid-1967:

> [The students] are not a coherent group, even though they unite—as they did this summer—around protest slogans … [T]hey are also, in many ways, more similar to their fathers, to a greater extent a reflection of established society, than their outspoken functionaries and opponents brandishing clubs would have you believe.[93]

Contrary to what they claimed, then, the other '68ers did not represent a 'silent majority' of students. Like their peers in SDS, they were a vocal minority, who dedicated much of their lives to politics. While the student body as a whole became more left-leaning in the late 1960s than at any previous point in the postwar decades, those organized in RCDS and other centre-right umbrella groups nevertheless represented a sizeable share of the student population, achieved considerable successes in student parliamentary elections, and contributed to on-campus and wider public debates in significant ways.

Reform vs. Revolution

Given how much organizational energy they dispensed on thwarting the radical Left, one of the most striking things about centre-right activists around 1968 was their reluctance to define themselves as 'conservatives', both at the time and with hindsight.[94] Instead, they embraced more ambiguous labels such as 'moderate',

1968, BAK, N1229/213; results summarized in *Der Spiegel*, 8 (19 February 1968), 40; *Der Spiegel*, 26 (19 June 1967), 28.

[92] 'Fritz wie Franz', *Der Spiegel*, 24 (10 June 1968), 54; a comparison between Dutschke and Amrehn a few months earlier had yielded similar results, see 'Gebrochenes Rückgrat', *Der Spiegel*, no. 7 (2 February 1968), 28; Tilman Fichter and Siegward Lönnendonker, 'Berlin: Hauptstadt der Revolte' (March 1980), available at http://web.fu-berlin.de/APO-archiv/Online/BlnHauptRev.htm (accessed on 15 June 2015).

[93] *Der Spiegel*, 26 (19 June 1967), 28.

[94] This reflected internal deliberations within the CDU in the 1960s. While the Bavarian CSU included the term in its party platform in 1968, the CDU deliberately did not. See Steber, *Die Hüter der Begriffe*, 310–11; also Schildt, *Konservatismus in Deutschland*, 213; some interviewees for this book embraced the label more explicitly in the 1970s. See e.g. former RCDS deputy national chair Erich Röper, 'Wider die Mode-Linken—Manifest eines Konservativen', *Berliner Rundschau*, 26 April 1970, copy in HIA, NOFU, Box 838.

'centrist', or 'progressive alternative' to the student Left.[95] In this way, students adopted political semantics that anticipated attempts by the two main West German political parties to claim the 'centre ground' of politics (*die Mitte*) that picked up steam from the 1980s onward. On West German campuses in the late 1960s, the left-wing radicalism of SDS indeed left plenty of space in the political centre to occupy, but projecting such centrism was also meant to demarcate these student groups from the right. As Meinhard Ade, who had participated in the January 1968 debate between Dutschke and Dahrendorf in Freiburg and who had founded a new centre-right student group in the city, explained in retrospect: 'We named ourselves the "Democratic Centre" to signal that we were not right-wing conservatives, not reactionaries, instead we saw ourselves as the centre.'[96]

Such reservations about the label 'conservative' were well founded, for the term had carried negative connotations in public discourse since the end of the war—one of the peculiarities of West German intellectual life after Hitler. After all, what was there to *conserve* in the wake of war, dictatorship, and genocide? After 1945, Weimar conservatives were routinely blamed for undermining republican stability and paving the way for the Nazi dictatorship. In the early years of the Federal Republic, therefore, conservatism was frequently associated with anti-liberalism. As a result, it was a concept that was of limited use in a country where showcasing liberal and 'Western' values was essential to signalling a decisive break with the past. It also did not help that, around 1968, in an era of widespread social and cultural change, conservatism was increasingly equated with anti-modernism and thus as out of step with the rapidly changing times.[97]

Although they shied away from embracing the term, the confrontation with SDS nevertheless led centre-right groups to adopt a classically conservative posture in many ways—notably the defence of existing institutions against a fundamental challenge by radicals.[98] As Jürgen Aretz, one of the founders of Bonn's *Aktion '68* (later named the Bonn Student Union, BSU), professed: 'I had the feeling, that things were developing in a way that you wouldn't want and thereby creating the conditions under which you wouldn't want to live. So, I tried to do my part [...] to keep things fairly balanced.'[99]

Much like Christian Democratic politics in the late 1940s and 1950s, which had been defined, above all, by a staunch anti-communism, the political identity of

---

[95] Deutsche Studenten Union, 'Wer ist, was will die DSU?' (Bonn, 1970), 45, available at http://dsu-slh.de/Wer%20ist,%20was%20will%20die%20DSU.pdf (accessed on 2 April 2018); HIA, GSC, Box 87, Aktion 20. Konvent: Die progressive Alternative, brochure.

[96] Ade interview.

[97] Steber, *Die Hüter der Begriffe*, 107–65, 310–11; Schildt, *Konservatismus in Deutschland*, 211–52; for critical reflections on the idea of the 'West' in German history, see Riccardo Bavaj and Martina Steber (eds.), *Germany and the 'West': The History of a Modern Concept* (New York and Oxford, 2015).

[98] On the classic definition of conservatism as a 'positional' ideology that seeks to defend existing institutions against a radical challenge, see Samuel P. Huntington, 'Conservatism as an Ideology', *The American Political Science Review*, 51, 2 (1957), 454–73.

[99] Aretz interview.

centre-right student groups around 1968 was shaped more by what they were against than what they were for. In some ways, they represented a counter-movement with a strongly positional identity. This identity was sustained by the constant articulation of what one was not, namely a left-wing revolutionary group, especially SDS—or, to be more precise, they were not whatever they *imagined* SDS to be.[100] Employing classic conservative tropes that contrasted their supposed sobriety with the Left's irrationality and emotionality, the Heidelberg Student Union, for one, appealed to all 'non-ideologized' and 'non-fanatic' members of the student body and 'instead of the revolution of the romantics' called for 'an evolution via rationalists'.[101] Or, as an article in the new centre-right publication *Alternativ* put it in more openly defamatory terms, centre-right student groups claimed to speak for all those students 'who do not smash windows, who go to the loo instead of the rectorate, who believe in the possibility and the meaning of reforms'.[102]

Christian Democratic student activists were also institutionally conservative in that they were adamant that the political system and institutions of the Federal Republic needed to be protected and that change could only come from within them. As a programmatic piece by RCDS published in 1968 put it: 'In contrast to SDS, RCDS offers moderate students the possibility to tackle the urgent need to further develop our society through the existing social institutions.'[103] As Wulf Schönbohm explained in retrospect: '[Students from SDS] were the definitive enemies of this system. They wanted to change the state, they wanted to change society and especially the economy. And we recognized that [...] very early. And that is why we were very early opponents of this organization. That was the conflict.'[104]

Their stated opposition to a radical shake-up of the political system did not mean, however, that centre-right students were unbending guardians of the status quo.[105] In fact, it was remarkable how much in the 1960s they shared the New Left

---

[100] In his pioneering article on the Cologne Student Union (KSU), Bartz rightly asserted that its identity was less defined by its opposition to the *real* SDS than to what SDS *symbolized* at the time. Bartz, 'Konservative Studenten und die Studentenbewegung', 255; on the importance of 'boundary construction' in stories told to nurture political identities, see Tilly, *Stories, Identities and Political Change*, 11.

[101] ArchAPO, SDS, file 'Konter-Revolutionäre—RCDS, NHB, u.a. Olympiade—Diverses', Heidelberger Studentenunion, leaflet, n.d. On the trope of left-wing irrationality, see René Ahlberg, *Akademische Lehrmeinungen und Studentenunruhen in der Bundesrepublik: Linker Irrationalismus in politologischen und soziologischen Theorien* (Freiburg, 1970); on the importance of terms such as 'hysterical', 'emotional', and 'irrational'—what she terms 'semantic nets'—in West German conservative thought, see Steber, *Hüter der Begriffe*, 195; on the particular emotional style of some of the leading critics of 1968, see further Biess, *Republik der Angst*, 284–94.

[102] HIA, Koenigs Papers, Box 1, *Alternativ: Studentenzeitung Berliner Hochschulen*, 1 (1969).

[103] ACDP, 4-6-16/1, Peter Radunski, 'Zum Selbstverständnis des RCDS: Politische und gesellschaftliche Bedingungen eines politischen Studentenverbandes'.

[104] Schönbohm interview.

[105] On conservatives' complex relationship to the status quo, see Biebricher, *Geistig-moralische Wende*, 17–44.

critique that fuelled the student protests across Western Europe and the United States. They bemoaned the political stagnation, bureaucratization, lack of participation, and disregard for human needs and individual happiness in capitalist liberal democratic societies. Western European domestic politics of the 1950s and early 1960s were indeed famously bland, with 'gray men in suits' often championing a conformist politics, emphasizing the importance of stability, and displaying a distinct lack of ideological imagination, as Martin Conway and others have argued.[106] It was against this background that youth and student protests first erupted across the continent. Christian Democratic students were convinced that this political unrest was not solely driven by neo-Marxist radicals, but had its roots in the 'immobility of state and society that they have uncovered'.[107] Much like the overwhelming majority of students of the Left, nearly half of all Christian Democratic students thought that the Grand Coalition under Chancellor Kurt Georg Kiesinger, which had governed since December 1966, had undermined healthy democratic debate and pluralism in the Federal Republic.[108] Citing Rudolf Augstein, the influential editor of the news magazine *Der Spiegel*, RCDS leaders bemoaned the fact that the Grand Coalition had reached 'a state of permanent inability to debate' and opined that this was the reason that students had taken their protests to the streets.[109]

In contrast to student thinkers of the Left (and many other critics), then, who traced the lack of political imagination back to the Adenauer years and the entire political architecture of the postwar years, centre-right students typically argued that it was a more recent phenomenon. This is not to say that they were unaccustomed to making the occasional stab at the former Chancellor, such as when the chair of RCDS in Tübingen wrote in 1967 that Christian Democrats 'should dare to experiment' again.[110] More often than not, however, they faulted the *post*-Adenauer era. Adenauer and the early Ludwig Erhard had promoted far-sighted political projects, such as European integration, the resistance against communist expansion in Europe, and the social market economy. Since then, West German politicians had run out of such dazzling ideas, they

[106] Martin Conway, 'The Rise and Fall of Western Europe's Democratic Age, 1945–1973', *Contemporary European History*, 13, 1 (2004), 67–88; see also Judt, *Postwar*, 241–77; Jan-Werner Müller, *Contesting Democracy: Political Ideas in Twentieth Century Europe* (New Haven and London, 2011), 143.

[107] 'Gesellschaftliche Immobilität in der Bundesrepublik', Beschlüsse der 18. Ord. Bundesversammlung 28.2.-3.3.1968, Archiv für christlich-demokratische Politik (ACDP), 4/6/9.

[108] According to a 1968 poll commissioned by *Der Spiegel*, 90 per cent of SDS and 48 per cent of RCDS students considered the Grand Coalition government anti-democratic. Cited in Thomas, *Protest Movements*, 92.

[109] Schönbohm, Radunski, and Runge, *Die herausgeforderte Demokratie,* 106; Rudolf Augstein, 'Warum sie demonstrieren', *Der Spiegel*, 26 (19 June 1968), 18.

[110] 'No experiments!' was a famous CDU/CSU election slogan of the 1957 federal elections. Matthias Frindte, in *RCDS-Brief*, 3 (1967), n.p.; for a discussion of more general critiques of politics under Adenauer, see Schildt, *Konservatismus in Deutschland*, 238–40.

suggested.[111] Looking back in the early 1990s, former West Berlin activist Christian Hacke (b. 1943) was still convinced that Adenauer had been the 'greatest German politician of the twentieth century' and that his immediate successors had lacked a political vision. 'Only the generation of the grandchildren offered constructive new ideas', he suggested.[112]

Hacke had a point about the state of the party prior to 1968 when a peculiar ideological emptiness prevailed among Christian Democrats, even taking into account their natural aversion to universalizing theories. In the late 1940s, by contrast, they had debated their basic principles quite vigorously, representing, as they did, a brand new and ideologically dynamic political formation that offered a radical alternative to both capitalism and communism and managed to overcome the traditional confessional divide of the bourgeois parties in Germany. These debates ceased almost entirely, however, after Adenauer secured the Chancellorship in 1949.[113]

Erhard, Adenauer's successor, had dabbled in conceptual thinking when he introduced the notion of the Federal Republic as a 'formed society' ['formierte Gesellschaft'] in 1965. However, it was an ill-named concept meant to describe a corporate structure in which pluralism was contained and state authority strengthened in the interest of the common good and economic life. Leftist and liberal critics lambasted the idea, and it never really caught on in conservative circles either.[114] The Grand Coalition's evident aversion to debate only further amplified the perception that the Federal Republic's entire political class, including the Christian Democrats, had run out of intellectual steam.

In the late 1960s, when confronted with a formidable opposition on campus in the shape of a theory-savvy New Left, Christian Democratic students began to see their mother party's intellectual poverty as a problem. They began to argue that, as the governing party of the entire postwar period, the CDU/CSU had done too little to address the discrepancy between the democratic model and the political reality of the Federal Republic. Furthermore, they contended that the party was too focused on the issues of the day and had not done enough to lay the theoretical and programmatic groundwork for a renewal of West German politics after reconstruction.[115] This left Christian Democrats particularly ill-prepared to deal

---

[111] ACDP, 4/6/16/1, Helmuth Pütz, 'Ein Pladoyer für "reale Utopien"'; similarly warm words about Adenauer in Schönbohm, Runge, and Radunski, Die herausgeforderte Demokratie, 27–8, 100–1.

[112] Christian Hacke, Weltmacht wider Willen: Die Außenpolitik der Bundesrepublik Deutschland (Frankfurt am Main and Berlin, 1993), 105.

[113] Conway, 'The Age of Christian Democracy', 45; Petra Hemmelmann, Der Kompass der CDU: Analyse der Grundsatz- und Wahlprogramme von Adenauer bis Merkel (Wiesbaden, 2017), 149–50.

[114] Wulf Schönbohm, Die CDU wird moderne Volkspartei (Stuttgart, 1985), 76; Schildt, Konservatismus in Deutschland, 241–2; For a later, more favourable analysis of this idea by a Christian Democratic student activist of the 1960s, see Warnfried Dettling, 'Die Kraft des Konservativen', Die Zeit, 47 (12 November 1998).

[115] Recent scholarship on the postwar CDU has confirmed that there was indeed a deeply rooted 'anti-programme-affect' within the party in the first postwar decades. A younger generation of party

with the challenge of protest, but repressive methods and a defensive attitude by state institutions towards youthful dissent would not calm the waters, they insisted. It was now time 'to take note of the neo-Marxist renaissance in German intellectual life, to hazard an intellectual engagement, and to refrain from a one-sided demonization' of the protesters.[116] In order for West German democracy to survive this major test, ordinary citizens had to be equipped for the dialogue with Marxism, they opined. Furthermore, the CDU had 'to address the only ideologically responsive part of society'—especially the young elites— 'with a contemporary model of democracy'. Christian Democrats had to persuade students of the 'necessity of and opportunities presented by systemic political engagement'.[117] 'A debate about our future is indispensable', Christian Democratic students concluded.[118]

In contrast to the Student Unions, which mostly confined their discussions to education policy and generic student issues, Christian Democratic student activists took an explicitly theoretical turn in 1968. Befitting an era that Tony Judt termed 'the great age of Theory' [sic], RCDS set up a new political strategy unit that year, first in West Berlin and then at the federal level, that was designed to tackle some of the existential questions of modern society in a theoretically informed way.[119] The impetus for this was twofold: wanting to place their own politics on a more conceptual footing while equipping Christian Democratic activists with at least the rudimentary intellectual background needed to endure in debates with the Left. The strategy unit's members were tasked with crafting language on the basic ideas and concepts of RCDS and the group's conception of man.

Under Adenauer, Christian Democrats had often invoked vague formulae, such as the party's 'Christian worldview', in lieu of a firm conceptual grounding. In the final years of his chancellorship, some CDU leaders had toyed with the idea of reinvigorating Christian Democracy by reemphasizing its connection with Christianity.[120] Although most of them had been socialized in confessional schools or youth groups, which had made the CDU/CSU their natural political

---

officials began to address this from the late 1950s onward, however. Bösch, *Adenauer CDU*; Steber, *Hüter der Begriffe*, 196.

[116] ACDP, 4/6/9, 'Gesellschaftliche Immobilität in der Bundesrepublik', Beschlüsse der 18. Ord. Bundesversammlung 28.2.-3.3.1968.

[117] 'Vorstellungen des RCDS-Bundesvorstandes ueber seine Arbeit im WS 1967/68', in ArchAPO RCDS, 18. Ord. Bundesdelegierten-Versammlung. Mappe 1968.

[118] ACDP 4/6/9, 'Gesellschaftliche Immobilität in der Bundesrepublik', Beschlüsse der 18. Ord. Bundesversammlung 28.2.-3.3.1968.

[119] ACDP, 4/6/13, 'Bericht des Bundesvorstandes über seine Arbeit im SS 1968'; on the cultural importance of theory in the 1960s, see further Judt, *Postwar*, 398; also Lawrence Black, '1968 and all That(cher). Cultures of Conservatism and the New Right in Britain', in von der Goltz and Waldschmidt-Nelson, *Inventing the Silent Majority*, 356-77.

[120] Thomas Großbölting, *Losing Heaven: Religion in Germany since 1945* (New York and Oxford, 2017), 60; Ronald J. Granieri, 'Politics in C Minor: The CDU/CSU between Germany and Europe since the Secular Sixties', *Central European History*, no. 42 (2009), 1-32. Adenauer was opposed to these endeavours, which were led by Rainer Barzel.

home, centre-right activists were mostly sceptical of such attempts. Given the loosening of Church ties among West German citizens and the erosion of traditional confessional milieus since the 1950s, appeals to a Christian foundation were no longer enough, they reasoned. 'Today, a predominantly Christian-based responsibility for politics has become obsolete', as one strategy paper put it. 'The RCDS idea of man is neither specifically Christian nor based on an original Christian basic belief, nor does it postulate a particular "Christian politics".'[121] In short, in the increasingly secular 1960s, the 'C' in Christian Democracy could no longer serve as the sole programmatic basis.

In a quest to come up with alternative political categories, centre-right students turned away from traditional sources of conservative or Christian Democratic intellectual sustenance. Rather than revisiting the writings of thinkers such as Carl Schmitt, the ordoliberals, the Catholic philosopher Jacques Maritain, the liberal conservatives of the postwar Ritter School—or indeed engaging with the neo-conservative body of thought that was beginning to take shape around 1968—they turned instead to the liberal intellectual Ralf Dahrendorf, whose memorable encounter with Dutschke they helped to engineer in January 1968.[122] Wolfgang Reeder (b. 1945) of the Bonn RCDS still gushed about the writings of the liberal sociologist nearly half a century later: 'Ralf Dahrendorf's *Society and Democracy in Germany* was clearly a defining literary testimony. [...] I found it a phenomenally, wonderfully clearly written book. I found it one of the most brilliant analyses covering all of society at that time.'[123]

This bestselling work, which was published in 1965 and has remained influential as an assessment of the early Federal Republic's shortcomings, identified a structural democratic deficit in postwar West Germany.[124] While political institutions had been formally democratized from above after 1945, West German culture and society had not yet caught up, Dahrendorf argued. In most areas of public life, he theorized, authoritarian tendencies prevailed, particularly in families and educational institutions. The democratization of private and public socializing institutions would therefore constitute the most important step towards liberalizing German society from below.

---

[121] ACDP, 04-006-16/1, Politischer Beirat, Helmut [sic] Pütz, Gesellschaftsreformprogramm: 'Menschenbild und Stellenwert des Individuums in Gesellschaft und Politik'; Helmuth Pütz, 'Menschenbild und Stellenwert des Individuums in Gesellschaft und Politik', *Sonde*, 3 (1969), 22–3.

[122] Martin Kempe, 'Ralf Dahrendorf: Gesellschaft und Demokratie in Deutschland-Zusammenfassung. March 1968'; Protokoll des Politischen Beirates des RCDS-Berlin, Arbeitspapier: Ausarbeitung von Kempe, 17 March 1968, in *Runge Private Papers*, file 'Politischer Beirat'. In the 1970s, centre-right students would increasingly turn to the works of Dahrendorf's teacher at the London School of Economics, Karl Popper—a subject explored on 186–7.

[123] Reeder interview.

[124] Ralf Dahrendorf, *Gesellschaft und Demokratie in Deutschland* (Munich, 1965); on Dahrendorf in contemporary debates, see Ulrich Herbert, 'Liberalisierung als Lernprozess. Die Bundesrepublik in der deutschen Geschichte—eine Skizze', in Herbert, *Wandlungsprozesse in Westdeutschland*, here 30; and Meifort, *Dahrendorf*, 118–24.

Dahrendorf's overall oeuvre championed the idea of an egalitarian and open society that would no longer suppress social and political conflicts to create stability, a feature that had been a hallmark of the Adenauer era. His ideas were radical in the sense that they envisaged fundamental social changes, but the basic goal of this philosophy was to work through and improve the existing institutions of parliamentary democracy. There were more than hints of Dahrendorf's logic in the RCDS's contention that a discrepancy existed between the democratic model and the political realities of the Federal Republic, their calls for a democratic restructuring of the education system, and their willingness to take on their opponents in the realm of ideas.[125]

Besides mining the work of this key liberal intellectual for inspiration, RCDS activists also expended a significant amount of energy on engaging with the political philosophy of their left-wing opponents.[126] They ploughed through the theoretical tomes of the German émigré philosopher Herbert Marcuse, for instance, who was the political mentor of the New Left and one of the world's most important living theorists.[127] His Marxist-inspired critique of the 'affluent society' contended that, while it had raised living standards with remarkable success, it stifled dissent and buried human beings' innate desire for a free and creative existence under a rampant and highly destructive materialism.[128] While he was not convinced by the solutions Marcuse advocated, Peter Philipp, the author of a detailed RCDS strategy paper on the New Left philosopher, found his analysis 'sharp and in many ways extremely accurate'.[129] Relying on an avant-garde of young intellectuals, who would help to cure people of their 'false needs', as Marcuse proposed, however, would produce an 'educational dictatorship', he contended. People could not be turned into 'free, conscious, and democratic' citizens by force.[130]

RCDS's own diagnosis of the Federal Republic's social and political ills never-theless included 'a little piece of Marcuse, if you will', as Peter Radunski put it in retrospect.[131] As he wrote in 1968, the human desire for a meaningful life was at odds with advanced industrial society's quest for rationalization and politics had failed to provide a 'spiritual idea for the individual's role in modern civilization'.[132]

---

[125] Schönbohm, Runge, and Radunski, Die herausgeforderte Demokratie, 34; Wolfgang Reeder, 'Thesen zur Bildungspolitik', in RCDS Bundesvorstand (ed.), RCDS—entschieden demokratisch: Geschichte, Programm und Politik, RCDS-Schriftenreihe, 8 (1971), 55–60.

[126] Horst Teltschik, 'Rudi Dutschke: Zusammenfassung seiner politischen Theorien' (September 1967), Jürgen-Bernd Runge Private Papers, file 'Politischer Beirat'.

[127] Douglas Kellner (ed.), Herbert Marcuse: Technology, War, and Fascism: Collected Papers of Herbert Marcuse, vol. 1 (Abingdon, 1998), xiii.

[128] Herbert Marcuse, One-dimensional Man: Studies in the Ideology of Advanced Industrial Society (Boston, MA, 1964).

[129] Peter Philipp, 'Herbert Marcuse: Zusammenfassung seiner gesellschaftskritischen Analyse', in Runge Private Papers, file 'Politischer Beirat', n.p.

[130] Ibid.   [131] Radunski interview.

[132] ACDP 4/6/42/2, Peter Radunski, 'Zum Selbstverständnis des RCDS', Rednerdienst, no. 1 (September 1968).

The West German postwar status quo with its short-termism and emphasis on material satisfaction, had neglected basic human desires. Material wealth could at best be an interim goal; Western societies needed 'creative, dynamic visions'.[133] RCDS's 1969 basic programme similarly defined the 'humanization' of society as a goal and called for opportunities for individual 'self-realization'.[134]

Horst Teltschik (b. 1940), a former deputy national chair of RCDS who would later go on to advise Chancellor Kohl on foreign policy, was more unequivocally critical of SDS's Marcuse-inspired worldview. In a detailed summary analysis of the group's ideology and strategy that he wrote in 1967, he charged:

> In the new critics of power itself, there is a malicious tendency towards force, to impose their will, the will of a minority with revolutionary methods. That is tyranny of a minority. In the name of greater freedom from social coercion, it imposes its coercion on others and destroys this freedom in the name of the construction of an ill-defined new society; in the name of protesting against violence, it uses violence.[135]

The federal leadership of RCDS used findings such as these to better equip Christian Democratic activists for their ideational struggle against the Left. Parallel to stepping up its intellectual efforts, RCDS started to run regular seminars for centre-right activists that taught the art and practice of political rhetoric and of countering arguments drawn from Marxist theory.[136] Ursula Männle (b. 1944), who had been state chair of the Bavarian RCDS in 1966/7, recalled that she ran such seminars regularly for Bavarian activists in the late 1960s. 'I hosted a lot of seminars and advanced trainings for younger students to prepare them for what happens at university and also [to educate them] about democracy by workers' councils. About theoretical engagement. I tried to give them theoretical equipment.'[137] RCDS offered similar event programming to secondary school students.[138] At one student seminar in July 1968, the attending activists first read a recently published piece on the political ideas of SDS by René Ahlberg, a sociologist and specialist on Marxist theory and Soviet communism. They

---

[133] ACDP, 4/6/16/1, Helmuth Pütz, 'Ein Pladoyer für "reale Utopien"'.

[134] RCDS Grundsatzprogramm (1969), Section I.2, available at https://www.kas.de/documents/252038/253252/7_file_storage_file_18226_1.pdf/d550a2e9-0af2-f69d-6a46-6c41c8fc3658?version=1.0&t=1539637748989 (accessed on 12 November 2019).

[135] ACDP, 04/006/016/1, Horst Teltschik, 'Der Sozialistische Deutsche Studentenbund (SDS): eine Analyse seiner Konzeption und Strategie' (31 August 1968), 12. Teltschik was elected deputy national chair of RCDS in March 1965.

[136] The first such seminar took place in October 1967. ArchAPO, RCDS, file '18. Ord. Bundesdelegierten-Versammlung (1968)', 'Vorstellungen des RCDS-Bundesvorstandes über seine Arbeit im WS 67/68'; ArchAPO, RCDS, file 'Zentrale Interna 1965–1968', Invitation letter from Detlef Stronk, 27 June 1968.

[137] Männle interview.

[138] Linde Apel, 'Jenseits von 1968' Politische Mobilisierung im Schwarzen Jahrzehnt', in Zeitgeschichte in Hamburg: Nachrichten aus der Forschungsstelle für Zeitgeschichte in Hamburg 2018 (Hamburg, 2019), 52–70.

then split into two teams—red and blue—to debate the pros and cons of political revolution.[139] In 1969, Wulf Schönbohm, who had been RCDS federal chair in 1967/8, published the fruits of these efforts as a handbook for centre-right activists that laid out how to take on radical leftists. The text presented seventeen of the most common political arguments made by activists of the Left—that the Basic Law, the Federal Republic's founding document, was at most a cover for an authoritarian, pre-fascist state, for instance, or that advanced industrial society constrained the free development of the individual—and then outlined what he considered to be the most effective arguments against such claims.[140] Centre-right activists were told, for instance, to point out that the very existence of hippies, beatniks, dropouts, and APO sympathizers proved that advanced industrial society left plenty of room for individual expression and for the development of a lifestyle that was at odds with political and social conventions.[141]

In spite of teaching its cadres to dispute New Left-inspired ideas in this rather formulaic fashion, RCDS at least attempted to answer the utopian impulses expressed in student demonstrations and the broader cultural revolt around 1968. Helmuth Pütz, one of the members of RCDS's strategy unit, drafted 'A Plea for "Real Utopias"', which explained how the centre-right might adopt the concept of 'utopia'.[142] For many in the conservative camp the term carried negative connotations, he conceded, because humans were inherently fallible and focusing on a distant, idealized end state bore the danger of justifying any means to get there. This was a critique conservatives routinely levelled not just against New Left philosophy, but also against Marxist-inspired thought in general. To make the striving for utopia palatable to a centre-right that was generally sceptical of blueprints, Pütz introduced the idea of 'real utopia', an 'anticipated utopia in the sense of goal-oriented action working towards an aspired state'.[143]

The phrase and its content were an unmistakable nod towards Ernst Bloch's 'concrete utopia', a concept that was very influential among leading SDS activists at the time, not least Dutschke, who engaged closely with Bloch.[144] Bloch had turned on its head the traditional understanding of utopia as a pre-existing ideal

---

[139] ACDP, 4-6-18/2, Invitation letter from Detlef Stronk, 1 July 1968; the respective piece was René Ahlberg, 'Die politische Konzeption des Sozialistischen Deutschen Studentenbundes', Beilage zur Wochenzeitung *Das Parlament* B20/68 (15 May 1968). The Office for the Protection of the Constitution had commissioned Ahlberg to write the piece a few months earlier. Aly, *Unser Kampf*, 39–40.

[140] Wulf Schönbohm, *Die Thesen der APO: Argumente gegen die radikale Linke* (Mainz, 1969).

[141] Schönbohm, *Die Thesen der APO*, 23.

[142] ACDP, 4/6/16/1, Helmuth Pütz, 'Ein Pladoyer für "reale Utopien"'; also ACDP, 04-006-63/1, *Kontrapunkt*, Information no. 2 (Frankfurt, October 1968), brochure by *Aktionskomitee Demokratischer Studenten* (ADS), a centre-right umbrella group at the Johann-Wolfgang-Goethe University in Frankfurt.

[143] ACDP, 4/6/16/1, Helmuth Pütz, 'Ein Pladoyer für "reale Utopien"'.

[144] The Marxist philosopher Ernst Bloch, like Dutschke exiled from the GDR from 1961 onward, was among the most important influences on Rudi Dutschke's political theory. They first met at a debate in Bad Boll in February 1968. 'Schwierigkeiten beim Aufrechtgehen', *Der Spiegel*, 8 (19 February

state, arguing instead that the process of getting there, which was driven by human beings, would determine its ultimate shape. Pütz took up Bloch's critique of utopia as a predestined telos, but he envisaged a process of changing society that was nevertheless very different from the Marxist philosopher's conception. The perfect end state could never be achieved, the centre-right student contended. Instead, continuous problem solving would improve the system gradually; the 'real utopias' that guided policy planning would routinely make way for new ones. This, then, was a mix of traditional conservative gradualism with liberal reformism in the Dahrendorf-mould couched in the language of utopia. Moreover, it was one that would show up, not only in RCDS's basic programme issued in 1969, but also in programmatic speeches given by none other than Helmut Kohl. The future Chancellor would make the rhetoric of 'real utopias' his own when he was honing his profile as an energetic, future-oriented reformer in the early 1970s.[145]

In the late summer of 1968, RCDS published a key document on its political self-conception. The piece drew together various ideas from the different papers that the members of the strategy unit had drafted and which unabashedly promoted the student association as an 'intellectual vanguard' (*vordenkende Gruppe in der Politik*). Rather than carrying the ideas of the CDU/CSU into the student body, student activists wanted to help redefine a party from below that they actually wanted to work in, it stated boldly. At the same time, Radunski, its lead author, insisted on the need for evolutionary rather than revolutionary changes to the West German political system—a juxtaposition that neatly captured the centre-right's desire for incremental change while directly contrasting their methods with those of the radical Left:

With [...] today's people in their concrete situation [...], RCDS wants to generate a real utopia and to achieve political progress without terror and with society. [...] RCDS wants to support policies and initiate social reforms, which bring about changes that together amount to a revolution. These reforms can be achieved with the resources of existing institutions. The answer of our democracy to the call for revolution must be reform, the revolution in tolerable doses.[146]

1968), 30–3; Jürgen Miermeister, *Ernst Bloch, Rudi Dutschke* (Leipzig, 1996). For Bloch's writings on utopia, see his *Geist der Utopie* (1918); and *Das Prinzip Hoffnung*, 3 vols (1938–1947).

[145] RCDS Grundsatzprogramm (1969), available at https://www.kas.de/documents/252038/253252/7_file_storage_file_18226_1.pdf/d550a2e9-0af2-f69d-6a46-6c41c8fc3658?version=1.0&t=1539637748989 (accessed on 12 November 2019). Just before his election as CDU chair, Kohl gave a speech on the party's relationship with intellectuals. It described the 'critical, open society' and 'active democracy' in the Federal Republic as the 'real utopias' he sought to realize. Helmut Kohl's spring 1973 speech in Trier, cited in Warnfried Dettling, *Das Erbe Kohls* (Eichborn, 1994), 109. Horst Teltschik worked as a speechwriter for Kohl at the time.

[146] ACDP, 4-6-16/1, Peter Radunski, 'Zum Selbstverständnis des RCDS: Politische und gesellschaftliche Bedingungen eines politischen Studentenverbandes'; also printed in ACDP, 04/6/42/2, RCDS-Rednerdienst, no. 1 (September 1968). A similar statement is included in Schönbohm, Runge, and

The student group's conceptual efforts did not end in 1968. RCDS issued its first basic programme in 1969—and thus nine years before the CDU would do so. Like Radunski's musings on the group's self-conception, it embraced the need for reform and suggested a number of specific ways in which Christian Democratic politics and West German democracy could be improved, notably through increased participation by ordinary citizens.[147]

In late 1968, a number of leading RCDS activists—among them Schönbohm and Radunski—also set up a new, and ultimately very influential, journal dedicated to carrying this reformist spirit further into the Christian Democratic parties. The quarterly *Sonde: Zeitschrift für Neue Christlich Demokratische Politik* was intended as a forum for intellectual debate on the centre-right and discussion about party reorganization. Its first editorial called for a new Christian Democratic politics based on new concepts and led by new personalities, who were intellectually open and flexible and embraced a new political style.[148] In the party's oppositional phase after 1969, *Sonde* quickly became *the* platform for young and ambitious inner-party reformers who advocated increased programmatic work as a form of Christian Democratic 'self-therapy'.[149] They regularly caused considerable furore with the publication of lists of bold theses on the need to broaden democratic participation and modernize party structures.[150] Several of its editors and lead authors would become intimately involved in the CDU's own programmatic endeavours in the 1970s and later occupied key strategic positions in the Kohl government.

Despite their principled opposition to SDS and rejection of all forms of 'ideology', being forced to engage with the ideas of the student Left in this age of theory ultimately pushed Christian Democratic students towards a far more ideational articulation of their own political principles than they had previously been inclined to put forward. The end result may still have been somewhat intellectually vacuous. RCDS's self-conception and basic program hardly defined exactly what was meant by 'reform' beyond vague paeans to a 'future-oriented politics' and 'social progress'. But this nevertheless represented a significant departure from the distinct lack of Christian Democratic programmatic debate in the 1950s and early 1960s. It was also very different from a traditional

---

Radunski, Die herausgeforderte Demokratie, 109, a book that in many ways presented a synthesis of RCDS's theoretical efforts.

[147] RCDS Grundsatzprogramm (1969).

[148] Editorial, *Sonde*, 1 (1968); also Wulf Schönbohm, '10 Jahre Sonde', *Sonde*, 4 (1978), 4–5.

[149] Helmuth Pütz, Peter Radunksi, and Wulf Schönbohm, '34 Thesen zur Reform der CDU', *Sonde*, 4 (1969), 8.

[150] 'RCDS startet "Sonde"', *FAZ*, 12 December 1968; Röper interview; Radunski interview; Schönbohm interview; Helmuth Pütz, Peter Radunksi, and Wulf Schönbohm, '34 Thesen zur Reform der CDU', *Sonde*, 4 (1969), 4–22; Helmuth Pütz, Peter Radunksi, Wulf Schönbohm, and Uwe Rainer Simon, '18 Thesen zur Reorganisation der CDU', *Sonde*, 3/4 (1973), 15–30; Wulf Schönbohm, 'Mehr Demokratie in der CDU', *Sonde*, 2 (1975), 29–35.

conservative stance that eschewed defining firm ideals and primarily sought inspiration in the past, not the future.[151]

Centre-right activists who were involved in this work later reported unanimously that it had lasting and productive effects, not least of all on them personally. For all his staunch criticism of his opponents' ideas at the time, even Horst Teltschik thought in retrospect that engaging with left-wing theoretical 'nonsense' paid off, because it turned centre-right activists into skilled debaters who defended parliamentary democracy in a more intellectual manner than their predecessors.[152]

Wolfgang Reeder, who had served as deputy national chair of RCDS in 1970/71, concurred that the confrontation with the Left had helped him to think more holistically about the virtues of liberal democracy and the social market economy. Before 1968, he had been expected to join the family business, but he chose to pursue a policy career instead and later set up his own economic consulting firm. In particular, it was the anti-capitalist impulse of the left-wing student movement that led to his explicit embrace of the market as an important component of presenting a political alternative to the Socialist system—beyond simply 'worshipping the holy Ludwig Erhard', as he put it.[153] After 1989/90, Reeder worked on economic reform in East Germany, and he explained that many of the rhetorical and conceptual skills he had acquired as a student activist had been useful when organizing the transition from a socialist command economy to a market-based system:

After the *Wende*, in debates with people in East Germany, I was in full command of Marxism-Leninism. And they always said to me: 'How do you know all this? Wasn't it all banned where you were?' And then I said: 'No, we dealt with it daily at university!' [...] We were repeatedly faced with a consistent counter model. And the confrontation with a consistent counter model naturally solidified and refined our own consciousness in dramatic ways. And I suspect that this ability to develop a consciousness of society as a whole would not have happened without the challenge from the Left.

Of Insiders and Outsiders

It was not just the engagement with left-wing ideas and theory, however, which shaped centre-right activists' long-term outlook. Numerous personal encounters

---

[151] In a famous tract published in 1952, Hans Mühlenfeld had described conservatism as 'politics without ideals'. See Schildt, *Konservatismus in Deutschland*, 213.

[152] Teltschik interview. Others made a very similar point. Schönbohm interview; Männle interview.

[153] Reeder interview; on RCDS's spirited defence of the social market economy during Reeder's tenure, see also *Hans Reckers Private Papers*, 'Soziale Marktwirtschaft: Antwort des 20. Jahrhunderts auf den Sozialismus (19. Jh.)', *RCDS-Info*, 15 (n.d.).

with their opponents were equally central to their political self-identification at the time and with hindsight. To be sure, genuinely close personal relationships between activists from different camps were quite rare. West Berlin RCDS chair Christian Hacke was one of the very few who had a girlfriend in SDS, for instance. He later recalled that they had been sneaking around and practically only met at night: 'Her people would have stoned her for going out with such a reactionary as an RCDS guy like Hacke, and my people would not have let that slide with me.'[154]

Although such recollections suggest that political tribalism was capable of reaching into the private realm, there were plenty of personal interactions. Far from being passive observers or mere students of New Left theory, RCDS activists engaged directly with their political rivals in numerous ways, not least in teach-ins that often pitted the SDS's call for revolution against Christian Democratic students' call for reform.[155] For instance, RCDS federal chair Wulf Schönbohm was invited to speak at the annual SDS convention in September 1967, where he described SDS and RCDS as 'political antipodes', and SDS activists in turn explained their political outlook at gatherings of conservative fraternity students.[156]

In fact, centre-right activists were almost always present at major SDS-run events. Peter Radunski recalled that he had spent most of his time following SDS activists around in the hope of breaking the spell they had on student audiences. 'I was always tagging along with them, practically like a vandal.'[157] In her biography of her late husband, Rudi Dutschke's US-born wife Gretchen Dutschke-Klotz—who otherwise did not mince her words when she held a grudge against somebody who had offended her or her husband—explicitly noted this presence and even described select Christian Democratic students with palpable fondness. She identified Jürgen-Bernd Runge (b. 1944), the one-time leader of West Berlin's RCDS chapter, as one of her husband's most effective and important counterparts and as somebody who enriched the political conversation: 'Runge countered Rudi at every event, and Rudi polemicized strongly but sincerely against him. In some ways it was admirable how Runge always fought against great disapproval and never gave up. His appearances stimulated the discussion.'[158]

---

[154] Hacke, '68: Fluch oder Segen?'.
[155] Hoover Institution Archives (HIA), German Subject Collection (GSC), box 87; 'RCDS—SDS. Evolution—Revolution', 7 Dec. 1967 (leaflet). Among the discussants were Schönbohm, Dutschke, SDS activist Wolfgang Lefèvre, and Runge.
[156] ArchAPO, RCDS, file 'BRD', 'Rede des RCDS-Bundesvorsitzenden Wulf Schönbohm auf der Delegiertenkonferenz des SDS am 4 September 1967 in Frankfurt/M'; 'Zur Ideologie des SDS: Ein Nachtrag zur Dreikönigstagung 1968', Akademische Blätter, 4 (1968), 69–70.
[157] Radunski interview.
[158] Gretchen Dutschke-Klotz, Wir hatten ein barbarisches, schönes Leben: Rudi Dutschke: Eine Biographie (Cologne, 2007), 121; the debates between the two were also covered in the national media, which juxtaposed the student leaders' different points of view. See, e.g., the statements by Runge and Dutschke featured in 'Zwei Beiträge zur Diskussion', Die Zeit, no. 23 (June 1967), available at http://www.zeit.de/1967/25/zwei-beitraege-zur-diskussion (accessed on 27 June 2015). On

The admiration was mutual, for many centre-right activists found similarly warm words for Dutschke. Radunski stressed that he had liked the SDS leader personally and interacted with him quite frequently, because both had studied under the same professors at the Free University. He recalled that they had lived only a short distance away from each other and had sometimes taken the same bus.[159] To Radunski, their cordial relationship and Dutschke's willingness to engage with him signified the openness of the 1968 Left—a trait which, he suggested, stood in marked contrast to subsequent cohorts of left-wing activists whose politics were much more rigid. 'So that was a generation that I was somewhat a part of, right? Later it was very, very different.'[160]

His recollections hint at a diffuse feeling of generational solidarity among student activists that, at least around 1968, was capable of transcending political dividing lines. 'The beginning was very discursive. [...] In the beginning, there was the feeling that we came from a somewhat similar kind of mental excitement.'[161] Finding a voice through encounters with authority, seizing speech, and developing personal confidence through participation in the student movement were common tropes among activists of the Left who later reflected on 1968.[162] Like them, Radunski described the years around 1968 as a personally transformative time. For him, however, it was the engagement and confrontation with the Left that sparked this personal transformation: 'We were no longer afraid of authority. Until then, I was like a dwarf, I would say. This movement gave me the strength suddenly to say "I can talk. [...] I can face people. I have an opinion".'[163] In his published autobiography he put it similarly: 'Like many others of my generation, the student revolt gave me the positive feeling that I was really needed.' He even described Dutschke as his 'role model, mentor or motivator', their considerable political differences notwithstanding:

> He was a young man of my age, who was at eye level with politicians and the media. Even if he failed, he really impressed me, and something inside me urged me to imitate him. Of all political actors that I observed in my youth, Rudi Dutschke impressed me the most.[164]

Dutschke-Klotz's difficult relationship with Dieter Kunzelmann and others from Kommune 1 and the negative way she portrayed them in her memoirs, see Reimann, *Kunzelmann*, 124–6.

[159] Interview mit Peter Radunski, Berlin, 26 October 2009.

[160] Radunski interview. This point is explored further in Chapter 5, see 184–5. Jens Litten, the one-time deputy leader of the SHB, argued similarly in 1969 when he stated that those left-wing activists who began to engage in politics before 2 June 1967 were much readier to compromise and open to dialogue than those who became active after the death of Ohnesorg. Litten, 'Die Generation des 2. Juni'.

[161] Radunski interview.

[162] Rebecca Clifford, Robert Gildea, and James Mark, 'Awakenings', in Gildea, Mark, and Warring, *Europe's 1968*, 21–45.

[163] Radunski interview.

[164] Radunski, *Aus der politischen Kulisse*, 64–6. As Berlin's Senator of Culture (1996–1999), Radunski signed off on designating Dutschke's final resting place in Dahlem an honorary grave, ibid., 67.

While others were more critical of the SDS icon, viewing him as a 'demagogue' whose zeal and social science jargon—'Dutschke-speak'—they, like other contemporaneous critics of the student Left, perceived as incomprehensible, it was far more common to find a mix of admiration and envy in recollections of Dutschke, who, more than any other individual, embodied left-wing radicalism in the eyes of centre-right activists.[165]

The envy they felt was sparked, above all, by the extensive media coverage dedicated to the activities of Dutschke and his SDS peers. Put simply: it stung that their competitors were so famous. According to a poll conducted by the Emnid polling institute in early 1968—and thus before the attempt on Dutschke's life on 11 April—98 per cent of university students and 77 per cent of West Germans between the ages of 15 and 25 had heard of the SDS leader.[166] Activists of the Left pointed out that much of the attention they received was negative, and that the conservative press, in particular, vilified them and turned them into targets of the public wrath—a charge that was far from unfounded, as the near-fatal attack on Dutschke made painfully clear. Meanwhile, their opponents on the centre-right were bothered by what they perceived as a complete lack of attention; they felt ignored.[167] '[W]e felt valued very little. [...] The Left were always the heroes, and, well, we were the little dummies', as Schönbohm put it bluntly with hindsight. 'There was no way to get into the media. They couldn't care less what the critics of the '68 movement said about its goals. The media only concentrated on Dutschke and the others.'[168]

Of course, such recollections severely underplayed the frequency—and considerable political sympathy—with which conservative-leaning papers, such as *Die Welt*, the *Frankfurter Allgemeine Zeitung* or *Rheinischer Merkur*, reported on the actions and goals of the centre-right around 1968. Nonetheless, he certainly had a point about the media's fascination with the left-wing stars of the student

---

[165] Members of the conservative faction of RCDS in West Berlin were particularly critical of Dutschke. Diepgen interview; Klemann interview; Härdtl interview. Centre-right activists often invoked Dutschke as a symbol of their broader relationship with the student Left. Activists from East Germany and other states in the Eastern bloc employed a similar strategy in interviews. They often used memories of Dutschke to convey the larger meaning of their relationship to the Western Left around 1968. See Mark and von der Goltz, 'Encounters', 150–1. On the incomprehensibility of the student Left's language as a common trope of critics of the protests. See Scharloth, *1968: Eine Kommunikationsgeschichte*, 301–7.

[166] See the report on the poll compiled by the Federal Government's Press and Information Office, 19 February 1968, BAK, N1229/213. The results were published in *Der Spiegel*, 8 (19 February 1968).

[167] Stuart Hilwig, 'The Revolt Against the Establishment: Students Versus the Press in West Germany and Italy', in Carole Fink, Philipp Gassert, and Detlef Junker (eds.), *1968: The World Transformed* (Cambridge, 1998), 321–50; Sedlmaier, *Consumption and Violence*, 168–204. Recent research on the media dynamics around 1968 has rightly stressed, however, that the student movement was also often covered quite favourably—and in many ways aided considerably—by a West German press that had become much more critical of authority since the 1950s. See von Hodenberg, *Konsens und Krise*.

[168] Schönbohm interview.

movement and their larger-than-life stature.[169] Their elevation had much to do with their protest repertoires. Inspired by French Marxist Guy Debord's Situationist International, the increasingly influential anti-authoritarian wing of SDS engaged in carefully planned and spectacular acts of protest aimed at exposing the repressive reality beneath the Federal Republic's democratic façade. Deliberate acts of provocation, often using irony and disrespectful humour, were intended to produce an overreaction on the part of state authorities, which, in turn, was designed to bolster the far-left critique of repressive forms of authority. Such protests were intentional spectacles and the news media lapped them up, making not just SDS theoretician Dutschke, but also the political clowns Fritz Teufel and Rainer Langhans true media icons in the second half of the 1960s.[170] The inhabitants of Kommune 1 graced the pages of the news magazines *Stern* and *Der Spiegel*, and Teufel's West Berlin trial for throwing stones at police on 2 June was covered nationally throughout 1967. Dutschke made it onto several covers of *Der Spiegel* and even of the business magazine *Capital*—a level of fame RCDS activists could only dream of.[171]

It was this near-blanket coverage that so irked their no less ambitious opponents on the centre-right. 'Student 1967—that was Rudi Dutschke', as the key centre-right text on the phenomenon of student unrest summed it up with barely concealed envy.[172] Schönbohm, one of its authors, duly complained in a letter to the editors of the liberal weekly *Die Zeit* that the paper's coverage contained 'Too much SDS—too little RCDS', and an open letter he penned to Rudi Dutschke mocked his rival for being a 'prominent politician'.[173] The RCDS national chair was noticeably keen to style himself as Dutschke's equal, referring to himself as the SDS figurehead's 'co-discussant' and '"reactionary" counterpart'. He went on: 'I saw you in a photo in *Der Spiegel* on your vacation in Sylt, in a neat soccer outfit sprinting through the area [...]', his turn of phrase hinting at how much he begrudged Dutschke his exposure in the press."[174]

Centre-right activists did not just blame the media for turning them into outsiders. Years later, they also still faulted their student opponents on campus

---

[169] For a heavily biased but nevertheless insightful examination of some of this coverage, see Stefan Winckler, '"Die Welt"—Ein Sprachrohr der schweigenden Mehrheit? Die Gegnerschaft zu den politischen Demonstrationen der Studenten 1967/68 aus publizistikwissenschaftlicher Sicht', in Winckler, Dirsch, and Becker, *Die 68er und ihre Gegner*, 183–207.

[170] Guy Debord, *The Society of the Spectacle* (St Petersburg, FL, 1970); Katrin Fahlenbrach, *Protest-Inszenierungen: Visuelle Kommunikation und kollektive Identitäten in Protestbewegungen* (Wiesbaden, 2002), 165–236; Simon Teune, 'Humour as a Guerrilla Tactic: The West German Student Movement's Mockery of the Establishment', *International Review of Social History*, 52 (2007), 115–32.

[171] Reimann, *Kunzelmann*, 169–70; Siegfried 'Stars der Revolte'; Stallmann, *Die Erfindung von '1968'*, 193–6.

[172] Schönbohm, Runge, and Radunski, *Die herausgeforderte Demokratie*, 9.

[173] Wulf Schönbohm, letter to the editors of *Die Zeit*, 8 December 1967; Wulf Schönbohm, 'Offener Brief an den Doktoranden Rudi Dutschke', 29 August 1967, printed in *RCDS-Brief*, 4 (1967), n.p.

[174] Wulf Schönbohm, 'Offener Brief an den Doktoranden Rudi Dutschke', 29 August 1967, printed in *RCDS-Brief*, 4 (1967), n.p.

and the general spirit of the era for marginalizing them. As Meinhard Ade put it, coming out as a Christian Democrat had pitted him firmly against the *Zeitgeist* in Freiburg. '[I]t was simply true that [by] joining RCDS [...] you made yourself into an outsider. It [...] wasn't considered good form.'[175] Interviewees thus portrayed themselves as rebels in their own right. Wulf Schönbohm related that he had grown up in Kassel, which had been 'staunchly Social Democratic' and where he attended a Steiner school [*Waldorfschule*] famous for its alternative pedagogy. In the late 1950s, he had begun to heckle demonstrations against nuclear weapons organized by the Campaign Against Atomic Death [*Kampf dem Atomtod*].[176] The atmosphere at West Berlin's Otto Suhr Institute of Political Science, where he arrived in 1964, had only crystallized his oppositional sense of self, he suggested. '[A]t the Otto Suhr Institute I very quickly became active, because the Left really got on my nerves with their arrogance and self-assurance.'[177]

Ursula Männle, who had been taught by the nuns at her Catholic boarding school that politics was 'unfeminine', similarly portrayed joining the Bavarian Christian Democrats as an act of 'resistance'—even though the party held the absolute majority of seats in the Bavarian state parliament at the time. When she later studied sociology at the Ludwig Maximilian University in Munich, she was suddenly surrounded by left-wing academics and students, she recalled. 'I was studying sociology there and really, they were all lefties. All lefties! And so I really found that rather shocking.'[178] She claimed that she had been ostracized in the department after asking for a letter of recommendation for a scholarship from the Konrad Adenauer Foundation, the Christian Democratic think tank. Being shunned for being 'right-wing' only strengthened her political commitment, however. 'It was so inescapable, there was resistance there, and then you really had to confront it. Yes, so that's how I also came to join RCDS.'[179]

At first glance, there is little contemporaneous evidence for such oppositional self-definitions. As late as 1960, twice as many West German students sympathized with the CDU than their contemporaries overall.[180] Four years later, the

[175] Ade interview; also Gauweiler, 'Wir waren für die das allerletzte'.

[176] On Schönbohm's family background, the family's flight, and his upbringing in Kassel, see also the autobiography of his older brother, CDU politician and military leader Jörg Schönbohm, *Wilde Schermut: Erinnerungen eines Unpolitischen* (Berlin, 2010), particularly 31, 81–3. On protests against nuclear weapons in the 1950s, see Holger Nehring, *Politics of Security: British and West German Protest Movements and the Early Cold War, 1945–1970* (Oxford, 2013).

[177] Schönbohm interview.

[178] Männle interview. On the politics of the local sociology department, see Elisabeth Zellmer, 'Protestieren und Polarisieren. Frauenbewegung und Feminismus der 1970er Jahre in München', in Kerstin Wolff, Eva-Maria Silies, and Julia Paulus (eds.), *Zeitgeschichte als Geschlechtergeschichte: Neue Perspektiven auf die Bundesrepublik* (Frankfurt am Main, 2012), 284–96.

[179] Männle interview.

[180] Bösch, *Die Adenauer-CDU*, 403; students had been even more conservative in the 1950s. Konrad H. Jarausch, *Deutsche Studenten*, 223.

sociologist Viggo Graf Blücher still described West German youths, including students, as overwhelmingly conformist and well-behaved.[181] In self-fashioning themselves as oppositional and anti-authoritarian figures, then, the interviewees no doubt appropriated popular tropes about left-wing activists' political socialization. Doing so was at least partly an attempt to contest who ought to count as a true 1960s rebel, at least in retrospect.

Inflated though these oppositional self-definitions no doubt were, however, they also built on actual experiences that were the product of the particular micro-contexts in which many of the most active centre-right students operated. Most interviewees could point to specific instances that had made them feel marginalized. This was especially true in the case of future Berlin Governing Mayor Eberhard Diepgen, who, at the age of twenty-one, had been driven out of office by a left-wing campaign. In February 1963, he was a law student at the Free University in West Berlin and at the centre of a major, but now largely forgotten, scandal that rocked the university in an early indication of the leftward tilt of student politics on the campus that was to come. In January of that year, the conservative-dominated student parliament had elected Diepgen, who was not only a Christian Democrat but also a member of the dueling fraternity Saravia, as chair of the student council. The fraternities, although a considerable force at universities across the country in the early 1960s (roughly 16 per cent of students in West Germany and West Berlin were members), had a difficult standing at the FU. Banned from operating on campus after the university's founding because of their ambiguous relationship to democratic values, most students eyed them with suspicion.[182] When Diepgen's Saravia membership became public knowledge in the context of his election, his opponents forced a referendum, in which over 70 per cent of FU students participated, thus placing the fraternities under considerable public scrutiny: 64.5 per cent of those who voted thought that the hierarchical educational model that lay at the fraternities' core was out of touch with the principles of a modern university and voted for Diepgen's dismissal from his seat as chair of the student council.[183]

Diepgen's ouster was the result of the specific context at the FU—a university founded as a symbol of freedom and democracy in the Cold War island city—and the contested role of the dueling fraternities within it. For many on the centre-right the perception of left-wing dominance emerged because of the particular places where they found themselves, be it in a sociology department or at a Steiner

---

[181] Viggo Graf Blücher, *Die Generation der Unbefangenen* (Düsseldorf, 1964); see also Wolfgang R. Krabbe, *Kritische Anhänger—Unbequeme Störer: Studien zur Politisierung deutscher Jugendlicher im 20. Jahrhundert* (Berlin, 2010), 115.

[182] James F. Tent, *The Free University of Berlin: A Political History* (Bloomington, IN, 1988), 298; c.f. von der Goltz, 'Other "68ers" in West Berlin'.

[183] See ACDP, 1-700-086-1, report of the student council on the official results of the referendum, 18 February 1963; also see Wilhelm Schumm, 'Nach der Urabstimmung', *FU Spiegel*, 30 (February 1963), 8.

school, for instance. Activists who were based at universities that were centres of left-wing protest, also had a more clearly honed sense of themselves as 'rebels' than those who were further removed from the action.[184]

For some, the subjects they chose to study, in particular, fed a sense of marginalization. Ingrid Reichart-Dreyer (b. 1946), who studied political science at the FU's Otto Suhr Institute, later recalled that 'The situation was difficult—to be a black there. [Black was the official colour of the Christian Democrats, AvdG] There was really exclusion.'[185] Teltschik, who studied political science, modern history, and international law at the FU, framed his stance in outright heroic terms, claiming that it had taken true courage to join the ranks of the centre-right and be open about it. 'I have always said, it was more courageous to be with us than to be with the others. Because whenever we made ourselves known, others were hostile to us.'[186]

Sociological research conducted around 1968 showed quite clearly that the levels of political activism and political preferences among students differed considerably between different departments. Up to 50 per cent of philosophy and sociology students sympathized with left-wing radicals in the late 1960s, but only 10 per cent of those studying dentistry did. Economists were the least radical and most likely to be conservative.[187] The majority of the most vocal centre-right activists on West German campuses around 1968—and, accordingly, most of those interviewed for this book—were not aspiring dentists, but students who at least minored in one of the 'left-wing' social sciences where most of their politicized student peers were also on the Left.

Many others majored in a relatively new, and rapidly expanding, subject: political science—a subject that also happened to be a favourite choice among SDS members.[188] Consequently, centre-right activists such as Horst Teltschik, Peter Radunski, and Wulf Schönbohm—who all majored in political science at the Free University in West Berlin whose programme and faculty had a particularly strong reputation—did not just encounter a left-wing radical like Dutschke at teach-ins. They also sat in some of the same seminars and had the same teachers as the SDS icon who was pursuing a doctorate in sociology, a field that was closely related to the new discipline.[189] Their sense of themselves as political outsiders—though no doubt overstated and honed in retrospect—thus had less to do with the broader political climate in the Federal Republic, or even with the overall political preferences of students in

---

[184] Röper interview. Röper was a student in Mainz and RCDS chair in Rhineland-Palatinate.
[185] Reichart-Dreyer interview.　　[186] Teltschik interview.
[187] Allerbeck, *Soziologie radikaler Studentenbewegungen*, 161; Jarausch, *Deutsche Studenten*, 234.
[188] Wienhaus, *Bildungswege zu '1968'*, 199. At the time, political science was conceived of as the academic underpinning of democracy and democratic education in West Germany. Arno Mohr, *Politikwissenschaft als Alternative: Stationen einer wissenschaftlichen Disziplin auf dem Wege zu ihrer Selbständigkeit in der Bundesrepublik Deutschland 1945-1965* (Bochum, 1988).
[189] Interviews with Teltschik, Radunski, and Schönbohm.

the 1960s, than with the specific ecosystems in which they operated, on campus and beyond.

Furthermore, some former activists suggested that their class and family educational background had set them apart from radical leftists, who, they claimed, were on the whole much more bourgeois. Radunski, for instance, whose grandparents, who raised him, had been of small means, pointed to the cashmere sweaters worn by Frank Wolff to suggest that activists of the student left had generally come from higher socioeconomic backgrounds.[190] Wolff was a gifted violinist, who, together with his brother K.D., served as national chair of SDS in 1967/8. Such retrospective verdicts, however, probably had at least as much to do with widespread stereotypes about 'champagne socialists' (*Salonkommunisten*) as with the class configurations among politicized students, for RCDS had its own equivalents to the Wolff brothers.[191] Christian Hacke, who served as chair of the West Berlin RCDS chapter in 1968/9, for one, 'grew up the complete opposite of petty-bourgeois', as he put it. Born in East Prussia, he was raised by his grandparents in a small town in the Black Forest. They lived in a villa owned by his great-grandfather who had been a Professor of Medicine at Freiburg University. 'In winter he drove with me in his Porsche (open-top, in 1950!) to the ski-jumping, and in summer to the motorbike racing on the Schauinsland [a mountain in the Black Forest]', Hacke recalled.[192] He later attended a boarding school housed in an old castle in Schleswig-Holstein. What is more, the father of Axel Wormit, who owned the Mercedes on which Dutschke and Dahrendorf debated in Freiburg in January 1968, was the head of the Prussian Cultural Heritage Foundation, one of Germany's premier cultural institutions.

While such upper middle-class family backgrounds were not the norm, the parents of other activists were doctors, teachers, civil servants, or had served as parliamentarians. To be sure, at a time of massive educational expansion in West Germany, there were clear *Bildungsaufsteiger* among them—first-generation students whose parents and grandparents had not attended universities or higher schools. However, there is little evidence to suggest that the socioeconomic backgrounds of centre-right activists differed markedly from that of left-wing activists in the 1960s. At a time when only around 5 per cent of students (compared to 49 per cent of over 16-year olds in the population as a whole) came from working-class households, while academic households made up 1.5 per cent of the population and 35 per cent of students, those from

---

[190] Radunski interview; Meinhard Ade made a similar point about the Wolff brothers. Ade interview.

[191] Sociologists who studied the radical Left could find no correlation between family income and radical outlook, Allerbeck, *Soziologie radikaler Studentenbewegungen*, 68; a collective biography of SDS members in West Berlin found that they were predominantly from middle class families. Only 7 per cent were the children of workers, which corresponded more or less to the overall numbers among students. Wienhaus, *Bildungswege zu '1968'*.

[192] Hacke, '68: Fluch oder Segen?'.

educated middle-class families were also prominently represented among activists of the centre-right.[193] In the 1960s, obtaining a university education was still the domain of a social elite, and this shaped the membership structure of all political student groups.

Feelings of outsiderdom among centre-right activists were also sustained by memories of having faced hostile treatment at the hands of their opponents. 'Of course, one was disparaged as a small-minded, fascist-type, and professor-dependent, and who knows what else', explained Wulf Schönbohm, who had experienced the student movement in West Berlin and Bonn at the time when the protests reached their peak. He recalled events at the Audimax, the main lecture hall on the Free University's campus, with up to 1,000 people, 'where, of course, as an RCDS-man, one is alone'. On such occasions, the Left used plenty of unfair tricks to make sure that his role was minimized, he claimed. 'Naturally, they manipulated the list of speakers. And everything was prepared by them. And whenever [a Christian Democratic student] appeared, then there was immediately yelling and booing. So, one had to have real nerves to get through this.'[194]

As Nina Verheyen demonstrated in her cultural history of discussion styles in the 1960s, political debates among students were not just shaped by the content of what was discussed, but also had a strong performative element. The discussants engaged in verbal combat with each other—an experience that would shape participants' long-term sense of self and habitus.[195] This applied to centre-right students, as well. Years later, Hacke still remembered having been weak at the knees when he entered the main lecture hall of the city's Technical University shortly after the assassination attempt on Dutschke. 'A fanatical crowd had gathered there', he recalled. He was there to voice criticism of the planned protest against the Springer publishing house, which the student Left blamed for inciting the assassin in the first place.

> My remarks disappeared in the hollering. They pushed and shoved me off the podium. My people linked arms with me, and to this day I still do not know how we left the Audimax unscathed. The terror sat in my bones for a long time.[196]

---

[193] BAK, 1363/II, Der deutsche Student: Kommentar des Instituts für Demoskopie Allensbach zur Spiegel-Umfrage (1966/67); Alexander Sedlmaier and Stephan Malinowski, '"1968" -A Catalyst of Consumer Society', *Cultural and Social History*, 8, 2 (2011), 255–74; Axel Schildt, *Die Sozialgeschichte der Bundesrepublik Deutschland bis 1989/90* (Munich, 2007), 52.

[194] Schönbohm interview. See also Schönbohm, Radunski, and Runge, *Die herausgeforderte Demokratie*, 80.

[195] Nina Verheyen, *Diskussionslust: Eine Kulturgeschichte des 'besseren Arguments' in Westdeutschland* (Göttingen, 2010), 292.

[196] Hacke, '68: Fluch oder Segen?'.

Such recollections of left-wing intimidation and martial confrontations with their student peers clearly built on established autobiographical tropes of outsiderdom and involved considerable hyperbole designed to ennoble the roles of centre-right activists.[197]

Nevertheless, Hacke's reminiscences highlight that, for all the evidence of dialogue and the mutual respect that did exist between SDS and RCDS activists, student politics quickly became more combative—and would become much more so over time. It was by no means solely the Left that created this climate of hostility, however. At the height of the student movement in 1967/8, it was quite common for centre-right speakers to bring security to events. They often appeared at political events in the company of a group of fraternity students who acted as stewards and bodyguards—a provocative gesture that only stoked the passions of their opponents and sometimes led to physical confrontations between activists from different camps.[198] One former RCDS activist who later became a critic of the organization, compared the practice to the Weimar-era 'Saalschutz', which had used violent means, if necessary, to protect political gatherings from interruption by rival political groups—a practice that was closely associated with the Nazis.[199]

Wighard Härdtl (b. 1944), who belonged to the RCDS's more conservative faction, later admitted that, at least in West Berlin, centre-right students also toyed with the idea of using physical force against their opponents. He recalled that in late May 1968, several hundred activists from various fraternities, among them Härdtl and Diepgen, hatched a plan to storm the rooms of the Free University's German department, which were being occupied by left-wing activists protesting against the planned emergency laws. Their plan was to use force to evict the left-wing occupiers, who had hoisted red flags on the building on Boltzmannstraße and renamed it the 'Rosa Luxemburg Institute'. Word got out, however, and the occupiers began to arm themselves with chair legs.[200] When the police showed up to calm the situation, the conservative students aborted the plan for fear of having to fight the police rather than their student opponents. 'So, with our basic convictions, we can't take on [...] the police! That meant we would have had to clear the police first. That meant we would have grappled with the police and the Left would have stood back and smirked.'[201] Instead, West Berlin newspapers, as they so often did, reported on the vandalism of the left-wing occupiers.[202]

On other occasions, when the police did not get involved, Christian Democratic activists were notably less restrained, even before the student movement reached

[197] Depkat, *Lebenswenden und Zeitenwenden*, 127.
[198] Hacke, '68: Fluch oder Segen?'; Runge interview.   [199] Runge interview.
[200] 'Das Germanische Seminar der FU besetzt', *Die Welt*, 1 June 1968, Berlin edition, 1.
[201] Härdtl interview; see also Diepgen interview.
[202] 'Zurück blieben nur die Parolen der Besatzer', *Die Welt*, Berlin edition, 1 June 1968, 8; Rudolf Müller, 'Wieder eine Besetzung an der FU?', *B.Z.*, 11 June 1968, 6.

its peak. On 8 February 1966, the day after the widely publicized incident in which left-wing protesters pelted West Berlin's Amerikahaus, an American cultural institute, with eggs to condemn the war in Vietnam, a pro-American counter-demonstration took place. Anti-Left demonstrators pushed a number of young, long-haired spectators into the nearby Zoologischer Garten station and forced them to purchase tickets to East Berlin's station at Friedrichstraße. SDS students were shocked by what they perceived as an unmistakable display of West Berlin's continued 'fascist potential', and the incident indeed hints at the potential for violence in counterdemonstrations by the right.[203] Contrary to what some of them would later suggest when arguing that only radical left-wing activism around 1968 was inherently violent and single-handedly birthed the terror of the 1970s, then, it is worth noting that centre-right activists did not necessarily have a principled commitment to non-violence.

Cordial or openly hostile, personal encounters between activists from different political camps had a real impact. The frequency and intensity of such encounters

Illustration 1.3 Christian Democratic activist and future (West) Berlin Governing Mayor Eberhard Diepgen arguing with a left-wing counter-demonstrator at a pro-American citizens' protest near Schöneberg Town Hall in West Berlin on 21 February 1968.

(ullstein bild—Rogge)

---

[203] Fichter and Lönnendonker, *Kleine Geschichte des SDS*, 178, note 147; on this incident see further von der Goltz, 'Other '68ers in West Berlin', 95–6.

highlights the degree to which activism on different sides developed in conjunction—even if activists pulled in different directions. They did not just observe each other from a distance or lead parallel political lives that never intersected; they sat in the same seminar rooms, debated each other in teach-ins, and campaigned in close physical proximity on campus. The political debate was often deeply personal around 1968—so much so that, years later, the other '68ers still defined themselves in relation to their opponents. Centre-right activists also mimicked the Left, even if often inadvertently. While they copied some of SDS's organizational and protest tactics deliberately (rallying pupils, staging go-ins), this mimicry was subtler in other ways. Activists on both sides fashioned themselves as radical outsiders and political rebels, as a persecuted minority marginalized by an allegedly hostile press and political environment. The relationship between the different sides veered between engagement, envy, emulation, and, with the radicalization of the left-wing student movement from 1967/8 onward, a growing estrangement that would only intensify in the 1970s.

Renegades

For some activists of the centre-right, personal encounters with their opponents had the opposite effect. Rather than entrenching their political identity, they helped to change it. A close and sustained engagement with the left-wing student movement could open up new possibilities for political action. In addition, the anti-Left hostility that they witnessed among their centre-right peers and parts of the West German public became a problem for some. This was especially true for activists who belonged to the left-leaning factions of RCDS or the Student Unions. It even produced some 'renegades', centre-right students who decided to turn their backs on RCDS and the Student Unions to embrace alternative forms of politics.

One such case, in particular, stood out. In May 1968, a whole faction of RCDS's West Berlin chapter, around a dozen people in total, announced that they were leaving the Association of Christian Democratic Students.[204] Among them were some of the FU's most committed and visible centre-right activists. Martin Kempe (b. 1943), who had been a member of RCDS's political strategy unit at the Free University, was one of them. Joining RCDS had been a natural choice for Kempe, who had been raised in a staunchly conservative environment in rural Lippe-Detmold and served for two years in a psychological operations unit of the

---

[204] 'Konflikt im RCDS', Der Tagesspiegel, 17 May 1968; 'Zwei Stellungnahmen zum Austritt des linken RCDS-Flügels aus dem Verband am 15.5.1968', FU Spiegel, 65 (June/July 1968), copy in Runge Private Papers; on the different West Berlin RCDS factions and the split, see also Seitenbecher, 'Die Reform als Revolution'. Three of these West Berlin 'renegades' were interviewed for this book. They were Martin Kempe (b. 1943), Jürgen-Bernd Runge (b. 1944), and Othmar Nikola Haberl (b. 1943).

Bundeswehr before arriving at the FU in 1966.[205] Given this background, left-wing student groups seemed initially off-putting and extreme to him. Over the next two years, however, witnessing the hostile reactions of the West Berlin authorities and the public to the student movement first-hand altered his political trajectory. As an intern at *Der Tagesspiegel*, one of West Berlin's major dailies, he was tasked with covering many of the key protest events of the student movement's heyday in 1967/8. He later recalled that this had made him realize that there was a huge discrepancy between actual events and the coverage in the conservative Springer press—and even the reporting in his own more moderate paper. He also saw with his own eyes much of the violence that West Berlin's increasingly militarized police force subjected student protesters to, including on 2 June 1967, when Kempe observed anti-Shah demonstrators being beaten in front of the Opera House.

The most troubling scenes Kempe witnessed took place in the aftermath of the 'International Vietnam Congress', which the SDS hosted on 17 and 18 February 1968 at the Technical University of West Berlin. Thousands of left-wing activists from across the globe came together to voice their opposition to the US-led war in Vietnam, which had reached its bloody zenith with the beginning of the Tet Offensive the previous month. At a protest march following the event, thousands of young activists marched through the city's streets to animated shouts of 'Ho-Ho-Ho-Chi Minh', a provocative display of direct action that many ordinary West Berliners perceived as menacing. Three days later, on 21 February 1968, the Berlin Senate and the Springer press organized a large counter-demonstration at Schöneberg Town Hall that 60,000 West Berlin citizens attended, many of whom had been given the day off to take part.[206] *Der Tagesspiegel* sent Kempe to cover the event, and he witnessed the attendees' deep hostility towards anyone who looked like a student. 'I experienced how emotionally charged the atmosphere was among the population. Everybody who looked even vaguely like a student had to fear for his life. [...] It was a horrible experience', he remembered.[207]

Demonstrators carried signs that labelled Dutschke 'The Enemy of the People [*Volksfeind*] no. 1'. Kempe saw how a young man named Lutz-Dieter Mende, whom the demonstrators mistook for Dutschke, was pushed to the ground. He eventually managed to flee, but the crowd suspected that 'Dutschke' was hiding in a police van and started rocking the vehicle so hard that it was nearly turned over. Kempe himself was caught up in the violent commotion when he attempted to help another young man, who had been trying to take pictures and was struck by an older demonstrator. Kempe was beaten and pushed around by members of the

---

[205] Kempe interview.   [206] Fichter and Lönnendonker, *Kleine Geschichte des SDS*, 126.
[207] Kempe interview.

crowd. The whole atmosphere reminded him of a 'pogrom'.[208] Less than two months later, the real Dutschke was shot and almost killed by a young right-wing extremist. This and other incidents he had witnessed since the previous year eventually led Kempe to rethink his political commitment, he explained:

> Experiences like these made me think 'the criticism of Springer is justified, the criticism of the febrile atmosphere [in West Berlin] is justified. The democratic right to demonstrate and to freedom of expression are really being threatened.' And within this confrontation between this incited anti-communist population and these students, for me the scales increasingly tipped towards the student movement. And that was the point at which I could not continue within RCDS. [...] It was an ongoing internal process, I just developed in a different direction given all these experiences.[209]

Partly pushed out by members of RCDS's more conservative faction, partly pulled away by his changing convictions, Kempe left RCDS shortly afterwards, in May 1968. He was followed by a number of his peers who had edged closer to the positions advanced by the student Left and now defined themselves as 'left-liberal'. Since around the time of Ohnesorg's death, they had worked covertly to transform RCDS from within, but had not succeeded in building a substantial following among its activists and outmanoeuvring the group's conservative wing led by Härdtl and Jürgen Klemann, who would later become a Berlin Senator.[210] 'The effort had to fail due to the apolitical-right-wing, [...] lethargic and formally democratic-conservative self-understanding of RCDS', their impassioned exit declaration asserted. 'RCDS never managed to go beyond simply negating SDS and did not offer a positive statement about changing the university and society with regards to advancing democratization.' Rather than being a motor for change, RCDS first and foremost defended the status quo, the Christian Democratic renegades alleged.[211]

Most of them would stay on a leftward trajectory in the years to come.[212] Although remaining wary of formal political organization, Martin Kempe went

---

[208] Kempe interview. This incident involving the fake Dutschke was reported widely at the time and captured by photographers. It soon entered the annals of the student movement. 'Kundgebung der Berliner Bevölkerung', *Colloquium*, 4 (April 1968), 2; Michael Ruetz, *'Ihr müsst diesen Typen nur ins Gesicht sehen' (Klaus Schütz, SPD): APO Berlin, 1966-1969* (Frankfurt am Main, 1980),116–17; Fichter and Lönnendonker, 'Berlin: Hauptstadt der Revolte'; Brown, *West Germany*, 236.

[209] Kempe interview.   [210] Härdtl interview; Klemann interview.

[211] 'Zwei Stellungnahmen zum Austritt des linken RCDS-Flügels aus dem Verband am 15.5.1968', *FU Spiegel*, 65 (June/July 1968), copy in Runge Private Papers; also the left-liberal strategy paper drafted by Benno Ennker, 'Zur Strategie und Taktik bei der BDV', ArchAPO, RCDS, file '18. Ord. Bundesdelegierten-Versammlung. Mappe 1968'. A handwritten note at the bottom of the paper said 'We should probably not leave this piece of paper lying around'; also Seitenbecher, 'Die Reform als Revolution'.

[212] After leaving RCDS and the CDU, Othmar Nikola Haberl joined the SPD, but soon left the party as well. He remained wary of formal political organization and focused on his academic pursuits, researching the history and politics of Eastern Europe. Haberl interview.

'into the factories' in the 1970s, trying to organize the printers employed by Mercator, *Der Tagesspiegel*'s publishing house. In 1979, he joined the staff of West Berlin's newly founded *die tageszeitung* (*taz*), a cooperative-owned daily that had emerged out of the remnants of the left-wing student movement. There he became close friends with the likes of Christian Semler, his former counterpart in the West Berlin SDS.[213]

Jürgen-Bernd Runge's conversion story was even more remarkable. Runge, RCDS chair at the Free University until January 1968 and a leading member of the centre-right *Aktion 20. Konvent*, was one of Rudi Dutschke's most vocal counterparts, earning him, as we have seen, appreciation even within SDS.[214] Like Kempe's, his upbringing in resolutely Catholic Paderborn had been very conservative, and he had taken his first political steps in a nationalist scout group (*Deutsche Pfadfinderjungenschaft 'Speerwache'*). He had dreamt of becoming a career army officer, before arriving at the FU in 1965 to study law and politics. As RCDS chair during the crucial phase of the student movement in West Berlin, however, he had to engage closely with the SDS-led student movement. Over time,

Illustration 1.4 Jürgen-Bernd Runge, RCDS chair at the Free University in West Berlin, speaking to the members of the university's *Konvent* (student parliament) on 26 April 1967.

(Michael Ruetz/Agentur focus)

---

[213] Kempe interview; on Christian Semler's political trajectory, see James Mark, Anna von der Goltz, and Anette Warring, 'Reflections', in Mark, Gildea, and Warring, *Europe's 1968*, 309–11.
[214] Dutschke-Klotz, *Wir hatten ein barbarisches, schönes Leben*, 121.

he was increasingly persuaded by the student Left's wide-ranging social and political critique and markedly less impressed by the centre-right's response.

> The RCDS did not collect intelligence per se [...] and the Left was different, which fascinated me. I had more friends, and therefore debating partners, on the Left [...] than I did in my own organization. I discussed and argued with them through the night, but they respected me.[215]

He recalled that, in late 1967, he participated in a radio debate with Dutschke. They fought bitterly on air.

> And then at the end of the program, Rudi says to me, 'So, we've earned a couple of drinks. Can we sit together?' And then we sat and talked the whole night and we had only argued before. And we got very personal in our conversation. And at the end, he said to me, 'You, in a year you'll be in SDS, I bet.'[216]

Dutschke's prediction did not quite come to pass; Runge never joined SDS. Along with Kempe, however, he left RCDS in May 1968 and veered leftward in the coming years. He briefly flirted with liberal politics and joined the Free Democrats' youth organization *Jungdemokraten*, but, over time, became more and more drawn to communist ideas. Just as he was ready to make his new stance official and join the German Communist Party (DKP) in the early 1970s, the East German Ministry of State Security made its move and recruited Runge as an 'informal collaborator'.[217] Western students who were toying with the idea of joining the DKP or its student organization MSB Spartakus were a convenient target for the Stasi, who made sure to approach them before the decision would disqualify them from a career in secret intelligence.[218] The former RCDS leader, now residing in Bonn and officially working for former West Berlin FDP chair William Borm—who, as was revealed much later, was also a high-level Stasi informant—would spend the next decade reporting to the East Germans from the West German capital under the codename 'IM Richard'.[219]

While the vast majority of RCDS activists interviewed for this book remained lifelong Christian Democrats and Runge's trajectory was therefore exceptional in

---

[215] Runge interview; also *Runge Private Papers*, Jürgen-Bernd Runge, 'Irrungen und Wirrungen: Ein Leben nicht nach Maß. Zwischenbilanz zum 25. Abi-Jubiläum am 28.12.1990' (27 December 1990).

[216] Runge interview.   [217] Runge interview.

[218] Georg Herbstritt, *Bundesbürger im Dienst der DDR-Spionage: Eine analytische Studie* (Göttingen, 2007), 128; Jens Gieseke, *The History of the Stasi: East Germany's Secret Police, 1945-1990*, trans. David Burnett (Oxford, 2014), 184–5.

[219] Der Bundesbeauftragte für die Unterlagen des Staatssicherheitsdienstes der ehemaligen Deutschen Demokratischen Republik (ed.), *Der Deutsche Bundestag 1949 bis 1989 in den Akten des Ministeriums für Staatssicherheit (MfS) der DDR* (Berlin, 2013), 72; see also the interview with Runge in the documentary Ute Bönnen and Gerald Endres, *Die Stasi in West-Berlin*, RBB, 5 August 2010.

most ways, his path from RCDS figurehead to Communist believer and Stasi informant highlights the remarkable contingency of activist biographies in this age of political commitment (as well as the German-German dimension of dissent during the country's Cold War division). Most importantly, stories like his and Kempe's illustrate that the dividing lines between activism of the Left and Right could be remarkably porous. This point has often been made with regard to leftist 'renegades' who veered to the right, most famously in the case of the former SDS activist and 1970s Red Army Faction leader Horst Mahler, who later became an extreme right-wing nationalist.[220] However, reverse life paths in this period have rarely been explored. The RCDS 'renegades' remind us that the political identities of student activists around 1968 were not fixed; experiencing the political upheaval of these years and being part of the same campus ecosystem as their opponents could have a profound impact. The years around 1968 had the potential to alter individual trajectories, sometimes radically so.

* * *

What, then, does all this tell us? Did it matter that centre-right students were present in 1968? That they set up new organizations to counter an insurgent Left? That they turned towards theory to advocate for reform rather than revolution? That they styled themselves as Dutschke's equals? Or that some of them were so deeply affected by the student movement that it led them to rethink their politics in fundamental ways? Do histories of student protest in the late 1960s stand to gain anything by reinserting activists into the narrative who are usually missing from depictions of these years or were later erased from them—such as those young men from Freiburg, who helped to put on the January 1968 debate between Dahrendorf and Dutschke with which this chapter opened?

The short answer is, of course, yes. Including centre-right students into histories of 1968 protest helps us to rethink this moment in important ways. Doing so, for one, shows that student activism in West Germany was less homogeneous than usually portrayed. From the outset, it involved committed activists with competing ideas and visions from different sides of the political spectrum. SDS clearly set the political agenda on campus in the late 1960s more than any other group. RCDS and the Student Unions were nevertheless important players whose members participated in many of the key protest events of these years. They organized major demonstrations (such as 'Action 1 July' or the sit-in against fare increases in Cologne's public transport system), took part in teach-ins, and engaged with the theoretical assumptions, ideas, and practices of the New Left.

---

[220] See Manuel Seitenbecher, *Mahler, Maschke und Co: Rechtes Denken in der 68er-Bewegung?* (Paderborn, 2013); interestingly, Klatch found similarly for the US case that, although most activists on the Left and Right maintained their beliefs and values as adults, among those who did change it was usually right-wing activists who moved leftward. Klatch, *A Generation Divided*, 8.

Centre-right activists were no uniform bloc, even if they feature in most of the existing scholarship—if they do at all—as one-dimensional characters, who enter the storyline at best sporadically to express their reactionary views and intransigence.[221] Just as there was substantial diversity within SDS and on the student Left more generally, the ways in which the centre-right responded to and engaged with the SDS-led student movement varied considerably as well. Some, like Wighard Härdtl, who was something of a hardliner within RCDS and *Aktion 20. Konvent*, thought that radical leftist students needed to be combated, even if it involved getting physical. Many of the leading centre-right activists, however, were more willing to engage with the Left, convinced that their student peers had initiated important debates about the Federal Republic's democratic deficits. Individuals like Peter Radunski felt a strong connection to and a generational solidarity with Rudi Dutschke, for instance, and were keen to emulate his example. For some activists, notably Martin Kempe and Jürgen-Bernd Runge, an intense engagement with the APO and a growing sense of unease about the darker and more violent aspects of West Germany's anti-communist climate led to a slow political conversion that would eventually alienate them from RCDS and the Student Unions and draw them more firmly into the Left's orbit. That such conversions were possible at all points to the fact that centre-right activists were intertwined with their counterparts in myriad ways.

All of this suggests that 1968 was a much broader phenomenon than is traditionally assumed—and one that is harder to dismiss as a moment that involved only a small radical minority and allegedly had few long-term consequences. Given how narrowly focused on left-wing radical groups much of the historiography has been to date, and given how much the importance of 1968 has been relativized in some recent surveys, this alone makes it a critical endeavour that broadens our view of what these years meant, whom they touched, and offers a fresh take on why they mattered.

Finally, the very presence of centre-right students around 1968 has larger repercussions for how we conceive of political generations around 1968. We may be accustomed to viewing these years as a period of heightened political contestation, of spirited intellectual debates, and heated clashes between individuals with different political views and philosophies, but we have paid hardly any attention to the fact that this contestation also played out among students. As this chapter has demonstrated, contestation was indeed key in 1968, but not just among activists on the Left and their older antagonists in the media and other positions of authority. It also took root among student activists of a similar age.

---

[221] This is most evident in an older literature written by former SDS activists themselves. Tilman Fichter and Siegward Lönnendonker, *Kleine Geschichte des SDS: Der Sozialistische Deutsche Studentenbund von 1946 bis zur Selbstauflösung* (Berlin, 1977), 178; Ruetz, 'Ihr müsst diesen Typen nur ins Gesicht sehen', 106. This tendency has also left some traces in more recent scholarly accounts, e.g., Thomas, *Protest Movements in 1960s West Germany*, 136.

Centre-right students and their peers in the SDS-led student movement disagreed, often vehemently, about what struggling for democracy meant just two decades after the collapse of the Third Reich. How exactly they viewed the Nazi past and the older generation, and how they first began to think of themselves as the other '68ers, is the subject to which we will turn next.

2

Talking About (My) Generation

In early 2018, Peter Gauweiler, who had served as deputy leader of the CSU from 2013–15, gave an interview to the conservative *Frankfurter Allgemeine Zeitung* to mark the fiftieth anniversary of 1968. Gauweiler had joined the Christian Democrats in 1968 and quickly risen to public prominence as chair of the Munich chapter of RCDS. The interviewer asked him to describe his relationship to the left-wing student movement at the time. Like other former centre-right students, Gauweiler related that he had actually felt a surprising bond with some left-wing activists—notably the communard Fritz Teufel, from whom he had once received a self-made art collage as a present. However, he also claimed that there had been at least one major difference between centre-right students and those on the Left, namely how each side had viewed the Nazi past.[1]

The residues of Nazi authoritarianism in West German society were a major issue for the Left. As early as 1959, SDS activist Reinhard Strecker had put together a travelling exhibit called *Unatoned Nazi Justice [Ungesühnte Nazijustiz]*. The exhibit was shown in ten West German cities over the next three years to educate the public about the continuities between the Nazi and West German judiciaries and the incomplete reckoning with Nazi crimes in the courts.[2] The desire to expose Nazi perpetrators in the Federal Republic, as well as protests against structural continuities with the Third Reich, were central to left-wing activism around 1968, even if recent studies have rightly pointed out that the Nazi past—especially having Nazi parents—was rarely the main cause of protest.[3]

From 1967 onward, students often boycotted or broke up lectures by professors suspected of continuing Nazi sympathies. Famous protest slogans of the movement

---

[1] Gauweiler, 'Wir waren für die das allerletzte', 50–2.

[2] Tilman Fichter, *SDS und SPD: Parteilichkeit jenseits der Partei* (Opladen, 1988), 306–9; Stephan Alexander Glienke, *Die Ausstellung 'Ungesühnte Nazijustiz' (1959–1962): Zur Geschichte der Aufarbeitung nationalsozialistischer Justizverbrechen* (Baden-Baden, 2008); Dominik Rigoll, *Staatsschutz in Westdeutschland: Von der Entnazifizierung zur Extremistenabwehr* (Göttingen, 2013), 145–64.

[3] Bernd-A. Rusinek, 'Von der Entdeckung der NS-Vergangenheit zum generellen Faschismusverdacht—akademische Diskurse in der Bundesrepublik der 60er Jahre', in Schildt, Lammers, Siegfried, *Dynamische Zeiten*, 114–47; Detlef Siegfried, '"Don't Trust Anyone Older Than 30?" Voices of Conflict and Consensus between Generations in 1960s West Germany', *Journal of Contemporary History*, 40, 4 (2005), 727–44; Michael Schmidtke, 'The German New Left and National Socialism', in *Coping with the Nazi Past: West German Debates on Nazism and Generational Conflict, 1955–1975*, edited by Philipp Gassert and Alan E. Steinweis (New York, 2006), 178; von Hodenberg, *Das andere Achtundsechzig*, 45–76.

such as 'Under the gowns, the musty odour of a thousand years' ['*Unter den Talaren, der Muff von 1000 Jahren*'] or the outcry attributed to future RAF leader Gudrun Ensslin's after Ohnesorg's death that 'This is the generation of Auschwitz—you cannot argue with them!' have often been cited as evidence that left-wing protesters were motivated, at least in part, by a desire to right the wrongs committed by their parents' generation in the 1930s and 1940s.[4]

Looking back in 2018, Gauweiler was adamant that the centre-right had approached the issue very differently. 'That was one of the arguments with the '68ers: They thought they were the new People's Court', he opined.[5] Rather than condemning the older generation because it was culpable for war crimes and genocide, he was convinced that members of this generation had suffered as well. This misery, combined with their positive record during West Germany's postwar reconstruction, he argued, had offset any historical guilt they had previously accrued.

Gauweiler invoked his own family history to make this point. His father had joined the Nazi party quite early and had fought in the *Wehrmacht*, he admitted to the interviewer, but

> [h]e lost his right arm in the war. Later he had a stroke, which crippled the other arm. He had lost all his siblings to the war. The young generation also paid a high price during the Third Reich, and in spite of all this worked to help the country rise from the ruins.[6]

Asked whether he had seen his parents' generation as perpetrators, he replied:

> I see it like this: They pulled us—in my case my sisters and me—from the rubble. Really we owe this generation, of which many survived two wars, everything. In addition there is the idea which was invoked by many a generation later, including on the far Left: everyone has the right to a second chance. Our parents' generation took this second chance, in spite of huge deprivation, with diligence and hard work.

Gauweiler's reminiscences touch on several major themes of public memory and the scholarship on the West German 1960s, notably the family experiences and wartime childhoods of those who joined the protests, the meaning of the Nazi past to their activism, and intergenerational relations in postwar West Germany.[7] They

---

[4] Ensslin, quoted in Klimke, *The Other Alliance*, 129; Hans Kundnani, *Utopia or Auschwitz: Germany's 1968 Generation and the Holocaust* (London, 2009).

[5] Gauweiler, 'Wir waren für die das allerletzte'.

[6] Gauweiler, 'Wir waren für die das allerletzte'.

[7] Bude, *Das Altern einer Generation;* Heinz Bude, 'The German *Kriegskinder*: Origins and Impact of the Generation of 1968', in *Generations in Conflict*, edited by Mark Roseman (Cambridge, 1995),

raise important questions about how centre-right activists made sense of their family background and upbringing in relation to their politics, at the time and with hindsight. Like their student peers on the Left, they were raised in a post-genocidal society. That given, how did they view and engage with Germany's violent past? If they were not animated by a desire to atone for Nazi crimes, as Gauweiler's recollections seem to suggest, then how did they frame the links between the country's past and present and between the war and postwar? If they did not seek to alleviate German guilt, then how did they conceive of the ethical dimension of their political mission? Had they all felt a similar sense of gratitude and connection to their parents' generation for 'pulling them from the rubble', as he put it? Was there no intergenerational conflict on the centre-right? If so, what does this mean for understanding generation and the meanings attached to the Nazi past around 1968 more generally?

Narrating the War, Postwar, and Cold War

There is a long scholarly tradition of linking the '68ers to the history of the Nazi regime and the Second World War, even beyond understanding efforts to come to terms with the Nazi past as the generational project of the '68ers. Since at least the 1980s, when the (auto)biographical mode of writing about these years emerged as a distinct genre and psychohistory was on the rise, there has been great interest in activists' formative years.[8] The widely-read works of sociologist Heinz Bude, which were based on a set of twenty-one interviews with left-wing activists and published in the 1990s, have been particularly influential.[9] According to Bude, the '68ers were in terms of 'temperament and mentality in fact a generation of *Kriegskinder*, children of the [Second World] war'.[10]

Bude's findings relied on an only slightly modified version of the Mannheimian model of political generations. Mannheim, in line with the theories on development popular in the 1920s, had singled out the years of adolescence as the formative phase of the individual. Bude, by contrast, drew on more recent insights from child psychology to argue that those wanting to understand the '68ers had to turn to their wartime childhoods to find their deeply anchored biographical

---

290–305; Hans-Ulrich Thamer, 'Die NS-Vergangenheit im politischen Diskurs der 68er-Bewegung, in Karl Teppe (ed.), *Westfälische Forschungen*, 48 (1998), 39–53; Gassert and Steinweis, *Coping with the Nazi Past.*

[8] Biographical treatments by former protagonists include Mosler, *Was wir wollten, was wir wurden*; Tobias Mündemann, *Die 68er... und was aus ihnen geworden ist* (Munich, 1988); academic studies that examined the lives of individual activists include Ronald Fraser, *1968: A Student Generation in Revolt* (New York, 1988); Passerini, *Autobiography of a Generation*: Jürgen Busche, *Die 68er: Eine Biografie* (Berlin, 2003).

[9] Bude, *Das Altern einer Generation*; Bude interviewed twenty-one people for this book, but only discussed six interviews in the actual text. Also Bude, 'The German *Kriegskinder*'.

[10] Bude, 'The German *Kriegskinder*', 293.

starting-point.[11] Distressing wartime experiences, such as sheltering from the Allies' aerial bombardment, had left an indelible mark, the sociologist suggested. In his most recent work, published in 2018, he maintained that, even as adults, the '68ers had remained trapped in war-related traumas. Raised by mothers marked by the hardships of war and postwar, who needed reassurance from their children, and with largely absent fathers, the '68ers had initially been prone to conformist behaviour. The lack of control [Kontrollloch] they experienced in the postwar years, however, predisposed them to later rebelliousness, he argued. This was the result of so many of them having grown up fatherless, according to Bude. 'The "no" of the paternal rulebook could no longer come to these children's rescue', as he put it somewhat paternalistically.[12] In the 1960s, he suggested, they finally acted out the emotional conflicts that they had not been able to express within their own families on a larger social stage.[13]

Given that biographical and psychopathological readings of the origins of 1968 have been a major feature of trying to make sense of the left-wing revolt, it is useful here to examine, at least briefly, the childhoods of activists of the centre-right and the ways in which they later invoked them to explain their politics. The aim is to problematize the idea, implicit in some works, that a simple causal link can be drawn between a wartime (or postwar) childhood and being active on the Left around 1968—in other words, that war children automatically turned into left-wing rebels. If such a causal link indeed existed, one would expect an absence of war-related traumas and for the early experiences of centre-right activists to have differed markedly from those of their age peers on the Left in general. As we will see, however, the differences often lay less in what activists experienced as children than in the ways in which they endowed such experiences with meaning later on.

Like those in their cohort who ended up on the Left, the young men and women who were involved in centre-right student politics around 1968 had childhoods that were marked by the events of the Second World War, the greatest outpouring of violence in history.[14] Between 1939 and 1945, Germans occupied much of Europe, enslaved other Europeans, and committed mass atrocities and a genocide against Europe's Jewish population, killing and maiming millions. Only in its final phase did the war take a heavy toll on the German home front. German civilians experienced the kind of suffering that the German armies had long inflicted on others in the war's final year. From the perspective of the German population, the final phase was the deadliest and most destructive: nearly half of German military

[11] Bude, 'The German Kriegskinder', 303.   [12] Bude, Adorno für Ruinenkinder, 48.
[13] Bude, Adorno für Ruinenkinder, 114–15.
[14] Richard Bessel and Dirk Schumann, 'Introduction: Violence, Normality and the Construction of Postwar Europe', in idem (eds.), Life after Death: Approaches to a Cultural and Social History of Europe during the 1940s and 1950s (Cambridge, 2003), 1–13; on the childhoods of left-wing '68ers, see Wienhaus, Bildungswege zu '1968', 127–31.

casualties occurred during the war's last ten months.[15] Major cities, including Berlin, Hamburg, and Dresden, were flattened, and hundreds of thousands died in Allied bombing raids. The hardships and disruption did not end with the German surrender in May 1945. Millions were homeless as a result of the bombing or were expelled from the East, and the country faced the issue of rehousing an unprecedented number of refugees; moreover, millions of German soldiers were still in captivity.

All of this meant that there was no neat dividing line between war and postwar, including in the families of centre-right activists.[16] Only the older activists interviewed for this book experienced the war consciously as young children, but it cast a long shadow over the lives of most of the interviewees. Many of them, as indeed most children who came of age in postwar West Germany, may have had a 'normal' upbringing in the sense that they grew up in families with both parents present and did not experience war-related displacement. Nevertheless, in one way or another, even their families had to negotiate the war's disruptive aftermath, and they often passed on to their children memories of personal suffering.[17]

Peter Radunski, who was a prominent activist in RCDS around 1968, was in many ways a quintessential war child. He was born in Berlin six months before war broke out in Europe with Germany's invasion of Poland. In his published autobiography, which recounted his path towards Christian Democratic politics and his illustrious career as the CDU's chief campaign strategist, he recorded vivid descriptions of his wartime childhood. As a young boy, he had experienced the full range of German suffering at the war's end, not least the massive Allied bombing raids on the German capital that intensified with the British Royal Air Force's Battle of Berlin in late 1943.

In 1943, I saw our neighbour's house in Berlin bombed to pieces, and how people crawled into our cellar through a shaft to get to safety. [. . .] Everywhere people were screaming—it characterized this dramatic night of bombing, which still shapes my memory of this period. [. . .] The city was burning all around us–the sight of the sea of flames remains with me to this day.[18]

---

[15] Ian Kershaw, *To Hell and Back: Europe 1914-1949* (London, 2016), 403; Nicholas Stargardt, *The German War: A Nation Under Arms, 1939-1945. Citizens and Soldiers* (New York, 2015); Richard Bessel, *Germany 1945: From War to Peace* (New York, 2009).

[16] In 1947, more than three million were still held as prisoners of war, the majority in the Soviet Union, the last of whom would not return until January 1956. Frank Biess, *Homecomings: Returning POWs and the Legacies of Defeat in Postwar Germany* (Princeton, NJ, 2006), 1–5; also Judt, *Postwar*; Frank Biess and Robert Moeller (eds.), *Histories of the Aftermath: The Legacies of the Second World War in Europe* (Oxford, 2010).

[17] Lu Seegers, '"Dead dads": Memory Narratives of War-related Fatherlessness in Germany', *European Review of History*, 22, 2 (2015), 259–76; see also Piotr Oseka, Polymeris Voglis, and Anna von der Goltz, 'Families', in Gildea, Mark, and Warring, *Europe's 1968*, 47.

[18] Radunski, *Aus der politischen Kulisse*, 12.

He further recalled that, in February 1945, while on the move with his grandmother, he witnessed the destruction of Dresden from an open field outside the city—a moment that had a lasting impact, he claimed: 'Thereafter, whenever people discussed war and peace, these images crossed my mind.'[19]

Born out of wedlock, Radunski never knew his father. His mother soon found a new partner, who acknowledged paternity, but he was among the 5.3 million *Wehrmacht* soldiers who were killed in the war.[20] In 1943, the four-year old Radunski was evacuated to Sensburg in East Prussia (today's Mrągowo in Poland), together with his mother and grandmother. Before the Soviet Red Army captured the town, Radunski and his grandmother fled to Saxony, but his mother fell into Soviet captivity. She was one of several thousand German women held captive on Soviet territory after the war and would not return to Berlin until late 1947.[21] Even then, she had difficulties readjusting to life in the city and eventually remarried in Alsace. The young Radunski remained in West Berlin and lived with his grandparents—an arrangement that was quite common in postwar Germany.[22]

As disorderly and remarkable as Radunski's childhood experiences may have been in many respects, they were not unusual for children in his cohort—including for students who ended up on the centre-right in the 1960s. Many of the RCDS activists whom Radunski encountered at the Free University in West Berlin had family experiences that were similar to his.[23] Flight, expulsion, and absent fathers (either as a result of death or of long-term captivity) were quite common. By the end of the war there were nearly two and a half million half-orphans in Germany. A third of German children fled, faced expulsion, or were resettled.[24] Given these overall numbers, it is not at all surprising that seven of the twenty-six activists interviewed for this book reported being expellees or having

---

[19] Radunski, *Aus der politischen Kulisse*, 12; Radunski interview.

[20] Rüdiger Overmans, *Deutsche militärische Verluste im Zweiten Weltkrieg* (Munich, 1999), 316. This figure included all members of the *Wehrmacht*, even those who hailed from beyond the German borders of 1937. The number of German military deaths from the pre-1937 Reich was 4.5 million. Schildt, *Sozialgeschichte*, 1.

[21] Biess, *Homecomings*, 45; Kurt Böhme, 'Zum Schicksal der weiblichen Kriegsgefangenen', in *Die deutschen Kriegsgefangenen*, edited by Erich Maschke (Bielefeld, 1974), 317–45.

[22] Radunski, *Aus der politischen Kulisse*, 12–14; Seegers, '"Dead dads"'; Lu Seegers, '*Vati blieb im Krieg*': *Vaterlosigkeit als generationelle Erfahrung im 20. Jahrhundert–Deutschland und Polen* (Göttingen, 2013).

[23] This was not limited to West Berlin. A Bonn oral history project that collected interviews with 21 former student activists in the early 2000s included six centre-right figures in its sample and half of them were expellees or fatherless. The family of Wolfgang Breyer (b. 1940) had fled from Silesia; Peter Gutjahr-Löser (b. 1940) had lost both parents by the time he was ten; and Jürgen Rosorius (b. 1944) had lost his father at the front. Horst-Pierre Bothien, *Protest und Provokation: Bonner Studenten 1967/1968* (Essen, 2007), 102–3; 125–6.

[24] All in all, roughly twelve million ethnic Germans fled or were expelled from Germany's Eastern territories, notably from Silesia, Eastern Pomerania, and East Prussia, as well as from the Sudetenland from 1944 onward. For the broader European context, see Keith Lowe, *Savage Continent: Europe in the Aftermath of WWII* (London, 2012).

had absent fathers—figures that are on slightly higher than those reported by activists of the Left.[25]

In narrating their childhoods in the late 2000s and early 2010s, in the wake of intense public debates over German wartime victimhood, interviewees for this book were able to draw on popular tropes of German suffering.[26] None described themselves explicitly as 'war children' or 'sons without fathers'—self-characterizations that members of this cohort increasingly began to use in the 1990s to frame memories of their childhoods. However, some who had experienced war-related displacement or grown up fatherless, especially the male interviewees, talked about these experiences at some length and suggested that they had shaped their political socialization in profound ways.[27] However, rather than stressing German victimhood in general, it was experiences with perceived communist repression—in the form of flight and expulsion from the East, family members held in Soviet captivity, or indoctrination under state socialism—that they highlighted to explain their political activism in the 1960s. In so doing, they were able to portray their opposition to SDS and related groups as instinctive.

Horst Teltschik, for one, who wrote treatises on Rudi Dutschke and Herbert Marcuse's political philosophy in 1968 to prep his centre-right student peers for debates, framed his family story as one defined by repeated Russian and Soviet aggression. Teltschik had been born in the Sudetenland, an area in Czechoslovakia that had been home to a German-speaking minority and that the Nazis had annexed in 1938. Like the other Sudeten Germans, his family was expelled by the Czechoslovaks in 1945. He spent most of his childhood on the shores of Bavaria's Lake Tegern, but recalled that his family's wartime and postwar experiences had made him stand out in these idyllic surroundings.[28] His mother had been on the move for nearly two years with her children before she settled in Bavaria and reunited with her husband. His father had been imprisoned by the Soviets, Teltschik recalled, and managed to escape, but was later captured in Austria and held by American troops. Teltschik's older brother, who had enlisted in the *Wehrmacht* in 1945, was also held in Soviet captivity for a time. In the

---

[25] Seegers, '"Dead dads"'; Schildt, *Sozialgeschichte*, 6; Hermann Schulz, Hartmut Radebold and Jürgen Reulecke, *Söhne ohne Väter: Erfahrungen der Kriegsgeneration* (Berlin, 2003), 115–16. Wienhaus found that roughly a fifth of SDS members in West Berlin had grown up fatherless. Wienhaus, *Bildungswege zu '1968'*.

[26] Bill Niven (ed.), *Germans as Victims: Remembering the Past in Contemporary Germany* (London, 2006); also Bernd Weisbrod's comments in Abosede George et al., 'AHR conversation', 1512.

[27] For the gendered dynamics of the discourse surrounding the 'war children', see Dorothee Wierling, '"Kriegskinder": westdeutsch, bürgerlich, männlich?', in *Die 'Generation der Kriegskinder': Historische Hintergründe und Deutungen*, edited by Lu Seegers and Jürgen Reulecke (Gießen, 2009), 141–55.

[28] This was in spite of the fact that many Sudeten Germans had settled in Bavaria and over a fifth of the state population were refugees in 1950. Schildt, *Sozialgeschichte*, 4; the figure for the Federal Republic as a whole was 16.5 per cent, see Andreas Kossert, *Kalte Heimat: Die Geschichte der deutschen Vertriebenen nach 1945* (Berlin, 2008), 196.

interview, Teltschik brought up the fact that his father had already been imprisoned by Russian troops during the First World War, thereby framing his entire family history around the theme of Russian and Soviet repression.

Wighard Härdtl, who was part of the conservative wing of RCDS in West Berlin in the late 1960s and later became a high-ranking civil servant, similarly framed his life story around negative encounters with communism. Like Teltschik's, his family were Sudeten Germans, but they had ended up in East Germany after the expulsions of ethnic Germans. They only fled to the Federal Republic in 1958. He insisted that his political socialization and anti-Left stance in 1968 could not be understood without taking into account these childhood experiences, not least his years living under state socialism in the GDR:

> I was exposed to communist indoctrination in school [...]. That was actually the reason [...] why I quickly became much more politically engaged when I was in the West. [...] In Mainz I was already a member of RCDS. [...] So in my case, from the very beginning my status as an expellee and a refugee, as well as having confronted communism head-on, shaped my experience even in childhood. That was really the starting point![29]

Härdtl was not the only RCDS activist who had grown up under communism.[30] Othmar Nikolai Haberl (b. 1943), who was active in RCDS in West Berlin at the same time, had also been socialized under a communist regime, in the Socialist Federal Republic of Yugoslavia. Born in Sarajevo to a Bosnian Serb mother and an ethnic German father, the family made use of Article 116, paragraph 2 of West Germany's Basic Law, which gave ethnic Germans citizenship, and moved to Paderborn in the mid-1950s. Haberl, who was one of the 'renegades' that left the West Berlin RCDS in May 1968, insisted that having grown up under communism explained why he had initially found his way into a centre-right student group:

> Paderborn was an arch-Catholic, arch-conservative, I would almost say arch-reactionary place in the '50s and '60s. And there I, as someone from a formerly communist state, was almost automatically pushed towards the right. As a result I ended up in the CDU as early as my high school days, and as a student joined RCDS.[31]

---

[29] Härdtl interview.
[30] Another prominent example is Jürgen Wohlrabe (1936–1995), one of the activists who spearheaded the CDU's response to West Berlin's radical Left around 1968. He had also spent his childhood and teenage years in the Soviet occupation zone and the GDR. See von der Goltz, ' "Other '68ers" in West Berlin'.
[31] Haberl interview.

These life stories are noteworthy, not least because so much has been made of the fact that some of the most prominent left-wing radicals of 1968, notably Dutschke and his friend Bernd Rabehl of the West Berlin SDS, had spent most of their childhoods in socialist East Germany—the implication being that having been exposed to communist indoctrination in their youth naturally led to their socialist activism later on.[32] Around 3.5 million East Germans arrived in the Federal Republic prior to 1961 and hundreds of thousands of ethnic Germans—so-called *Aussiedler*—migrated from socialist countries in the same period. That given, it is only logical that similar East-West biographies could also be found among student activists of the centre-right.[33] Rather than turning them into fervent young socialists, interviewees for this book who had experienced state socialism first-hand conveyed that it had pushed them towards the right.

Besides framing their life stories around German wartime suffering and negative postwar experiences with communism, former activists often invoked major milestones of Europe's Cold War history to narrate the story of their politicization. Only the centre-right 'renegades', who veered leftward in the wake of 1968, gave equal weight to events commonly associated with critiques of authoritarianism in the Federal Republic, such as the *Spiegel* affair of 1962/3. This public scandal saw the news magazine's editor Rudolf Augstein imprisoned for several months and the paper accused of treason, sparking a major debate about free expression in a democracy.[34] In most interviews for this book and other autobiographical accounts of former centre-right activists, by contrast, events that symbolized communist cruelty, such as the crushing of the East German Uprising of 17 June 1953, the Soviet invasion of Hungary in 1956, and the construction of the Berlin Wall in August 1961, were the most frequently cited historical reference points.[35]

Apart from recounting the bombing of Berlin and Dresden and the family's displacement, Radunski's autobiography, for instance, noted his presence during several iconic Cold War moments. As a child in West Berlin in 1948, the young Radunski allegedly witnessed Ernst Reuter's famous speech during the Soviet blockade in which the Mayor called on the 'peoples of this world...to look

---

[32] Some scholars also point to their East German heritage in an attempt to explain activists' later trajectories, which, at least in the case of Rabehl, included a sharp rightward turn. Wolfgang Kraushaar, *Achtundsechzig: Eine Bilanz* (Berlin, 2008), 44.

[33] Patrick Major, *Behind the Berlin Wall: East Germany and the Frontiers of Power* (Oxford, 2009), chapter 3; on the Aussiedler, Wolfgang Seifert, 'Geschichte der Zuwanderung nach Deutschland nach 1950', *Bundeszentrale für politische Bildung* (31 May 2012), available at http://www.bpb.de/politik/grundfragen/deutsche-verhaeltnisse-eine-sozialkunde/138012/geschichte-der-zuwanderung-nach-deutschland-nach-1950 (accessed on 9 October 2018); Schildt, *Sozialgeschichte*, 14.

[34] Kempe interview; Runge interview.

[35] Strikingly, American conservative students listed many of the same moments, often citing Hungary's 1956 as the most important event in their political socialization. Klatch, *A Generation Divided*, 87. Some younger West German interviewees, who were active in the 1970s, also mentioned the crushing of the Prague Spring as an important moment in their politicization.

upon this city'—a key moment in (West) Berlin's transformation into *the* symbol of the Cold War. On 17 June 1953, the teenage Radunski cycled to the Brandenburg Gate to get a glimpse of the tanks on the Eastern side of the border, where workers' protests against a 10 per cent rise in work norms had turned into a broader revolt against the communist regime. And his first political demonstration, he noted, was a protest, organized by various West Berlin schools, of about 2,000 high school students marching against the crushing of the anti-Soviet Hungarian Uprising in 1956. They marched towards Brandenburg Gate, determined to cross over into East Berlin, but, according to Radunski, were stopped at the last moment by none other than a megaphone-wielding Willy Brandt, then the SPD's representative to the state parliament of West Berlin.[36] All the early political experiences he included in his autobiography thus conveyed a staunch anti-communist mindset.

Eberhard Diepgen (b. 1941), in whose cabinet Radunski would serve as a senator in the 1990s when the former was Governing Mayor of Berlin, recounted strikingly similar instances of communist repression in an interview. Raised in West Berlin's Wedding neighbourhood, he recalled seeing Soviet tanks roll in on the other side of the border on 17 June 1953 and being shaken deeply by events in Hungary three years later. Interviewed more than half a century after the Soviet intervention in the country, he still vividly remembered hearing the voices of reform socialist Imre Nagy and the Hungarian General Pál Maléter, who supported Nagy's reformist cause, on the radio. Several other interviewees from across West Germany related similar recollections of raptly following the Hungarian events in 1956.[37]

The Hungarian Uprising was a frequent reference point, but the construction of the Berlin Wall in August 1961 was a particularly important staging post in many accounts—one that signalled the centrality of German division to centre-right student politics around 1968.[38] Radunski related that the news of the Wall's construction had reached him while he had been on a language course in France. The event sparked '[e]ndless personal and political deliberations. I was in the thick of the political action. The change of circumstances affected me emotionally, as it did many students in Germany, who came to Berlin now

---

[36] Radunski, *Aus der politischen Kulisse*, 26–7.

[37] Klemann interview; Kempe interview; Radunski interview; by the mid-1950s, the majority of West German households owned a radio. Schildt, *Sozialgeschichte*, 26–7. Ignaz Bender also protested against Nagy's and Maléter's execution outside the Soviet Embassy near Bonn in 1958. 'Mohikaners Wandlung', *Der Spiegel*, 27 (1958), 15–16; Bender interview.

[38] The impact of Germany's division on activists' biographies was also a persistent theme in the Bonn interviews conducted by Bothien. See the interviews with Peter Gutjahr-Löser, Wolfgang Breyer, and Jürgen Rosorius in Bothien, *Protest und Provokation*.

more than ever', he explained. He joined RCDS very shortly afterwards, in the fall of 1961.[39] 'Many people who thought like me met there.'[40]

Detlef Stronk (b. 1945) similarly remembered hearing about the building of the Wall while he had been abroad. This highlights that participating in international school exchanges was quite common for members of this cohort, who had been socialized by various postwar educational programs to embrace intercultural understanding and responsible citizenship in an increasingly integrated Europe.[41] Stronk grew up near Munich, was active in RCDS and the centre-right Munich Student Union in the late 1960s, and served as the head of Diepgen's West Berlin State Chancellery in the 1980s. Like Radunski, he claimed in his memoirs that the Wall became central to his politics even while he still lived far away:

> [Berlin] only really entered my consciousness [...] on 13 August 1961. I was 16 years old and in England as a schoolboy. In faint chimes over my old long wave radio, I heard that the communists had begun constructing the Wall. I was deeply moved by this event and it shaped my political beliefs.[42]

Horst Teltschik also emphasized that, throughout the 1960s, the existence of the Wall and division of the city shaped not just his daily life as a student in West Berlin but also his general political stance. Moreover, Teltschik credited the two years he had served in a *Bundeswehr* tank battalion close to the Czechoslovak border with honing his sense of what the Cold War and European division meant in concrete terms. He served in 1961 and 1962, two years that were among the most tense of the entire Cold War. In the wake of the construction of the Berlin Wall, the tanks in his battalion had been fully equipped with weapons and filled with petrol, he recalled. 'So [...] we were ready for war. And aged 21, 22, at that. As such, I experienced these crises as a soldier, as a conscript.'[43] He was also convinced that his time in the military had affected his personal style, which later helped him to assert himself among his student peers. Towards the end of his service, Teltschik had commanded 120 soldiers. Those who had served, especially in higher ranks, 'had a natural air of authority' when they arrived at university, he suggested.[44]

---

[39] Radunski, *Aus der politischen Kulisse*, 37–8.   [40] Radunski, *Aus der politischen Kulisse*, 47.

[41] Belinda Davis, 'A Whole World Opening Up: Transcultural Contact, Difference, and the Politicization of "New Left" Activists', in *Changing the World, Changing Oneself: Political Protest and Collective Identities in the 1960s/70s West Germany and U.S.*, edited by Belinda Davis, Wilfried Mausbach, Martin Klimke, and Carla MacDougall (New York and Oxford, 2010), 255–73; Richard Ivan Jobs, *Backpack Ambassadors: How Youth Travel Intergrated Europe* (Chicago and London, 2017), 101; Christina Norwig, *Die erste europäische Generation: Europakonstruktionen in der Europäischen Jugendkampagne 1951–1958* (Göttingen, 2016). A number of the interviewees for this book talked about intra-European travel, pen friendships, and student exchanges in their youth.

[42] Stronk, *Berlin in den Achtziger Jahren*, 18.   [43] Teltschik interview.

[44] Teltschik interview.

Several of the leading activists in West Berlin's RCDS chapter at the time had indeed served more than the compulsory eighteen months. Wulf Schönbohm, national chair of RCDS in 1967/8, had signed up for the three-year temporary career officer track and made it to the rank of lieutenant. He had four siblings and did not want to burden his parents financially; the *Bundeswehr* paid him and also gave him severance pay when he left, which went towards financing his studies. Schönbohm was already twenty-three when he arrived at the Free University and had held 'leadership responsibilities [...]. So I already felt older and more mature', he explained.[45]

While such military backgrounds stood in marked contrast to the widespread image of Cold War West Berlin as a haven for young draft dodgers (the city's four-power status meant that men with a permanent residence certificate were exempt from military service), they were not unusual in a country with a conscription army. After all, contrary to later decades, conscientious objection was still a marginal phenomenon at this time. While opting for community service (*Zivildienst*) would become much more widespread from the 1970s onward, prior to 1968, no more than a few thousand chose this route annually. The vast majority of young West German men in the 1960s served in the military.[46] What is more, even in the West Berlin SDS there was a surprisingly large number of reserve officers, notably the media-savvy communard Rainer Langhans.[47] Contrary to their contemporaries on the centre-right, however, few leftist radicals suggested at the time—or indeed in retrospect—that their military service had socialized them in a positive manner or that Cold War-era military norms had shaped their political commitment, ideas about masculinity, and leadership style in productive ways.

The Nazi Past and Totalitarianism

The frequent emphasis on service in the West German army, anti-communism, German division, and repression in the Eastern bloc as motifs that shaped centre-right activists' political outlook stood in marked contrast to the ways in which activists of the Left typically narrated the stories of their politicization. In interviews and other autobiographical accounts produced after the events of 1968,

---

[45] Schönbohm interview. His older brother was Jörg Schönbohm, who made it to the rank of Lieutenant General. He was the first commander of the Bundeswehr Eastern Command in 1990 and oversaw the integration of the East German National People's Army (Nationale Volksarmee, NVA) into the Bundeswehr. Schönbohm, *Wilde Schwermut*.

[46] James Sheehan, *Where Have All the Soldiers Gone? The Transformation of Modern Europe* (Boston and New York, 2009), 178. On West Berlin as a haven for those escaping the draft, see Alexandra Richie, *Faust's Metropolis: A History of Berlin* (London, 1999), 777–8; David Clay Large, *Berlin* (New York, 2000), 482; on conscientious objection in the 1960s, Patrick Bernhard, *Zivildienst zwischen Reform und Revolte: Eine bundesdeutsche Institution im gesellschaftlichen Wandel 1961–1982* (Munich 2005).

[47] Siegfried, *Time is on My Side*, 257, fn. 187.

left-wing '68ers often traced the roots of their political socialization to the Nazi past and the powerful residues it had left in postwar society. Since public commemorations of 1968 became widespread in the 1980s, the idea that the '68ers had been the first to break the public silence about Nazi crimes has often been held up as one of the era's main achievements, not least by former activists themselves.

Seen from this vantage point, the revolt of 1968 was the younger generation's struggle for restitution. Prominent left-wing radicals whose own parents had been Nazis and who spoke about the political conflicts that had arisen in their own families as a result—activists such as Bernward Vesper, Hannes Heer, or K.D. Wolff—emerged as archetypes and embodiments of generational conflict around 1968.[48] Scholars who studied the student Left of 1968 often adopted these narratives, as did many popular accounts. In the words of Heinz Bude, the '68ers were haunted by the 'feeling, implanted so early in life, of being born guilty', making 1968 a sort of proxy revolt. The notion of 1968 as a surrogate event fit into a larger pattern of interpretation that took firm hold in the 1980s, one that understood 1968 as a chapter in a longer German 'family saga' in which the children rebelled to atone for their parents' crimes.[49]

However firmly this notion may be established in popular memory and parts of the older scholarship, more recent work has emphasized that the idea relied on a heavy dose of retrospective invention. In effect, the family experiences of a small number of activists, who had openly fought with their Nazi parents, were transfigured into the collective tale of an entire generation. The idea of the '68ers as silence breakers, who instigated the public and private reckoning with the Nazi past, helped to cast this generation in decidedly heroic terms.

We now know, however, that the '68ers had a much more complex relationship to the Nazi past—one that involved denouncing the crimes of the perpetrators alongside allusions to German victimhood that were more in line with the self-exculpatory discourses of the 1950s.[50] Moreover, few left-wing activists experienced overt political conflicts within their own families, even when family members had participated in Nazi crimes or were otherwise implicated in the regime. Their rebellion usually targeted their abstract parents—in the form of the older generation at large, representatives of state authority, etc.—rather than their actual ones. More often than not, as Christina von Hodenberg argued recently,

---

[48] Jureit, *Generationenforschung*, 92; Behre, *Bewegte Erinnerung*; Oseka, Voglis, and von der Goltz, 'Families', 49–50; von Hodenberg, *Das andere Achtundsechzig*.

[49] Bude, 'The German *Kriegskinder*', 302 and 304; Bude, *Das Altern einer Generation*.

[50] Gassert and Steinweis, *Coping with the Nazi Past*; Kundnani, *Utopia or Auschwitz*; for a powerful analysis of how the Nazi past was discussed in the Federal Republic before 1968, see Robert G. Moeller, *War Stories: The Search for a Usable Past in the Federal Republic of Germany* (Berkeley, CA, 2001).

children were complicit in keeping silent about their relatives' past in order to protect their feelings and preserve family relationships.[51]

If overt political conflicts about the Nazi past between left-wing activists and their parents were already much rarer than long assumed, they were absent pretty much entirely in the families of centre-right activists. Not a single interviewee for this book reported having argued with his or her parents over National Socialism around 1968, and the theme is largely absent from centre-right publications of the time. Only Jürgen-Bernd Runge recalled falling out with his parents over politics, but this had only occurred *after* Runge had turned his back on centre-right politics and moved towards the left in the wake of 1968. Moreover, it involved the parents rejecting their son's political choices, rather than the son breaking with his father over the latter's early SA membership.[52]

Given how central the trope of conflict with Nazi parents has been to making sense of 1968, former centre-right activists nevertheless invoked it explicitly in their autobiographical recollections. However, like Peter Gauweiler, quoted at the beginning of this chapter, they overwhelmingly did so to emphasize that it did not capture their own family dynamics. Meinhard Ade, who had debated with Dutschke and Dahrendorf in Freiburg, was adamant about this. He had grown up in a small town in Baden near the Swiss border. His father's family had been Social Democrats, and his maternal grandfather had been a member of the pro-Weimar Catholic Centre Party. Ade presented this as evidence of his family's lack of involvement in the Nazi regime. His father had never joined the Nazi party; he had been conscripted into the *Wehrmacht* and died on the Eastern front, he explained.

So I had no points of interaction with those who needed to have a showdown with their fathers. A: I had no father, and B: My father was not implicated; my family was not implicated at all. Because of that the theme of generational conflict didn't affect me.[53]

---

[51] Sociologists, who studied the West German student Left, had already found near the time that only around 10 per cent of activists reported that fighting about the Nazi past with their parents had led them towards activism. Allerbeck, *Soziologie radikaler Studentenbewegungen*, 108; see further Siegfried, '"Don't Trust Anyone Older Than 30?"; Oseka, Voglis, and von der Goltz, 'Families'; von Hodenberg, *Das andere Achtundsechzig*.

[52] Runge interview. This finding chimes with sociological surveys conducted among left-wing activists at the time, which showed that political conflicts within the family that did occur were usually the result and not the cause of children's political engagement. Allerbeck, *Soziologie radikaler Studentenbewegungen*, 117. A couple of other interviewees mentioned tensions with their parents over the Nazi past, but reported that these surfaced after 1968. Stronk interview; Klemann interview. These findings are also supported by the Bonn interviews conducted by Bothien. He interviewed six centre-right activists from the city. None reported family conflicts over the Nazi past. Bothien, *Protest und Provokation*.

[53] Ade interview.

Activists raised in Catholic families that, unlike Ade, could not point to Weimar-era party political affiliations to suggest an anti-Nazi lineage, sometimes explained that their parents' Catholic faith had inoculated them against Nazi ideology. In so doing, they drew on post-war portrayals of Catholicism and the Church as inherently anti-fascist.[54] Ursula Männle (b. 1944), for instance, who served as chair of the Bavarian RCDS in the late 1960s, did not provide specific details about her parents' conduct during the Nazi years, but explained simply that, as Catholics, they had felt threatened by the Nazis.[55] Maria-Theresia van Schewick (b. 1948), who grew up near Bonn and served as deputy national chair of RCDS in the early 1970s, likewise stated that, as a staunch Catholic, her father could not have been a Nazi. A talented astrophysicist, he had worked with Wernher von Braun on the prestigious Nazi rocket development program, but his religious faith had shielded him from blind faith in the regime, she insisted. 'So my father, and this is also proven, never had a picture of Hitler in his office, instead always the Madonna of Kevelaer [a Catholic pilgrimage site in the Lower Rhine region], so in that sense he was Catholic to the core.'[56]

Others distanced themselves from the Nazi past in yet other ways. Similar to Gauweiler, they insisted that the whole idea of passing moral judgement on the older generation was problematic. In doing so, the student Left had not helped Germans to come to terms with the past but actually mimicked the Nazi movement's bullying tactics, they suggested. Jürgen Aretz (b. 1946), for one, who grew up in a small town near Mönchengladbach and was a founding member of Bonn's centre-right *Aktion '68*, repeatedly criticized the student Left for their alleged 'blanket judgement from their moral high horse' of the older generation and their 'persecution' of professors suspected of Nazi sympathies.[57]

In this respect, the other '68ers were, in fact, closely aligned with some of their most prominent older teachers. Notable among these were Jewish returnees such as Richard Löwenthal and Ernst Fraenkel, who had fled Germany in the 1930s and returned from exile after the war to teach the new subject of political science at West German universities. Deeply sceptical, as they were, of mass politics, the growing radicalism of the left-wing student movement in the 1960s reminded them of the anti-democratic right in the 1920s and 1930s, and, worse, of the early Nazis.[58] Teltschik, who served as Löwenthal's academic assistant at the FU,

---

[54] Although fewer Catholics than Protestants had voted for the Nazis prior to 1933, the relationship between Catholic Germans and the Nazi regime was much more complex—and often much closer—than such portrayals suggest. See Chappell, *Catholic Modern*, 59–143; Thomas Brodie, *German Catholicism at War, 1939–1945* (Oxford, 2018); Derek Hastings, *Catholicism and the Roots of Nazism: Religious Identity and National Socialism* (Oxford, 2010).

[55] Männle interview; also Bender interview.   [56] Van Schewick interview.

[57] Aretz interview; Bothien, *Protest und Provokation*, 123; von Hodenberg, *Das andere Achtundsechzig*, 58.

[58] On Fraenkel see 'FU-Professor: Gegen die SA-Methoden des SDS zur Wehr setzen! Morgenpost-Interview mit Ernst Fraenkel', *Berliner Morgenpost*, 17 September 1967, 1; Michael Wildt, 'Die Angst vor dem Volk. Ernst Fraenkel in der deutschen Nachkriegsgesellschaft', in Monika Boll and Raphael

recalled approvingly that: '[H]e once said to me, Mr Teltschik, I have experienced this all before, only under different auspices. And he meant the Nazis. Namely the intolerance, the aggressiveness.'[59] Teltschik thus suggested that the student Left had perpetuated some of the Nazis' worst traits.

Some also questioned the relevance of the Nazi past to student activism around 1968 by claiming that it had already been fully dealt with by then—and suggesting that they had contributed to this reckoning. A number of major criminal trials of Nazi perpetrators, including that of members of a Nazi paramilitary death squad in Ulm in 1958, the Eichmann trial in Jerusalem in 1961, and the Frankfurt Auschwitz trials of 1963–5, had indeed put the issue of Germans' widespread complicity in genocide on the public agenda well before the climactic years of the student movement.[60] Teltschik therefore insisted that he had been engaged with the subject long before the student Left embraced it. '[I]t really annoyed me that they said they were the first to try to reassess the National Socialist era [...] I already did that as a teenager. [Already then] I dealt with it.' To make this point, he related that, during his time in the Catholic Youth, he had organized a film screening of Alain Resnais' documentary film *Night and Fog* (1956), which showed the abandoned grounds of the concentration camps in Auschwitz and Majdanek. 'And I caused great disgust among the adults with this film, [...] along the lines of: a young fellow is screening a concentration camp liberation film for us. He does not know how it really was! Some left the room indignant.'[61]

Wolfgang Bergsdorf, who was active in RCDS in Bonn in the 1960s and who later worked closely with Teltschik when both were senior advisers and confidants of Helmut Kohl, similarly reported that schools and public education had dealt sufficiently with the topic well before 1968. Bergsdorf's father had died during the war, and his grandfather, who helped to raise him, had been a Centre Party delegate in the Düsseldorf state parliament until 1933, a party background which Bergsdorf presented as evidence of his family's anti-Nazi attitude. Neither his family nor West German society at large had failed to reckon with German crimes, he suggested.

> Then and now I was of the opinion that we didn't really omit anything. I mean, our political education confronted the National Socialist past very thoroughly and indeed as early as the 1950s. And I thought it was really rigorous.[62]

Gross (eds.), '*Ich staune, dass Sie in dieser Luft atmen können': Jüdische Intellektuelle in Deutschland nach 1945* (Frankfurt am Main, 2013), 317–44; Abbott Gleason, *Totalitarianism: The Inner History of the Cold War* (New York and Oxford, 1995) 159. For Löwenthal's views, see Richard Löwenthal, *Romantischer Rückfall: Wege und Irrwege einer rückwärts gewendeten Revolution* (Stuttgart, 1970); and Wehrs, *Protest der Professoren*, 73–4, 116.

[59]   Teltschik interview. See also Härdtl interview; Reichart-Dreyer interview.

[60]   Marc von Miquel, *Ahnden oder amnestieren? Westdeutsche Justiz und Vergangenheitsbewältigung in den sechziger Jahren* (Göttingen, 2004).

[61]   Teltschik interview.   [62]   Bergsdorf interview.

To make the case, he related that, when he was merely thirteen years old, he had been deeply affected by reading the diary of Anne Frank, an influential text that chronicled a young Jewish girl's life in hiding in the Netherlands under Nazi occupation.[63] Tellingly, however, he was quick to assert that another book had left an equally strong impression on him when he was young: Wolfgang Leonhard's *Child of the Revolution*. This was an autobiographical account by a key member of the Ulbricht Group, a unit of exiled members of the Communist Party of Germany, who returned from the Soviet Union just before the German surrender and laid the groundwork for the re-establishment of communist organizations in Berlin.[64] Leonhard had become disillusioned with the Stalinist system, fled from East Germany in 1949, and later taught Soviet history at Yale. *Child of the Revolution* was first published in the Federal Republic in 1955 and distributed to a broad audience by the Federal Agency for Civic Education, which embraced its fervent anti-Stalinist message. 'I read it around 1958 and that was what shaped me', Bergsdorf recalled.[65]

By invoking the writings of Anne Frank and Wolfgang Leonhard in the same breath, Bergsdorf framed his political engagement not as having been animated by an unswerving desire to confront the Nazi past—as an activist of the Left might have done with hindsight—but rather as part of the anti-totalitarian logic of the early Cold War, which saw the Nazi past and communist present as twin evils.[66] Totalitarianism theory, which held that Nazism and Communism were genetically identical because each was intent on achieving total domination of their subjects, was arguably the most powerful intellectual framework of the early Cold War, not least in the Federal Republic. While left-wing activists increasingly began to question this theory in the 1960s, it remained central to centre-right activists' view of the world. It began to encompass not just Soviet and East German communism, but the West German radical Left as well. Teltschik summed up his convictions of 1968 thus: '[M]y conclusion was of course utterly simple: never again war, never again fascism, but also: never communism.'[67]

[63] The first German edition of the diary had appeared in 1950. *Das Tagebuch der Anne Frank* (Heidelberg, 1950).

[64] Wolfgang Leonhard, *Die Revolution entlässt ihre Kinder* (Cologne, 1955); Wolfgang Leonhard, *Child of the Revolution* (London, 1957).

[65] Bergsdorf interview. After he finished his studies, Bergsdorf worked as a researcher for the *Kuratorium Unteilbares Deutschland*, an influential pressure group set up on the occasion of the first anniversary of 17 June 1953, to mobilize the West German population for the goal of German unification. Christoph Meyer, *Die deutschlandpolitische Doppelstrategie: Wilhelm Wolfgang Schütz und das Kuratorium Unteilbares Deutschland 1954–1972* (Landsberg am Lech, 1997).

[66] Gleason calls totalitarianism 'the great mobilizing and unifying concept of the Cold War'. See his *Totalitarianism*, 3; on its role in the FRG especially 157–66. Erich Röper (b. 1939), who was chair of RCDS in Rhineland-Palatinate in the 1960s, was the only interviewee who pointed to a desire to confront Nazi-era racism as a direct source of his activism. His father, who had been leader of the German People's Party (DVP) in Hamburg before 1933, was half Jewish. Röper interview.

[67] Teltschik interview.

This anti-totalitarian framing did not just sustain opposition to the radical Left, it also had the potential to further subdue any conflicts that might otherwise have arisen in families where the parents were directly implicated in the Nazi regime. Wolfgang Reeder, for one, credited his father (along with reading the anti-totalitarian French existentialist Albert Camus) with instilling in him a deep understanding of the dangerous appeal of totalitarian ideologies. As a centre-right activist in Bonn in the late 1960s and deputy national chair of RCDS in 1970/71, his anti-totalitarian thinking fuelled his struggle against the student Left and bolstered his assertive centrism.[68] Reeder's father had been a member of the Nazi party, but he had repented after the war and often spoken to young people about the flawed attraction of the movement and its ideology.

> My father [...] showed me through his example a clear awareness, a historical consciousness, of National Socialism. He [...] did set an example and in doing so sparked my very substantial interest in National Socialism, as well as in another totalitarian regime, Communism. [...] It gave me a clear awareness of the fact that there are totalitarian movements on both the Left and the Right and that meaningful political consciousness develops between these totalitarian movements or as an alternative to these movements.[69]

Like Reeder, Detlef Stronk admired his father in spite of his Nazi past. The latter had been an Officer in the *Wehrmacht*, even serving as an adjutant to Hermann Göring, and had been awarded the Knight's Cross.[70] His father did not repent until many decades later and instead continued to extol the Third Reich's supposedly positive sides. Stronk nonetheless described him as an important role model. Highly educated and active in communal politics after the war, he served as mayor of a small town near Munich and was awarded the Order of Merit of the Federal Republic of Germany. He even had a small street named after him, Stronk emphasized. 'This means that he also really sparked my interest in the common good and that of the republic.'[71]

As we can see, then, regardless of whether or not their own parents were implicated in the Nazi regime, centre-right activists did not report experiencing political conflicts over the Nazi past within their own families. On the contrary, they relied on various narrative strategies to distance their families—and, ultimately, themselves—from Nazi crimes and to emphasize that dealing with the issue should not count as an achievement of the Left. Some invoked their family's anti-Nazi political lineage or religious faith or highlighted the ways in which they had personally already dealt with the issue prior to 1968. Others subsumed critiques of

---

[68]   On Camus's anti-totalitarianism, Gleason, *Totalitarianism*, 144, 151–4.
[69]   Reeder interview.   [70]   Stronk, *Berlin in den Achtziger Jahren*, 16.
[71]   Stronk interview.

the Nazi past under the general umbrella of totalitarianism to suggest that the struggle against communism in all its forms had been the most pressing issue at the time. And some argued that any crimes committed during the Third Reich had been offset by family members' postwar conduct or their suffering during the war and its aftermath.

Given this mindset, it is only logical that centre-right activism in the 1960s was not focused on exposing Nazi perpetrators in the Federal Republic or protesting structural continuities to the Third Reich. To be sure, in 1969, RCDS and the Student Unions, like their student peers on the Left, marched in protest against the neo-fascist National Democratic Party (NPD), which had made considerable gains in state elections between 1966 and 1968 and threatened to pass the 5 per cent hurdle needed to gain seats in the Bundestag in 1969.[72] At the same time, however, they vehemently rejected SDS's assertion that its escalating struggle against the West German system represented a delayed anti-fascist resistance.[73] Resisting the fascist threat in the present and dealing with the Nazi past meant something different entirely to centre-right activists: it meant preventing the collapse of liberal democracy—'another Weimar'—by bolstering the Federal Republic's character as a 'militant democracy' armed against its enemies on both Left and Right.[74]

'Militant democracy' was the main idea behind the Grand Coalition's proposed emergency laws, which the Bundestag passed with the necessary two-thirds majority on 30 May 1968. Rallying against this controversial amendment to the Basic Law had been the glue that held together, albeit temporarily, the diverse strands of the extraparliamentary opposition movement of left-wing student activists and trade union members. Various drafts of the legislation had been debated since 1958, and the version that was eventually enacted ten years later granted the executive far-reaching emergency powers to curtail citizens' basic freedoms in moments of grave national crisis. To warn against what they saw as the deeply anti-democratic and authoritarian thrust of the legislation, APO

---

[72] ACDP, 4-6-10, Beschlüsse der 19. Ord. BV (Maerz 1969), 35–7; ACDP, 4-6-53-3, Leaflet no. 3 on the RCDS's Anti-Radicalism Action. By 1967, the NPD had gained seats in six of the ten state parliaments. In April 1968, it gained nearly 10 per cent in the state elections in Baden-Württemberg, its highest result to that date. On the NPD's ideology and electoral strategy, see Lutz Niethammer, *Angepasster Faschismus: Politische Praxis der NPD* (Frankfurt am Main, 1969); John D. Nagle, *The National Democratic Party: Right Radicalism in the Federal Republic of Germany* (Berkeley, Los Angeles, and London, 1970).

[73] ACDP, 04/006/016/1, Horst Teltschik, 'Der Sozialistische Deutsche Studentenbund (SDS): eine Analyse seiner Konzeption und Strategie' (31 August 1968), 9–10; Nina Grunenberg, 'Der verspätete Anti-Faschismus und die 68er: die BRD', in Nina Grunenberg (ed.), *Antifaschismus—ein deutscher Mythos* (Reinbek near Hamburg, 1993), 39–53.

[74] On the idea of preventing 'another Weimar' in the early Federal Republic, see Sebastian Ullrich, *Der Weimar-Komplex: Das Scheitern der ersten deutschen Demokratie und die politische Kultur der Bundesrepublik 1945–1959* (Göttingen, 2009); on the anti-communist origins of 'military democracy', see Udi Greenberg, 'Militant Democracy and Human Rights', *New German Critique*, 42, 3 (2015), 169–95.

activists often invoked the infamous Article 48 of the Weimar constitution. It had given the Reich President the authority to take emergency measures without prior consultation of the Reichstag and led to a creeping dissolution of the parliamentary process in the early 1930s—and, ultimately, the establishment of the Nazi dictatorship. To their left-wing critics, the *Notstandsgesetze* of 1968—pointedly abbreviated 'NS Laws' by opponents of the legislation—vividly illustrated that, in the absence of a functioning parliamentary opposition, the Federal Republic was on the verge of a new fascist takeover.[75]

Centre-right activists, by contrast, did not just think that the laws posed no threat; they were adamant that the measures were urgently required to guard West German democracy against internal and external threats. They were not alone in thinking this: approximately half of all West German students favoured the legislation.[76] Christian Democratic politicians had been its champions, and centre-right students supported the project with considerable fervour. They opposed demonstrations against the legislation and pointed out that the Allies had made the passing of such laws a precondition for the transfer of full sovereignty to the Federal Republic.[77] Several interviewees for this book recalled speaking up in defence of the laws at various teach-ins and student rallies that had often become very heated.[78]

Furthermore, for centre-right activists, dealing with Nazism did not mean making a scandal of the Nazi careers of prominent West German bureaucrats and politicians, especially if they were Christian Democrats. Contrary to their left-wing opponents, Christian Democratic students did not criticize Chancellor Kiesinger for his erstwhile membership in the Nazi party or his work in the propaganda department of the Nazi Foreign Office. His past was the subject of considerable public controversy at the time, memorably illustrated by the fact that Beate Klarsfeld, the wife of French Nazi hunter Serge Klarsfeld, slapped Kiesinger in the face while shouting 'Nazi! Nazi!' at the annual convention of the CDU in November 1968.[79] As one former Christian Democratic student activist put it

---

[75] Thomas, *Protest Movements*, 87–92.

[76] Polling data varied over time on this issue. A poll of 1,000 students conducted by Allensbach between the summer of 1966 and the first half of 1967 found that 55 per cent of students viewed the planned emergency laws positively. 'Was denken die Studenten?', *Der Spiegel*, 26 (19 June 1967), 38. Three separate polls of more than 3,000 students in total, conducted by the Mannheim pollster Rudolf Wildenmann prior to the spring of 1968, showed that 42 per cent of students were in favour of the legislation. See the summary analysis of these polls for the Federal Minister of Education and Science, 26 April 1968, in BAK, B138/10262.

[77] ACDP, 4-66-1, RCDS Press Release (11 May 1968); ACDP, 4-6-8, Nachtrag zu den Beschlüssen der 17. Ordentlichen Bundesversammlung in Heidelberg (March 1967); see also Thomas, *Protest Movements*, 87.

[78] Radunski, *Aus der politischen Kulisse*, 56; Laepple interview; Stronk interview; Röper interview.

[79] Marie-Luise Scherer, 'Beate Klarsfelds privater Feldzug', *Die Zeit*, 17 (25 April 1969); Gassert, *Kiesinger*, 631–59; RCDS activists grew more critical of the former Chancellor after his ouster from federal office in 1969, but never attacked him over his Nazi past. Friedrich-Karl-Fromme, 'Das Salz in der CDU-Suppe', *FAZ* (12 September 1970).

later, to him Klarsfeld's slap had not represented a 'moral win' but rather 'an expression of exuberant hatred and impotence towards a generation on whom the young passed sweeping judgment'.[80]

Ten years later, RCDS would similarly reject accusations against the Christian Democratic Minister President of Baden-Württemberg, Hans Filbinger, who was eventually forced to resign amidst controversy surrounding death sentences he had passed as a judge in the Nazi-era navy. The constructive role he had played in the Federal Republic ought to shield the CDU politician from 'pharisaic snooping around in his political conscience', Christian Democratic students opined at the time.[81] And when the 'Provo of the CDU' Klaus Laepple stood trial for his role in the Cologne tram riots in early 1967, he chose as his lawyer Robert Servatius, who had defended some of the main Nazi perpetrators at Nuremberg and, more recently, Adolf Eichmann in Jerusalem. This demonstrates how different the sensibilities surrounding the subject were on the centre-right. Servatius was one of Cologne's most prominent defence lawyers in the 1960s and had never been a member of the Nazi party, but it is probably safe to assume that the symbolism of seeking counsel from a man whose fame rested on having defended one of the chief organizers of the Nazi genocide just a few years prior would have struck activists from the SDS as far more problematic.[82]

Nor were centre-right students averse to invoking the spectre of Nazi crimes to score political points in the present—not unlike their peers in SDS who regularly used the issue to advance more current agendas. This became particularly evident when left-wing students held events to mark the thirty-fifth anniversary of Hitler's appointment as Reich Chancellor in January 1933. In early 1968, SDS organized a series of events that focused on the Nazi past of Federal President Heinrich Lübke. By this point, revelations about Lübke's role in drawing up architectural plans for Nazi concentration camps, notably the one in the coastal city of Peenemünde, had fuelled left-wing outrage against the 'concentration camp contractor' [KZ-Baumeister] for over a year. Many of these were based on documents provided by the Socialist regime in East Germany. In early February 1968, SDS put on an 'anti-Lübke week' to discuss the latest revelations about the President's past and,

---

[80] Hacke, *Weltmacht wider Willen*, 141.

[81] Günther Heckelmann, 'Demokratie widersteht Systemüberwindern', *Deutschland-Union-Dienst*, 125 (4 July 1978), 7. Whereas 'pharisaic' might be perceived by contemporary readers as the conscious use of a term freighted with antisemitism, this would probably be a misreading in this particular context. It was in common usage at the time as a term that denoted hypocrisy, self-righteousness, and petty criticism.

[82] Eva Schmidt-Häuer, 'Der "Provo" von der CDU', *Die Zeit*, 1 (6 January 1967), 7; on Servatius's involvement in the Eichmann case, both at the trial and beyond, see Willi Winkler, 'Adolf Eichmann und seine Verteidiger: Ein kleiner Nachtrag zur Rechtsgeschichte', *Einsicht: Bulletin des Fritz-Bauer-Instituts*, 5 (2011), 33–41.

by association, to lay bare the larger continuities between the Third Reich and Federal Republic.[83]

Under the leadership of Bonn history student and prominent SDS activist Hannes Heer, the local SDS chapter invited Friedrich Karl Kaul, a well-known East German jurist licensed to practice law in the West, as one of the main speakers.[84] Amongst other major appearances in West German courts, Kaul had been a co-plaintiff in the Frankfurt Auschwitz trial, representing former camp inmates who had settled in East Germany.[85] SDS brought him to Bonn to discuss if it was lawful that mail sent from the GDR, which included information on Lübke's Nazi past, was being confiscated by the West German authorities.

During the actual event on 6 February 1968, however, Kaul was barely able to get a word in on the subject of West German surveillance practices. Centre-right activists from the local RCDS chapter and *Aktion '68* staged a go-in. Appropriating a protest practice SDS used widely at the time to intimidate professors suspected of having fascist ties, centre-right students interrupted the lawyer's remarks with shouts and questions.[86] A number of them then jumped on their chairs and unrolled banners that condemned Kaul for condoning GDR repression. 'Freedom for the political prisoners of the GDR. What are you doing, Mr. Kaul?', asked one. Another one directly offset Nazi crimes against state socialist offences in the present and charged Kaul, who had a Jewish mother and had been imprisoned in Dachau in the 1930s, with hypocrisy in speaking out against the Nazis' persecution of the Jews without simultaneously condemning political oppression in East Germany: 'Prof. Kaul: Against the murder of Jews in Auschwitz—in favour of murder at the Wall.'[87] Clearly unsettled and

---

[83] Anette Weinke, *Die Verfolgung von NS-Tätern im geteilten Deutschland: Vergangenheitsbewältigungen 1949–1969, oder: eine deutsch-deutsche Beziehungsgeschichte im Kalten Krieg* (Paderborn, 2002); Davis, 'New Leftists and West Germany', in Gassert and Steinweis, *Coping with the Nazi Past*, 213; Schmidtke, 'The German New Left and National Socialism', 179; Rusinek, 'Von der Entdeckung der NS-Vergangenheit', 121–2.

[84] Heer would later become one of the leadings experts behind an important—and quite controversial—exhibition on the complicity of German soldiers in the Holocaust. Hannes Heer and Klaus Naumann, eds, *Vernichtungskrieg: Verbrechen der Wehrmacht 1941–1944* (Hamburg, 1995); on Heer's activism, continued interest in the Nazi past, and trajectory, see Stallmann, *Die Erfindung von '1968'*, 120–6; on the Kaul event in Bonn and Heer's activist biography, see also von Hodenberg, *Das andere Achtundsechzig*, 45–52.

[85] See the entry for 'Kaul, Friedrich Karl', in *Wer war Wer in der DDR?*, available at https://www.bundesstiftung-aufarbeitung.de/wer-war-wer-in-der-ddr-%2363%3B-1424.html?ID=1654 (accessed on 21 July 2017); F.K. Kaul, *Ich klage an: Der berühmte DDR-Anwalt berichtet als Nebenkläger und Verteidiger in westdeutschen Strafprozessen* (Hamburg, 1971); Friedrich Karl Kaul, *Auschwitz trial in Frankfurt-on-Main: summing up and reply of Friedrich Karl Kaul, legal representative of the co-plaintiffs resident in the German Democratic Republic in the criminal proceedings against Mulka and others before the criminal court at the Provincial Court in Frankfurt-on-Main* (Dresden, 1965).

[86] Schmidtke, *Der Aufbruch der jungen Intelligenz*, 147; a few months later, the Bonn RCDS spoke out against Lübke as President, however. Rolf-Peter Henkel, 'Die jungen linken Christdemokraten', *Bonner Rundschau* (27 April 1968).

[87] 'Anwalt Kaul kam kaum zu Wort. Hörsaal nach 10 Minuten verlassen', *Bonner Generalanzeiger* (7 February 1968).

Illustration 2.1 Centre-right student protests during an SDS-run event with East German star lawyer Friedrich Karl Kaul in Bonn on 6 February 1968. The banners state 'Freedom for the political prisoners of the GDR. What are you doing, Mr. Kaul?' and 'Prof. Kaul: Against the murder of Jews in Auschwitz—in favour of murder at the Wall.'

(dpa Picture-Alliance)

unaccustomed to vocal student dissent—dissent SDS duly condemned as 'terror against Kaul', thus taking a page out of the Right's playbook in turn—the GDR jurist left the event after a few minutes.[88]

In staunchly anti-totalitarian fashion (and quite oblivious to scale), centre-right students portrayed Auschwitz and the Berlin Wall as two equivalent symbols of crimes committed in the name of ideology. Much like student activists from SDS, who did not shy away from attacking victims of Nazi-era persecution for their 'fascist' views in the present, they disregarded Kaul's own experiences in Dachau when denouncing him for defending former Auschwitz inmates while enabling inhumane practices in the GDR.

As several scholars have pointed out, the 1968 student movement, through its insistence on structural continuities in German society across the divide of 1945, in many ways helped, but in other ways also hindered, efforts to come to terms with the Nazi past, not least through stretching the term fascism in such a way that

---

[88] Universitätsarchiv Bonn, AStA 081-167, SDS Leaflet 'Terror gegen Kaul' (7 February 1968). On the Kaul episode also Bothien, *Protest und Provokation*, 85–7; von Hodenberg, *Das andere Achtundsechzig*, 47–8.

removed much of the concept's analytical value.[89] The anti-Kaul protest in Bonn suggests that centre-right students had a no less warped view of the subject. SDS seized on the anniversary of the Nazi seizure of power to discuss the 'fascistic' surveillance practices of the Federal Republic (with the help, we should note, of materials provided by a regime that was neither a model of transparency nor a stranger to spying on its citizens). Meanwhile, the centre-right used the anniversary of Hitler's appointment to indict the GDR.[90] The impulse to further current agendas outdid the desire to honour the experiences of the Nazis' victims, educate the public about the regime's persecutory practices, and to reckon with ordinary Germans' complicity. The Nazi past, in this instance and others, served as a cudgel with which to beat one's opponents—and this was true across the political spectrum.

Intergenerational Conflict and Affinity

The presence of the Nazi past in West Germany's 1960s was one major reason why generational conflict emerged as a chief paradigm to make sense of student unrest. This went hand in hand with intense public scrutiny of what made student protesters tick. From the moment the protests erupted, social scientists began to look back in time to ask if there was anything in the backgrounds of student activists that predisposed them to participating in this anti-authoritarian rebellion.[91] They profiled the typical protester in considerable depth, often after being tasked to do so by media outlets wanting to understand the phenomenon of student unrest or government institutions seeking to craft an effective response.[92] Based on the

---

[89] Konrad Jarausch, 'Critical Memory and Civil Society: The Impact of the 1960s on German Debates about the Past', in Gassert and Steinweis, Coping with the Nazi Past, 11–30, and Schmidtke, 'The German New Left and National Socialism', 176–93; Schmidtke, Der Aufbruch der jungen Intelligenz, 148.

[90] The discourse about the Nazi past—in different ways, but on both the Left and Right—was also shaped by the German-German entanglements and competition that were hallmarks of the Cold War era. On this tendency see further Jürgen Danyel (ed.), Die geteilte Vergangenheit: Zum Umgang mit Nationalsozialismus und Widerstand in beiden deutschen Staaten (Berlin, 1995); Herf, Divided Memory; Detlef Siegfried, 'Zwischen Aufarbeitung und Schlussstrich. Der Umgang mit der NS-Vergangenheit in den beiden deutschen Staaten 1958 bis 1969', in Schildt, Lammers, Siegfried, Dynamische Zeiten, 77–113.

[91] Rudolf Wildenmann und Max Kaase, 'Die unruhige Generation': Eine Untersuchung zu Politik und Demokratie in der Bundesrepublik (Mannheim, 1968); Allerbeck, Soziologie radikaler Studentenbewegungen; Erwin K. Scheuch. 'Soziologische Aspekte der Unruhe unter den Studenten', Aus Politik und Zeitgeschichte: Beilage zur Wochenzeitung Das Parlament (1968), 36, 3–25; see further Nehring, 'Generation as a Political Argument'; von der Goltz, Talkin' 'Bout My Generation.

[92] Der Spiegel (ed.), Der deutsche Student: Situation, Einstellungen und Verhaltensweisen. Ergebnisse einer Repräsentativerhebung an 26 deutschen Universitäten und Hochschulen. Durchgeführt vom Institut für Demoskopie, Allensbach 1966-67 (Hamburg, 1967); BAK, B145/5474, Bruno Heck, Federal Minister of Family Affairs, in a letter to the leader of the Federal Government's Press and Information Office, Karl-Günther von Hase, 20 September 1967, which listed some of the different polls and studies commissioned by the federal government. Amongst others, they had commissioned

information they collected, scholars generated a variety of different explanations for the rise in (left-wing) political activity among students, including plenty of pathological readings of youthful dissent that identified supposed character defects or parental neglect as the key to understanding student rebels.[93]

The most common explanation by far, however, was that their status as the first postwar generation explained students' rebelliousness in the late 1960s. In stark contrast to those who would later portray the '68ers as 'war children', this paradigm emphasized that theirs was a generation that had grown up during peacetime and amidst an unprecedented and seemingly eternal prosperity—a period that Germany's neighbours to the west referred to as the *trentes glorieuses*. This generational location, many scholars and commentators argued at the time, afforded young people a privilege not available to their parents, especially in Germany, namely the luxury to contest liberal democracy and the market economy. Young people directed their ire at democracy, so the argument ran, because they had not borne the hardships of postwar reconstruction.[94]

Given the omnipresence of 'generation' as an explanatory framework for student protest, both in the 1960s and in the decades since, it is only logical that centre-right activists have also framed their own political project in generational terms. For one, a number of interviewees for this book described their relationship to older Christian Democrats as one defined by generational conflict. Radunski related that they had referred to older conservatives within the party as the 'late harvest of Weimar' because they had seemed like outdated products of an entirely different era.[95] Schönbohm recalled that simply wearing a full beard had been enough to make him deeply suspect in the eyes of older party members like Franz Amrehn (b. 1912), the West Berlin CDU chair whose anti-communism was particularly virulent. 'Here in Berlin: Franz Amrehn. Oh my God, that was a real 1950s mentality', he explained with hindsight. Even the more conservative Härdtl, RCDS chair in West Berlin in 1967/68, framed the relationship to older party members in similar terms. Although he insisted that he had not been as much of an 'RCDS revolutionary [*RCDS-Revoluzzer*]' as Schönbohm, he recalled that 'for us students Franz Amrehn [...] was something of an ossified fossil', less

the conservative Allensbach polling institute and the Mannheim-based political scientist Rudolf Wildenmann to conduct empirical studies that were to form the basis of the government's response. See also BAK, B145/5474, the memorandum entitled 'Studentenumfrage' (19 October 1967); and Heck to Herbert Wehner, Federal Minister for Intra-German Relations (12 December 1967).

[93] Allerbeck, *Soziologie radikaler Studentenbewegungen*, 52–3; similar ideas were propagated by US social scientists at the time. William A. Westley and Nathan B. Epstein, *The Silent Majority: Families of Emotionally Healthy College Students* (San Francisco, CA, 1969).

[94] Erwin K. Scheuch (ed.), *Die Widertäufer der Wohlstandsgesellschaft: Eine kritische Untersuchung der 'Neuen Linken' und ihrer Dogmen* (Cologne, 1968); Löwenthal, *Romantischer Rückfall*.

[95] Radunski interview; also Radunski cited in Gerhard Sport, 'Der Maskenbildner der Union', *Die Zeit*, 19 (4 May 1984).

in terms of his concrete political views than in terms of his style, 'his demeanour... this drabness'.[96]

Ascribing even the smallest signs of domestic opposition to communist infiltration from East Germany was rooted deeply in the West German politics of the preceding decade. Not even RCDS, whose members' commitment to the anticommunist cause was often deeply personal, were exempt from such treatment.[97] At one CDU board meeting, Amrehn and Chancellor Kiesinger speculated that the more left-leaning RCDS members had been implanted in West Berlin by the East German regime. It was almost as if they had anticipated Runge's subsequent conversion from RCDS leader to Stasi collaborator.[98]

Some centre-right activists insisted that they had therefore been involved in two age-specific political conflicts at the same time, one with their left-wing peers on campus and one with older conservatives within their party. This perception fuelled their sense of outsiderdom, but it also bolstered their idea of themselves as an avant-garde. In the words of former West Berlin Christian Democratic student Ingrid Reichart-Dreyer: 'So it was dual: on the one hand, you are black [i.e. Christian Democratic, AvdG] and forced out, so therefore you are excluded [on campus]. And in that instance, on the conservative spectrum, I was, then again, too progressive.'[99] Schönbohm equally described having fought a battle on two fronts: 'At university we were the "fascists": "Schönbohm, the fascist." And within the CDU, around '67/'68, we were the lefties.'[100]

The media fed such (self-)perceptions throughout 1968. The West German press, which often framed its reporting on student protest in terms of a conflict between the generations, took great delight in running counter-intuitive stories about young conservatives shedding their customary deference.[101] At a time of educational expansion, students were widely considered a bellwether of where the

---

[96] Härdtl interview.

[97] See Eric D. Weitz, 'The Ever-Present Other: Communism in the Making of West Germany', in Hanna Schissler (ed.), *The Miracle Years: A Cultural History of West Germany, 1949-1968* (Princeton, NJ, 2001), 219–32; Stefan Creuzberger and Dierk Hoffmann (eds.), *'Geistige Gefahr' und 'Immunisierung der Gesellschaft': Antikommunismus und politische Kultur in der frühen Bundesrepublik* (Berlin, Munich, and Boston, MA, 2014); for a concrete example see Holger Nehring, 'The British and West German Protests against Nuclear Weapons and the Cultures of the Cold War, 1957–64', *Contemporary British History*, 19, 2 (2005), 223–41.

[98] Kiesinger in a meeting of the party's federal board on 10 May 1968. *Kiesinger: 'Wir leben in einer veränderten Welt' (1965–1969), Die Protokolle des CDU-Bundesvorstandes*, vol. 5, edited by Günter Buchstab (Düsseldorf, 2005), 914; also Bösch, *Die Adenauer-CDU*, 406.

[99] Reichart-Dreyer interview.

[100] Interview mit Wulf Schönbohm, Berlin (20 February 2008); see also Wulf Schönbohm, 'Die 68er: politische Verirrungen und gesellschaftliche Veränderungen', in *APuZ*, 14–15 (2008); over the years, several of his former peers equally described their erstwhile position as a war on two fronts. See e.g. Peter Gauweiler, quoted in Gunter Hofmann, 'Nach links Flaggen zeigen', *Die Zeit*, 21 (20 May 1988); http://www.zeit.de/1988/21/nach-links-flagge-zeigen; and Jürgen Rosorius, quoted in 'Die '68er der CDU/CSU aus der APO-Zeit treffen sich', *dpa* (11 May 1988).

[101] Rolf-Peter Henkel, 'Die jungen linken Christdemokraten', *Bonner Rundschau* (27 April 1968); Annamarie Doherr, 'Unzumutbar für die Partei. Berliner RCDS will CDU-Führung zu öffentlicher Diskussion zwingen', *Frankfurter Rundschau* (9 May 1968).

country was headed. If even the conservatives among them were turning into rebels, the prospects for political stability seemed truly dire. The conservative *Münchner Merkur* was sure to detect 'a hint of the APO' even among the traditionally conservative Bavarian Christian Democrats.[102] When Härdtl charged the West Berlin CDU with an 'authoritarian intervention in the affairs of RCDS' for refusing to send out mail from the student group whose content deviated from the official party line, *Der Spiegel* duly covered the episode. The news magazine clearly relished reporting on what it termed Härdtl's 'declaration of war' to West Berlin party leader Amrehn: 'Berlin's CDU, which, up to now, was proud of its scholars and was not without joy about the alienation of the young, left-wing intelligentsia of the SPD, now also had an uprising in its own ranks', the influential weekly observed with thinly veiled *Schadenfreude*.[103] A photograph of Härdtl in a turtleneck sweater—a fashion staple associated with the French existentialists— accompanied the article. As Frank Bösch aptly observed in his study of the postwar CDU, then, something akin to the anti-authoritarian 'spirit of 1968' rocked the party in these years.[104]

Media portrayals of youthful unrest among Christian Democrats and personal recollections that framed the position of centre-right students around 1968 as a two-pronged generational clash, however, overplay the conflicts on the centre-right. For most activists this was especially true at home, because they overwhelmingly perpetuated their families' broader political traditions. Not a single interviewee for this book came from a left-wing parental home. Not all grew up in politicized homes and some had mixed backgrounds that included Social Democratic or liberal-leaning family members alongside others who had supported the Catholic Centre Party or one of the national bourgeois parties during the Weimar years. The majority, however, grew up in families with clear or implicit conservative leanings, and many had parents who supported the Christian Democrats. Ingrid Reichart-Dreyer, who grew up in a small town in Schleswig-Holstein, told a story that was far from atypical: 'I received an intensive [...] political socialization through my upbringing. My parents are both CDU members. At that time my mother was one of only a few women [in the party], and my father was a founder member in the village. And then, in 1965, I also joined.'[105]

These findings do not set centre-right activists apart, but correspond to what we know about the political socialization of left-wing student activists of the 1960s, in West Germany and other countries that witnessed protest movements in these years. None of the numerous sociological studies of student activists conducted at the time was able to find empirical proof of generational conflict as a major

---

[102] Heinz Brockert, 'Ein Hauch von APO in der CSU', *Münchner Merkur* (11 December 1969); also Eckart Spoo, 'RCDS greift "Bayernkurier" an', *Frankfurter Rundschau* (27 January 1970).

[103] 'RCDS: Aufstand im Haus', *Der Spiegel*, 20 (1968), 52.

[104] Bösch, *Die Adenauer CDU*, 408–16; Bösch, *Macht und Machtverlust*, 96.

[105] Reichart-Dreyer interview.

driving force of activism.[106] There was some evidence to suggest that there had been a swing to the left in the overall political preferences of students in West Germany—more students reported that they sympathized with the SPD or FDP than their parents—but politically heterogeneous families were still the exception, not the rule. Even in the dynamic 1960s, then, most students' political convictions were shaped to a large extent by the families in which they had grown up.[107] Accordingly, SDS supporters were more likely than other students to come from Social Democratic or Liberal homes; far fewer had conservative parents, especially conservative fathers.[108] The reverse was true in the case of centre-right students— a conservative family background clearly predominated among activists.

Intergenerational relations within the CDU were also more cordial in the 1960s than the press reports about young Christian Democratic rebels suggested. It was the fact that they occurred at all in a party that had been unaccustomed to internal debate and dominated almost entirely by the geriatric Adenauer until a few years prior that generated press interest. Whatever political differences existed within the Christian Democratic parties at a time of significant social and economic change and shifting electoral fortune, fundamental clashes between members of clearly delineated age groups—between old conservatives and student reformers, as it were—were not the norm around 1968. Accordingly, far from all interviewees for this book related stories of inner-party strife along generational lines. Härdtl, for one, whose rebellious antics *Der Spiegel* had so savoured, downplayed his own contentious instincts in the 1960s with hindsight. It was no more than a 'certain kind of insubordination'. 'These were not disputes of principles', he stressed.[109]

Sources from the period suggest much the same. In fact, the CDU leadership relied quite heavily on the advice and expertise of Christian Democratic student leaders to make sense of the protests and craft the government's response to them, both at the federal and state level. Hans Filbinger, the Governor of Baden-Württemberg, for one, personally commissioned student leader Ignaz Bender to write a study about the phenomenon of student unrest in West Germany and the Western world more broadly to help inform his government's response. Bender observed numerous protest events first-hand throughout 1968 to gather information for Filbinger while on Baden-Württemberg's payroll. He kept this fact secret from the student activists he observed out of a fear of appearing like a lackey of the

---

[106] Konrad Jarausch, *Deutsche Studenten: 1800–1970* (Frankfurt/Main, 1984), 233; Klatch, *A Generation Divided*, 43.

[107] BAK, B138/10262, Dr Raabe to the Minister of Education and Research (26 April 1968), summarizing the findings of three separate polls conducted by Rudolf Wildenmann; Allerbeck, *Soziologie radikaler Studentenbewegungen*, 99; political beliefs were not inherited directly from parents, however. For a more in-depth conceptual discussion, see Paul Allen Beck and M. Kent Jennings, 'Family Traditions, Political Periods, and the Development of Partisan Orientations', *The Journal of Politics*, 53, 3 (1991), 742–63.

[108] Allerbeck, *Soziologie radikaler Studentenbewegungen*, 50, 108. Numerous sociological studies came to similar conclusions about student activists in the US Jarausch, *Deutsche Studenten*, 233.

[109] Härdtl interview.

'establishment'.[110] Wulf Schönbohm, Peter Radunski, and Jürgen-Bernd Runge, three of the leading Christian Democratic activists in West Berlin, also received funding for their own widely-read study, *Democracy Challenged [Die herausgeforderte Demokratie]*, from a state-run institute tasked with political education in Mainz, the capital of Rhineland-Palatinate where Helmut Kohl had been the leader of the Christian Democrats since 1966.[111]

In reality, therefore, the other '68ers were not just instigators but already beneficiaries of a cautious inner-party opening that was slowly getting under way. The '68ers of the Left, who often claimed in retrospect that everything they had done had been brand new, had actually been influenced heavily by older left-wing intellectuals and the public climate of critical reflection that had begun to take shape in the Federal Republic in the late 1950s.[112] Similarly, Christian Democratic students benefitted from a new openness to reform within the CDU that began to take hold in the late 1960s. The need to enter into a Grand Coalition government with the Social Democrats in December 1966 provided a major impetus for party renewal. That same month, the party began a process of internal deliberation that culminated in the Berlin Program of 1968, the first official program of the CDU since 1953. The text was hardly revolutionary, but it called for greater participation of ordinary citizens in political decision-making processes and emphasized that 'critical engagement, particularly of the younger generation, is an essential contribution for the advancement of our democracy'.[113] While the Berlin Program by no means represented a Bad Godesberg-style overhaul of the party's basic principles, it was still a marker on the CDU's journey towards becoming a more programmatic party with a more open culture of internal debate—a journey that, in the 1970s and 1980s, the other '68ers would then help to chart, in turn.[114]

Moreover, the party's new openness in the late 1960s was at least partly carried by a generational change that preceded the arrival of the '68ers on the political scene. Younger men—for this change remained almost exclusively male at the time—born around 1930 began to occupy more senior positions within the party when the first cohort of postwar functionaries, who had been socialized during the late Wilhelmine period and the Weimar years, reached retirement age. The newcomers slowly introduced a more critical tone and greater internal debate. This culminated in more far-reaching reforms and inner-party democratization

---

[110] Bender interview; Ignaz Bender, *Der Protest der 'großen' Minderheit: Eine Studie zu den Ursachen der Studentenunruhen, verfasst im Auftrag des Kultusministeriums Baden-Württemberg* (May 1969), copy in Bender Private Papers.

[111] Schönbohm, Runge and Radunski, *Die herausgeforderte Demokratie*.

[112] von Hodenberg, *Konsens und Krise*.

[113] CDU, Berliner Programm, 1. Fassung (1968), IV, no. 24, ACDP 07-001-22059, available online at http://www.kas.de/upload/ACDP/CDU/Programme_Beschluesse/1968_Berliner-Programm.pdf (accessed on 28 November 2017).

[114] Pridham, *Christian Democracy*, 178–80; see further Chapter 6.

during the party's oppositional phase in the 1970s.[115] Franz Amrehn may have attributed all student dissent to infiltration from the GDR, but a figure like Kohl (b. 1930), who was building a profile as an energetic young reformer, pushed back vehemently against similar sentiments in the closed meetings of the party's board. On 21 June 1968, the future Federal Chancellor declared: 'The CDU establishment has an idea of the universities that is absolutely out of step with the times. At the moment, we have an attitude among the German population—and this also reaches into the CDU—where the term "student" is becoming a curse word.' In contrast, he stated that he was in favour of 'everything that improves the position of RCDS'.[116] Voices like his attenuated the potential for generational clashes between older Christian Democrats and younger student 'rebels'.[117]

Centre-right student activists of the 1960s generally felt a strong intellectual and stylistic kinship to the so-called '45ers—party figures like Kohl or the sociologist Dahrendorf, whose works they so admired. Several studies of this generation have demonstrated that the '45ers only became a self-conscious unit in response to encountering the radicalism of the left-wing student movement.[118] To delineate themselves clearly from the left-wing student activists of 1968, who rediscovered utopian thought and sought to infuse West German politics with a new fervour, the '45ers began to define themselves as sober pragmatists and rational democrats. Only they had learned the correct lessons from the political fanaticism of the Nazi years and the great political uncertainty and anxiety that followed the collapse of the regime in 1945, they began to insist.[119] While the '68ers' commitment to liberal democracy was at best ambiguous, so their argument ran, the '45ers' belief in parliamentary democracy was absolute, resting, as it did, on having experienced the Nazi dictatorship and the upheaval of the postwar years.

Many of the most influential West German social science studies written about the student movement in the 1960s—often by scholars who were self-conscious '45ers themselves—analysed the student movement through this generational

---

[115] Bösch, *Die Adenauer CDU*, 408, 415; Pridham, *Christian Democracy in Western Germany*, 178–9; Steber, *Hüter der Begriffe*, 196. For a fuller discussion of the transformation of the CDU in the 1970s, see Chapters 5 and 6.

[116] Minutes of the meeting of the party's federal board on 21 June 1968. *Kiesinger: 'Wir leben in einer veränderten Welt' (1965–1969), Die Protokolle des CDU-Bundesvorstandes*, vol. 5, edited by Günter Buchstab (Düsseldorf, 2005), 994.

[117] Recent research suggests that even Kiesinger was quite open towards the student movement. Gassert, *Kiesinger*; see also Kiesinger's comments during the meeting of the CDU's federal board on 10 May 1968, in *Kiesinger: 'Wir leben in einer veränderten Welt'*, 882–3.

[118] Moses, *German Intellectuals and the Nazi Past*; Wehrs, *Protest der Professoren*; Riccardo Bavaj, 'Young, Old, and In-Between. Liberal Scholars and "Generation Building" at the Time of West Germany's Student Revolt', in von der Goltz', *Talkin' 'bout My Generation'*, 177–94; Thomas Kroll, 'Generationenverhältnisse und politischer Konflikt während der Studentenrevolte von 1968 in der Bundesrepublik Deutschland', in Annemarie Steidl et al. (eds.), *Übergänge und Schnittmengen: Arbeit, Migration, Bevölkerung und Wissenschaftsgeschichte in Diskussion* (Vienna, 2008), 319–46.

[119] Dirk Moses, 'Das Pathos der Nüchternheit: Die Rolle der 45-Generation im Prozess der Liberalisierung der Bundesrepublik', *Frankfurter Rundschau*, 2 July 2002.

frame. They portrayed student dissent as the inflated political remonstration of young intellectuals who had never faced the hardships of war, displacement, and deprivation and therefore had the luxury of feeling moral outrage about the imperfections of liberal democracy and the capitalist economic system.[120]

While left-wing activists at the time usually rejected such generational inter-pretations as dismissive and politically charged, centre-right students took many cues from these analyses in their own critiques of the left-wing student movement and in their self-descriptions.[121] This was in spite of the fact that they were the same age as the 1968 activists examined in these studies. Of course, interpretations that rested on age-specific experiences as determinants of political outlook, if accurate, should have applied equally to them as well. Nevertheless, the key texts that summarized Christian Democratic students' responses to the phenomenon of student unrest in the late 1960s were all infused with generational interpretations that sounded eerily similar to those of the '45ers. As Schönbohm, Runge, and Radunski claimed in *Democracy Challenged*, the sixties generation of student activists showed no appreciation of the difficult beginnings of the Federal Republic and was therefore not able to accurately assess the achievements of the Adenauer era; its representatives took democracy for granted, they charged.[122]

In his Filbinger-commissioned study, Bender relied even more overtly on the idea of specific generational experiences as markers of political difference. Those who had experienced the Third Reich and the collapse of 1945 had

> measured the established state and social order [...] against this gloomy past. The Basic Law seemed like a constitutional model compared with the dictator-ship of the Third Reich or the totalitarianism of communist states in the postwar, the Federal Republic of Germany like an impeccable democratic constitutional state.[123]

The students of the 1960s, on the other hand, were a 'generation without memory', he observed:

---

[120] Scheuch, *Widertäufer der Wohlstandsgesellschaft*. Most of the contributors to this influential anthology were '45ers and their years of birth were prominently listed in this work. Richard Löwenthal, who, having been born in 1912, was not a '45er, nevertheless viewed the student movement in very similar terms. See his *Romantischer Rückfall*, 25–9. Such analyses often drew on the classic work by Helmut Schelsky that had defined the previous generation as 'sceptical' and sober. Helmut Schelsky, *Die skeptische Generation: Eine Soziologie der deutschen Jugend* (Düsseldorf and Cologne, 1957); see further Franz-Werner Kersting, 'Helmut Schelskys "Skeptische Generation" von 1957: Zur Publikations- und Wirkungsgeschichte eines Standardwerkes', *VfZ*, 50, 3 (2002), 465–95; also Bavaj, 'Young, Old, and In-Between'.

[121] Rudi Dutschke, 'Die geschichtlichen Bedingungen für den internationalen Emanzipationskampf', in *1968: Eine Enzyklopädie*, edited by Rudolf Sievers (Frankfurt am Main, 2004), 259; see further Nehring, 'Generation as a Political Argument'.

[122] Schönbohm, Runge, and Radunski, *Die herausgeforderte Demokratie*, 27–8.

[123] Bender, *Der Protest der 'großen' Minderheit*, 23–29, here 24.

For them, those terrible years are history. They no longer have any idea of the dangers and hardships that their fathers had to go through. [. . .] The benchmark is no longer that previous worse period, the benchmark is now the better state of things that it is possible to imagine. Since the possible has become self-evident, one now grasps for the impossible.

An article that Radunski wrote for the first issue of the new Christian Democratic journal *Sonde* in late 1968 drew perhaps the most explicit link between the other '68ers and the '45ers. The piece argued that the division among late 1960s student activists in many ways mirrored that between the 1960s activist Left and the previous generation of intellectuals. There were two starkly contrasting styles to be found 'among the present generation of students', Radunski observed: the 'pragmatism of the postwar period and the new forms of ideologization and fanaticism'.[124] Like those who were older, centre-right students of the late 1960s subscribed firmly to the former, he insisted.

Musings such as these highlight that invoking generation in assessments of the student movement often had more to do with the desire to express political affinity and to justify a particular political programme than it did with the actual age-specific experiences and characteristics of the protagonists thus described.[125] Political and stylistic affinity clearly trumped age-specific factors in Radunski's analysis of what made him and his centre-right student peers tick. Like the '45ers, the other '68ers began to develop a collective sense of self through their encounters with the student Left and turned to the concept of generation to give their experiences, political programme, and aspirations narrative shape.

* * *

As this chapter has shown, those who were involved in centre-right student groups around 1968 had often been predisposed towards this type of partisan engagement by their families. It is very telling that no interviewee for this book came from a left-wing parental home; most grew up in families with conservative leanings and had parents who supported the Christian Democrats.

In many other ways, however, they were actually remarkably similar to their activist contemporaries on the Left—and not just in that they mostly followed family political traditions. Their childhoods were shaped by the Second World War and its chaotic aftermath; a sizeable number fled their homelands, or experienced expulsion or war-related fatherlessness; some had spent part of

---

[124] Peter Radunski, 'Protest im 4. Semester', *Sonde: Neue Christlich Demokratische Politik* 1 (1968), 34; In making this point, Radunski quoted a verdict by Federal Minister for Research and Education Gerhard Stoltenberg, 'Student und Politik', in: *Aus Politik und Zeitgeschichte* 18 (1968).
[125] See Nehring, 'Generation as a Political Argument'.

their early lives under state socialism or served in the *Bundeswehr* prior to entering student politics; and some came from Nazi families, while others did not.

We need to integrate these insights into how we conceive of the 1968 generation, because the left-wing revolt has all too often been portrayed as the delayed symptom of a familial psychodrama. Some scholars have even suggested that the '68ers rebelled in a specific way or embraced a particular political program, because they had been collectively traumatized as children.[126] Even leaving aside the problems associated with using trauma as a category of collective experience, such interpretations easily lapse into a kind of psychological determinism where specific wartime or postwar experiences supposedly led straight to a particular way of doing politics around 1968. The point here has been to show that the other '68ers had experiences that were often very similar to the ones that had supposedly led activists directly into the arms of SDS and other groups of the Left.

The other '68ers fashioned very different political identities from these early influences, however. Activists of the Left often pointed to Nazi-era residues in postwar society as a major driving force of their politicization. Centre-right activists, by contrast, typically downplayed the salience of the Nazi past and highlighted instead that combating the socialist regime(s) to the east of the 'Iron Curtain' had been the most pressing political issue. They did so regardless of whether or not their own families had been complicit in the Nazi regime. They narrated the story of their politicization along the major milestones of Europe's Cold War history and constructed stories about their childhood and youth that symbolized communist repression—family members held in Soviet captivity, the 17 June 1953 uprising, Hungary's 1956, or Germany's division. The argument here is not that they were shaped irreversibly by these events—as more deterministic treatments of generation would have it—but that they fashioned a narrative about their political socialization that highlighted these events at the expense of others. All this ultimately tells us more about what the other '68ers thought they had done in 1968 than about why they got involved in politics in the first place.[127]

Finally, this chapter has shown that centre-right activists already began to think of themselves as a distinct generation-unit of student activists in the late 1960s. Nudged by social scientists and a press that regularly interpreted the protests as a conflict between generations, activists of the centre-right began to conceive of themselves as an age-specific community with distinct characteristics. In doing so, they were inspired by the '45ers, who had begun to articulate their collective traits

---

[126] See Schulz, Radebold and Reulecke, *Söhne ohne Väter*, 149, who argue that both 1968 and second-wave feminism were the direct result of widespread fatherlessness in Germany after the war. See also Karin Wetterau, *68 – Täterkinder und Rebellen: Familienroman einer Revolte* (Bielefeld, 2017). As much recent research has shown, not all German children had uniform experiences or were traumatized during the war. For a powerful critique of using the notion of 'trauma' to understand the collective experiences of Germans in wartime, see Nicholas Stargardt, *Witnesses of War: Children's Lives Under the Nazis* (London, 2004); and Stargardt, *The German War*, 2.

[127] Portelli, *The Death of Luigi Trastulli*, 52; Abrams, *Oral History Theory*, 7, 90.

after encountering left-wing student rebels. This laid the groundwork for later commemorations of the student movement that imagined former activists as the other '68ers. At a time when 'generation' was on everybody's lips, it was an obvious way of making sense of one's politics—and it would only become a more appealing framework over time.

3

Between Adenauer and Coca-Cola

In January 1968, Bonn's *Aktion '68*, one of the new centre-right umbrella groups set up on West German campuses from 1967 onward, landed a spectacular coup when it hosted a free concert in the university cafeteria. The performance was by none other than *The Rattles*, one of West Germany's most commercially success-ful rock bands at the time. One of *Aktion '68*'s members had formerly managed the famous band and was able to persuade them to appear on the campus.[1] Over 1,000 students showed up and squeezed into a space designed for a few hundred to revel in the 'beat ecstasy', as the local student paper reported.[2] The stunt helped the new centre-right group to win the largest number of seats in elections to the Bonn student parliament, held shortly thereafter.

Exactly one year later, in January 1969, a piece entitled 'Housewife and Mother: Stereotypes of Femininity. Thoughts on Emancipation and Discrimination' ran in the Christian Democratic student magazine *Facts*. 'Using classic circular argu-ments, conservative and reactionary family ideologues exploit the fact that today's woman is still raised and judged based on family-oriented values to reason that women are "naturally" more family-oriented', its anonymous author explained.[3] The monothematic publications of the fashion and leisure industry groomed women for their constricted roles, the article went on. 'The staid housewife romanticism of the old days is simply revived in a consumption-friendly variant through images of the fashionable and cosmetically enhanced nibble and petting female [*Nasch- und Streichelweibchen*].' It then called for the overcoming of 'authoritarian-patriarchal structures', a task the author identified as one of the most important challenges to contemporary society. However, they also cautioned that it had to be tackled by democrats and not left up to 'extremist groups' of the Left. 'Emancipation does not equal revolution', the piece concluded.[4]

Calls to smash the patriarchy, references to musical 'ecstasy', and constructivist readings of gender roles that critiqued the consumer industry are likely not the first things that readers would associate with centre-right students in the 1960s. As

---

[1] Aretz interview.

[2] *Akut: Nachrichtenblatt der Bonner Studentenschaft*, 38 (February 1968), 11.

[3] HIS, Sammlung Studentenbewegung, Studentische Verbände, RCDS, 'Hausfrau und Mutter, Stereotypen der Weiblichkeit. Gedanken zur Emanzipation und Diskriminierung', *Facts*, (20 January 1969), 4.

[4] The original piece was published anonymously, but, a few years later, parts of the article were reprinted under the byline of Thomas G. Vetterlein as 'Sie heiratet ja doch', *Demokratische Blätter*, 2 (WS 1971/72). 4. It is unclear if Vetterlein was the author of the original text.

The Other '68ers: Student Protest and Christian Democracy in West Germany. Anna von der Goltz,
Oxford University Press (2021). © Anna von der Goltz. DOI: 10.1093/oso/9780198849520.003.0004

we saw in the first chapter, they were certainly on the move politically in the latter part of the decade, questioning the status quo and calling for greater democratic participation. What does their apparent embrace of feminist rhetoric and pop music mean for our understanding of their involvement in 1968? Was the personal political for centre-right students? Did they embrace the cultural revolt and women's emancipation?

This chapter focuses on the experiences of centre-right women and the cultural practices of centre-right students more generally to assess to what extent they participated in the broader cultural moment that was 1968. The first part of the chapter examines different forms of cultural expression and everyday aesthetics, such as corporeal habits, fashion, music, and design, to investigate whether centre-right activists viewed these as political. The second part of the chapter deals with sexuality: how centre-right activists talked about sexuality as well as their attitudes towards the evident modernization of sexuality in West Germany in this period. The final section centres women's experiences. It analyses changing gender roles and centre-right women's attitudes towards the emerging women's movement to understand why at least some on the centre-right thought that emancipation did not necessarily equal revolution.

Reforming the World, (Not) Changing the Self?

The years around 1968 were about much more than young activists trying to affect change through organized politics and formal institutions.[5] The student Left's critique of West German society grew ever more all-encompassing and increasingly extended into the private and personal realm. Activists believed that the conformism of western societies was structural and that authoritarian traits were deeply ingrained, including in individual people. Accordingly, they were convinced that changing the world required changing the self.

Inspired by New Left ideas, not least Marcuse's, about the need to create new people freed from their capitalist conditioning and 'false needs', leftist students championed a radical individualism aimed at breaking internal chains and developed new forms of cultural protest, such as new artistic and musical happenings. These practices expanded the realm of what was understood as political, and activists increasingly expressed their radical ideas in corporeal terms: long loose hair on women and long hair on men, beards, colourful and exotic clothes, casual

---

[5] Brown, *West Germany and the Global 1960s*; Davis et al., *Changing the World, Changing Oneself*; Reichardt, *Authentizität und Gemeinschaft*; Timothy Brown and Andrew Lison (eds.), *The Global Sixties in Sound and Vision: Media, Counterculture, Revolt* (London, 2014), 1; Biess, *Republik der Angst*, chapters 6 and 7.

behaviour, and an ostentatious informality became distinctive displays and embodiments of a new kind of politics in the late 1960s.[6]

Changing oneself and one's social relationships in an effort to broaden one's consciousness and radically transform the world neither fit centre-right activists' gradualist inclinations nor their much narrower and more traditional conception of what politics entailed. While some on the 1968 Left and growing numbers of people within the emerging alternative scene began to embrace recreational drug use to facilitate a sense of community, awakening, and self-actualization, for instance, centre-right activists, for the most part, rejected such self-experiments and their political premise.[7] Peter Radunski, for one, who, as we saw in the previous chapters, was in many other ways drawn to the student Left, stressed that this attraction did not extend to forms of radical cultural experimentation. 'The line for me, the borderline was: the widening of the senses with LSD and so on.'[8] His one-time co-author Jürgen-Bernd Runge, a centre-right renegade, did try drugs. Tellingly though, he did not experiment until a few years after he had broken off his ties to the Christian Democrats and when he was hitchhiking in Goa, India's hippie enclave.[9]

Centre-right interviewees for this book did not just recall shunning consciousness-altering substances; they generally emphasized that they had subscribed to conventional social norms and rituals at a time when these were widely being questioned in a quest for a more authentic self.[10] Such retrospective self-descriptions were reinforced by the exceedingly polite and formal manner in which the interviewees for this book usually received me, as well as by the distinctly bourgeois settings in which most of the interviews took place: neatly kept suburban bungalows or one-family homes in which the wives of male interviewees often served refreshments, restaurants in upmarket hotels, or office suites. These scenes stood in contrast to the ostentatious insistence on authenticity, egalitarian habitus—not just expressed through the use of the informal 'du' in conversation—and expressed scepticism towards suspected performances of social conformism on my part that I often encountered in many of the equally bourgeois, but mostly urban apartments in old buildings where I interviewed left-wing '68ers for a previous book.[11]

Around 1968, in fact, some on the centre-right had consciously adopted a conventional bourgeois posture to distinguish themselves from their more casual

---

[6] Reichardt, *Authentizität und Gemeinschaft*, 634–49; Fahlenbrach, *Protest-Inszenierungen*, 12.

[7] Will Morris, 'Spiel Appeal: Play, Drug Use and the Culture of 1968 in West Germany', *Journal of Contemporary History*, 49, 4 (2014), 770–93; Reichardt, *Authentizität und Gemeinschaft*, 831–54.

[8] Radunski interview.

[9] *Runge Private Papers*, Jürgen-Bernd Runge, 'Die Etappen meiner Indien-Trampreise 1971. 5 Monate: vom 31. Juli bis zum 21. Dezember 1971' [7 January 2010].

[10] Reichardt, *Authentizität und Gemeinschaft*, 55–66; Charles Taylor, *The Ethics of Authenticity* (Cambridge, 1992).

[11] Gildea, Mark, and Warring, *Europe's 1968*.

peers on the Left—such as when the alleged Christian Democratic 'Provo' Klaus Laepple entered a Cologne courtroom in early 1967 wearing a smart blazer and carrying a briefcase to demonstrate to the judge that he was no ordinary student rebel. Or when Horst Teltschik, who had grown a beard in high school that, he remembered, had earned him the nickname 'Fidel', shaved again as a student because beards conjured up images of left-wing protest and were frowned upon within the CDU.[12] When he taught seminars in political science at the Free University in the late 1960s, he always dressed quite conservatively in the classroom and elsewhere on campus, he stressed. '[I] did not have to walk around as grubby as they were. So, I consciously wore a tie to the lectures that I gave.'[13] Likewise, while still in RCDS and fashioning himself as Dutschke's centre-right counterpart, Jürgen-Bernd Runge was in his 'bow tie phase', as he later recalled with notable ironic detachment to distance himself from his former political self.[14] Christian Democratic students in Bonn—one of the centre-right's strongholds— took it even further when they set up an 'Association for Elevating Table Manners in the Cafeteria'. Wolfgang Reeder, one of the club's founders, outlined its members' motivations thus:

> We found that the behaviour and appearance of the students was not appropriate. And we then commissioned many of us to bring ordinary, white tablecloths, ordinary dinnerware and cutlery. And we all came in dark suits and the ladies in evening wear. And we made a show of it![15]

While he claimed that they were trying to be ironic and self-deprecating by performing a stereotype of Christian Democrats as obstinate reactionaries, he equally stressed that the stunt was meant to delineate them from their 'slovenly colleagues from the [leftist] camp'. The symbolic practices, habitus, and styles of activists from different political camps differed considerably—and could be carefully cultivated features of cultural distinction.[16]

Tangible though these stylistic differences may have been, we should be careful not to overemphasize them. Stereotypes of longhaired communards in shaggy

---

[12] Teltschik interview; Heiko Gebhardt, 'Wir waren Demokraten', *Stern* (1 May 1988), 190; Jürgen Wahl, 'Impressionen von einer Revolution in verträglicher Dosis', *Christ und Welt/Rheinischer Merkur* (20 May 1988). His friend Wulf Schönbohm recalled that he was told explicitly that as a CDU man he could not have a beard and should shave. Schönbohm interview; Radunski confirmed that Schönbohm's beard made him suspect. They initially thought he was a 'left-wing U-boat'. Radunski interview.

[13] Teltschik interview.

[14] Runge interview; see the photograph of the bow-tied Runge in chapter 1 (66). On ironic detachment as a mode of self-reflection, Portelli, 'What makes oral history different?', 54.

[15] Reeder interview; Lawrence Black notes a similar penchant for bow-ties and ball gowns among otherwise quite rebellious young British Conservative activists in the late 1960s. See Black, '1968 and All That(cher)', 363.

[16] Pierre Bourdieu, *Distinction: A Social Critique of the Judgement of Taste* (Cambridge, MA, 1984).

clothing on one side and neatly dressed, bow-tied conservative youth dining on white tablecloth on the other fail to capture the breadth and intricacies of cultural change in the 1960s. The dynamic modernization of West German society had already taken off in the late 1950s, and it brought greater social liberalization and pluralism in its wake. Demographic changes and the growing opportunities for consumption and leisure pursuits went hand in hand with an erosion of traditional milieus and a fundamental transformation of mentalities. They opened up countless new ways to express oneself, particularly among West German youth.[17]

Centre-right women, for instance, embraced the mini skirt, a new piece of clothing popularized by the British designer Mary Quandt that quickly turned into a symbol of growing female confidence. Like the full beard on men, however, the mini skirt often connoted 'leftist' in the popular imagination, especially outside major cities. 'The leaflet-distributing ladies of the RCDS should not wear mini-skirts because it would be suspected that they belong to the APO', cautioned a female RCDS activist in Erlangen in May 1968, but quickly added 'why actually, is unclear'.[18]

On the other side, men on the Left were much slower to shed their suit jackets and ties than the iconography of the protest movement suggests, and most activists of the centre-right eventually adopted a more casual style, particularly from the late 1960s onward. When pollsters from the Allensbach Institute personally interviewed 1,000 West German students in mid-1966 for a study commissioned by *Der Spiegel*, they observed that most students' style was impossible to distinguish from that of their white-collar age peers. The pollsters from the conservative institute were tasked explicitly with recording their impressions of students' appearance. Eighty-nine per cent dressed in a way they considered 'normal', they noted, and only around 2 per cent of students appeared 'shabby' to them. Only 1 per cent of those interviewed, most of them students in the humanities and social sciences, sported a 'Beatles haircut', they documented.[19]

Photographs from the mid-1960s indeed suggest that student activists across the political divide often still dressed quite formally, with male students clean shaven and sporting short hair and suit jackets and women neat skirts or dresses, including at demonstrations.[20] Pictures from the 1970s, by contrast, illustrate that woolly sweaters, full beards, and longer hair on men had lost their countercultural

---

[17] Axel Schildt, *Moderne Zeiten: Freizeit, Massenmedien und Zeitgeist in der Bundesrepublik der 50er Jahre* (Hamburg, 1995); idem, 'Materieller Wohlstand—pragmatische Politik—kulturelle Umbrüche. Die 60er Jahre der Bundesrepublik', in Schildt, Siegfried, and Lammers, *Dynamische Zeiten*, 21–53; Sedlmaier and Malinowski, '"1968"—A Catalyst of Consumer Society'.

[18] ACDP, 4/6/14/1, Helga Griesheimer, 'Ein unsachlicher Veranstaltungsbericht zum Monat Mai 68', in: *Forum-Aktuell*. A young woman in a mini skirt is also featured prominently in an MSU brochure, in: IfZ, ED738/23.

[19] 'Was denken die Studenten', *Der Spiegel*, 26 (19 June 1967), 29; BAK, ZSG 132, 1363/II, 'Der deutsche Student: Kommentar des Instituts für Demoskopie Allensbach zur Spiegel-Umfrage'.

[20] E.g. the photographs of SDS activists Christoph Strawe and Heidrun Lotz in April 1968, in Bothien, *Protest und Provokation*, 15; also Reichardt, *Authentizität und Gemeinschaft*, 631.

connotation and become mainstream within a few short years. At a time when subcultural styles had become ever more differentiated, aesthetic choices that might still have been marked as 'shabby' in the late 1960s were no longer perceived as such. This was also true among Christian Democratic student leaders, who now looked much more dishevelled than their 1960s predecessors.[21] By 1976, Christian Democratic students in Heidelberg sought to garner votes for their group with a sketch of a young man with scruffy hair and a full beard, who, they stressed, had been a member of the local RCDS for several years.[22] Such portrayals involved some wishful thinking and were no doubt partly intended to counter persistent stereotypes about male reactionaries populating the group. Nevertheless, it is clear that the broader social and cultural changes of the 1960s, which, as recent research has rightly emphasized, were not so much the result as a cause of 1968, reached centre-right students with considerable force.[23]

Rock 'n' roll—a musical style Germans captured under the Anglicism 'beat'—in particular, was a big part of the cultural shift that marked the 1960s. Although they were far less adventurous when it came to cultural (self-)experiments than their peers on the Left, centre-right students embraced the popular music of the era. Many older conservative cultural critics had initially viewed the music and style of British bands such as *The Beatles*, the even more scandalous *The Rolling Stones* and *The Who* as a dangerous attack on authority and traditional German values. Nonetheless, their music quickly developed mass appeal among young West Germans—an appeal that offered fewer and fewer clues as to fans' political views or affiliation, as Detlef Siegfried and others have shown.[24] Contemporary press reports may have conflated the rise of 'beat' music and left-wing protest in West Germany, because both phenomena occurred more or less simultaneously, but the dynamism and anti-authoritarian habitus of rock bands also spoke to centre-right students who were growing restive in this period. Many centre-right interviewees recalled going to rock concerts and being touched by the rebellious sounds of the years around 1968. Wulf Schönbohm, who was federal chair of

---

[21] Similar observations were made regarding the evolving styles of fraternity students. Joachim Neander, 'Die Burschenschaften wandeln sich', *Burschenschaftliche Blätter*, 83, 10/11 (1968), 207–8; Detlef Siegfried cites a number of surveys to illustrate the spread of long hair among West German men in the 1970s. Siegfried, *Time Is on My Side*, 394–6; also Reichardt, *Authentizität und Gemeinschaft*, 646–7. Tellingly, long hair and t-shirts were also *de rigeur* among British and French conservative students in the 1970s. See Daniel Gordon, 'Liquidating May '68. Generational Trajectories of the 2007 Presidential Elections', in *Modern and Contemporary France* 16, 2 (2008), 143–59; Black, '1968 and all That(cher)'.

[22] See the brochure 'Wahlen' (1976), in ACDP, 04-037-006/4.

[23] von Hodenberg and Siegfried (eds.), *Wo '1968' liegt. Reform und Revolte in der Geschichte der Bundesrepublik* (Göttingen, 2006); Schildt, Siegfried, and Lammers, *Dynamische Zeiten*; Frese, Paulus, and Teppe, *Demokratisierung und gesellschaftlicher Aufbruch*.

[24] Siegfried, *Time Is On My Side*, 238–55; idem, 'Vom Teenager zur Pop-Revolution: Politisierungstendenzen in der westdeutschen Jugendkultur 1959 bis 1968', in Schildt, Siegfried, Lammers, *Dynamische Zeiten*, 582–623; Brown, *West Germany and the Global 1960s*, 155–92; and Beate Kutschke and Barley Norton (eds.), *Music and Protest in 1968* (Cambridge, 2013).

RCDS in 1967/68, for one, recalled seeing *The Beatles* at the Star-Club when, in the early 1960s, he lived in Hamburg as a trainee officer in the *Bundeswehr*, and liking 'the music quite a bit'.[25]

Friedbert Pflüger, a leading figure in Christian Democratic student politics in the 1970s, later recalled having been quite offended by assumptions others made about his musical preferences, which they assumed to be much more square and traditional because of his politics. He recalled that he had once taken a woman home who, upon finding a Santana record in his collection, told him that she was surprised to learn that he listened to a band that had played at the infamous Woodstock festival of 1969:

[She said:] 'What? A right-winger listens to Santana?' She could not conceive of that. She probably thought that [it would be] Roy Black or something like that, I do not know what she envisioned. Or Tony Marshall or something. She couldn't get over it; she had a completely different picture of someone on the right.[26]

Given such stereotypes about conservatives' anti-modernism, championing popular music could be a useful tool for centre-right activists to project a progressive image and even garner votes. After all, when Bonn's *Aktion '68* hosted *The Rattles* in the university cafeteria in January 1968, they were showcasing the fun-loving and apolitical image of a group that saw itself primarily as an advocate of student interests. This 'happening' turned into a huge success for the newly founded student organization, which quickly became a household name in Bonn. The university's official student newspaper opined that the musical ecstasy provided by *The Rattles* had been far more important than *Aktion '68*'s political platform in garnering student support:

Regardless of political conviction, the beat proved once again to be a means of strong attraction for a mass event [. . .]. Political discussions did not even occur. The masses fell into the beat ecstasy [. . .]. Maybe the electoral success of Aktion '68 can be explained by the fact that so many undecided people rewarded the successful happening with their vote.[27]

In May 1968, the RCDS in West Berlin similarly tried to woo students with popular sounds, even if their 'bop' with 'May wine [a sweet punch, AvdG] and

---

[25] Schönbohm interview.

[26] Pflüger interview. Roy Black was a German schlager singer, whose romantic single *Ganz in Weiss*, a song about a white wedding, was one of the biggest German hits of 1966/7. Tony Marshall was also a schlager singer. He rose to fame with a song called *Pretty Maid* in 1971.

[27] *Akut: Nachrichtenblatt der Bonner Studentenschaft*, 38 (February 1968), 11.

hard beat' remained much smaller in scale and did not pay off in the same way at the polls.[28]

Conscious of the need to shed lingering suspicions of conservative stuffiness, student groups of the centre-right went to considerable lengths to project a modern and forward-looking image in all sorts of other ways as well. Aesthetic choices mattered greatly in this respect. When former RCDS leaders Wulf Schönbohm, Peter Radunski, and others set up their new journal *Sonde* in late 1968, they did not just envisage the publication as a forum for Christian Democratic debate and new intellectual content. They also sought to express its progressive spirit through its unusual elongated format—a move that in some ways replicated the performative character of a New Left publication like *Kursbuch* whose experimental design was in itself a medium of protest.[29] Radunski later recalled that '[W]hen designing the *Sonde*, I always had the picture in my mind that a chic, elegant female student wore this small, overlong newspaper as a fashion accessory under her arm. A little aesthetic cannot harm politics', he stated.[30]

The Student Unions were often even savvier when it came to appropriating styles more commonly associated with the Left. In late May and early June 1968, Cologne's *Aktion '67*, for instance, organized an exhibition of original student posters from what would soon be known simply as the 'French May'. Over the previous weeks, the French capital had been rocked by student protests and workers' strikes, bringing life in the capital almost to a standstill. Louis F. Peters, a centre-right student from Cologne was in Paris at this time and got involved with student activists from the Sorbonne who occupied the Odéon theatre. Before he left Paris, he took numerous posters that had been produced in the École des Beaux Arts from the walls around the Sorbonne and brought them with him to Germany to stage the first ever display of such works.[31]

Around the same time, the Bonn Student Union began to lure its readers with colourful and playful imagery in a glossy new magazine, tellingly named *Pop-Kurier*. Its design differed from many left-wing publications of the time, which typically adopted a grittier, DIY aesthetic, but its editors were clearly determined to highlight that they equally kept up with the changing times. A 1969 election special featured local centre-right activist Maria-Theresia van Schewick on the cover. With her fashionably short crop and beret, the 20-year old's look was reminiscent of Jean Seberg, the protagonist of Jean-Luc Godard's 1960 film *Breathless*, one of the earliest pieces of French New Wave cinema that quickly

---

[28] HIA, GSC, Box 85, invitation signed by Peter Philipp (29 April 1968).

[29] Peter Schweppe, 'The Politics of Removal: Kursbuch and the West German Protest Movement', *The Sixties*, 7, 2 (2014), 138–54.

[30] Radunski, *Aus der politischen Kulisse*, 40. Radunski here erroneously dates the publication of the first issue of *Sonde* to 1971.

[31] Holl and Glunz, *1968 am Rhein*, 74–5.

Illustration 3.1 The Bonn Student Union's magazine *Pop-Kurier* (January 1969). On the cover: Maria-Theresia ('Musch') van Schewick, BSU activist and future RCDS national deputy chair.

(Hoover Institution Archives, German subject collection, box no. 85)

became a classic. Van Schewick favoured this style privately, too. She later proudly recalled that she had driven a Citroën 2 CV—a coveted mark of distinction among students at the time who sought to project their individuality—and smoked Gauloises without a filter, another symbol of French liberté.[32] A photograph in the same election special showed a 24-year old male candidate for the Bonn student parliament in a self-consciously casual pose, a cigarette dangling from one hand, the other making the 'peace' sign with two fingers. Instead of a suit or formal jacket, he was wearing a white T-shirt—then a new item of clothing with considerable symbolic capital.[33]

'None of Us Thought that You Weren't Supposed to Sleep with the Same Woman Twice'

For the most part, it was not images of a casual and de-militarized masculinity that sought to project social progressiveness.[34] Images of young women—often, like van Schewick, centre-right activists themselves—promoted this goal more effortlessly. At a time when a so-called 'sex wave' swept across West Germany, flooding the public sphere with sexually explicit articles and imagery, centre-right publications, too, realized that sex—and more specifically female nudity—sells.[35]

From 1967/68 onward, they increasingly featured images of young women in suggestive poses. In 1968, Detlef Stronk, who had run the Munich Student Union's victorious campaign in 1967 and who would later run Eberhard Diepgen's campaigns in West Berlin, passed on campaign advice to Christian Democratic students across the country that made the objective explicit. To replicate the MSU's success, he recommended 'A cheeky election newspaper with a sexy girl on the front page and the slogan below: "Let's do it! Vote..."' Make sure to obtain first-class (!!!) photos of the candidates!'[36]

Many groups took the hint. A brochure issued by the Bonn RCDS in November 1969, for instance, included a still from the 1968 film *Go for it, Baby* (*Zur Sache,*

---

[32] van Schewick interview; on the symbolism of the 2 CV among students, see Siegfried, *Time Is On My Side*, 273–4.

[33] HIA, GSC, Pop-Kurier, Wahlexpress (28 January 1969). On the symbolic value of the T-shirt in 1960s West Germany see the autobiographical reminiscences of author and SDS activist Peter Schneider. Peter Schneider, *Rebellion und Wahn: Mein '68* (Cologne, 2008), 19.

[34] Ute Frevert, 'Umbruch der Geschlechterverhältnisse? Die 60er Jahre als geschlechterpolitischer Experimentierraum', in Schildt, Siegfried, Lammers, *Dynamische Zeiten*, 658; Siegfried, *Time Is On My Side*, 255–62; Reichardt, *Authentizität und Gemeinschaft*, 638–9.

[35] See Dagmar Herzog, *Sex after Fascism: Memory and Morality in Twentieth-century Germany* (Princeton, NJ, 2005), 141–54; Sibylle Steinbacher, *Wie der Sex nach Deutschland kam: Der Kampf um Sittlichkeit und Anstand in der frühen Bundesrepublik* (Munich, 2011).

[36] ArchAPO, RCDS, file 'RCDS-Brief', Detlef Stronk, 'Einige Erfahrungen aus dem siegreichen Münchner Wahlkampf', *RCDS-Brief*, 6 (1968), n.p.; the Munich Student Union had won the largest number of seats in the local student parliament with this very imagery and slogan. See the MSU brochure in IfZ, ED 0738–23.

Schätzchen), a cult product of the New German Cinema. The photograph showed the lead actor Uschi Glas in her underwear.[37] Centre-right groups also used similar images of female nudity in an explicit attempt to woo students away from their opponents on the left. 'Wouldn't you be tempted by the other side(s)?', the Munich Student Union asked in 1969 next to a picture of a pigtailed, naked young woman shown from behind.[38]

Early on, such images were still quite tame, although they were already accompanied by slogans full of sexual innuendo. A 1968 brochure by the Göttingen RCDS, for instance, featured two attractive, but rather prim blondes in white, ruffled night dresses above the slogan 'You should know what this is about...'[39] The imagery quickly became more risqué, however. In a nod to the popular adult magazine *Playboy*, the Cologne Student Union graced its campaign materials with an 'election bunny', a young woman who was pictured with her shirt fully unbuttoned and her breasts partially exposed.[40] In late 1968, the Action Committee of Democratic Students (*Aktionskomitee Demokratischer Studenten*, ADS), a Frankfurt am Main-based centre-right student group, advertised with the help of a scantily-clad blonde with long, loose hair and sultry look.[41] By 1971, the student paper of the RCDS in Bonn presented its own blonde 'starlet', now completely topless, alongside images of other semi-naked women.[42] The contrast between such sexualized imagery and the overly sober and old-fashioned photographs of the male candidates for the student parliament that were featured in the same issue (among them future Christian Democratic stars, such as Gerd Langguth and Peter Hintze) obviously did not strike the editors as insensitive or discriminating at the time. Nor did it seem to raise fears that the men would look boring in comparison. As we will see below, however, this kind of juxtaposition would create tensions between male and female activists once centre-right groups began to grapple with the critique of overly sexualized and sexist advertising that originated in second-wave feminism and the women's movement.[43]

---

[37] ACDP, 01/365/068 'Zur Sache', Broschüre zur Wahl vom 24.–27. November 1969; on the film's reception, Heiko Stoff, '"Ungeheuer schlaff". Der Film "Zur Sache, Schätzchen" (1968)—Über Leistungsdenken und Gedankenspiele', in: *Zeithistorische Forschungen*, 11, 3 (2014), 500–7. Glas was a fitting choice for the cover; she later revealed that she had been very critical of the countercultural spirit of '1968'. Uschi Glas, 'In der Früh pünktlich ans Film-Set zu kommen und auch noch geduscht zu sein, das war damals verpönt', in: *Süddeutsche Zeitung Magazin*, 8, (2008), available at http://sz-magazin.sueddeutsche.de/texte/anzeigen/4493/Uschi-Glas (accessed on 10 April 2014).

[38] HIA, GSC, box 85, P.S.: Presse der Studenten 1/2 (8 May 1969).

[39] ACDP, 004/6/121/4, brochure of the RCDS Göttingen (1968).

[40] Holl and Glunz, *1968 am Rhein*, 73.

[41] ACDP, 4/6/63/1, ADS leaflet *Kontrapunkt*, Information no. 2, Frankfurt (October 1968).

[42] HIA, GSC, Box 85, *Aktuell* (20 January 1971).

[43] Langguth, for one, had already demonstrated his insensitivity in this regard as chair of the Bonn Student Council. When thirty female students from SDS set up a 'Working Group Emancipation', Langguth published its programme in the official student newspaper *Akut*, but illustrated the article with pictures of bare-breasted women. See von Hodenberg, *Das andere Achtundsechzig*, 105.

While this sexualized imagery was very similar to many of the visuals in left-wing student publications at the time, former centre-right students often suggested that their attitudes towards sexuality and sexual practices had actually differed markedly from the radical Left's permissiveness and promiscuity. From 1967 onward, new sites of political and cultural experimentation emerged on the West German Left. Most famous were the so-called communes—shared living spaces in which radical left-wing activists sought to overcome the constraints of the nuclear family and put their ideas of a better society into practice by revolutionizing the self.[44] Such living collectives, most famously West Berlin's Kommune 1, whose inhabitants had been active in the anti-authoritarian wing of the local SDS until they were ousted in May 1967, caught the attention of a national news media fascinated by sensationalized tales of sexual debauchery and drug consumption.[45] The members of Kommune 1 became true media stars and their commune a kind of negative foil onto which bourgeois readers and audiences projected their fears of social disorder. This despite the fact that, as recent research has emphasized, the lived reality of communal life was much more timid and sexually repressed than its glossy representations.[46]

The media portrayal of the communards nevertheless gave centre-right activists the chance to differentiate themselves by emphasizing their rejection of the more radical cultural practices of the era. For all their alleged criticism of their authoritarian elders in the Christian Democratic parties, they did not seek to overthrow all social norms, especially not monogamous, heterosexual relationships. 'Of course, I rejected this whole communal thing. I was rather on the conservative side. I wanted to marry and have children, and that is how it played out. Of course, these bourgeois virtues were very important', recalled Detlef Stronk who had been active in RCDS and the Munich Student Union.[47] 'I was [...] socialized in a very conventional bourgeois way. And in terms of communal living, I would have never even thought of that. So, I would have nothing to do with it', concurred Jürgen Klemann of the West Berlin RCDS.[48] Like some others, Horst Teltschik invoked his Catholic upbringing to explain why he personally rejected the possibilities for sexual libertinism, which, he was nevertheless keen to stress, certainly existed at the time for a young man of his age.

There was no one who slept freely with girls in our RCDS. I had a girlfriend and was absolutely faithful. So, I did not like that. Of course, that was also due to my

---

[44] Reichardt *Authentizität und Gemeinschaft*, 104–15; 351–408; for other European examples, see John Davis and Juliane Fürst, 'Drop-outs', in Gildea, Mark, and Warring, *Europe's 1968*, 193–210.
[45] Reimann, *Kunzelmann*, 123–44; Siegfried, *Time Is On My Side*, 506–20; and idem, 'Stars der Revolte'; Sedlmaier, *Consumption and Violence*.
[46] Reimann, *Kunzelmann*, 170; Reichardt, *Authentizität und Gemeinschaft*, 679–85.
[47] Stronk interview. Wulf Schönbohm made very similar observations about these cultural-political boundaries in a 1988 interview. 'Die 68er der CDU', *Zeit-Magazin*, 33 (12 August 1988).
[48] Klemann interview.

Catholic upbringing. But, I mean, the opportunity would surely have been there. I do not know if others did it.[49]

Martin Kempe, one of the Christian Democratic renegades from West Berlin, recalled that he had only begun to experiment with 'free love' once he had left RCDS along with other 'renegades' in May 1968. His political conversion and departure from the group went hand in hand with a personal and emotional transformation that reached deeply into his private life.

I mean, the era of '68 was not just a political movement, but also a cultural movement, with free love and so forth. And of course I joined in too. And in retrospect I have to say, in RCDS and the people there, that was just boring. [...] So I experienced [...] [the exit from the group] as a kind of liberation, an expansion of my potential for development, of my interests, my knowledge, my feeling. [...] That basically was my belated [...] libertarian phase in terms of lifestyle, so well, what do I know, well, lots of girlfriends and such.[50]

As much as they emphasized their rejection of the alleged promiscuity on the Left, some centre-right men clearly also begrudged their political opponents what they imagined to be an infinite number of sexual conquests. As Wulf Schönbohm admitted to an interviewer twenty years later: 'We observed the experiments in communal living with a mixture of fascination, jealousy, and condemnation.'[51] Former activists often suggested that the Left's superior public profile had drawn admiring and sexually available women into the Left's orbit.

Studies by West German sexologists and reports in the press had likely amplified these impressions. In 1968, *Der Spiegel* reported on a survey that the Hamburg-based Institute of Sexuality Research had conducted among West German students from twelve universities throughout 1966. The researchers had found that women who identified as socialist were the most sexually liberated and most sexually adventurous group. Eighty per cent of female socialist students had intercourse, the paper reported, while conservative women were significantly less sexually experienced and adventurous. The differences between men with divergent political views were much less pronounced, the study had found.[52] Such reports help to explain a long-standing sense of inferiority. 'There weren't that many girls back then. Unfortunately, I have to say, because as a young student it would have been quite pleasurable. I have to admit that the Left had the chic women back then', as one former activist who later went into politics put it, his

---

[49] Teltschik interview.   [50] Kempe interview.
[51] 'Die 68er der CDU', *Die Zeit*, 33 (12 August 1988).
[52] Hans Giese and Gunter Schmidt, *Studenten-Sexualiät: Verhalten und Einstellung: Eine Umfrage an 12 westdeutschen Universitäten* (Reinbek near Hamburg, 1968), 295–6. 'Studenten: Sex-Report', *Spiegel*, 35 (1968), 46–50.

envy still palpable many decades later.[53] Another interviewee, who was a prominent figure in RCDS in the 1970s, concurred. 'I always thought the girls on the Left were much better. The good women always go to the communists. I suffered from this', he admitted.[54]

Such sexual anxieties were also reflected in contemporary RCDS materials. In the 1970s, the RCDS issued a poster that depicted a topless man with longish, messy hair and moustache, smoking a cigarillo and wearing an RCDS button, his arm wrapped proudly around the buttocks of an attractive naked woman pictured from behind. A slogan printed over her naked buttocks read 'Types we also attract'. Another slogan printed underneath the man read 'Types who vote RCDS'. It is probably safe to assume that the scene it depicted was quite far

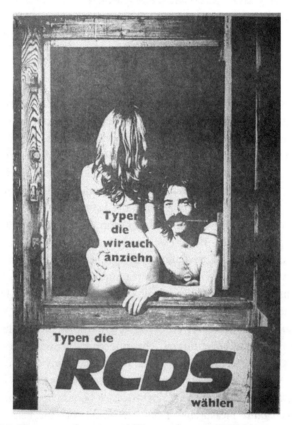

Illustration 3.2 'Types we also attract.' 'Types who vote RCDS.'
(RCDS poster, n. d. [1970s])

---

[53] Anonymous interview.
[54] Anonymous interview. Similar recollections in Hacke, '68: Fluch oder Segen?'.

removed from the lived experience of most Christian Democratic 'types'. But it tells us a great deal about male insecurities, the attempt to counter persistent stereotypes, and the ways in which centre-right men projected onto their peers on the Left a manly coolness and confident, casual sexuality that they envied.

Although centre-right activists did not seek to attack bourgeois morality per se, the changing times nevertheless went hand in hand with a rethinking and loosening of numerous social conventions. For many, this involved a distancing from the Christian moral teachings that had provided the ethical foundations of their upbringing. Many interviewees for this book, much like centre-right activists in the 1960s more generally, had been socialized in religious institutions—very often Catholic—from church schools to confessional youth organizations that initially thrived in postwar Germany. This web of religious socialization became increasingly frayed after 1968 as Germans, especially young people, left the churches in droves. But even prior to the Second Vatican Council and the height of the youth revolt of the late 1960s, the binding force of social conventions based on strict religious norms had weakened considerably as a result of demographic shifts, the economic miracle, and the resulting erosion of traditional confessional milieus.[55]

The questioning of religiously inspired social norms played out most clearly when it came to the issue of sexual relations before marriage, which centre-right activists, along with the overwhelming majority of West German students, approved of in the late 1960s.[56] The penal code had not yet caught up with these liberalized attitudes, however. Until 1972, §180 of the West German criminal code—also known as the 'pimping law' [Kuppeleiparagraph]—meant that parents, landlords, and hotel owners could face several years in prison if they allowed unmarried couples to sleep in the same room or cohabitate. Christian Democratic activists recalled that, like many of their sexually active student peers, they had found ways around this. 'Of course, for us that was completely out of the question, and we would not even dream that we would take part in that and of course we took our freedoms', remembered Meinhard Ade of the Freiburg RCDS. Invoking a much-cited, radical slogan of the time, he suggested that the centre-right's desire to uphold societal norms and create distance to the radical Left had its limits. 'None of us thought that you weren't supposed to sleep with the same woman twice. But we also didn't think that we weren't supposed to sleep with any woman.'[57]

---

[55] Mark Edward Ruff, *The Wayward Flock: Catholic Youth in Postwar West Germany* (Chapel Hill, NC, and London, 2005), 6; Großbölting, *Losing Heaven*, 94–110.

[56] The above-mentioned Hamburg survey found that fewer than 10 per cent of those surveyed thought that premarital sex was impermissible or morally wrong. Giese and Schmidt, *Studenten-Sexualität*, 218.

[57] Ade interview.

Detlef Stronk, who had been raised Catholic, related that the quest to overcome rigid social norms based on religious teachings united students of the Left and Right. 'This piece of liberation, against the religious insistence in matters of sexuality, with my attitude towards life, I was fully in line with the Left.'[58] Ursula Männle of the Bavarian RCDS likewise recalled that, in the 1960s, she threw overboard most of the moral principles that had been instilled in her in an all-girls convent school. Contrary to many of her male student peers, who married and had children early, she lived with her partner without marrying him for many decades. 'So, things like that, I disregarded. And that was not easy at all coming from the family background that I came from.'[59] Even former Bonn student leader Wolfgang Reeder, a Protestant, who stressed that Christian ethics in other ways continued to be an important source of his political beliefs, declared that the Church's moral teachings on sexuality had become 'irrelevant' to him by 1968. 'So, for us too, who openly embraced the "C" [the Christian element in Christian Democracy], these classical moral values no longer played any role. They did not matter to us at all.' His girlfriends all took the contraceptive pill. 'That was completely natural', he remembered.[60]

Opinion surveys conducted in the late 1960s indeed showed that, in spite of considerable societal resistance and the Catholic Church's opposition to 'unlawful birth control methods' (as laid out in Pope Paul VI's encyclical letter Humanae vitae issued on 25 July 1968), only a tiny fraction of students was still opposed to the use of contraceptives. 'The question of the morality of contraception is no longer seriously discussed even among the most restrictive groups of students', reported the Institute of Sexuality Research in 1968.[61]

As a case in point, Ingrid Reichart-Dreyer, one of the few visible women activists in the West Berlin RCDS in the late 1960s, recalled matter-of-factly that she had, of course, been on the pill. She generally portrayed her attitude towards the body and sexuality as having been very relaxed. Her parents had been quite open in matters of sexuality and had often taken her on vacation to the Baltic coast's nudist beaches, she related. As a result, she saw no need to politicize sexuality, as parts of the radical Left were prone to do, or to revolutionize attitudes towards the body. She had once visited West Berlin's Kommune 2, which partly

---

[58] Stronk interview; see also Karl Gabriel, 'Zwischen Aufbruch und Absturz in die Moderne. Die katholische Kirche in den 60er Jahren', in Schildt, Siegfried, Lammers, Dynamische Zeiten, 538; Chappel, Catholic Modern.

[59] Männle interview.

[60] Reeder interview. Although Reeder was Protestant, this is similar to what Mark Edward Ruff terms 'cafeteria Catholicism'. He argued that young people in postwar West Germany increasingly decided themselves which parts of religious teaching to adopt and which parts to discard. Ruff, The Wayward Flock, 62.

[61] Giese and Schmidt, Studenten-Sexualität, 288. Only 5 per cent of female students and 3 per cent of male students rejected the use of contraceptives or thought it was morally wrong, ibid., 204 and 220. On Humanae vitae and its reception among West German Catholics, see Benjamin Ziemann, Encounters with Modernity: The Catholic Church in West Germany 1945–1975 (Oxford, 2014).

financed its activities through selling re-prints of the works of radical psychoanalyst Wilhelm Reich, the founder of the 1930s 'Sexpol' movement. But the debates she witnessed there had not spoken to her at all, she insisted.[62]

> I mean, I didn't find that part of the Revolution that revolutionary because my parents had actually done it a generation ago. [...] So this part of the Left I found pretty old-fashioned. [...] I didn't need to wage the Revolution against my parents.[63]

Recollections such as these highlight the extent to which centre-right activists, much like their age peers on the Left, already practised a liberalized sexuality that is often wrongly portrayed as the unintended consequence of the overt sexual hedonism and politicization of sexuality on the 1968 radical Left.[64]

They also show that there was no clear-cut generational divide in the West German conservative milieu when it came to matters of sexuality, at least not between students of the 1960s and their parents. To be sure, some activists recalled conflicts with their parents over matters of style and sexuality. Maria-Theresia van Schewick, who had graced the cover of the *Pop-Kurier*, for one, remembered that her mother had called her a whore and slapped her when she first saw her wearing makeup.[65] More often than not, though, as Christina von Hodenberg has argued recently, the split did not occur between the '68ers and their own— often already more liberally inclined—parents, but rather between the young and the very old.[66] The conservative backlash against social and cultural change, particularly against the 'sex wave', that did occur in West Germany in the 1960s was indeed mostly driven by much older Germans. The Protestant Concern for Germany Campaign, for one, campaigned against 'sexual propaganda in schools and universities', organized doctors' protests against the contraceptive pill, and warned against 'a dictatorship of indecency'.[67] The *Aktion Saubere Leinwand*, under the leadership of the Christian Democratic politician Adolf Süsterhenn (b. 1905) denounced 'sexual terror' and called for the censorship of sexually explicit films.[68] The journalist Gabriele Strecker (b. 1904), another older Christian Democratic commentator, was dismayed by both the mini skirt and the increasingly androgynous styles of West German youth that, to her, threatened established gender norms

[62] Kommune 2, *Versuch der Revolutionierung des bürgerlichen Individuums* (Berlin, 1969).
[63] Reichart-Dreyer interview.
[64] Giese and Schmidt, *Studenten-Sexualität*; Gunter Schmidt (ed.), *Kinder der sexuellen Revolution: Kontinuität und Wandel studentischer Sexualität 1966–1996* (Giessen, 2000).
[65] van Schewick interview; also Ruff, *The Wayward Flock*, 107–10.
[66] von Hodenberg, *Das andere Achtundsechzig*, 170–83.
[67] Evangelisches Zentral Archiv Berlin (EZA), rep. 81/3, no. 213 and rep. 87, no. 1107.
[68] Herzog, *Sex after Fascism*, 148.

and the social order.[69] In the 1970s, some West German religious groups also staged street protests against the legalization of abortion.[70]

By contrast, there were no culture wars about sexual relationships, contraception and reproductive rights among students. Although less libertarian than their socialist or Social Democratic student peers, opinion surveys showed that the majority of West German students who self-identified as conservative or religious and denominationally bound had no problem with premarital sex, masturbation or the use of contraceptives and even tolerated homosexual sex.[71] As early as 1966, a few years before a major reform of West German criminal law changed the notorious §175 of the West German penal code that criminalized even consensual sex between adult men, the Christian Democratic student newspaper *Civis* was notably relaxed about the prospect of decriminalization. Several Western European states had already legalized homosexual sex, the paper explained, and the warnings of conservative guardians of morality against a general dissolution of values had turned out to be misplaced. 'The marriages were not shattered, the armed forces were not demoralized; homosexuality had not been proven to be contagious, the birth rates did not fall. The youth remained "normal,"' the paper commented matter-of-factly.[72]

Centre-right activists also got involved in campaigns for heterosexual autonomy. In 1967, Christian Democratic students and other centre-right activists in Bonn were closely involved in a high-profile campaign to make the contraceptive pill more easily available. The Schering pharmaceutical company had introduced the oral contraceptive that would become known simply as 'the pill' to West Germany in 1961. There were no legal restrictions on who could get a prescription. However, most doctors initially followed a restrictive practice and only prescribed the pill to married women under influence from the strong moralizing discourses that accompanied its introduction to the West German market.[73]

---

[69] On Strecker, see further von der Goltz, 'Von alten Kämpfern'; having been born in 1904, Strecker belonged to the older generation that von Hodenberg portrays as most socially conservative in her book, von Hodenberg, *Das andere Achtundsechzig*.

[70] Jana Ebeling, 'Religiöser Straßenprotest? Medien und Kirchen im Streit um den § 218 in den 1970er Jahren', in *Jenseits der Kirche: Die Öffnung religiöser Räume seit 1945*, edited by Frank Bösch and Lucian Hölscher (Göttingen, 2013), 253–84.

[71] Attitudes towards sexuality diverged much less strongly among West German students of the Left and Right than they did in the United States in the same period. Giese and Schmidt, *Studenten-Sexualiät*, 207–9.

[72] Hamburger Institut für Sozialforschung (HIS), A-ZC-1521, 'Strafrechtsreform §175', in: CIVIS (1966), no 11; at this time, two-thirds of West German students surveyed by researchers (and half of those who said they had strong religious beliefs or confessional ties) stated that they favoured a liberalization of existing laws on homosexuality. Giese and Schmidt, *Studenten-Sexualiät*, 204, 221, and 289. On homosexuality and law reform see further Michael Kandora, 'Homosexualität und Sittengesetz', in Herbert, *Wandlungsprozesse in Westdeutschland*, 379–401.

[73] 'Anti-Baby-Pillen nur für Ehefrauen?', *Der Spiegel*, 9 (1964), 79–89. On this debate and the role of the pill in the protest movement of the 1960s, Silies, *Liebe, Lust und Last*, 349–75; 'AStA sucht Anti-Baby-Pillen', *Frankfurter Rundschau* (13 October 1967), 24.

Single women continued to risk unwanted pregnancies or had to obtain the pill on the black market.

In October 1967, the 23-year old Christian Democrat Jürgen Rosorius, one of the best-known student activists in the West German capital, spearheaded a bipartisan campaign to make the pill more easily available to unmarried students.[74] Rosorius was the speaker of the Bonn student parliament at the time and had a liberal bent. During his tenure, its members voted unanimously to collect addresses of doctors who would be willing to write a prescription. Local doctors did not exactly line up to register at first, leading the student council to place an advertisement in the left-wing daily *Frankfurter Rundschau*.[75] Maria-Theresia van Schewick, who worked on student welfare issues at the time, recalled that she had also used her family's good name and conservative credentials to solicit potential doctors' names over the phone.[76] The goal of the campaign was to 'finally break the taboo' and to enable women to obtain the medication 'without having to listen to a philippic from moral apostles in white coats'.[77] Once the names had been collected, a committee appointed by the student council passed them on to interested female students upon request.[78]

The RCDS-championed campaign had a huge echo in the media, not least because one of the participating doctors, a dentist from Bamberg, was happy to send prescriptions via mail and agreed to be photographed by the press. Most of the major West German dailies and magazines ran stories about him and the Bonn pill campaign.[79] By December, the student council's welfare division reported that two to three women per day made use of the service and likely shared the information with other peers. The requests came from local students, but also from other parts of the country.[80] Other West German student parliaments soon initiated similar campaigns. In July 1968, the influential left-wing magazine *konkret* started a similar initiative which extended to unmarried non-students.[81] Only afterwards did the number of West German women on the pill begin to rise exponentially.[82] As we have seen, centre-right students'

[74] '"Pillen-Aktion" an der Uni Bonn', *Akut*, 35 (October 1967), 17; von Hodenberg, *Das andere Achtundsechzig*, 160–1; Bothien, *Protest und Provokation*, 125.
[75] 'AStA sucht Anti-Baby-Pillen', in *Frankfurter Rundschau* (13 October 1967), 24; 'Rezept frei Haus', *Der Spiegel*, 48 (1967), 84; see also Silies, *Liebe, Lust und Last*, 167–8.
[76] van Schewick interview.   [77] 'Die Pillen von Bonn', *Stern*, 47 (1967), 222–3.
[78] Private Papers Jürgen Rosorius, 'AStA "verschreibt" Anti-Baby Pille', newspaper clipping (4 October 1967).
[79] 'Rezept frei Haus', *Der Spiegel*, 48 (1967), 84; 'Die Pille vom Zahnarzt', *Constanze*, 47 (1967), 8–9; Universitätsarchiv Bonn, Sammlung Flugblatt, no. 3364, 1 January 1968; also Silies, *Liebe, Lust und Last*, 167–8.
[80] Universitätsarchiv Bonn, AStA 47, no. 32, Letter from Sozialreferat AstA Bonn to the Österreichische Hochschülerschaft (9 December 1967); AStA 47, no. 33, Letter from Sozialreferat to F.B., 30 November 1967.
[81] Silies, *Liebe, Lust und Last*, 136 and 165–6.
[82] In 1967, only 10 per cent of West German women between the ages of 15 und 44 took the pill. By 1972, the number had risen to 30 per cent. See Silies, *Liebe, Lust und Last*, 103.

embrace of a liberalized sexuality was not the result of being nudged by their more hedonistic peers on the Left.

Changing Gender Roles and Women Activists

Men dominated centre-right student politics in the 1960s. While approximately a quarter of RCDS members were female—a number that was close to the percentage of female students in the Federal Republic overall[83]—most of the committed and visible activists on university campuses were male. 'It was by and large a male affair', remembered Wolfgang Reeder.[84] The same was true of the Student Unions, whose professionally designed publications featured plenty of women as objects of male desire, but whose organization remained firmly in the hands of young men.[85] The local chapters of centre-right student groups were often run by small 'male cliques'; the few women who were involved primarily took on auxiliary or welfare-oriented roles.[86] 'We had very few women. They were the water-carriers', declared Wulf Schönbohm.[87] Meinhard Ade of the Freiburg RCDS concurred that 'Few of our members [were] women. We would have liked, really liked to have had more.' However, he also pointed out that they were not an exception in this regard. 'It wasn't much different for the others, the SDS did not have that many more [women activists].'[88]

Ade was correct about this, at least when it came to the male dominance in leadership positions, which was by no means confined to the centre-right groups of the time, something that has been noted frequently in the recent scholarship on 1968. Left-wing activism, not least in SDS, was strongly male dominated.[89] Although 1968 gave rise to the women's movement, the daughters of the revolt were less publicly visible than their male peers, especially in the early days of the student movement. The men's masculine display, verbal combat, and militaristic fantasies of street battles projected a virile heroism, which could be as alienating and off-putting to women activists as it was enticing to much of the media. The

---

[83] In 1965, only 27 per cent of West German students were women. Wehler, *Deutsche Gesellschaftsgeschichte*, 5, 175.

[84] Reeder interview.

[85] The BSU, for instance, featured Maria-Theresia van Schewick on the cover of its magazine *Pop-Kurier*, but its leader Jürgen Aretz was quick to downplay her political role when interviewed. Aretz interview.

[86] Härdtl interview. Härdtl's wife, who was a student at the Free University of Berlin in the 1960s, also chimed in with observations about women's secondary roles in centre-right student politics during the interview.

[87] Schönbohm interview.   [88] Ade interview.

[89] See Julia Paulus, Eva-Maria Silies, and Kerstin Wolff (eds.), *Zeitgeschichte als Geschlechtergeschichte: Neue Perspektiven auf die Bundesrepublik* (Frankfurt am Main, 2012); Sara M. Evans, 'Sons, Daughters, and Patriarchy: Gender and the 1968 Generation', *AHR*, 114, 2 (2009), 331–47; Brown, *West Germany and the Global Sixties*; Ute Kätzel, *Die 68erinnen: Porträt einer rebellischen Frauengeneration* (Berlin, 2002).

latter typically focused its extensive coverage of the international youth protests on male figureheads, such as Rudi Dutschke or the 'bearded, young, brash, gun-toting, self-confident' international star Che Guevara.[90]

In spite of the predominance of men, the women that were active on the centre-right in the 1960s nevertheless shared with their male peers the sense that their initial entry into student politics had been driven first and foremost by a desire to oppose the left-wing student movement. A recently published collection of 58 autobiographical interviews with Christian Democratic women includes a number of testimonies by women born in the 1940s which stress that resisting the left-wing student movement had played a pivotal role in activist political biographies. Beatrix Philipp (b. 1945), who later became a Bundestag delegate for North-Rhine Westphalia, recalled confronting the Left while a student in Freiburg and Frankfurt am Main. She portrayed a particular encounter with Franco-German activist Daniel Cohn-Bendit as leading to a kind of epiphany. Listening to Cohn-Bendit explain his political goals, she became convinced that the left-wing movement was destructive. 'My experiences with the APO led me to the conclusion: I wanted to do more than just go and vote and not leave the shaping of our society up to left-wing ideologues.'[91] Erika Steinbach (b. 1943), a Hessian Christian Democrat who would later gain notoriety as a zealous and hard-line advocate of expellee interests, similarly explained that her entry into politics had been sparked by her opposition to what she termed the 1968 'riots' in Frankfurt am Main.[92]

In an interview and in a commemorative piece about 1968, Ursula Männle, one of the very few female activists in RCDS who held a leadership role in those years, likewise framed her recollections of centre-right activism as anti-Left 'resistance'. She had served as state chair of the Bavarian RCDS from 1966–67, making her the highest-ranking female Christian Democratic student nationally. To this day, she sees the political conflict with the left-wing student movement as providing the key to her political biography.[93] At the same time, however, Männle recalled that being one of the few leading centre-right women in student politics at the time had gone hand in hand with a certain experiential overlap with women of the Left, who were subjected to casual sexism and outright misogyny even in student groups that advocated against other forms of political repression. In groups like SDS,

[90] Evans, 'Sons, Daughters, and Patriarchy', 337.

[91] Beatrix Philipp, 'Ich bin eine 1968erin!', in *Mut zur Verantwortung: Frauen gestalten Politik in der CDU*, edited by Beate Neuss and Hildigung Neubert (Cologne, Weimar, and Vienna, 2013), 347–54, here 348. Herlind Gundelach (b. 1949), who later served as a Senator in Hamburg, ascribed a similarly central role to being exposed to the APO as a student in Bonn. Herlind Gundelach, 'Mein Weg in die Politik – Erfahrungen und Erkenntnisse', in Neuss and Neubert, *Mut zur Verantwortung*, 441–60, here 442.

[92] Erika Steinbach, 'Recht und Ordnung sind Substanz eines pfleglichen Miteinanders', Neuss and Neubert, *Mut zur Verantwortung*, 281–302, here 281.

[93] Männle interview; Ursula Männle, 'Unkonventionelle Anmerkungen', in *Politische Studien*, 59, 422 (2008), 33–5.

women activists were famously assigned auxiliary roles by the men and often confined to the side-lines at political events. Männle had experienced much the same from an early age. The nuns at the Catholic all-girls boarding school where she was educated portrayed political engagement as an exclusively male domain. Being politically active was 'unfeminine', they told Männle. Like many of her peers on the Left, she recalled having rebelled against this mantra early on.[94]

When she joined RCDS in the mid-1960s, she repeatedly confronted being marginalized or excluded by her male peers. On a Christian Democratic study trip to Israel, for instance, some travellers had the chance to meet David Ben-Gurion, one of the founders of the state of Israel. Männle had long been interested in German-Israeli relations but was told that only the men could go to the meeting with the former Israeli Prime Minister. She claimed that, prior to that moment, she had not perceived discrimination against women as a problem in the organization, 'but there I experienced it very clearly', she recalled.[95] She continued to make similar observations throughout her time in student politics. 'The men led. And they were in their role. Well, women were also handing out leaflets

Illustration 3.3 Former Bavarian RCDS chair Ursula Männle speaking at the fiftieth anniversary of the Hanns-Seidel Foundation, a think tank affiliated with the CSU that she chaired from 2014 until 2019 (Munich, 20 January 2017).

(dpa Picture-Alliance)

---

[94] Männle interview. For similar autobiographical recollections from a British left-wing activist and feminist, see Sheila Rowbotham, *Promise of a Dream* (London, 2000).
[95] Männle interview.

and manning the stands, but when it came to discussions only the men spoke. Only! [. . .] Women were really the exception.'[96]

In West Germany, as indeed across much of the globe, from the United States to Japan, this kind of marginalization and discrimination eventually led to forceful confrontations between male and female activists. These confrontations sparked the formation of a broad array of 'autonomous' women's groups dedicated to fighting not just global imperialism but also the patriarchy.[97] The emergence of the women's movement has often been celebrated as one of the enduring cultural legacies of 1968. This 'new' women's movement may have emerged in the context of the left-wing student movement, but it formed in explicit opposition to the perceived chauvinism of its male leaders.

Given how similar her experiences in RCDS were, Männle was initially curious about the politics of women's liberation. During her sociology degree at Ludwig-Maximilians University in Munich, in a department that was dominated by left-wing academics, Männle was increasingly confronted with ideas about social change and the structural situation of women.[98] This slowly affected her relationship with her male peers, whom she began to criticize openly, not least for making women's physical attractiveness a precondition for career advancement. In doing so, she mimicked left-wing activists at the time who made issues surrounding the female body central to their critique of patriarchal structures. Feminist activists began to question the sexualized marketing of women's bodies that had become prevalent in advertising and generally railed against stereotypical depictions of women.[99] 'The personal is political' was the unofficial slogan of this generation of women activists.[100]

In several particularly memorable acts of protest in 1968, 1969, and 1970, American and British feminists disrupted the Miss America pageants in Atlantic City and the Miss World Contest in London's Royal Albert Hall to denounce what they perceived as a degrading 'cattle parade' that reduced women to objects of beauty and male desire.[101] A few years later, Männle made a similar argument

---

[96] Männle interview. On male dominance in political debates, see Verheyen, *Diskussionslust*, 236.

[97] Evans, 'Sons, Daughters, and Patriarchy'; Heinrich-Böll-Stiftung and Feministisches Institut (eds.), *Wie weit flog die Tomate? Eine 68erinnen-Gala der Reflexion* (Berlin, 1999).

[98] Elisabeth Zellmer, 'Protestieren und Polarisieren. Frauenbewegung und Feminismus der 1970er Jahre in München', in Paulus, Silies, and Wolff, *Zeitgeschichte als Geschlechtergeschichte*, 284–96.

[99] Silke Eilers, '"Sie kommen". Selbst- und Fremdbilder der Neuen Frauenbewegung', in *Das Jahrhundert der Bilder*, vol. 2: *1949 bis heute*, edited by Gerhard Paul (Bonn, 2008), 461.

[100] 'The personal is political' was one of the most famous slogans of second-wave feminism. It was popularized in an essay written by New York radical feminist Carol Hanisch. Carol Hanisch, 'The Personal is Political', in *Notes from the Second Year: Women's Liberation: Major Writings of the Radical Feminists*, edited by Shulamith Firestone and Anne Koedt (New York, 1970), 76–8; on the origins of the phrase, see further Carol Hanisch, 'The Personal Is Political. The Women's Liberation Movement Classic with a New Explanatory Introduction' (2006), http://www.carolhanisch.org/CHwritings/PIP.html (accessed on 7 March 2017).

[101] Geoff Eley, *Forging Democracy: The History of the Left in Europe 1850–2000* (Oxford, 2002), 366–83.

about internal Christian Democratic Party elections, which, she contended, dis-advantaged women if they lacked the 'correct' physical attributes. Such elections were 'Mis(s)-Contests', she wrote a piece in which she suggested that, in her eyes, the personal was indeed political—at least to some degree.[102] A male colleague had once opined in her presence that he wanted to be able to picture female candidates in bed. In addition, the 'physical downsides' of female politicians were regularly discussed in a 'derogatory manner during nightly debates at the beer table (. . . she with her drooping breasts)', Männle wrote in an article about women's roles in politics. She then asked rather provocatively if 'anybody ever asked the women whether they approve of the collection of more or less fat bellies, half-bald heads etc.?' Männle later recalled that her critique had been inspired by the operative double standard in judging the appearance of a male politician like the archcon-servative leader of the CSU Franz Josef Strauss and his deputy, Mathilde Berghofer-Weichner, who—contrary to Strauss who was also hardly convention-ally attractive—was often degraded for her lack of desirability.[103]

Männle was not the only centre-right student to make notions of the female body and everyday sexism points of contention. The feminist critique of using women's bodies for marketing purposes began to reach them, too, as we saw at the beginning of this chapter. Some also questioned the biological reading of gender differences and called for the overcoming of patriarchy. To be sure, understanding women as a subjugated social class that had to liberate itself from the yoke of male subjugation came more naturally to young leftist women who believed in global forms of structural oppression, and not all centre-right women activists developed a feminist consciousness. Dorothee Buchhaas-Birkholz (b. 1952), who had served as RCDS national deputy from 1974–75, for one, later claimed that she had never faced any obstacles or difficulties in Christian Democratic student politics because she was a woman. 'No, that was not an issue at all. Never!' There had been no machismo in RCDS, she insisted. 'We didn't have that. We didn't have that at all. [. . .] I never experienced it that way at all.'[104]

Articles that called for the abolition of authoritarian-patriarchal structures and Männle's outcry against casual sexism within her party, on the other hand, illustrate that some elements of the feminist critique had indeed reached centre-right student groups by the early 1970s. By then, the founding texts of 'second-wave' feminism—books such as Simone de Beauvoir's *The Second Sex*, first published in German in 1951, and Betty Friedan's *The Feminine Mystique*, available in German translation from 1966—had been in wide circulation for a

---

[102] Ursula Männle, 'Weibchen oder Feigenblatt. Die Frau in der Politik', in *Für eine humane Gesellschaft: Beiträge zum Programmdenken der jungen Generation*, edited by Wulf Schönbohm and Matthias Wissmann (Frankfurt am Main, 1976), 97.
[103] Männle interview.   [104] Buchhaas-Birkholz interview.

number of years.[105] The 'first wave' of feminism of the late-nineteenth- and early twentieth century had focused on opening up political and professional opportunities and on legal rights, notably suffrage. But the German bourgeois variant, in particular, had still defined the differences between the sexes as innate and essentially positive; femininity was seen as virtuous and worth preserving. 'Second-wave' feminists, like de Beauvoir, by contrast, questioned the very notion of femininity.[106] She viewed the differences between men and women as the product of a specific form of socialization by a society that considered women inferior to men. 'One is not born, but rather becomes, a woman', she famously stated.[107]

This constructivist reading of gender roles changed the language of politics—and it even percolated into conservative circles. An article published in *Akademische Blätter*, the communal journal of nearly forty different fraternities and student corporations, directly quoted de Beauvoir's well-known dictum in an essay.[108] This particular piece, written by one Barbara Langhoff, the wife of a fraternity student (fraternities and corporations were male communities by definition), in many ways stood out in a publication otherwise dedicated to debating the concept of the nation and regularly adorned with images of the bricked-up Brandenburg Gate or the old hunting lodges of German aristocrats.[109] In early 1972, however, Langhoff informed its readership that student couples increasingly practised equality in their daily lives. They strove to share the housework and childcare and women sought self-realization through their work, the author, who was a practising lawyer, explained. She then called on the men to join in the struggle for full gender equality. Any lingering differences between men and women, she argued with reference to de Beauvoir, were the products of socialization. 'It starts with the toys: dolls for little Eva, cars for the real boys. [...] This is how girls are guided towards things that allegedly fit them from the youngest age. They must be kind, pretty, and domestic.'[110] Advertisements on television and in illustrated magazines and the 'fashion diktat' did their share to create a particular kind of woman, Langhoff went on. The discussion of such ideas in a leading

---

[105] Simone de Beauvoir, *Das andere Geschlecht: Sitte und Sexus der Frau* (Hamburg, 1951); Betty Friedan, *Der Weiblichkeitswahn: Ein vehementer Protest gegen das Wunschbild von der Frau* (Reinbek near Hamburg, 1966).

[106] On the different emphases of first- and second-wave feminists, see Ingrid Biermann, *Von Differenz zur Gleichheit: Frauenbewegung und Inklusionspolitiken im 19. und 20. Jahrhundert* (Bielefeld, 2009), 115; Kristina Schulz, *Der lange Atem der Provokation. Die Frauenbewegung in der Bundesrepublik und in Frankreich 1968–1976* (Frankfurt am Main, 2002), 203.

[107] Simone de Beauvoir, *The Second Sex*, translated and edited by H.M. Parshley (New York, 1953).

[108] Barbara Langhoff, 'Die Stellung der Frau in der heutigen Gesellschaft', *Akademische Blätter* no. 1 (1972), 8–10.

[109] The *Akademische Blätter* was the official publication of the *Verband der Vereine Deutscher Studenten*, also known as the Kyffhäuserverband. On notions of masculinity in the fraternities, see Dietrich Heither, *Verbündete Männer: Die Deutsche Burschenschaft. Weltanschauung, Politik und Brauchtum* (Cologne, 2001), 276–322.

[110] Langhoff, 'Die Stellung der Frau'.

fraternity publication was a stark indication of how far the debate about women's issues had progressed since the 1950s societal consensus that had defined women exclusively as mothers and spiritual guardians of the family.[111]

At the same time, however, the article provided evidence of the considerable societal obstacles that remained. This was especially true in conservative student groups whose male leadership cliques often favoured a far more traditional gender regime. Langhoff trod conspicuously lightly, for instance, when discussing every-day displays of male 'chivalry'. In what can only be read as an effort to calm male fears about women's emancipation leading to a loss of feminine charm or an assertive self-sufficiency that threatened to undermine male caretaker roles, she wrote: 'I still like it if a man helps me into my coat, even though I could manage it myself.' She went on to suggest that women with a newfound self-confidence might even be more attractive to men and conceded that 'in our increasingly confusing and confused world […] the role of the wife and mother is more important than ever.'[112] Hers, then, was a highly mixed message about what women were supposed to strive for and one that still channelled a notion of an innate femininity worth preserving—second-wave feminism 'lite', in other words.

In the same year, Maria-Theresia van Schewick, who had helped to make the contraceptive pill available to unmarried students in Bonn and beyond in the late 1960s, published a deeply personal piece that attempted a rhetorical balancing act similar to Langhoff's. As an activist in the Bonn Student Union, van Schewick had often used her good looks to promote the centre-right cause. When she was featured in the group's glossy *Pop-Kurier* in early 1969, her profile as a student parliamentary candidate advertised her 'feminine charm and feminine skill' and invited potential voters to visit her for a 'personal "viewing"'.[113] In an article she penned in 1972, the year that she was elected national deputy chair of RCDS, she still projected an image of unthreatening femininity. 'The author does not object to her cigarette being lit for her or her suitcase being carried. Emancipation does not go that far, after all', she stressed.[114] Nonetheless, van Schewick now explicitly identified as an 'emancipated girl' and revealed that this was not easy in a conservative milieu. Her confidence and assertiveness often created trouble with the men she got involved with romantically, she explained. The mother of one boyfriend, for instance, had objected to her encouraging the young man to help with the dishes. She had fought with another boyfriend who wanted a traditional marriage where the wife took care of the home and children. She did not want to

---

[111] Robert G. Moeller, *Protecting Motherhood: Women and the Family in the Politics of Postwar West Germany* (Berkeley and Los Angeles, CA, 1993).

[112] Langhoff, 'Die Stellung der Frau'.

[113] *Pop-Kurier*, Wahlexpress (28 January 1969); van Schewick interview.

[114] Marie-Theresia van Schewick, 'Entwicklung eines emanzipierten Mädchens', *Demokratische Blätter*, 3 (1972).

give up her career, she reasoned, and then asked if a man would ever be happy to wait with the dinner when she got back from a conference. She mused:

> But males expect all of this and more from a woman. And if she is not willing to provide it, then it will be difficult for her to find a life partner. And lifelong loneliness is a high price to pay for emancipation. But isn't the price that a woman pays to get a man at least as steep?[115]

She was certainly not the only one who felt torn between her desire for self-fulfilment and autonomy and her quest for a partner whose general political outlook she shared. Ingrid Reichart-Dreyer reported that she had faced similar difficulties in her encounters with Christian Democratic men. In the late 1960s and early 1970s, they would ask her if she had spent the day folding laundry and run away from her at social functions, she remembered. Conservative men of her generation could not handle intellectually ambitious and successful women, she observed in retrospect.[116] Although they did not make it explicit, both Reichart-Dreyer and van Schewick's experiences overlapped with those of politicized and emancipated women from a left-wing milieu who often suffered increasingly contentious relationships and break-ups because of their expressed desire for equality and autonomy.[117]

In spite of the obstacles they faced and their initially wary embrace of an explicitly feminist politics, many centre-right women activists reported having grown more passionate about women's issues over time. Reichart-Dreyer, for one, went into academia after a semi-successful career in local politics in West Berlin. There, she channelled her personal experiences of discrimination into her scholarly work, publishing on gender issues and barriers to women's participation in Christian Democratic politics.[118] Her trajectory in some ways reflected a broader shift in the representation of women's issues in Christian Democratic politics. The success of the women's movement made it difficult for West German political parties across the board to ignore the legitimate demands of women. Christian Democratic women, on the whole, became noticeably more politicized from the 1970s onward. The Women's Union, one of the party's auxiliary organizations,

---

[115] van Schewick, 'Entwicklung eines emanzipierten Mädchens'.
[116] Reichart-Dreyer interview.   [117] See von Hodenberg, Das andere Achtundsechzig, 127–9.
[118] Ingrid Reichart-Dreyer, 'Relevanz vorherrschender Geschlechtsleitbilder in der Programmarbeit der CDU', in Die politische Steuerung des Geschlechterregimes: Beiträge zur Theorie politischer Institutionen, edited by Annette Henninger and Helga Ostendorf (Wiesbaden, 2005), 57–73; Ingrid Reichart-Dreyer, 'War die K-Frage in den C-Parteien eine F-G-V-Frage?', femina politica, 1 (2002), 97–101; one of her pieces on women's participation in the CDU explicitly stated that her analysis was informed by personal experiences. Ingrid Reichart-Dreyer, 'Partizipation von Frauen in der CDU', in Gefährtinnen der Macht: Politische Partizipation von Frauen im vereinigten Deutschland: Eine Zwischenbilanz, edited by Eva Malecky-Lewy and Virginia Penrose (Berlin, 1995), 40; van Schewick and Männle also reported becoming more interested and passionate about women's issues over time. van Schewick interview; Männle interview.

which had previously focused on organizing charity and social functions, grew much more active in shaping the party's domestic policy agenda.[119]

Women also slowly occupied more leadership positions within the party. So much so, in fact, that when the *Frankfurter Rundschau* asked Jürgen Habermas to name the most important legacies of 1968 around the time of the twentieth anniversary of the student movement, the critical theorist famously replied: 'Mrs. [Rita] Süßmuth.' Süßmuth was at that time the President of the Women's Union and a proponent of a rather liberal family policy as Christian Democratic Minister of Family Affairs, Senior Citizens, Women and Youth. A figure like her would 'scarcely have been thinkable [. . .] prior to 1968', Habermas argued.[120]

Süßmuth was indeed a prime example of feminism's broad reach and significant long-term impact on the CDU. In one of the first major interviews she gave after her appointment in 1985, she revealed that Simone de Beauvoir was her greatest role model, and she often spoke about the great influence the women's movement had had on her personally and politically.[121] Left-wing critics at the time were confounded by her brand of 'conservative feminism' and saw it as mere co-optation, but the early interest of figures such as van Schewick and Männle in the ideas of second-wave feminism illustrates that it was part of a longer Christian Democratic tradition—and one that perhaps in some ways foreshadowed the subsequent rise of Angela Merkel, CDU leader from 2000 to 2018 and Germany's first female Chancellor.[122]

Such evidence of the women's movement's broad social and cultural reach notwithstanding, there remained important issues and stylistic differences that separated centre-right women from their sisters on the Left in the wake of 1968,

[119] Sarah Elise Wiliarty, *The CDU and the Politics of Gender in Germany: Bringing Women to the Party* (Cambridge, 2010), 106–7; Bösch, *Macht und Machtverlust*, 240–5.

[120] Jürgen Habermas, Interview, *Frankfurter Rundschau*, 11 March 1988; English version published in Jürgen Habermas, 'Political Culture in Germany since 1968: An Interview with Dr. Rainer Erd for the Frankfurter Rundschau', in idem, *The New Conservatism: Cultural Criticism and the Historians' Debate*, edited and translated by Shierry Weber Nicholsen (Cambridge, 1989).

[121] 'Simone de Beauvoir ist mein großes Vorbild', *Die Zeit*, 37 (1985); Margit Gerste, 'Knochenarbeit für die Männer-Partei', *Die Zeit*, 1 (1986); Rita Süßmuth, *Das Gift des Politischen: Gedanken und Erinnerungen* (Munich, 2015), 70–4, 72, 102–3.

[122] Mechthild Jansen, ' "Konservativer Feminismus" mit Rita Süßmuth?', in *Blätter für deutsche und internationale Politik*, 2 (1986), 184–201. On the role of gender in the rise and politics of Angela Merkel, see Joyce Marie Mushaben, *Becoming Madam Chancellor: Angela Merkel and the Berlin Republic* (Cambridge, 2017). Left-wing commentators have continued to be confounded by Christian Democratic women in leadership positions. When Ursula von der Leyen was elected as the first female President of the European Commission in July 2019, the front page of the left-wing daily *taz* summed up the Left's astonishment thus: 'So haben wir uns das Ende des Patriarchats aber nicht vorgestellt: Christliche Damen Union sichert sich die Macht in Deutschland und Europa. Linksliberale Parteien sehen dagegen alt aus', *taz*, 18 July 2019, 1. Conservative women were indeed often the first to benefit from the women's movement by gaining political power. See Belinda Davis, 'The Personal Is Political: Gender, Politics, and Political Activism in Modern German History' in *Gendering Modern German History: Rewriting Historiography*, edited by Karen Hagemann and Jean H. Quataert (Oxford, 2007), 107–27.

not least in the realm of symbolic politics. For centre-right men, the gulf was even deeper. Former RCDS federal chair Wulf Schönbohm remembered having been repelled by the 'hysterical broads [...] [who] were the worst, these fanatic ones'.[123] Männle, on the other hand, felt that the leftist women's movement of the 1970s had forced her to think more deeply about and eventually confront the sexism within her party's ranks. 'I thought that they provided an important impetus', she stated. At the same time, however, she stressed that there were things she found off-putting about left-wing women and the movement. Like Schönbohm, she thought that left-wing feminists 'behaved incredibly aggressively' back then, and she 'didn't want to be identified with that'.[124]

During the widely publicized protests against the Miss America Contest in Atlantic City in 1969, members of a radical New York women's group had staged a counter pageant at which they threw 'oppressive' feminine objects, including bras, girdles, and makeup into a trashcan. The scene entered popular mythology as an act of 'bra burning'.[125] Männle invoked this incident and explained that, to her, it had seemed excessive and like 'adolescent behaviour'. 'For me a bra wasn't a symbol of oppression or something along those lines. Perhaps I didn't have the right consciousness.'[126] Echoing a broader conservative critique of alleged left-wing excess and ostentation, van Schewick made a similar point and agreed that left-wing feminists 'overdid it' with their attacks on femininity—a trait she thought worth celebrating despite identifying as 'emancipated'.

'I never understood why I was supposed to walk around without a bra', she said. 'I think that nice lingerie is something wonderful and always thought so. [...] I was proud of my breasts. [...] I didn't get how my running around without a bra would advance emancipation.'[127]

However, the most divisive issue that separated left-wing feminists from female centre-right activists was not 'bra burning' but abortion. In the late 1960s and early 1970s, the West German women's movement was highly diverse, consisting of numerous only loosely connected groups across the country. In the 1970s, the movement increasingly coalesced into a more unified whole around the campaign to legalize abortion in the Federal Republic.[128] The Weimar-era §218 of the penal code was still in place then, and it threatened women who terminated a pregnancy with imprisonment for up to five years.

---

[123] Schönbohm interview.   [124] Männle interview.
[125] Bonnie J. Dow, 'Feminism, Miss America, and Media Mythology', *Rhetoric & Public Affairs*, 6, 1 (2003), 127–49.
[126] Männle interview.   [127] van Schewick interview.
[128] Schulz, *Der Lange Atem Der Provokation*; Eva-Maria Silies, 'Ein, zwei, viele Bewegungen? Die Diversität der Neuen Frauenbewegung in den 1970er Jahren in der Bundesrepublik', in *Linksalternatives Milieu und Neue Soziale Bewegungen in den 1970er Jahren*, edited by Cordia Baumann, Sebastian Gehrig, and Nicholas Büchse (Heidelberg, 2011), 87–106.

In spring 1971, the issue began to occupy a prominent place on the public agenda when, inspired by a similar French campaign that took place in April of that year, three West German grassroots feminist organizations launched a national campaign of self-incrimination. In the pages of the popular magazine *Stern*, 374 women, many of them celebrities, confessed to having had an illegal abortion.[129] Young centre-right women were, for the most part, not opposed to abortion on grounds of principle. Polls showed that 83 per cent of West German women and even the majority of Catholics supported legalization in the early 1970s, and student activists were not prominently represented at the few street protests against legalization.[130] Nevertheless, the issue had the capacity to drive a wedge between women on the centre-right and left-wing feminists. This partly had to do with how liberally each side thought the right to terminate a pregnancy should be interpreted, but it was also the result of differing political styles. The women's movement's focus on abortion seemed excessive and one-sided to centre-right activists. Asked what differentiated her own stance from that of left-wing women, Männle replied: 'It was the debate about §218. The §218 debate crystallized [the differences]. It made it easier for conservative women to draw a line.'[131] Van Schewick concurred that the legalization of abortion was not an issue around which she would have chosen to rally publicly, even though she did not object to sexual promiscuity and thought that the contraceptive pill should be freely available. 'I can say clearly: I live a colourful life. [...] But [...] [abortion] wasn't the question for me. I didn't sense that it was something that one took into the streets.'[132] To put it differently, for van Schewick, not everything that was personal was also political.

Männle, more than anything else, objected to the anti-§218 campaign's most prominent slogan 'My belly is mine!', the premise of which, that women had an absolute right to control their own bodies, she perceived as flawed. 'It was a rallying cry', she insisted, and it made it difficult to voice a more nuanced position.[133] Like other conservative commentators at the time, she argued that the *Stern* campaign was primarily a media stunt that distracted from a more serious and substantial debate on the issue.[134] Most of the women on the 6 June 1971 cover of the magazine were celebrities, among them the famous actors Senta Berger, Romy Schneider, and Veruschka von Lehndorff. Alice Schwarzer, a

---

[129] 'Wir haben gegen den §218 verstossen', *Stern*, 24 (6 June 1971), cover page and 16–23.
[130] Ebeling, 'Religiöser Straßenprotest?'; Wehler, *Deutsche Gesellschaftsgeschichte*, 5, 177. Despite official Church condemnations, 51 per cent of Catholics polled in 1971 believed that women should have the right to terminate a pregnancy and the numbers were much higher if extenuating social or economic circumstances existed or the child was at risk of suffering from serious mental or physical defects. See further Kimba Allie Tichenor, 'Protecting Unborn Life in the Secular Age: The Catholic Church and the West German Abortion Debate, 1969–1989', *Central European History*, 47, 3 (2014), 617. Older Christian Democratic women, including those organized in the Women's Union, by contrast, were strongly opposed to legalization. See Bösch, *Macht und Machtverlust*, 246.
[131] Männle interview.   [132] van Schewick interview.   [133] Männle interview.
[134] See e.g. Herbert Kremp, '218–zu ernst fuer die Schickeria', *Die Welt* (15 June 1971).

journalist who had previously worked in France and whose name has since become synonymous with West German feminism, had organized it. 'Alice Schwarzer and the actresses. [...] [I]t was the leading media women, film stars and so on, but not the kind of women one identified with, it wasn't the normal woman', according to Männle.[135]

While the feminist campaign to abolish §218 was initially successful in terms of creating public awareness around the issue and galvanizing the women's movement, it did not ultimately lead to the legalization of abortion. After the Social-Liberal coalition in the Bundestag passed a new law in 1974 that legalized abortions in the first twelve weeks of pregnancy, the Christian Democrats sued against the law. West Germany's highest court declared it unconstitutional a year later. In 1976, a new law, based more closely on Christian Democratic ideas on the subject, was passed. This law did not decriminalize abortion but declared that women and their doctors would not be punished for terminating a pregnancy in the first twelve weeks in cases where there were extenuating circumstances. This outcome, which remained in place until the early 1990s, was in many ways much closer to the ideas of female centre-right activists than those of the more radical West German women's movement—even though it was originally passed with the votes of the Social-Liberal coalition.

In the 1980s, after Kohl's election victory, Christian Democratic women resisted attempts by the party's conservative wing to further restrict access to abortion. When seventy-four male Christian Democratic *Bundestag* delegates put forward a bill that would have restricted medical insurance payments for certain abortion procedures, all eighteen female Christian Democratic delegates opposed the measure—Ursula Männle prominently among them. As *Der Spiegel* commented at the time: 'Their male fellow party members find the new self-confidence of the women in the CDU almost unnerving.' Occasional displays of female solidarity across the aisle also made the men worry about a 'women's alliance' across parliament, the paper reported. As if Christian Democratic women 'would catch some sort of bacillus', the paper quoted Männle as saying in disbelief.[136] This female solidarity, however limited it may have been in other respects, highlights the need to pay closer attention to the intersections of centre-right women and second-wave feminism and their participation in the broader cultural moment that was 1968.[137]

*   *   *

There were discernible and meaningful differences between the cultural styles and aesthetic preferences of activists of the centre-right and those at the forefront of

---

[135] Männle interview.
[136] 'CDU-Frauen: Irgendein Bazillus', *Der Spiegel*, 19 (1984) 29–31; see also Biebricher, *Geistig-moralische Wende*, 191.
[137] On the 'female 1968', see von Hodenberg, *Das andere Achtundsechzig*, 103–50.

the SDS-led student movement. Students of the centre-right remained wary of forms of overt cultural (self)-experimentation that parts of the radical Left practised, be it drug use, communal living, or a politicized sexual promiscuity meant to upend capitalism's influence in the private realm. They generally favoured a narrower understanding of what was political and did not believe that the self needed to be altered to change larger social and political structures. The experiences of some of the Christian Democratic renegades, whose political conversions went hand in hand with a cultural and emotional transformation, are telling in this regard. Martin Kempe, for one, did not just think differently; he later recalled that he had felt differently and lived differently after leaving RCDS. Cultural and political preferences were clearly related around 1968. As the housing style and social habitus of the interviewees for this book suggest, the nexus between the two has continued to shape aesthetic preferences since then. Aesthetic choices could also be deliberate performances of cultural distinction. Centre-right activists sometimes adopted a more formal and self-consciously bourgeois style to demarcate themselves from their political opponents, such as when Bonn centre-right students set up an 'Association for Elevating Table Manners in the Cafeteria'.

The differences, however, are clearest when the cultural preferences of centre-right activists are contrasted with a highly generalized—and partly imagined—portrayal of their allegedly scruffy and hedonistic opponents on the Left, whose lives were seen as marked by a constant stream of sex, drugs, and rock 'n' roll. In reality, as recent research has emphasized, the private lives of most left-wing activists were much more ordinary; 'free love' often remained no more than an ideal, and left-wing student demonstrators donned neat suits, dresses, and hairstyles for far longer than the later iconography of the protest movement suggested.

More importantly, however, for our purposes at least, the hair of centre-right men also grew longer over time as social anxieties over the de-militarization of masculinity dissipated.[138] Similarly, in the late 1960s, centre-right women embraced the mini skirt—a symbol of women's rising confidence—and were surprised when they noticed that older West Germans now suspected them of being on the Left. Centre-right students put on rock concerts and adopted pop or experimental designs for their publications. They also campaigned to make the contraceptive pill available to unmarried students, used sexualized imagery for marketing purposes, and, despite upholding the norm of heterosexual, monogamous relationships, generally practised an already liberalized sexuality. This confirms that many of the cultural and social changes associated with 1968 had already been under way for some time when the protest movement reached its peak. They were not the result of political agitation by a culturally experimental Left, but rather consequences of a dynamic modernization of West German

---

[138] Siegfried, *Time Is On My Side*, 255–62; Bodo Mrozek, *Jugend—Pop—Kultur: Eine transnationale Geschichte* (Frankfurt am Main, 2019), 682–711.

society that had taken off in the late 1950s and led to wide-ranging changes in collective social values, especially among the youth. Moreover, this was an international development that was observed in great detail and with considerable anxiety by conservative pollsters and social scientists, not just in West Germany.[139]

In his 1966 film *Masculin—Féminin*, the French filmmaker Jean-Luc Godard famously suggested that young activists of the Left were the 'children of Marx and Coca-Cola', because they embraced the new possibilities for consumption available to them at a time of seemingly endless prosperity in spite of their neo-Marxist politics. This chapter has attempted to show that a related observation can be made about centre-right students. They were the children of Adenauer and Coca-Cola: a generation that still considered the conservative postwar Chancellor a role model, but one that was affected just as much by consumer society and the social and cultural changes it wrought.[140]

Even though centre-right activists did not strive to make the personal political in the same way as the student Left, the influence of the nascent women's movement on centre-right women shows that they also broadened their understanding of what politics was. They may not have gone as far as throwing actual tomatoes at the men—as left-wing activist Sigrid Damm-Rüger famously did at the 1968 SDS convention[141]—but they began to toss some verbal tomatoes. They criticized sexualized (political) marketing campaigns and the casual sexism within their ranks, embraced a more constructivist reading of gender roles, and wrote about their subjective experiences in student newspapers otherwise dedicated to more traditional political content. This illustrates the extent to which the world of centre-right groups was shaken up not just by the far-reaching social and cultural changes of the period, but also by the emergence of an explicitly feminist politics.

Finally, the case of the centre-right women highlights that the Mannheimian model of political generations, with its male-centredness and emphasis on bipolarity and political antagonism, fails to capture the nuances and fluidities of activist identities and experiences around 1968. Much like their student peers on the Left, male and female centre-right activists experienced 1968 differently, at least in part. This difference allowed for the creation of new gender-based allegiances and conflicts that do not fit neatly into a model of political generations

---

[139] Helmut Klages, *Wertorientierungen im Wandel: Rückblick, Gegenwartsanalyse, Prognosen* (Frankfurt am Main, 1984); Ronald Inglehart, *The Silent Revolution: Changing Values and Political Styles Among Western Publics* (Princeton, NJ, 1977); for critical historical assessments of such surveys, see Norbert Grube, 'Seines Glückes Schmied? Entstehungs- und Verwendungskontexte von Allensbacher Umfragen zum Wertewandel 1947–2001' and Helmut Thome, 'Wandel gesellschaftlicher Wertvorstellungen aus der Sicht der empirischen Sozialforschung', in *Gab es den Wertewandel? Neue Forschungen zum gesellschaftlich-kulturellen Wandel seit den 1960er Jahren*, edited by Bernhard Dietz, Christopher Neumaier, and Andreas Rödder (Munich, 2014), 95–120 and 41–68.

[140] Godard's dictum is often referenced in studies of youth culture in the 1960s, e.g. in Schildt and Siegfried's, *Between Marx and Coca-Cola*; Siegfried, *Time Is On My Side*, 9.

[141] Heinrich-Böll-Stiftung and Feministisches Institut, *Wie weit flog die Tomate?*

that rests on a strict left-right binary.[142] Later on, centre-right women were far less vocal in 'generationalizing' their experiences of activism around 1968. The memory of the other '68ers that took shape from the 1980s onward was predominantly male. Excavating the role of centre-right women around 1968 therefore remains an important task, not least because of the powerful ways in which the (West) German centre-right has shaped discourses and policy on women's issues for much of the past half century—long before Christian Democrats nominated Germany's first female candidate for Chancellor in 2005.

[142] Karin Hausen, *Geschlechtergeschichte als Gesellschaftsgeschichte* (Göttingen, 2012), 371–91.

4

From Berlin to Saigon and Back

On 6 December 1966, raucous scenes took place at the Free University of Berlin, one of the epicentres of student protest in West Germany. Since the previous year, the vibrant and vocal student-led protest movement in the city had mobilized a growing number of activists against the US-led war in Vietnam, the escalating Cold War struggle to prevent a communist takeover of South Vietnam. Now Nguyen Quy Anh, the South Vietnamese Ambassador to Bonn, had come to the West Berlin campus to participate in a student-run event. In front of approximately 100 listeners, the diplomat likened the situation in his home country to that in divided Germany and invoked the Berlin blockade of 1948–49. Much as in West Berlin, he argued, South Vietnamese freedom and independence could not be sustained without US involvement.[1] In linking the fate of Saigon to that of the emblematic European Cold War city, the Ambassador invoked a mantra frequently voiced in the era of containment. US Secretary of Defense Robert McNamara, for one, had argued since 1964 that the defence of West Berlin started at the Mekong.[2]

Soon after the representative of the American-backed Thieu regime had made this claim, several hundred supporters of the local SDS interrupted his appearance. Amid shouts of 'Long live the National Liberation Front!' (as the communist Viet Cong was also known), students associated with the New Left group entered the room and demanded an open debate. The atmosphere in the now overcrowded hall grew more and more tense. At one point, SDS figurehead Dutschke leaped onto the podium, grabbed the microphone, and began to criticize the war.[3] A scuffle ensued onstage, which led the Ambassador to end the discussion abruptly and hastily exit the building through the back.[4] The next day's press coverage duly focused on the disruption and Dutschke's role at the event.[5] It was on this occasion that the first-ever detailed profile of the soon-to-be iconic student

---

[1] 'SDS-Studenten störten an der FU', *Der Tagesspiegel*, 7 December 1966.

[2] Alexander Troche, *'Berlin wird am Mekong verteidigt'. Die Ostasienpolitik der Bundesrepublik in China, Taiwan und Süd-Vietnam, 1954–1966* (Düsseldorf, 2000).

[3] Dutschke-Klotz, *Wir hatten ein barbarisches, schönes Leben*, 114; see Landesarchiv Berlin (henceforth LAB), B. Rep. 014, 3213, report to the Free University's Chancellor by RCDS member Othmar Nikola Haberl, 15 December 1966 and the report by SDS member Klaus Gilgenmann (12 December 1966).

[4] LAB, B. Rep. 014, 843, 'Bericht des Rektors der FU für den 1. Untersuchungsausschuss des Abgeordnetenhauses von Berlin, V. Wahlperiode'.

[5] See the press clippings in LAB, B. Rep. 014, 3213.

The Other '68ers: Student Protest and Christian Democracy in West Germany. Anna von der Goltz, Oxford University Press (2021). © Anna von der Goltz. DOI: 10.1093/oso/9780198849520.003.0005

Illustration 4.1 SDS activist Rudi Dutschke (right) with the South Vietnamese Ambassador to Bonn at an RCDS-organized event at the Free University in West Berlin in December 1966.
(ullstein bild—Sakowitz)

leader ran in one of the papers owned by the right-wing Springer publishing house. An accompanying photograph in the West Berlin tabloid *B. Z.* showed the 'star agitator of the SDS' and 'bogey of the middle classes incarnate [*leibhaftige Bürgerschreck*]' in a leather jacket, standing next to the Ambassador and facing a flurry of flashbulbs.[6]

As in the aftermath of the Dahrendorf-Dutschke debate in Freiburg a little over a year later, the fact that Dutschke and his SDS peers had not been the only students present was largely lost in this highly personalized coverage. In fact, just as in January 1968, young Christian Democrats had played a crucial role on

---

[6] Udo Bergdoll, 'Dutschke dreht an einem dollen Ding...', *B. Z.*, 21 December 1966, 2.

6 December 1966. Activists from the local RCDS had organized the entire event and invited Nguyen Quy Anh to talk about the political situation in his home country, and they had also been involved in the scuffle on stage. Wighard Härdtl had been one of the organizers and later remembered that it was the first time he had come face to face with the SDS leader. Invoking an image of Dutschke akin to later media portrayals—of the now iconic activist as a kind of German Che Guevara—Härdtl described the scene this way: 'The Ambassador was trying to give his presentation. And up in the front row, I noticed a wild looking, dark-haired man with fanatical eyes. [...] It was my first encounter with Rudi Dutschke.'[7] When Dutschke leaped onto the podium, Härdtl tried to pull him down by force.[8] Soon afterward, other SDS activists began to get up on stage and RCDS members formed a protective circle around the diplomat, who made his premature exit soon after.[9]

Wulf Schönbohm later admitted that, in an early example of centre-right students mimicking left-wing tactics, they had planned the whole event to provoke their opponents and generate publicity. The Christian Democratic students had scheduled it to coincide with a student-run 'Vietnam Week', in which the SDS had taken the lead. Given the vitality of the SDS-led anti-war movement in the city, they had anticipated disruptions, he explained. 'Of course we knew that if we, the RCDS, hosted an event with the South Vietnamese Ambassador, it would be a provocation for the Left. But we liked that idea—that he would come marching in and then mayhem would break loose.'[10] Their plan worked out spectacularly well, at least in the short run. The protests against the diplomat generated a university-wide inquiry, as well as substantial coverage in the national press, which focused on the transgressions and alleged intolerance of the Left. According to a report filed by Othmar Nikola Haberl, another West Berlin Christian Democratic activist who had been present, the local RCDS was very pleased with its 'great action', because it had helped to promote the group's public profile.[11]

The events surrounding the South Vietnamese Ambassador's contentious West Berlin visit of late 1966 not only confirm that centre-right activists were inter-twined with their counterparts on the Left in myriad ways. They also point to another important but little-understood facet of 1968 that this chapter explores more fully: centre-right activists not only disagreed with left-wing students' visions for the Federal Republic's domestic political future, they also had a very different conception of internationalism. Like their student peers on the Left, they

---

[7] Härdtl interview.

[8] Härdtl interview; Dutschke-Klotz, *Wir hatten ein barbarisches, schönes Leben*, 114.

[9] LAB, B. Rep. 014, 843, 'Bericht des Rektors der FU für den 1. Untersuchungsausschuss des Abgeordnetenhauses von Berlin, V. Wahlperiode'.

[10] Schönbohm interview.

[11] ArchAPO, RCDS, file 'LV Berlin FU', Othmar Haberl, report about the RCDS election cam-paign, 1966.

were convinced that their own political struggles were intimately connected to others around the globe, but they conceived of these connections in fundamentally different ways.

The literature on West Germany's 1960s—as indeed the international historiography on this tumultuous era as a whole—has tilted heavily towards global and transnational approaches in the past two decades. Various recent studies have highlighted the extent to which West German student activists looked beyond national borders and were inspired by individuals and ideas from other countries, not just from the United States and Europe but also from what was then called the 'Third World'. For the most part, however, the Left has been the sole focus of such works, in German historiography and beyond.[12] Conservative and centre-right movements are still rarely discussed as a part of what has come to be known as the Global 1960s.[13] As Martin Durham and Margaret Power have pointed out, both the interconnectedness of transnationalism with the study of social movements of the Left, and the assumption that the right is by definition nationalistic have stunted research on transnational conservatism until quite recently.[14]

This chapter seeks to broaden, and ultimately correct, our view of student internationalism around 1968 by showing that the West German centre-right had its own mental map of the world—one that differed substantially from the far more familiar version of their left-wing student peers. While the very idea of internationalism is often conflated with leftist ideology, the argument here is that centre-right activists were heirs to what Glenda Sluga has called a 'liberal, nation-embracing, and anticommunist version of internationalism' that had characterized much of the twentieth century.[15]

---

[12] Timothy S. Brown, 1968. Transnational and Global Perspectives, Version: 1.0, in: Docupedia-Zeitgeschichte, 11.06.2012 http://docupedia.de/zg/brown_1968_v1_en_2012 (accessed on 19 September 2016); Klimke, The Other Alliance; Slobodian, Foreign Front; Dorothee Weitbrecht, Aufbruch in die Dritte Welt: Der Internationalismus der Studentenbewegung von 1968 in der Bundesrepublik (Göttingen, 2012); Brown, West Germany and the Global Sixties; Macartney, War in the Postwar.

[13] See, e.g., the special issue on 'The International 1960s', The American Historical Review 114:1 & 2 (2009); Gerd Rainer Horn, The Spirit of '68: Rebellion in Western Europe and North America, 1956–1976 (Oxford, 2007); Jeremi Suri, Power and Protest: Global Revolution and the Rise of Detente (Cambridge, MA, 2003). Newer studies that place a specific national case in a global context also tend to exclude activists of the right, e.g. Brown, West Germany and the Global Sixties; much the same can be said about the literature on the 'Global 1970s'. Niall Ferguson, Charles Maier, Erez Manela, and Daniel Sargent (eds.), The Shock of the Global: The 1970s in Perspective (Cambridge, MA, 2011); Thomas Borstelmann's US-centric global history of the 1970s, by contrast, pays close attention to the conservative ascendancy. See his The 1970s: A New Global History From Civil Rights to Economic Inequality (Princeton, NJ, 2012); for more recent comparative and transnational approaches to the study of conservatism, see von der Goltz and Waldschmidt-Nelson, Inventing the Silent Majority; Steber, Hüter der Begriffe; and Johannes Großmann, Die Internationale der Konservativen: Transnationale Elitenzirkel und private Außenpolitik in Westeuropa seit 1945 (Munich, 2014).

[14] Martin Durham and Margaret Power, 'Introduction', in idem (eds.), New Perspectives on the Transnational Right (London, 2010); 1–10, here 1; c.f. von der Goltz and Waldschmidt-Nelson, 'Introduction', in idem (eds.), Inventing the Silent Majority, 6.

[15] Glenda Sluga, Internationalism in the Age of Nationalism (Philadelphia, PA, 2013), 5.

It explores three areas on the centre-right's mental map in closer detail: the powerful ways in which the Cold War binary structured the centre-right's view of the world, paying special attention to the US-led war in Vietnam, which centre-right students often supported with fervour; the Europeanism of conservative and Christian Democratic student groups, which was bolstered, at least in part, by the fact that such groups across the west of the continent faced a similar challenge in the shape of left-wing insurgencies on university campuses; and, finally, centre-right students' extensive, but little-known, campaigns for human rights.

Cold War Imaginaries

While students of the Left increasingly began to question the binary framework of the Cold War and turned their attention to the Global South, the East-West conflict continued to structure the political imagination of the centre-right. Given their generally reformist and anti-communist impulses, it is hardly surprising that student activists of the centre-right did not buy into the radical Left's revolutionary internationalism and the increasingly militant anti-imperialist rhetoric of the student movement's heyday. Not least because, contrary to other western European countries, Germany had already lost its overseas colonies in the wake of the First World War, they rejected the idea that the Federal Republic was in any way imperialist or that anti-imperialism was a salient theme for West German students. This position became particularly clear in the wake of the Six Day War of 1967, when Israel began to occupy a central place in the left-wing student movement's anti-imperialist thinking. When some student activists began disrupting a number of events featuring Israel's first Ambassador to the Federal Republic, Asher Ben-Natan, for instance, Christian Democratic students were quick to stage counter-demonstrations, issued statements that condemned the disruptions, and hosted teach-ins with Ben-Natan.[16]

However, centre-right students' rejection of anti-imperialism as an overarching political concept did not mean that they were generally unsympathetic to the anti-colonial cause. In a relatively short time span of roughly three decades (1945–75), a world of European colonial empires was transformed into a world of nation-states—a development that did not leave centre-right students unmoved. Ignaz Bender, the young Christian Democrat who spearheaded 'Action 1 July' in 1965 and helped to organize the Dutschke-Dahrendorf debate of January 1968, for one,

---

[16] ACDP, 4/6/44/3, RCDS press release, 36, 19 June 1969; Schönbohm, Radunski, and Runge, *Die herausgeforderte Demokratie*, 71. The RCDS had established ties with Israeli student organizations in 1965. ACDP, 4/6/13/1, 'Bericht von der Israel-Reise' [1966]; on the anti-Zionist turn of activists of the far Left in 1967, see Aribert Reimann, 'Letters from Amman: Dieter Kunzelmann and the Origins of German Anti-Zionism during the Late 1960s', in *A Revolution of Perception?: Consequences and Echoes of 1968*, edited by Ingrid Gilcher-Holtey (Oxford, 2014), 69–88.

had a keen interest in anti-colonial liberation movements of the era. He was a leading member of the International Committee of the Association of German Students in the early 1960s and, as such, had extensive international ties. In his memoirs, he proudly stressed that he had helped to get Agostinho Neto, the leader of the Angolan movement for independence from Portugal and the first president of independent Angola, to give a talk at the University of Freiburg in 1963. This had been the first time that the leader of an African independence movement gave a speech in West Germany.[17] Bender also participated in a solidarity campaign for the South African anti-Apartheid activist (and former University of Tübingen student and SDS member) Neville Alexander, who would spend ten years in Robben Island prison alongside Nelson Mandela.[18]

Bender did not just lay claim to the anti-colonial cause in retrospect. As early as 1958, he had voiced concerns about the brutal conduct of French troops during the Algerian War of Independence and the censorship of the issue in the French press. Bender was then editor of Bonn University's student newspaper *Spuren*, and he penned an editorial that chronicled the torture and murder of Algerians at the hands of the French in highly graphic terms. The piece was so unusual that it raised French suspicions that Bender had ties to fighters from the Algerian National Liberation Front (*Front de Libération Nationale*, FLN) who were then in hiding in the Federal Republic.[19] Reports about French atrocities in the North African country circulated widely in the West German press at the time, and Bender had also read first-hand reports by the Committee of Spiritual Resistance and the French-Algerian journalist Henri Alleg, a member of the French Communist Party.[20] He was particularly appalled by the silence about French crimes in France itself. 'Many innocent people fell victim to terrorist justice. They were murdered recklessly and brutally. Had no one become aware of this guilt?', Bender asked in his article.[21] However, not just the French were guilty, he went on to caution. The entire western community had shied away from protesting the violence out of fear that an independent Algeria might embrace communism or

---

[17] Bender Papers, 'Mit Agostino [sic] Neto fuer die Unabhängigkeit Afrikas', Memoirs, unpublished MS. See also Ignaz Bender, *Weltordnung: Der Weg zu einer besser geordneten Welt* (Baden-Baden, 2017).

[18] 'Solidarität mit dem Südafrikaner Dr. Neville Alexander', Bender Memoirs, unpublished MS; Weitbrecht, *Aufbruch in die Dritte Welt*. 121; Slobodian, *Foreign Front*, 22–4, 214, fn. 39.

[19] I. B. [Ignaz Bender], 'Grauenvolles geschah in Algerien', *Spuren*, 7/8 (1958), 27–9; Mathilde von Bülow, *West Germany, Cold War Europe and the Algerian War* (Cambridge, 2016), 84–103; 153–324; some West German activists of the Left indeed supported FLN fighters at the time. See Claus Leggewie, '*Kofferträger': Das Algerien-Projekt der Linken im Adenauer-Deutschland* (Berlin, 1984). Bender was later told that the West German Military Counterintelligence Service had put him under surveillance, allegedly to stop potential reprisals against him by terrorist pro-French groups. Bender interview.

[20] Henri Alleg, *La question* (Lausanne, 1958); Comité résistance, spirituelle, *Des rappelés témoignent* (Clichy, Seine, 1957); Bender interview.

[21] I.B. [Ignaz Bender], 'Grauenvolles geschah in Algerien', *Spuren*, 7/8 (1958), 27–9.

of jeopardizing the relationship to France. Informing West German students about the events was a means to atone, he suggested.

Bender's article echoed a powerful trope championed in FLN propaganda and increasingly also by French critics of the war at the time, namely that the torture and extra-judicial killings in Algeria were comparable to the Nazi genocide. Given that there were many former anti-Nazi resistance fighters among the French troops in Algeria, this was a highly controversial claim. As Mathilde von Bülow has shown recently, it was also a comparison that older West German Christian Democrats and the conservative press rejected.[22] Bender, by contrast, agreed that French torture in Algeria was comparable to the Nazi campaign of mass murder. 'In the concentration camps [...] these kinds of things happened, as well', he wrote.

Bender's account thus transcended the anti-totalitarian logic of the Cold War by suggesting that the crimes committed by the Western democracies in their colonies were equivalent to Nazi violence. As a young Christian Democrat he nevertheless added quickly that communist regimes equally violated human rights. 'And they are happening today behind the Iron Curtain and will perhaps happen tomorrow in another, Western country.' In the end, his anti-communist instincts prevailed, for the piece ended with an anti-communist rallying cry. If one did not enter the world 'to call every man brother, others will come along and call him "comrade,"' he warned[23]—a rhetorical move that foreshadowed Christian Democratic human rights campaigns of the 1970s, as we shall see later in this chapter.

One the one hand, Bender's advocacy on behalf of the anti-colonial movements of the era and his vocal condemnation of French torture in Algeria was something of a novelty for a young Christian Democrat in this period. On the other, his anti-communism and focus on political repression in the socialist dictatorships of the Eastern bloc were far more typical for a young activist of his political stripes. Like many of his peers, he narrated the story of his political socialization along some of the Cold War's major European milestones, such as the East German Uprising of 17 June 1953 and the Soviet's crushing of the revolt in Hungary in 1956.[24] To centre-right students like Bender, the victims and central sites of Europe's Cold War division were the equivalent of what Fidel Castro and Che Guevara and the city of Havana or Mao's China represented to activists of the radical Left, who drew much of their political inspiration from 'Third World' revolutions.[25]

---

[22] von Bülow, *West Germany, Cold War Europe and the Algerian War*, 113–14.

[23] Bender, 'Grauenvolles geschah in Algerien'.

[24] 'Mohikaners Wandlung', *Der Spiegel*, 27 (1958), 15–16; Bender interview.

[25] John Davis, 'Silent Minority? British Conservative Students in the Age of Campus Protest', in *Inventing the 'Silent Majority' in Western Europe and the United States*, edited by von der Goltz and Waldschmidt-Nelson, 63–80; on the Left's fascination with Cuba and Mao's China, see Slobodian, *Foreign Front*; and Jennifer Ruth Hosek, *Sun, Sex and Socialism: Cuba in the German Imaginary* (Toronto; Buffalo, 2012).

As the frontline city of Cold War Europe, divided Berlin indeed elicited a particular fascination among students of the centre-right. While West German students with left-wing political leanings flocked to the island city for other reasons—notably its cosmopolitan reputation and the prospect of avoiding conscription—it was the barbed-wire symbolism of the walled city that caught the imagination of the centre-right, representing, as it did, the inhumanity of socialism in practice.[26] Since the late 1940s, a strong anti-communist consensus had defined politics in West Berlin, and many West Berliners were still haunted by memories of Soviet occupation in 1945 and the blockade of 1948/9. For a young activist of the centre-right, the city was the perfect place to demonstrate anti-communist commitment.

Radunski, who had grown up in West Berlin, conveyed that the city's division had a profound impact on his political trajectory. On 13 August 1961 the world woke up to the news that the East German regime had walled off the western half of Berlin, leading to '[n]ever-ending personal and political deliberations. The changed situation touched me emotionally, much like the other students who now came to Berlin more than ever', Radunski recalled in his autobiography.[27] In the mid-1960s, the growing number of young visitors to West Berlin included young Christian Democratic and conservative students from across Western Europe for whom the RCDS hosted regular 'Berlin Seminars' to foster greater awareness of the day-to-day realities of German division after the construction of the Wall.[28] Their intense focus on the Berlin Wall and Germany's Cold War division represented a marked contrast to activists of the Left, whose main points of political reference often lay outside Germany's and Europe's borders—be it the Free Speech Movement in the United States or anti-colonial liberation movements in Latin America, Asia, and Africa. 'We had a different socialization into these topics [of international student politics in the 1960s]. Our socialization was the Wall', Radunski asserted.[29]

Radunski's peer Horst Teltschik, who, in the 1980s, would become something of a shadow Foreign Minister under Chancellor Kohl, equally stressed the important ways in which Berlin's division shaped his views as a student of political science at the city's Free University.[30] He arrived in West Berlin in the fall of 1962, just one year after the Wall had gone up. He later said that throughout his time

---

[26] Some of the material on West Berlin and the Vietnam War in this section previously appeared in my article 'The "other '68ers" in West Berlin: Christian Democratic Students and the Cold War City', *Central European History* 50, 1 (2017), 86–112.

[27] Radunski, *Hinter der Kulisse*, 37.

[28] ACDP, 4-6-7, 'Rechenschaftsbericht des Bundesvorsitzenden Gert Hammer' [1966], 10; also Dieter Ibielski and Wolfgang Kirsch, 'Geschichte: Der RCDS als vordenkende Gruppe in der Politik', in Wolfgang Kirsch, ed., *RCDS-entschieden demokratisch: Geschichte, Programm und Politik*, RCDS-Schriftenreihe no. 8 (n.d. [1971]), 37.

[29] Radunski interview.

[30] Wirsching, *Abschied vom Provisorium*, 182. On Teltschik's important role in the 1980s, see further 238–42.

there, he found it impossible to ignore what was happening on the other side of the barrier; the repression that ordinary East Germans suffered had been ever-present to him, Teltschik recalled. As a West German living in the city, Teltschik could visit its Eastern half even before the Quadripartite Agreement on Berlin came into effect in 1972, and he did so frequently, meeting various people that an East German friend put him in touch with. 'I always met with friends from the GDR and from East Berlin in East Berlin. So I experienced first-hand how much GDR citizens suffered', he explained. Even young children already knew what was permissible to say in the company of strangers, Teltschik remembered. '[T]his showed the whole brutality and inhumanity of the system. I'm saying this, because of course it shaped my conflict with the Left.'[31]

Teltschik recalled that, viewed from the vantage point of West Berlin, he had found the radical Left's revolutionary internationalism particularly misguided, because, to him, there had appeared to be far more pressing problems closer to home. He charged the Left with having been wilfully ignorant about conditions in the Eastern bloc while cultivating a romanticized, naïve, and deeply flawed revolutionary internationalism. This trope would become popular among later critics of 1968 but was already circulating in centre-right publications at the time.[32]

> I never understood it. Including Dutschke, who came from the GDR. [...] The Wall had just been built. Against the backdrop of the Wall, barbed wire, the Wall dead, the Soviet intervention against the Prague Spring in '68—that it wasn't an issue! Vietnam was a huge issue. [...] [O]vernight the U.S. was suddenly the devil. Just Vietnam, Vietnam, Vietnam. [...]The Wall, human rights abuses in East Berlin, in Moscow. That's who my enemies were, actually.[33]

In spite of his strong anti-communist commitment, Teltschik was adamant, however, that centre-right students, and the RCDS in particular, had not simply remained stuck in the rigid Cold War mindset of the 1950s. Indeed, in the 1960s, not only did Christian Democratic students speak out against the 'irrational anti-communism' of the previous decade, but they also supported the legalization of

---

[31] Teltschik interview.

[32] Centre-right student papers regularly carried reports about opposition movements in the Eastern bloc and often featured articles that accused the West German Left of ignorance about the concerns of Eastern dissidents, see e.g. HIS, A-ZC-96, 'Verständigungsschwierigkeiten', *Colloquium*, 4 (1967); HIA, GSC, box 87, 'Prag liegt näher', *Colloquium*, 4 (1968), 2–3; *Actio: Eine deutsche Studentenzeitschrift*, 4, 2/3 (1968). Some leading SDS members have since conceded that they had often been oblivious to the postwar anxieties of the West Berlin population and showed little concern about what went on to the east of the Iron Curtain. Fichter and Lönnendonker, *Kleine Geschichte des SDS*, 88; Christian Semler, '1968 im Westen – was ging uns die DDR an?', *Aus Politik und Zeitgeschichte*, B 45 (2003), 3–5.

[33] Teltschik interview. Peter Gauweiler argued very similarly in a more recent piece. Gauweiler, 'Wir waren für die das allerletzte'.

the West German Communist Party, which had been banned in 1956.[34] Moreover, even before the Social-Liberal coalition under Willy Brandt began to pursue its *Neue Ostpolitik* of rapprochement with the Soviets and Eastern bloc in 1969, the RCDS had begun to favour closer ties with the German Democratic Republic. As early as 1967, the RCDS was advocating German-German contacts on all levels and signalling its openness towards establishing formal relations with the East German Socialist youth organization Free German Youth (FDJ).[35] In doing so, the student activists edged closer to the stance of the Social Democrats at the time, who held the Foreign Ministry during the Grand Coalition years and began to lay the ground for Brandt's later initiatives. Most Christian Democratic politicians, on the other hand, opposed any accommodation with the GDR—a position that would initially only harden once the SPD began to implement its new course after 1969.[36]

In contrast to its mother party, in 1968 the West Berlin RCDS chapter debated the desirability of recognizing the Oder-Neisse Line, thereby calling into question the long-standing official policy of seeking a restoration of the German borders of 1937.[37] RCDS's basic program of 1969 similarly called for recognizing Poland's western border and for the total revocation of the Hallstein Doctrine according to which the FRG did not maintain diplomatic relations with countries that recognized the GDR (the Soviet Union being an exception).[38] Older party representatives were not amused by the students' proposals. When the West Berlin RCDS chapter stopped placing all written mentions of the GDR in inverted commas, for instance—speaking of the 'GDR' was the party's preferred way of identifying a state that the Federal Republic did not officially recognize—it caused such a spat that the CDU decided to suspend its monthly subsidies to the students.[39]

---

[34] HIA, BFW, box 84, 'RCDS-SDS', in *Akut: Nachrichtenblatt der Bonner Studentenschaft*, 40 (May/June 1968); ACDP, 4/6/8, 'Nachtrag zu den Beschlüssen der 17. ord. Delegiertenversammlung vom 16.-20. März 1967 in Heidelberg'.

[35] ACDP, 4/6/1/2, Wulf Schönbohm, 'Innerdeutsche Politik im Wandel'; *Runge Private Papers*, file Politischer Beirat, Martin Kempe, 'Protokoll des Außenpolitischen Arbeitskreises des Bundesverbandes des RCDS, 19.-21. Januar 1968'; Ibielski and Kirsch, 'Geschichte: Der RCDS als vordenkende Gruppe in der Politik', 41–2.

[36] However, some moderates within the CDU were more open-minded about the future of German-German relations at the time, which has led some scholars (notably former Christian Democratic student activist Christian Hacke, who became a leading scholar of German foreign relations) to re-interpret *Ostpolitik* as the brainchild of Kiesinger's Grand Coalition. Hacke, *Weltmacht wider Willen*, 152–62. Most of the scholarship, however, disagrees with this assessment—while acknowledging that not all Christian Democrats were vehemently opposed to rapprochement. See Julia von Dannenberg, *The Foundations of Ostpolitik: The Making of the Moscow Treaty Between West Germany and the USSR* (Oxford, 2008), 101; and Clay Clemens, *Reluctant Realists: The CDU/CSU and West German Ostpolitik* (Durham and London, 1989).

[37] ACDP, 4-6-1-2, Wulf Schönbohm, 'Innerdeutsche Politik im Wandel'; Runge Papers, file 'Politischer Beirat', Martin Kempe, 'Protokoll des Außenpolitischen Arbeitskreises des Bundesverbandes des RCDS, 19.-21. Januar 1968'.

[38] 'Grundsatzprogramm des RCDS: 39 Thesen zur Reform und zu den Zukunftsaufgaben deutscher Politik', in Wolfgang Kirsch (ed.), *RCDS-entschieden demokratisch: Geschichte, Programm und Politik*, RCDS-Schriftenreihe, 8 (1970), 53–4.

[39] Karsten Plog, 'Revolution in kleinen Dosen. Der Linksruck an den Universitäten schreckt auch den RCDS auf', *Die Welt*, 3 April 1968, 5. 'Streit zwischen CDU und RCDS: Immer Ärger mit den

Their more relaxed and pragmatic attitude towards state socialist regimes was also reflected in the considerable interest centre-right students displayed in reform communist movements to the east of the 'Iron Curtain', particularly in the Prague Spring, the attempt to build 'socialism with a human face' in Czechoslovakia. They paid close attention to the liberalization of the Czechoslovak economy that began in the mid-1960s and interpreted the reformist cause adopted by Communist Party leader Alexander Dubček in 1968 (reflected in the relaxation of censorship laws, for instance) as a cautious first step towards Western-style democracy. Some young Christian Democrats even openly revered Dubček—so much so that Chancellor Kiesinger expressed consternation about the phenomenon in internal discussions with party leadership.[40] All this led to a somewhat bizarre spectacle during the World Festival of Youth and Students in Sofia, organized by the Communist-controlled International Union of Students and the World Federation of Democratic Youth in the summer of 1968. West German Christian Democratic students, who brandished their anti-communist credentials at home, now applauded the official Czechoslovak delegation when they came in carrying pictures of the Communist Party leader. Members of the anti-authoritarian wing of the West German SDS, on the other hand, displayed their preference for alternative revolutionary socialist models from the 'Third World' when they shouted 'Castro-Mao-Guevara' instead.[41] Such were the intricacies of student internationalism in the 1960s.

This was not the only instance of such a counter-intuitive link being drawn between the Western centre-right and reform socialists in the Eastern bloc. The West Berlin paper *Colloquium*, a popular student publication with a strong anti-totalitarian bent and avowedly centrist politics, for one, argued explicitly in April 1968 that the reformers in Prague had more in common with the Western centre-right than with their socialist peers in the West.[42] Pointing, for example, to a speech Rudi Dutschke gave in Prague in the spring of 1968 that famously fell flat, the paper honed in on instances of political misunderstanding between West German SDS activists and Communist Czechoslovak student leaders. In doing so, it suggested that student activists in the East were much more reasonable and realistic than many of their Western counterparts:

Jungen', *Stuttgarter Zeitung* (5 July 1968), 7; Annamarie Doherr, 'Unzumutbar für die Partei: Berliner RCDS will CDU-Führung zu öffentlicher Diskussion zwingen', *Frankfurter Rundschau* (9 May 1968).

[40] *Runge Private Papers*, file 'Politischer Beirat', Frank Breitsprecher, 'Liberalisierungstendenzen in der tschechischen Wirtschaft'; see also Detlef Stronk, 'Die Notwendigkeit einer konkreten Humanisierung', in Kirsch, *RCDS-entschieden demokratisch: Geschichte, Programm und Politik*, 17; Kiesinger's remarks in a meeting of the CDU's federal board on 21 June 1968. *Kiesinger: 'Wir leben in einer veränderten Welt' (1965–1969)*, ed. by Buchstab, 969–70.

[41] Slobodian, *Foreign Front*, 195.

[42] On the history and politics of *Colloquium*, a publication that had its roots in East Berlin dissident circles of the late 1940s, see James F. Tent, *The Free University of Berlin: A Political History* (Bloomington and Indianapolis, 1988), 78–9.

> The students in the socialist countries understand much better how to sensibly combine protest and working within the system. The liberalization there, incidentally, is primarily driven by forces of a type that over here are condemned as managers, slaves to practical constraints, positivists, and one-track specialists.[43]

The Western 'would-be-revolutionary elite' should stop growing 'Castro beards' and 'change their travel plans for a cheaper ticket to Prague', the paper suggested. 'But over there the students have often laughed mockingly at the strange and unrealistic theories of their guests from the SDS', *Colloquium* noted with thinly veiled glee.

The Soviet military intervention of 21 August 1968 saved centre-right activists and commentators from having to think more deeply about the—at best complicated—relationship between Dubček's attempt to build 'socialism with a human face' and liberal democracy. The brutal clampdown on the Czechoslovak experiment made August 1968 a symbol of communist repression akin to 1953 and 1956. The powerful sounds and images of Soviet tanks and overwhelmingly non-violent Czechoslovak resistance disseminated via Western radio and television broadcasts reinforced this symbolism. Rather than exemplifying the promises of a more humane form of socialism, as it had once done, 'Prague '68' became a stick with which to beat the socialist Left. The Czechoslovak reformers had sought to combine socialism and democracy, but their movement had been crushed violently, which raised larger questions about socialism's ability to coexist with a free society, Christian Democratic students pointed out. 'Can socialism be a political solution for a generation that wants freedom, if socialism has historically always been the political enemy of free development? We will ask all those who propagate socialism in Germany for their measures to safeguard freedom', Teltschik wrote in guidelines for student speakers on how to attack the APO for its lacklustre response to the Soviet intervention.[44]

Over the next ten years and more, Christian Democratic students would frequently commemorate the Soviet intervention in Czechoslovakia to highlight communism's repressive nature and what they regarded as indelible proof of the wholly antithetical relationship between socialism and democracy.[45] Some observers would later see the Prague Spring as a more meaningful aspect of the

---

[43] 'Prag liegt näher', *Colloqium*, 4 (April 1968), 2–3; on Dutschke's reception in Prague, see Paulina Bren, '1968 in East and West: Visions of Political Change and Student Protest from across the Iron Curtain', in *Transnational Moments of Change: Europe 1945, 1968, 1989*, edited by Gerd-Rainer Horn and Padraic Kenney (Oxford, 2004), 119–36; James Mark and Anna von der Goltz, 'Encounters', in Gildea, Mark, and Warring, *Europe's 1968*, 151.

[44] ACDP, 4/6/42/2, Horst Teltschik, 'Die Argumentation der Außerparlamentarischen Opposition (APO) zur Entwicklung in der CSSR', Rednerdienst, 4 (November 1968).

[45] See the picture of an RCDS demonstration in front of the Soviet Embassy in August 1969 on the cover of *Facts: Zeitung des RCDS* (20 October 1969); ACDP, 4/6/44/3, RCDS Pressemitteilung, 41, 22 August 1969; 'Vor 10 Jahren: Prager Frühling', *Der Grüne Punkt: Hochschulzeitung des RCDS Berlin* (Sommersemester 1978), 2.

international 1968 than the French May, including some left-wing activists, like Dutschke, who came to regret their erstwhile indifference towards dissident movements in the Eastern bloc.[46] Centre-right activists have thus been able to claim that, in this respect at least, they had been on the 'right side of history' in 1968.[47] In the words of Wulf Schönbohm: 'When Dubček and the attempt to build "socialism with a human face" were bludgeoned in Prague in '68, [...] [the student Left, AvdG] was not at all interested.'[48] In a 2018 interview, Peter Gauweiler drew a particularly stark contrast between the Left and Right's internationalism—a contrast that the events in Prague made particularly visible, he claimed:

[The student Left] chanted for the liberation of humanity, while at the same time parading through the streets under pictures of mass murderers. I still remember how we held a big demonstration in 1968 against the Russians' [sic] intervention in Prague. For the APO, this was highly suspicious, as the people of Prague were pro-American.[49]

Former Christian Democratic activists have often made a similar point about the radical Left's fascination with Mao Zedong's Cultural Revolution and the lack of concern for the violence that accompanied it. Indeed, this became one of the most difficult aspects of political commitment around 1968 that many left-wing activists have since had to wrestle with, especially those who belonged to one of the manifold Maoist groups founded after the dissolution of the SDS.[50] For their part, centre-right groups at the time had not been above tongue-in-cheek appropriations of Maoism, peppering their leaflets with lesser-known quotations from the chairman, inviting students to join them on 'the long march for persistent reform', and even using Mao's image in their own advertising on occasion.[51] However, they later invoked Mao and Maoism purely to draw a sharp line between themselves and the Left.

---

[46] Jacques Rupnik's interview with Rudi Dutschke (1978), printed in 'The misunderstanding of 1968', *Transit*, 35 (Summer 2008), https://www.eurozine.com/the-misunderstanding-of-1968/; on such left-wing regrets James Mark, Anna von der Goltz, and Anette Warring, 'Reflections', in Gildea, Mark, and Warring, *Europe's 1968*, 283–325.

[47] Kurt Faltlhauser, 'Die 68er-Bewegung: Persönliche und gesellschaftliche Wirkungen', *Politische Studien*, 59/422 (2008), 27–8.

[48] Schönbohm interview.   [49] Gauweiler, 'Wir waren für die das allerletzte'.

[50] Götz Aly's semi-autobiographical (and very polemical) indictment of the student Left in 1968 is a case in point. See his *Unser Kampf: 1968-ein irritierter Blick zurück* (Frankfurt, 2008); on repentant (and unrepentant) ex-Maoists, see also Mark, von der Goltz, and Warring, 'Reflections'; and David Spreen, *Cold War Imaginaries: Mao's China and the Making of a Postcolonial Far Left in Divided Germany* (PhD dissertation, University of Michigan, 2019).

[51] See e.g. Universitätsarchiv Bonn, *BSU-Kurier*, SP-Wahlen 1970 Special; see the 1971 Young Union advertisement from Hamburg printed in Apel, 'Jenseits von 1968', 65.

Detlef Stronk, for one, who was involved in the RCDS and MSU at the time, recalled that he had been a 'fierce opponent of Mao Zedong's. When the Left shouted "Mao, Mao, Mao Zedong!", I said "He is a criminal!" And I am right. He was one of the biggest criminals of all time, together with Hitler and Stalin.'[52] Horst Teltschik equally contrasted his stance on Communist China with that of the Left and was adamant that his student peers should have known better. Teltschik pointed out that Jürgen Domes, a conservative political scientist and expert on Chinese history and politics, whose research dealt with the Cultural Revolution's considerable violence, taught at the Free University during the height of the Left's Mao cult and was attacked by the local student Left for his allegedly reactionary politics.[53] By contrast, Teltschik, who had admired Domes, wrote his thesis on the Sino-Soviet split and later claimed that he had always been repelled by the Chinese Communist leader. Teltschik was generally scathing about the Left's view of the world:

And this was another thing that really vexed me about the APO and the Left. There was the Cultural Revolution in China with millions of dead people. And at the same time they marched down Kurfürstendamm with Mao posters. Mao, Mao, Ho Chi Minh! I always said to myself: Boy, how can they?! It was something that was so foreign to me, because I always felt that I was naturally against dictatorship and injustice and against terror. [. . .] The Left was totally blind. They suppressed it. All of it. Eastern Europe, [the] Warsaw Pact, the GDR, China, the Cultural Revolution, all of it.[54]

Only a few years after 1968, while the Cultural Revolution was still underway, Western conservatives, including leading West German Christian Democrats, began to embrace Chairman Mao and China with considerable enthusiasm. By this point, they had come to the conclusion that the Asian communists would make useful allies in their quest to contain the Soviet Union—an especially urgent issue to West German Christian Democrats critical of Brandt's *Ostpolitik*. RCDS had, in fact, called for establishing bilateral diplomatic relations with China as early as 1969.[55] A few years later, the Christian Democratic former Foreign and Defence Minister Gerhard Schröder was the first West German politician to visit communist China, just five months after US President Richard Nixon's trip 'that changed the world' in 1972. The newly-minted CDU leader Helmut Kohl followed in 1974. In January 1975, Franz Josef Strauss, the leader of the Bavarian Christian Democrats, then became the first West German politician to secure a coveted

[52] Stronk interview.

[53] Jürgen Domes, *Politik und Herrschaft in Rotchina* (Stuttgart, Berlin, Cologne, and Mainz, 1965).

[54] Teltschik interview. Erich Röper also remembered being influenced by the writings of Jürgen Domes and inviting the China scholar to an event in Mainz. Röper interview.

[55] Ibielski and Kirsch, 'Geschichte: Der RCDS als vordenkende Gruppe in der Politik', 44.

meeting with Mao Zedong.[56] Christian Democrats could of course rationalize this new openness towards China as a contribution to Cold War détente, and they did not glorify Maoism and parade around the streets with Mao posters. Given their scathing verdicts about the Left's fascination with Mao and the Cultural Revolution, it is nevertheless noteworthy that they had no qualms about meeting with the chairman and his deputies. At no point before the Tiananmen Square massacre in 1989 did the Chinese human rights record complicate this Christian Democratic embrace.[57] Nor did the Christian Democratic opening to China during the Cultural Revolution seem to confound former activists' complimentary portrayals of their own form of internationalism around 1968.

The American War in Vietnam

While centre-right activists regularly stressed their superior judgement regarding Prague '68 and the Chinese Cultural Revolution, claiming a similarly finely tuned moral compass when it came to their stance on the war in Vietnam has been a more difficult endeavour. Opposition to the war became the focal point of left-wing student activity from 1965 onwards, who articulated it in increasingly moralistic terms through frequent comparisons between the American-led war and the murder of the Jews at Auschwitz.[58]

In autobiographical accounts, be they interviews or memoirs, and in commemorative publications concerning the centre-right's 1968, by contrast, references to the war are often conspicuous by their absence. Archival sources from the period, however, make clear that West German centre-right activists, like their conservative student peers across the Atlantic, supported the war with considerable fervour.[59] As the RCDS national chair declared in 1966:

[56] Bernd Schaefer, 'Sino-West German Relations during the Mao Era', CWIHP e-Dossier, no. 56 (3 November 2014), available at https://www.wilsoncenter.org/publication/sino-west-german-relations-during-the-mao-era. For the broader context see Margaret Macmillan, *Nixon & Mao: The Week that Changed the World* (New York, 2007). At the time of Kohl's visit to China, Teltschik was an aide to Kohl.

[57] Frank Bösch, *Zeitenwende 1979: Als die Welt von heute begann* (Munich, 2019), 154 and 182.

[58] Wilfried Mausbach, 'Auschwitz and Vietnam: West German Protest against America's War in the 1960s', in *America, the Vietnam War, and the World: Comparative and International Perspectives*, edited by Wilfried Mausbach, Andreas W. Daum, and Lloyd C. Gardner (New York, 2003), 279–98; on anti-Vietnam war activism generally, Thomas, *Protest Movements*, 69–86; and Slobodian, *Foreign Front*, 85–9. The Vietnam issue was particularly charged in divided Germany. By contrast, John Davis found that the war played a relatively minor role for British Conservative students active in campus politics in the 1960s, Davis, 'Silent Minority?'.

[59] On American conservatives and the Vietnam War and students' pro-war campaigns, see Sandra Scanlon, *The Pro-War Movement: Domestic Support for the Vietnam War and the Making of Modern American Conservatism* (Amherst, MA, 2013).

We believe that America's policy is necessary and that the American war in Vietnam is essential in order to enable South Vietnam to develop freely and to have a chance for freedom. We are certain that the chance for freedom will no longer exist in South Vietnam once the communists have flooded the country and hold power.[60]

One young Christian Democrat even went as far as embracing the left-wing slogan 'Vietnam is the Spain of our time'—an internationally popular mantra meant to express the moral urgency that fuelled anti-Vietnam War activism in the 1960s. Whereas the SDS likened 1960s US imperialism to General Francisco Franco's role in the Spanish Civil War of 1936–39 and endorsed the international fight against what many perceived as a new form of fascism, activist Jürgen Wahl saw parallels between the Communist quest for world revolution in Spain and Vietnam. Just as a Republican victory in the Spanish Civil War would have extended Moscow's influence further into Europe, he argued, so a North Vietnamese victory would only be the first step towards the worldwide victory of Communism.[61]

Even if his alarmist tone and vaguely Francoist sympathies were something of a rarity, former activists usually admitted that they had shared this anti-communist reasoning and been in favour of this now largely discredited military intervention when prompted in the oral history interviews. 'Well, when it came to the Vietnam War, I was convinced back then that it was indeed about containing and limiting communist expansion', as Wolfgang Reeder explained.[62] 'As far as the Vietnam War was concerned, we were—and this was certainly one of our weaknesses—[...] on the side of the Americans. The basic mood was one of unwavering anti-communism, of course', recalled Meinhard Ade of the Freiburg RCDS.[63] Jürgen Aretz, one of the founders of the Bonn Student Union, was less self-critical. Nearly fifty years later, he was still convinced that much of the student opposition to the war had been the result of Soviet and East German propaganda, which had used the war to whip up anti-Americanism in the West. At the time, Aretz explained, he had thought that 'the attack [on Vietnam] was justified. [...] With hindsight I think that things were much more nuanced, of course. But to pretend that the Americans waged a criminal war, I still wouldn't subscribe to that today. I think that is wrong.'[64]

This strongly pro-American and anti-communist reading of the war was particularly pronounced among activists in West Berlin, who thought that the fate of the island city was linked directly to the American venture in Southeast Asia. In line with the 'domino theory', according to which the fall of one country

---

[60] ACDP, 4-6-7, 'Rechenschaftsbericht des Bundesvorsitzenden Gert Hammer' [1966], 25.

[61] See ACDP, 4/7/75/2, Jürgen Wahl, memorandum for the Christian Democratic Young Union (1968).

[62] Reeder interview.   [63] Ade interview.   [64] Aretz interview.

to communism would have ripple effects elsewhere, and in an effort to put pressure on the West German government to lend military support, US Secretary of Defense Robert McNamara had suggested that, should Saigon fall, West Berlin would be next.[65]

Although the Erhard government remained reluctant to intervene militarily in the former French colony, the Federal Republic sent considerable funds and humanitarian assistance to South Vietnam. By 1965, it was the second largest donor to the country, topped only by the United States, and it would remain in that position until the end of the conflict.[66] Moreover, the US-led war enjoyed strong cross-party support and public backing in the Federal Republic, at least in the mid-1960s.[67] In line with this cross-party consensus, Christian Democratic students in West Berlin fully bought into the idea that the US military effort in Vietnam had to be supported in the name of anti-communism. 'All states that back South Vietnam militarily, especially the United States of America, deserve the gratitude of freedom-minded individuals, because here it becomes clear that they are still willing to resist militant communism's claim to power', argued the West Berlin RCDS in February 1966.[68] Christian Democratic students were convinced that West Germans—and West Berliners, in particular—owed a considerable debt of gratitude to their (former) occupiers, who had helped to spread democracy after 1945. They portrayed their pro-American stance and support for the war as a given. 'The Americans always guaranteed the freedom of West Berlin. [...] And those who guarantee your security and your life [...], you put them on a pedestal', explained Jürgen Klemann, a Christian Democratic student activist from West Berlin, who later became a senator in the city.[69]

RCDS activists did not just voice support for the war in internal memoranda. They also began to organize pro-war campaigns, which began soon after SDS activity around the issue commenced in earnest. In January 1966, RCDS set up an 'Action Committee on Peace and Freedom for South Vietnam' tasked with 'countering all efforts to defame US policy in Vietnam'.[70] Aided by funds from the local America Houses, US cultural institutions in West Germany that were often the object of left-wing protest against the war, the Action Committee engaged in a wide range of activities, including soliciting donations for South Vietnamese orphans. This latter campaign foreshadowed West German Christian Democrats' vocal support for accepting the Vietnamese 'boat people' as refugees in the Federal Republic when they fled the country en masse after the war had

---

[65] Troche, 'Berlin wird am Mekong verteidigt'.
[66] Troche, 'Berlin wird am Mekong verteidigt', 433.
[67] Troche, 'Berlin wird am Mekong verteidigt', 348–59.
[68] ACDP, I-700-841-2, RCDS FU leaflet (n.d.) [February 1966] 'Demonstration für den Frieden?'
[69] Klemann interview.   [70] ACDP, 4/6/40/2, Statute of the Action Committee.

ended in 1975.[71] RCDS also cooperated with the Union of Vietnamese Students in the Federal Republic and sought personal ties to student leaders in Saigon.[72] Christian Democratic students disseminated thousands of leaflets in an attempt to proselytize on behalf of pro-Vietnam war sentiment among students across the country and staged numerous pro-American demonstrations.[73] Klemann later

Illustration 4.2 Young Christian Democrats, including RCDS activists, at a demonstration against communist aggression in South Vietnam in Hamburg on 14 April 1975. The banners call for peace and human rights in Vietnam.
(ullstein bild—dpa)

---

[71] As Frank Bösch has shown, the CDU was the party that advocated most forcefully for accepting these South Vietnamese refugees. The left-wing magazine *konkret*, by contrast, was often quite dismissive of them, denouncing the refugees as 'US collaborators', for instance. Frank Bösch, 'Engagement für Flüchtlinge: Die Aufnahme vietnamesischer "Boat People" in der Bundesrepublik', *Zeithistorische Forschungen/Studies in Contemporary History*, 14 (2017)c 13–40, here 29; also Bösch, *Zeitenwende 1979*, 185–96. Christian Democratic students also campaigned on behalf of the 'boat people'. 'Wir können nicht mehr schweigen', *Demokratische Blätter*, 1 (1979), 21–2.

[72] ACDP, 4/6/7, annual report of RCDS chair Gert Hammer [1966]; and ACDP, 4/6/40/2, Wulf Schönbohm to Lutz Bähr, 28 July 1966; Bähr to Schönbohm, 14 July 1966; ACDP, 4/6/40/2, Vu Duy-Tu to Erich Röper, 2 June 1966. The YAF ran similar campaigns in the United States. See Scanlon, *Pro-War Movement*, 253.

[73] 'Flugblattaktion des RCDS', *FAZ*, 18 February 1966; ACDP, 4/6/40/2, Werner Gries to Wolfgang Weltin, 2 February 1966.

remembered 'bravely defending the American engagement for freedom' in front of predominantly anti-war audiences. Photographs taken in February 1966 show him giving a pro-war speech to listeners in Heidelberg, some of whom held signs that denounced the American 'terror' in Vietnam.[74]

Some of these demonstrations, such as the December 1966 event with the South Vietnamese Ambassador discussed at the beginning of this chapter, were staged as direct answers to anti-war events organized by the APO. On 5 February 1966, for instance, SDS staged its first high-profile moment of direct action in its anti-Vietnam war campaign. During a demonstration of 2,000 students in the centre of West Berlin, demonstrators blocked the traffic on Kurfürstendamm, and several hundred of them subsequently made their way to the America House.[75] In a widely reported incident, a handful of demonstrators took down the American flag and pelted the building with eggs, causing considerable outrage in the local and national press. Both the Free University's Chancellor and Governing Mayor Brandt condemned the demonstration and apologized to the US Commander in Berlin.[76] A few days later, on 8 February, the CDU, Young Union (JU), and RCDS organized a counter-demonstration in front of the America House to display the enduring pro-American sympathies of West Berlin's youth. In a speech he delivered at the site, Jürgen Wohlrabe (1936–1995), the combative leader of the local chapter of the Young Union and a former RCDS activist, fashioned himself as the true voice of the young generation in West Berlin. He even claimed to speak for young East Germans on the other side of the Berlin Wall who, he insisted, were being silenced by the socialist regime:

Three days ago a shameful act took place at this site. The flag, the highest symbol of our American protection force, was defiled by the boorish behaviour of a small group of students. As a representative of the young generation of our free Berlin, and also as a spokesman for those who are not allowed to open their mouths today, I want to emphasize: We condemn this act in the strongest possible terms! We know that these splinter groups stand in sharp contrast to the convictions of the vast majority of Berliners. Those who demonstrate for peace in this way and, by uncritically adopting the slogans of red China, work for the communists, are not taken seriously in our Berlin.[77]

---

[74] Klemann Papers, personal photograph.

[75] Reinhild Kreis, *Orte für Amerika: Die deutsch-amerikanischen Institute und Amerikahäuser in der Bundesrepublik seit den 1960er Jahren* (Stuttgart, 2012), 337–60.

[76] Fichter and Lönnendonker, 'Berlin: Hauptstadt der Revolte'; Troche, '*Berlin wird am Mekong verteidigt*', 352; Slobodian, *Foreign Front*, 87.

[77] ACDP, I-700-007-1, Rede an die Berliner und die Jugend Berlins, 7.2.1966 [sic] bei einer 'Vietnam-Gegendemonstration'. Curiously, the draft of this speech in Wohlrabe's personal papers features a title page adorned with a swastika and introduces the Christian Democrat as 'Führer' and 'Gauleiter' of West Berlin. One might speculate that this was meant to be an ironic—if rather tasteless— take on the Left's frequent labeling of the Christian Democrat as 'fascist'. See e.g. Rudi Dutschke's

As we can see, the claim of speaking for one's generation and representing the true convictions of the country's youth on international issues was made on different sides of the political spectrum.

A primary goal of speeches like these and of the overall work of the RCDS's Action Committee was to highlight the positive reasons for US involvement in the former French colony and to help craft a counter-narrative to the increasingly negative coverage of the war in the West German press. This coverage, the Action Committee argued, completely distorted the nature of the war and obscured who actually perpetrated most of the atrocities in Indochina:

> The acts of terror by communist gangs against their own population, against innocent women and children, the support of the [South Vietnamese] under-ground movement by the communist regime in North Vietnam and the delivery of Soviet and red Chinese weapons are kept completely quiet. Based on a total misjudgment of the historical truth and the real will of the South Vietnamese people, fanatical partisans are portrayed as freedom fighters.[78]

Left-wing student campaigns against the war were indeed helping to create a counter-public that was highly critical of the whole premise of the American presence.[79] In effect, groups like the Action Committee were now attempting to create a 'counter-counter-public' on campus. West German students eventually supported the protests against the war in Vietnam in growing numbers. In 1966, though, the issue still proved a suitable vehicle for centre-right students to mobilize those who did not support the anti-war movement for their own cause: '[T]he stance of the RCDS on the question of South Vietnam really secures new members for us, especially those who actually guarantee a high level of involvement', reported the head of the Baden-Württemberg chapter in February 1966.[80]

In subsequent years, however, the escalation of the war amid growing concerns over the aerial bombardment of Vietnamese civilians and the US military's use of napalm made it more and more difficult to rally in support of the war.[81] RCDS slowly adopted a more qualified stance towards the war from 1967 onward, and some members even began to question their unconditional support of the Americans. In his Filbinger-commissioned study on the origins of student protest,

testimony to the investigation committee of Berlin's state parliament in February 1968, cited in Scharloth, 1968, 133.

[78] ACDP, 4/6/40/2, Declaration of the Baden-Württemberg chapter of RCDS.

[79] Jürgen Horlemann and Peter Gäng, *Vietnam: Genesis eines Konflikts* (Frankfurt am Main, 1966).

[80] ACDP, 4/6/40/2, Werner Gries to Wolfgang Weltin, 2 February 1966.

[81] Bernd Greiner, *War Without Fronts: The USA in Vietnam*, translated from the German by Anne Wyburd with Victoria Fern (New Haven, CT, 2009).

for instance, Bender invoked Germany's own wartime experience to critique the increasingly brutal warfare in Vietnam:

> [The younger generation] cannot understand why the Federal Republic did not take a clearer position on the war in Vietnam. Even if it was particularly hard to reach a balanced judgement on these questions: it would probably have befitted the Federal Republic to have condemned the way in which all sides, including the USA, were conducting the war at that time, because the war had reached a degree of inhumanity for which the Federal Republic ought to have had a particular understanding, given its own experience with the consequences of total war.[82]

One particularly vocal critic of the war was Jürgen-Bernd Runge, even before he became a Christian Democratic 'renegade'. In retrospect, he pointed to Vietnam to make sense of his unusual political trajectory. Doubts about the war had played a big role in his political conversion, he explained. In 1966, SDS activists Jürgen Horlemann and Peter Gäng published a thoroughly researched and widely read book on the origins of the war, and Runge felt compelled to keep up.[83] 'The Left wrote books [...], and I defended the American position and had few arguments. And that made me angry', as he put it. Runge recalled that he had spent several weeks in various libraries to read up on the official US position, '[b]ut I could not prove what I wanted to prove'.[84] As a result, he began to adopt a more nuanced stance, he explained, criticizing both the North Vietnamese and the US-backed government in the South.[85] His more critical approach towards the United States never gained majority support within the association, however. While some activists began to raise doubts about the American engagement and overall opposition to anti-war protest grew much more muted, most student activists never abandoned their basic commitment to supporting the American presence in Southeast Asia. Only many years later would more former Christian Democratic student activists reflect back on their erstwhile stance and admit openly that the Federal Republic's—and their own—backing of the war had been flawed.[86]

Europe

For all their emphatic pro-Americanism on display over the question of Vietnam, centre-right students had remarkably few tangible ties to the United States. A trip

---

[82] Bender, *Der Protest der 'großen' Minderheit*, 39–40.   [83] Horlemann and Gäng, *Vietnam*.
[84] Runge interview.
[85] ArchAPO, RCDS, file 'Berlin Flugblätter Juni-Juli 1967', West Berlin RCDS leaflet about the decision of the university convention regarding Vietnam; ArchAPO, RCDS, file '18 Ord Bundesdelegierten-Versammlung Mappe 1968', press release on Vietnam by RCDS delegates, among them Runge.
[86] Faltlhauser, 'Die 68er-Bewegung', 27–8; Hacke, '68: Fluch oder Segen?', 47. With some exceptions, most of my interviewees were critical of their unconditional support for the war.

by a group of young Christian Democrats to Washington, D.C. and New York City in the summer of 1969, where they watched Apollo 11's moon landing on television and quizzed Greenwich Village hippies about their 'attitudes about life, society, and its consequences' was something of an exception.[87] Theirs was largely an instinctive and principled pro-Americanism sustained by gratitude for the US role in democratizing West Germany after 1945, memories of John F. Kennedy's 'Ich bin ein Berliner' speech in 1963, and one that harkened back to Adenauer's policy of seeking deeper integration of the Federal Republic into the West. It was not based on more personalized forms of internationalism, such as political friendships, personal exchanges, deep organizational linkages to North American student organizations, or a strong intellectual commitment to understanding recent debates and events in the United States. As Martin Klimke has shown in considerable detail, SDS activists, by contrast—often erroneously portrayed as 'anti-American' for their critique of US imperialism—had close and continual links to the American Students for a Democratic Society (with whom they shared an acronym) and adopted much of their protest repertoire from US protest movements.[88] The events in Berkeley, Oakland or in the streets of Chicago did not have nearly the same influence on the West German centre-right. 'There was no exchange to speak of', recalled Horst Teltschik. 'Of course we knew what happened in Berkeley, but it was all far away.'[89]

As a case in point, one of the few traces of their reception of the Black liberation struggle in the archives of the centre-right was an extremely ill-judged appropriation of the slogan 'Black is beautiful', a mantra that had originally sought to express the fight for a more positive perception of African American bodies in a society dominated by whites. Christian Democratic students duly stripped it of its anti-racism and began to use the English-language slogan on behalf of a party whose official political colour was black—just as some activists continued to link their own political marginalization on campus to being 'Black'.[90]

Nor did West German centre-right students pay much attention to the extremely vibrant conservative student movement in the United States at the time. As in West Germany, its members similarly rallied in favour of the war in Vietnam and confronted a resurgent campus Left—and no doubt would have had a thing or two to teach the West Germans when it came to organizing a

---

[87] ACDP, 4/64/1481, Junge Union Deutschland, Studienfahrt in die USA vom 17. Juli bis 1. August 1969. There are few other archival sources that suggest concrete ties to the United States in the late 1960s. Some interviewees mentioned individual trips to the country, but usually did not attribute much political significance to them.

[88] Klimke, *The Other Alliance*.   [89] Teltschik interview; also Schönbohm interview.

[90] From the late 1960s, Christian Democratic youth and student groups issued leaflets with images of black—and white—women next to the caption 'Black is beautiful', ACDP, Bildarchiv, no. 5472/2; RCDS Bonn (ed.), *Wahl-Reflex* (WS 1967/68). In 1972 elections, the CDU campaigned with the slogan at the national level. ACDP, Plakatsammlung, no. 10-001-1550. The Young Union was still using the slogan in 2008. http://www.spiegel.de/lebenundlernen/schule/innenansicht-der-jungen-union-black-is-beautiful-a-589823.html (accessed on 12 July 2017); see 62 and 100.

successful counter-movement. RCDS and the Student Unions did not seek out American conservative student groups such as the College Republican National Committee or the increasingly influential Young Americans for Freedom (YAF), which had been founded in 1960. The West Germans' political moderation and reformist zeal meant that they felt little ideological affinity for a Republican Party or conservative youth organizations like YAF that stressed not only a militant anti-communism, but also the need for limited government and traditional conservative principles.[91]

This did not mean, however, that West German centre-right students did not have personal or political ties that transcended the Federal Republic's borders. Rather than gazing across the Atlantic, however, they first and foremost looked to their Western European neighbours for allies and inspiration. Much has been made in recent years about the Europeanism of 1968.[92] Some scholars have gone as far as to portray 1968 as the cradle of an affective form of European integration, as the era that gave birth to a 'European identity among the young protesters' that was sustained beyond 1989.[93] However, the West German student Left's keen interest in US protest movements and in developments in the 'Third World' in the 1960s, along with its relative lack of focus on protest events to the east of the Iron Curtain, raises at least some doubts about the extent to which ideas of a united Europe truly animated left-wing students around 1968. Despite often being held up as one of the archetypical transnational Europeans in the literature on 1968, even Daniel Cohn-Bendit conceded as much in a 2018 interview: 'Europe was not an issue, not at all. [...] We enjoyed the mobility, travelled back and forth [...] yes. But "Europe" was not on our minds much, not as a grand idea and not as the basis for political institutions either.'[94]

In fact, 'Europe' was a far more salient theme for centre-right students around this time—and not just in that they regularly denounced the continent's political division and the socialist dictatorships in its eastern half. In 1968, RCDS called directly on the Christian Democrats to make a united Europe its chief political goal. In doing so, the organization was following in the footsteps of the Christian

---

[91] On the history of American student right in the 1960s, see Gregory L. Schneider, *Cadres for Conservatism: Young Americans for Freedom and the Rise of the Contemporary Right* (New York, 1999); John A. Andrew III, *The Other Side of the Sixties: Young Americans for Freedom and the Rise of Conservative Politics* (New Brunswick, NJ, 1997); and Klatch, *Generation Divided*.

[92] Gildea, Mark, and Warring, *Europe's 1968*; Richard Ivan Jobs, 'Youth Movements: Travel, Protest, and Europe in 1968', *The American Historical Review*, 114, 2 (2009), 376–404. In his study of British Conservative student activists in the late 1960s, John Davis also found that they were remarkably pro-European and had extensive personal networks that spanned the continent. Davis, 'Silent Minority?'.

[93] Jobs, *Backpack Ambassadors*, 98.

[94] Daniel Cohn-Bendit and Claus Leggewie, '1968: Power to the Imagination', *The New York Review of Books* (10 May 2018), 6; on Cohn-Bendit as the archetypical European, see Richard Ivan Jobs, 'The Grand Tour of Daniel Cohn-Bendit and the Europeanism of 1968', in *May 68: Rethinking France's Last Revolution*, edited by Julian Jackson, James S. Williams, and Anna-Louise Milne (London, 2011), 231–44.

Democratic parties of the late 1940s, which had been a major driving force behind the project of European integration.[95]

In contrast to their peers on the Left who often utilized more informal networks and personal travel to forge connections to movements in other countries, centre-right students relied primarily on formal channels of international exchange to liaise with student activists from other Western European democracies. The RCDS was a founding member of the International Union of Christian Democrat and Conservative Students (ICCS), which had been set up in 1961 and which organized regular meetings between like-minded students from Scandinavia, the United Kingdom, Austria, Belgium, and the Netherlands.[96] Such formal exchanges could leave lasting personal impressions. Wolfgang Reeder, for one, recalled being deeply impressed by the willingness to engage, superior debating skills, and eloquence of students from some of Western Europe's older democracies, notably Britain. Activists there knew how to combine politics with socializing and possessed remarkable rhetorical skills, he remembered.[97] Other former activists recalled the meetings with their European peers mostly for the social bonhomie and heavy drinking that accompanied such international encounters. Whereas they might otherwise have had difficulties translating their different brands of Conservatism and Christian Democracy to each other, this generation of activists was keener than ever to strengthen transnational ties.[98]

More than anything else, it was their similar experiences of being put on the defensive by a resurgent student Left that strengthened the bonds between West German Christian Democratic students and their peers across the continent. '[I]n response to extreme left-wing disruptions in the universities of Europe', ICCS increased its activities markedly in the late 1960s, a report published in the organization's main publication explained in 1974.[99] Left-wing mobilization indeed posed a formidable common challenge. Student protests were rocking campuses in London, Aarhus, Leuven, and West Berlin. The fact that left-wing protest around 1968 was itself strongly transnational thus shrunk the political distance between different national student groups that opposed it. 'Europe has to be seen as a unit in this regard as well. That is why the RCDS is trying to activate a

---

[95] Ibielski and Kirsch, 'Geschichte: Der RCDS als vordenkende Gruppe in der Politik', 43. On the Catholic and Christian Democratic origins of European integration, see Wolfram Kaiser, *Christian Democracy and the Origins of European Union* (Cambridge, 2007); and Richard Vinen, *Bourgeois Politics in France 1945–1951* (Cambridge, 1995), 152.

[96] It was renamed European Union of Christian Democrat and Conservative Students (ECCS) in 1970, and renamed European Democrat Students (EDS) in 1975. For an organizational overview: Holger Thuss and Bence Bauer, *Students on the Right Way: European Democrat Students 1961–2011* (Brussels, 2012).

[97] Reeder interview.

[98] On this issue of 'translation' of conservative ideas see BAK, B138/33493, Friedbert Pflüger's foreword in *Taurus*, no. 6 (1977); and Steber, *Hüter der Begriffe*.

[99] 'What is ECCS?', *Taurus*, 1, 1 (1974), ACDP, 4/6/13/2.

European International of Students. All students that seek a free, democratic, and parliamentary Europe can collaborate', RCDS delegates to the association's annual federal convention agreed in 1969.[100] They envisaged this new body as a counterweight to the Prague-based, pro-Communist International Union of Students after the dissolution of its main Western competitor, the International Student Conference (ISC), in February 1969 had left a political vacuum on the right.[101]

Although the new organization never quite got off the ground, the 'fight against the extreme Left [...] [remained] an absolute link' between European Conservative and Christian Democratic student groups well into the 1970s, as Friedbert Pflüger recalled.[102] He served as deputy chair of their renamed international association, the European Democrat Students (EDS), and worked hand in hand with other young Europeans, not least the Swedish centre-right activist Carl Bildt, who chaired EDS and later became the leader of Sweden's Moderate Party and the country's first conservative Prime Minister in over half a century. The cooperation at the European level ran smoothly, not just because conservative and Christian Democratic students faced similar challenges across the continent, but also because the different national organizations came up with near-identical answers to the left-wing insurgency. The staunchly anti-communist Bildt, for one, co-founded a new centre-right umbrella group at Stockholm University in 1968 to protest against the Left's occupation of a university building.[103] He thus had much in common with his West German peers, whose activism was similarly animated by the desire to keep a vibrant student Left in check and sought new organizational platforms, like the Student Unions, to accomplish this.

The Danish Conservative Students group also defined its politics in ways that were remarkably similar to the reformist ideas of RCDS. Rather than adopting a purely reactionary posture, it portrayed itself as politically moderate and stressed that it shared the Left's call for far-reaching changes in the Danish education system, but preferred a 'gradual alteration of society' to a revolutionary transformation. Much like members of RCDS, who regularly pored over—and often envied—the extensive news coverage of their opponents, the Danes also felt sidelined by the 'sensation-seeking' news media. The press had more interest in 'reporting a demonstration or a revolt than [...] in a group of persons who in a

---

[100] ACDP, 4/6/10, 'Europäische Allianz der gemäßigten Studenten', Beschlüsse der 19. Ordentlichen Delegierten-Versammlung des RCDS, 11.-15. März 1969 in Soest-Westfalen, 42.

[101] The ISC had been in crisis ever since it had been revealed two years earlier that the organization had had received financial aid from the American Central Intelligence Agency. See Philip G. Altbach, 'The International Student Movement', *Journal of Contemporary History*, 5, 1 (1970), 156–74.

[102] Pflüger interview.

[103] The name of Bildt's Stockholm centre-right student group was *Borgerliga Studenter—Opposition '68*. Michael Weiss, 'Bildt in a Day', *Foreign Policy* (8 May 2014), http://foreignpolicy.com/2014/05/08/bildt-in-a-day/ (accessed on 18 October 2016).

democratical [sic] way are achieving results through negotiations', Poul Juelsbjerg, the International Secretary of the Danish Conservative Students, bemoaned.[104]

Their British peers from the Federation of Conservative Students (FCS) were equally adamant that the left-wing critique of modern industrial society had to be taken seriously and that the spirit of generational rebellion transcended political partisanship. In a leaflet drawn up just after an ICCS conference held in early July 1968 at Swinton Park, a castle in rural northern England that served as an education centre for the British Conservative Party, the FCS framed their argument in very similar ways to West German Christian Democratic students:

> The recent increase in student unrest is not merely a left-wing militant move by a very small minority to overthrow western society. It is evidence of a deep-rooted dissatisfaction with many aspects of modern life and with the inability of governments to deal with them. Certainly, the left-wing students have been setting the pace in this reappraisal but conservative and Christian-democratic students have entered the dialogue and have responded to the increase in political activity and argument. Students combine in their disappointment at the way the older generation is handling the problems of modern society.[105]

They went on to state that 'Conservative and Christian-democrat students can also take a radical view of society [... which] would not be purely destructive'. Even the London-based left-liberal *Guardian* noted with astonishment that such utterings about a generational rift between the young and old made the gathering of centre-right students sound 'remarkably like [...] [a] reunion of [the prominent New Leftist] Tariq Ali and his mates'.[106]

The same could be said about many of the topics discussed at an international student conference that RCDS hosted in Bonn in February 1970. With over 300 student attendees from eighteen countries and a reception hosted by former Chancellor Kiesinger, this was the largest event Christian Democratic students had organized to that day. The participants identified the belief in a 'permanent reform of society [...] by evolutionary means' as their binding conviction, and they called on European politicians to help young reformers defeat the left-wing revolutionaries by 'making parties and institutions more transparent, strengthening democracy within parties, communicating more with their citizens, and increasing the incentive to become politically active'.[107]

---

[104] ACDP, 9/3/61, Poul Juelsbjerg, 'The political situation of students in Denmark', *SG-Bulletin* 9 (1969/70).
[105] ACDP 9/3/62, Federation of Conservative Students (FCS) leaflet on 'Student Unrest' [1968]; on Swinton and young British Conservatives, Black, '1968 and all That(cher)'.
[106] 'Student Power Takes a Swing to the Right', *The Guardian* (9 July 1968).
[107] ACDP, 4/6/43/1, *Aktuell* (24 April 1970).

The organizers also paid attention to the extra-European world, particularly the growing economic divide between North and South. In 1968, British Conservative students had already suggested that the 'attitude to the third world where the economic gap between the richer and poorer nations is increasing' and the need for 'policies alleviating hunger and encouraging economic growth in developing countries' were areas of agreement with the student Left.[108] Ignaz Bender had argued around the same time that a rising awareness of global economic inequality was a major source of student unrest in Western industrialized countries.[109] In 1970, the RCDS made 'overcoming the North-South conflict' one of the three central themes of its international meeting in Bonn.[110] This did not mean, of course, that centre-right students suddenly embraced the Left's fascination with 'Third World' revolutionary movements. Nonetheless, their emphasis on improving living conditions in the world's poorest countries signified a growing interest in the Global South and a renewed attempt to place their political endeavours on a new moral footing.

Human Rights Activism

This expansion of the centre-right's mental map was reflected not least in expressions of concern over human rights violations abroad. These were a major feature of centre-right activism from the late 1960s onward, both at the European and the domestic level. In concert with their European peers in EDS, Christian Democratic students in the Federal Republic condemned human rights violations committed by the military regime in Greece, which had been in power since the coup of April 1967; called on the West German federal government to bring the Khmer Rouge's genocide in Cambodia in front of the United Nations (UN) in the 1970s; and seized on a report by the UN Commission on Human Rights to rail against torture and other grave violations of human rights by the Pinochet regime in Chile.[111] As early as 1969, Ignaz Bender, who had already spoken out on torture in Algeria in the late 1950s, criticized West German foreign policy for its lack of moral engagement with human rights. The federal government had long

---

[108] ACDP 9/3/62, Federation of Conservative Students (FCS) leaflet on 'Student Unrest' [1968].

[109] Bender, *Der Protest der 'großen' Minderheit*, 35.

[110] ACDP, 4/6/43/1, 'Dokumentation: Internationale Studentenkonferenz in Bonn-Bad Godesberg vom 19.-22. Februar 1970', *Aktuell* (24 April 1970). On the growing importance of the North-South constellation in the eyes of young activists at this time, Charles S. Maier, '1968, Did It Matter?', in Vladimir Tismaneanu (ed.), *Promises of 1968: Crisis, Illusion, and Utopia* (Budapest and New York, 2011), 403–23.

[111] Bericht über Gruppenaktivitäten, RCDS-Brief, no. 1 (1968); 'RCDS: Bundesregierung soll Kambodscha Völkermord vor die UNO bringen', *Demokratische Blätter* 13 (April/May 1977), 11; Michael Roik, 'Menschenrechtsverletzungen in Chile', *Demokratische Blätter*, 13 (April/May 1977), 10–11.

advocated for the rights of Germans to self-determination but not for the human rights of non-Germans in other states, he lamented.[112]

Centre-right activists were part of the turn towards international human rights activism that began in the late 1960s and exploded in the 1970s, when human rights became the object of an unprecedented wave of popular mobilization across much of the globe.[113] This was the period in which Amnesty International (AI), the first notable non-governmental human rights organization, became a major international force, attracting thousands of volunteers and winning the Nobel Peace Prize in 1977. Similarly-oriented grassroots organizations mushroomed, not least in Europe and North America. Furthermore, the Helsinki Final Act, the concluding document of the 1975 Conference on Security and Cooperation in Europe, made the protection of civil rights a cornerstone of global governance. This global movement was reinforced in 1977, when the new US administration of Jimmy Carter identified the protection of human rights as a central pillar of its foreign policy strategy.[114]

Much of the burgeoning scholarship on the history of human rights has portrayed the unprecedented breakthrough of the issue in the 1970s as a left-wing cause. Jan Eckel, in particular, has interpreted the newfound enthusiasm for human rights as stemming from a deep disillusionment with social and political utopianism on the Left that began to set in soon after 1968. Left-wing activists had grown tired of endless theoretical discussions about revolutionizing the 'system' and the intense factionalism and turn towards violence in their ranks, he argued. As a result, they were searching for new ways of effecting change. Adopting human rights activism—and the brand of activism that AI, in particular, represented—allowed them to preserve their idealism while embracing political pragmatism and focusing on achieving meaningful results on a smaller scale.[115] Human rights in many ways represented a major departure for the Left.

However, writing centre-right activists back into the history of human rights in the 1970s, as this chapter does, highlights that—like 1968 itself—it was a politically versatile phenomenon. The politics of human rights organizations like Amnesty International, for instance, were in many ways closely aligned with centre-right self-conceptions around 1968—even though the group is often associated with the post-utopian Left. The anti-political image AI projected sat very

---

[112] Bender, *Der Protest der 'großen', Minderheit*, 39.

[113] Stefan-Ludwig Hoffmann, 'Introduction' in idem (ed.), *Human Rights in the Twentieth Century* (Cambridge, 2011), 20; Jan Eckel and Samuel Moyn (eds.), *The Breakthrough: Human Rights in the 1970s* (Philadelphia, PA, 2014).

[114] Samuel Moyn, 'The Return of the Prodigal: The 1970s as a Turning Point in Human Rights History', in Eckel and Moyn, *The Breakthrough*, 1–14.

[115] Jan Eckel, 'The International League for the Rights of Man, Amnesty International, and the Changing Fate of Human Rights Activism from the 1940s through the 1970s', *Humanity*, 4, 2 (2013), 183–214; Jan Eckel, *The Ambivalence of Good: Human Rights in International Politics since the 1940s* (Oxford, 2019).

comfortably with activists who had long since railed against ideology and the Left's revolutionary aspirations. Working to 'make the world a slightly less wicked place'—AI's motto—was also very much in line with the centre-right's gradualist impulses.[116] In fact, Christian Democratic student publications regularly called for donations to the human rights group. As early as 1973—several years before AI achieved truly global stature—for instance, the leading Christian Democratic student magazine declared its 'solidarity' with Amnesty's 'prisoners of the month', a Somali, a Greek, and a Soviet citizen, and asked its readers to write letters on their behalf to their respective country's head of government.[117]

Reintegrating centre-right activists into the history of 1970s human rights activism also highlights that it stemmed from sources other than left-wing disillusionment. Embracing the cause of human rights required no major pivot for centre-right activists after 1968—if any turn at all. Talking about human rights allowed them to continue to push many of the themes Christian Democrats had long since championed, not least the inviolability and dignity of the 'human person' against the totalitarian collective, a concept that was derived from Catholic social teaching. Moreover, anti-communism could easily be reframed as a human rights issue.[118] In postwar West Germany, in particular, appeals to human rights had been made constantly. But these had primarily been on behalf of other Germans, notably those living in the GDR, the expellees, bombing victims, and POWs held captive in the Soviet Union, as Lora Wildenthal has shown.[119] Younger centre-right activists built on these traditions when stepping up their human rights work in the wake of 1968; they were able to reinvigorate the longstanding centre-right critique of socialist regimes in a now universally popular political vocabulary.

A long article published in a national Christian Democratic student magazine in 1977, for instance, portrayed the German-German border as the 'most inhumane border in the world'. It also chronicled the individual suffering of East

---

[116] Tom Buchanan, '"The Truth will set you free": The making of Amnesty International', *Journal of Contemporary History*, 37, 4 (2002), 575–97; Eckel, 'The International League for the Rights of Man'.

[117] 'Die Arbeit von Menschenrechtsorganisationen unterstützen', *Demokratische Blätter* 13 (April/May 1977), 13; 'Die Gefangenen des Monats', *Demokratische Blätter*, 1 (1973), 4.

[118] Some recent studies have indeed called into question the idea that human rights were primarily a left-wing project. To be sure, human rights became the secular doctrine of the Left in the 1970s, while conservative governments, for the most part, did not associate their foreign policy with human rights, but this had not always been the case. The emergence of the European human rights regime in the postwar years had been part and parcel of a moment of Christian Democratic hegemony in Western Europe, not least of all in the Federal Republic. The postwar development of human rights talk had a distinctly conservative, Christian Democratic, and specifically anti-communist, lineage that has often been overlooked as a result of the scholarly focus on its progressive and secular uses. See particularly Samuel Moyn, *Christian Human Rights* (Philadelphia, PA, 2015); Duranti, *The Conservative Human Rights Revolution*; Udi Greenberg, 'Militant Democracy and Human Rights', *New German Critique*, 42, 3 (2015) 169–95; Mikael Rask Madsen, '"Legal Diplomacy" – Law, Politics and the Genesis of Postwar European Human Rights', in Hoffmann, *Human Rights in the Twentieth Century*, 62–84.

[119] Lora Wildenthal, *The Language of Human Rights in West Germany* (Philadelphia, PA, 2013), 9.

Germans who had tried to flee to the West, reported that the children of attempted escapees were put up for adoption, and condemned the suppression of religion in the GDR in the strongest terms. This portrayal of the inner-German border as a human rights issue built on earlier Cold War campaigns that had focused on the human suffering imposed by the 'Schandmauer' [wall of shame]. Such campaigns had often centred on the 'Wall dead', failed escapees like the young Peter Fechter, whose case became an anti-communist cause célèbre in West Germany after he had been shot near Checkpoint Charlie on 17 August 1962 and had lain dying on the Eastern side of the border for nearly an hour.[120]

The figure of the Eastern European or Soviet dissident—who, in the words of Stefan-Ludwig Hoffmann, 'replaced the revolutionary as the political paragon' in the 1970s and became the object of worldwide fascination and hero-worship—also perfectly matched the centre-right's Cold War-framed world view and longstanding focus on human rights violations in the Eastern bloc.[121] Many activists of the student Left had had a much more complicated relation-ship with those openly critical of Communist rule, as well as considerable difficulty embracing dissident-directed reform movements in the Eastern bloc, not least the Prague Spring. Numerous left-wing activists discovered the virtues of Eastern dissidence only in the 1970s and 1980s, a delay that would become the subject of intense soul-searching and self-critique later on.[122] Centre-right activists, by contrast, had long seen critics of state socialism as natural allies. In the 1970s, when the politics of empathy became a key component of global human rights activism, they often highlighted the fate of individual East German dissidents. These included the prominent East German reform socialists Rudolf Bahro and Robert Havemann, who faced repressive measures ranging from imprisonment to house arrest, and the Protestant pastor Oskar Brüsewitz, whose self-immolation in protest against the oppression of religion in the GDR in August 1976 had shocked the world.[123]

Christian Democratic students also cooperated on the publication of a docu-mentary report on human rights violations in the Soviet Union with the International Society for Human Rights, West Germany's most important anti-communist human rights organization founded in Frankfurt in the early 1970s. And they ran individualized campaigns in support of Soviet dissidents such as Boris Evdokimov, a historian and publicist, who had been committed to a psychiatric asylum in the USSR for his political views, and Vladimir Maksimov, a dissident writer, who had been stripped of his Soviet citizenship

---

[120] Pertti Ahonen, 'The Berlin Wall and the Battle for Legitimacy in Divided Germany', *German Politics and Society*, 'Special Issue: The Berlin Wall after Fifty Years', 1961–2011, 29, 2, 40–56.
[121] Hoffmann, 'Introduction', 23.
[122] Mark and von der Goltz, 'Encounters'; Mark, von der Goltz, and Warring, 'Reflections'.
[123] 'Die unmenschlichste Grenze der Welt', *Demokratische Blätter* 18 (January 1978), 12–16.

in 1973 and now lived in exile in Paris and published the dissident magazine *Continent*.[124]

Although anti-communism remained a major focus of their human rights work, Christian Democratic students were careful to project ideological equidistance, especially in the second half of the 1970s, when they always struck a delicate balance between their campaigns against human rights violations by left-wing and right-wing regimes. This method was almost certainly appropriated from AI, whose credo was that the guarantee of human rights should be independent from ideological or political systems.[125] AI's founder, Peter Benenson, had homed in on abuses by right-wing regimes at a time when Western politics were almost solely guided by anti-communism; now, Christian Democratic students contended that the Left's focus on crimes committed by regimes of the right and by Western 'imperialists' threatened to obscure human rights violations in the communist bloc.

As early as 1971, Gerd Langguth, the recently elected national chair of RCDS—and, as we will see in the next chapter, a particularly zealous anti-Left campaigner—presented the Soviet Ambassador with a chronicle of alleged transgressions committed by the Soviet Union. He contended that the West German public received too little information about human rights violations in the Eastern bloc.[126] That the Left ignored the misconduct of communist dictatorships and voiced selective outrage when right-wing regimes committed human rights violations remained a central trope of centre-right activism in the 1970s.

Nevertheless, Christian Democratic students increasingly coupled their campaigns for Eastern dissidents with condemnation of right-wing repression in different parts of the world.[127] What was new about the centre-right's human rights talk in the 1970s, then, was that it went well beyond anti-communism. It was framed in decidedly global terms. In part, this framing built on an earlier interest in the Vietnam war, such as when Christian Democratic students advocated on behalf of the 'boat people', refugees from socialist Vietnam, in the late 1970s.[128]

For most of the 1970s, however, Latin America was an even bigger focus than Southeast Asia. In the mid-1970s, the undisputed international symbol of despotism was the right-wing regime of General Augusto Pinochet in Chile—a state with which Germany had a long-standing relationship since a wave of German

---

[124] Beschlüsse der 27. O. BDV, Bonn, 5–7 March 1976, ACDP, 4/6/45/1; RCDS leaflet 'Freiheit für Boris Ewdokimov', in HIA, Koenigs Papers, Box 3. On the history of this controversial society, see Jürgen Wüst, *Menschenrechtsarbeit im Zwielicht: Zwischen Staatssicherheit und Antifaschismus* (Bonn, 1999).

[125] Jan Eckel, 'The Rebirth of Politics from the Spirit of Morality: Explaining the Human Rights Revolution of the 1970s', in Eckel and Moyn, *The Breakthrough*, 256.

[126] ACDP Press Archive, Gerd Langguth, Open Letter to Soviet Ambassador Valentin Michajlovič Falin (10 December 1971).

[127] ACDP Press Archive, 'RCDS fordert Freilassung politischer Gefangener in Chile und der Sowjetunion', RCDS press release (2 June 1977).

[128] 'Wir können nicht mehr schweigen', *Demokratische Blätter*, 1 (1979), 21–2.

emigration to the Andean country in the mid-nineteenth century. Pinochet and his military junta had deposed the elected Chilean Socialist leader Salvador Allende in a bloody coup on 11 September 1973. Between 1973 and 1989, thousands of Allende supporters were killed and many thousands more imprisoned and tortured. Roughly 200,000 Chileans—2 per cent of the population—were forced into exile. Pinochet's brutal dictatorship gave rise to one of the longest and most intense human rights campaigns the world had seen to that day.[129]

Its intensity was at least as much the result of the dictatorship's brutality as the upshot of what Allende's Chile had come to symbolize for many on the international Left. The Unidad Popular (UP) had gained power democratically in 1970, and Allende attempted to build socialism by constitutional means. For many activists of the Left, in Western and Eastern Europe alike, Allende's experiment renewed the promise of democratic socialism—a promise that had been damaged heavily, not least in Europe, with the crushing of the Prague Spring in 1968.[130] When Pinochet ended the Left's dream by force, Chile came to symbolize another socialist utopia upended by brutal violence. Contrary to the Prague events, however, this time the culprits were not to be found in Moscow; they were the 'imperialistic forces of fascism' represented by the Chilean military, the American CIA, and multinational corporations.[131] It was therefore no surprise that the Chile solidarity campaign in West Germany was dominated heavily by activists of the far Left, especially by members of the so-called 'K-groups', an array of newly-founded communist groups, often Maoist in orientation, that emerged in the wake of 1968. The campaign was dominated by displays of solidarity with victims from the UP.

Centre-right activists, on the other hand, had a rather different take on the events in Chile, but one that was fuelled by a similar sense of urgency. To them, the premature end of Allende's socialist experiment was further proof, if any were still needed after Prague, that socialism and democracy could not be combined. The centre-right's engagement with Chilean politics was not due to a simple anti-socialist reflex, however; it built on a long tradition of engagement with the Latin American country. The Federal Republic had given substantial aid to Chile since the Cuban Revolution out of a fear that Chile, too, was threatened by socialism. West German Christian Democrats were particularly invested in the country, maintaining close ties to the Chilean Christian Democrats, in spite of major

---

[129] Patrick William Kelly, 'The 1973 Chilean coup and the origins of transnational human rights activism', *Journal of Global History*, 8 (2013), 165–86, here 177; Jan Eckel, '"Under a Magnifying Glass": The International Human Rights Campaign against Chile in the Seventies', in Hoffmann, *Human Rights in the Twentieth Century*, 321–42; Eckel, *The Ambivalence of Good*.

[130] Kim Christinaens, Idesbald Goddeeris, and Magaly Rodríguez García (eds.), *European Solidarity with Chile 1970s–1980s* (Frankfurt am Main, 2014).

[131] Eckel, '"Under a Magnifying Glass"; Georg Dufner, "West Germany: Professions of Political Faith, the Solidarity Movement and New Left Imaginaries", in Christinaens, Goddeeris, and Rodríguez García, *European Solidarity with Chile*, 163–86.

philosophical differences between the two parties. Theirs was one of the 'closest of all the transatlantic partnerships' maintained by the Christian Democrats prior to the 1973 coup.[132] While centre-right activists condemned the coup and Pinochet's regime of state terror, they laid much of the blame at the feet of Allende. The deposed socialist leader, they suggested, had increased polarization in Chilean politics and plunged the country into political and economic chaos. They maintained that the coup was at least partly the result of the civil war-like atmosphere Allende had created.[133]

While some prominent conservative Christian Democratic politicians in West Germany went much further, downplaying the junta's violence and even offering praise for Pinochet, the RCDS leadership was careful not to appear supportive of the military regime.[134] Instead, they expressed solidarity with the Christian Democrats of former Chilean President Eduardo Frei, who had preceded Allende in office and was now in opposition to the military regime.[135] Frei's government had been avowedly reformist, pursuing its own version of a 'third way' with substantial reform efforts in the education and health sectors.[136] When the Bavarian Christian Democratic hardliner Franz Josef Strauss embarked on a controversial visit to internationally isolated Chile in 1977, met with Pinochet, and snubbed Frei publicly after meeting with him, the RCDS helped Frei to disseminate his version of the encounter to the West German media.[137]

To symbolize what their alternative version of solidarity with Chile was about, Christian Democratic student activists chose a young Chilean named Juan Bosco Maino Canales as the public face of their campaign against human rights abuses in the Andean country. The 25-year old activist was the leader of the United Popular Action Movement, which had originally formed as a splinter group of the Christian Democratic Party of Chile. He was arrested by Pinochet's secret police in May 1976 and disappeared.[138] Throughout 1977, the peak year of human rights campaigning globally, Christian Democratic students collected signatures and

---

[132] Georg Dufner, 'Chile as a Litmus Test: East and West German Foreign Policy and Cold War Rivalry in Latin America', in Agnes Bresselau von Bressensdorf, Christian Ostermann, and Elke Seefried (eds.), *West Germany, the Global South and the Cold War* (Munich, 2017), 77–118, here 87.

[133] Gerd Langguth, letter to the editor, *Weser Kurier* (15 November 1973).

[134] Gerd Langguth, letter to the editor, *Weser Kurier* (15 November 1973). By contrast, Christian Democratic hardliners Franz Josef Strauss and Alfred Dregger, as well as former Interior Minister Bruno Heck, expressed sympathy for the coup and downplayed its violence. See further Dufner, 'West Germany', 176–7; Michael Stolle, 'Inbegriff des Unrechtsstaates. Zur Wahrnehmung der chilenischen Diktatur in der deutschsprachigen Presse zwischen 1973 und 1989', *Zeitschrift für Geschichtswissenschaft*, 51/9 (2003), 800.

[135] 'Chile: Christdemokraten verfolgt', *Demokratische Blätter*, 1 (1978), 12.

[136] Stolle, 'Inbegriff des Unrechtsstaates', 793–813.

[137] 'Arbeiten lernen', *Spiegel*, 49 (1977), 23–4.

[138] HIA, Koenigs Papers, Box 3, 'Freiheit für Juan Bosco Maino Canales', RCDS leaflet; for details of the investigation of Maino Canales' disappearance and suspected death, see *Report of the Chilean National Commision on Truth and Reconciliaton* (Notre Dame, Indiana: University of Notre Dame Press, 1993), vol. II/II, Part 3, chapter 2, A.2.e.1.1., 599–600 (available at https://web.archive.org/web/20050323183301/http://www.usip.org/library/tc/doc/reports/chile/chile_1993_pt3_ch2_a2_e.html).

Illustration 4.3 The Fight for Human Rights . . . everywhere . . .

EDS and RCDS poster asking for signatures on a campaign to free Chilean activist Juan Bosco Maino Canales and Soviet dissident Boris Evdokimov.

(ACSP, Pl S 8835 [1977])

called for the release of Maino Canales alongside that of detained Soviet dissident Evdokimov. Exiled members of the Chilean opposition spoke at RCDS events alongside the Soviet dissident Maksimov and the exiled GDR dissident and poet

Siegmar Faust, who had spent several years in prison in East Germany for his political views.[139] Such Christian Democratic campaigns against human rights violations naturally had a strong domestic angle. When left-wing activists disrupted an event with Maksimov that the RCDS had organized in Hamburg, the scenes served as a politically expedient reminder of the Left's cynicism and alleged disregard for human rights violations by regimes of the Left.[140]

Articulating their political critiques in the powerful and evocative language of human rights, then, offered Christian Democratic activists the welcome chance to reclaim the moral high ground. Announcing a new campaign that they organized in concert with EDS, entitled 'Fighting for human rights...everywhere!', RCDS national chair Günther Heckelmann unabashedly spelled out the political opportunities inherent in this type of campaigning:

> This kind of human rights activism offers us the possibility to advocate aggressively for our political and moral agenda. We have to make clear that for us criticizing human rights [violations] has to stand apart and be independent from the ideological traits of those who suppress them. It does not matter if it is a communist state, such as the USSR, or a purely fascist system, such as Chile, that violates human rights.[141]

When Christian Democratic students campaigned on behalf of the Vietnamese 'boat people' a year later, they used the same playbook, drawing a sharp contrast between their own advocacy on behalf of these refugees and the Left's alleged 'cynicism' for ignoring refugees who did not fit political purity tests.[142]

The chance to paint left-wing activism as morally inferior was a welcome opportunity indeed. In the 1960s, the student Left had successfully focused the public debate onto questions of political morality. They had done this by linking the Vietnam War to Auschwitz, for instance, and by denouncing the exploitative nature of capitalism, imperialism, and the Federal Republic's contribution to such global systems of structural oppression. Campaigning against international human rights violations by left-wing and right-wing regimes alike—and pointing out all the ways in which the student Left's ideological blindness allegedly undermined its professed humanitarianism—allowed centre-right activists to place their activism on a moral foundation. Moreover, it allowed them to project an image of

---

[139] ACDP Press Archive, 'RCDS fordert Freilassung politischer Gefangener in Chile und der Sowjetunion', RCDS press release (2 June 1977).

[140] ACDP Press Archive, 'Schwere Krawalle an der Universität Hamburg. Neun Verletzte bei der Veranstaltung mit dem sowjetischen Regimekritiker Maximov', RCDS Press Release, no. 24 (30 June 1977).

[141] ACDP, 4/6/54/2, Heckelmann, letter to RCDS group- and state chairs (4 May 1978).

[142] A text box that accompanied the main article on the 'boat people' included dismissive quotations on the Vietnamese refugees by the communist student group MSB Spartakus. 'Wir können nicht mehr schweigen', Demokratische Blätter, 1 (1979), 22.

floating above the political fray in an era of intense polarization. Human rights were thus clearly a vehicle for advancing other political projects.

However, it would miss the point to draw too sharp a contrast between an inherently cynical and self-interested human rights practice on the centre-right and a more unambiguously altruistic activism on the Left. Adopting the cause of human rights was not just a reactive move made for political expedience after the Left had embraced it. On the contrary, the centre-right's interest in human rights was propelled by a longstanding anti-communist commitment—one that was at least partly driven by personal or family experiences with flight, expulsion, and political repression in the socialist bloc.[143] Students' advocacy on behalf of imprisoned Chilean Christian Democrats, too, was based on longstanding ties to the country. What is more, for all the genuine identification with the struggles of individuals abroad, selective outrage was also a feature of the Left's human right's work. Self-interest was often as strong a driving force as the desire to help people in need, as Jan Eckel has shown.[144] Human rights served a purpose for the Left as well, allowing disillusioned activists to reinvigorate their critique of capitalist liberal democracy and to break free from political debates about the correct path towards revolution that felt increasingly stale.

Human rights activism in 1970s West Germany was thus more multifaceted than it is often portrayed. It was not just a project driven by a post-utopian Left, but a far more politically versatile phenomenon. Centre-right activists also spoke the language of international human rights in this period and campaigned fervently on behalf of prisoners of conscience and victims of human rights abuses across the globe. In doing so, they gave the postwar conservative and Christian Democratic version of anti-communist human rights a more self-consciously global and overtly apolitical form.

*   *   *

The '68ers have often been described as the first global and transnational generation, but we need a more nuanced understanding of what this meant.[145] Much as it did for their student peers on the Left, the world of centre-right students had opened up considerably in the 1950s and 1960s. Growing opportunities for intra-European travel and school exchanges had broadened their horizons, and they later linked their activism to global concerns, including decolonization, the

---

[143] See 79–86; as Frank Bösch has shown, West German advocates of accepting the Vietnamese 'boat people' as refugees in the late 1970s and 1980s, especially Christian Democratic politicians, often based their stance on experiences with flight and expulsion. Bösch, 'Engagement für Flüchtlinge'; also Bösch, *Zeitenwende 1979*, 195, 197, 210; also Duranti, *The Conservative Human Rights Revolution*, 404.

[144] Eckel, *The Ambivalence of Good*.

[145] Fietze, '1968 als Symbol der ersten globalen Generation'.

Vietnam War, and human rights.[146] Centre-right students, then, were not just a part of West Germany's 1968, but of the Global 1960s, too.

And yet, their mental map of the world differed in fundamental ways from that of their political opponents—even if it included some of the same landmarks, such as Vietnam and Chile. While activists of the Left often looked south to anti-colonial liberation movements, convinced that the Federal Republic was a cog in the global machinery of imperialist oppression, centre-right students did not question the Cold War framework in fundamental ways and often found their political inspiration much closer to home.

While they may not have been ardent cold warriors in the vein of the 1950s—as their more pragmatic approach to the GDR and interest in movements of socialist reform in the Eastern bloc signified—they were convinced that socialism and democracy were antithetical to one another. Anti-communist conviction animated much of their activism, and they viewed global politics first and foremost through that lens. As a result, they opposed any movement that couched its goals in communist rhetoric, be it domestic student groups or the North Vietnamese, and their human rights activism in the 1970s always included a prominent anti-communist angle. To them, the walled-in city of West Berlin was a powerful symbol of defiance in the face of communist repression, and Germany's division generally continued to structure much of their thinking. Although emphatically pro-American, centre-right students had few concrete ties to the United States, but they had close and sustained links to their Christian Democratic and conservative peers in Western Europe. Bound together by a common left-wing challenge, they socialized, exchanged ideas, and ran joint campaigns, including ones against human rights violations. The centre-right's evident Europeanism, in particular, should give us pause when trying to understand the legacies of student internationalism in 1968. Historians have frequently portrayed left-wing '68ers as forerunners of European unity who anticipated the post-1989 coming together of a divided continent. As this chapter has shown, however, this was more clearly the case for student activists of the centre-right, who made Europe's division a much more central aspect of their campaigning in the late 1960s than the Left did at the time. While the radical Left sought to overcome Europe's division more indirectly, via a socialist revolution that would transform the West alongside the East, centre-right activists focused their critique on the repressive nature of the regimes in the socialist bloc.[147]

---

[146] Belinda Davis has argued persuasively that the internationalist impulses of the left-wing '68ers at least partly stemmed from their upbringing, which included increased opportunities for travel and exchange across borders. Much the same was true for activists of the centre-right. See Davis, '"A whole world opening up"'.

[147] They also admitted, however, that the Western model of liberal democracy had to be improved to become more attractive to citizens in the Eastern bloc. See 'Grundsatzprogramm des RCDS: 39 Thesen zur Reform und zu den Zukunftsaufgaben deutscher Politik', 52.

All of this matters because, for better or worse, the centre-right's vision of internationalism was the one that won out in the long run. If we strip this statement of the normative baggage and political point scoring that all too often accompany assessments of 1968 and its legacies, it is difficult not to come to this conclusion. Centre-right activists may not have got their way on Vietnam when Saigon fell in 1975, but Latin America's military dictatorships eventually crumbled without a speedy return of democratic socialism. More importantly, European politics developed in ways that the centre-right welcomed. In 1989, dissident-directed reform movements, people power, symptoms of socialist collapse, and a reformer in the Kremlin coalesced to bring about the demise of Europe's state socialist regimes, while leaving Western political systems largely unchanged. This was an outcome that the centre-right was more than comfortable with—in contrast to a West German Left for whom 1989 and its aftermath was a moment of considerable political disappointment.[148]

What is more, in Germany, this transformation occurred under Christian Democratic auspices. Former student activists of the 1960s played key roles in shaping the course of unification and helped to craft the post-Cold War order in Europe. Horst Teltschik, who railed against the Left's revolutionary internationalism around 1968 and who reported that his experience as a student in West Berlin had profoundly influenced him, shaped Chancellor Kohl's foreign and German policy more than any other figure. In the 1980s, he helped to orchestrate a closer West German relationship to the United States and was intimately involved in the negotiations surrounding German unification.[149] When historians seek to understand the links between 1968 and 1989—and indeed the internationalism of West German activists around 1968 and its legacies—the centre-right deserves to be a much bigger part of the story. Studying their vision of internationalism helps to explain why the world looks the way it does today—and much less like the way the revolutionary Left envisaged it around 1968.

---

[148] This is not to suggest that German unification and the end of the Cold War had no effect on the western part of Germany or other Western European societies. For an analysis of the far-reaching economic, social, and political effects of unification on West Germany—what he terms 'cotransformation'— see Philipp Ther, *Europe Since 1989* (Princeton, NJ, 2016), 259–87; on left-wing disappointment after 1989, see Konrad Sziedat, *Erwartungen im Umbruch: Die westdeutsche Linke und das Ende des 'real existierenden Sozialismus'* (Munich, 2019).

[149] Wirsching, *Abschied vom Provisorium*, 182, 512, 659. See also Teltschik, *329 Tage*; Hacke, *Weltmacht wider Willen*, 441; Mary Sarotte, *1989: The Struggle to Create Post-Cold War Europe* (Princeton, NJ, 2009), 159. For a more detailed discussion of Teltschik's trajectory, see 238–42.

5

Combative Politics

On 26 January 1972, during prime time, viewers of the West German public television channel ZDF witnessed a spectacle that filled many of them with deep unease. The right-leaning news program *ZDF Magazin* showed rowdy scenes from a 'Spartakus Tribunal' that RCDS had staged at the University of Hamburg one week earlier. Viewers saw its national chair, Gerd Langguth (1946–2013), speaking on a heavily barricaded podium in a large auditorium. Like many young centre-right men at the time, the 25-year old student of political science from Bonn sported longish hair, and he also wore a brown jacket and a red scarf. In spite of looking almost indistinguishable from many members of his enraged student audience, Langguth was drowned out by incessant shouting. The RCDS chair gave his best to remain composed in the face of left-wing students loudly and repeatedly demanding 'D-I-S-C-U-S-S-I-O-N' while he calmly painted the Marxist Student Association (MSB) Spartakus as a threat to the constitution.[1]

Set up the previous year by a group of activists that included former members of the traditionalist wing of SDS, MSB Spartakus was the student wing of the newly founded German Communist Party (DKP). Unlike SDS, MSB Spartakus espoused the ideas of the old Left rather than the New Left and had close ties to the East German socialist regime. Despite this, it was remarkably successful in student council elections during much of the 1970s.[2] By 1972, it had forty chapters across the country. Hamburg, a city that was home to around 10 per cent of West Germany's 30,000 DKP members, was a particular stronghold. The MSB Spartakus was the strongest parliamentary student group at the local university in 1971/72.[3]

An article in the conservative daily *Die Welt* emphasized the Herculean nature of Langguth's efforts inside this left-leaning university. Viewers might not have realized, the paper contended, that

---

[1] On the symbolic value of 'discussing' on the 1968 Left, including its strategic uses, see Scharloth, *1968: Eine Kommunikationsgeschichte*, 211–54.

[2] Helmut Bilstein et al., *Organisierter Kommunismus in der Bundesrepublik Deutschland: DKP-SDAJ-MSB Spartakus-KPD/KPDml/KBW/KB*, 4th edition (Opladen, 1977); Anne Rohstock, *Von der 'Ordinarienuniversität' zur 'Revolutionszentrale': Hochschulreform und Hochschulrevolte in Bayern und Hessen 1957–1976* (Munich, 2010), 365–6.

[3] Rigoll, *Staatsschutz in Westdeutschland*, 281; Westdeutsche Rektorenkonferenz (ed.), 'Übersicht über die Ergebnisse der Wahlen zu den Studentenvertretungen im Sommersemester 1971', *Dokumentation*, 25 (1971), 10.

The Other '68ers: Student Protest and Christian Democracy in West Germany. Anna von der Goltz, Oxford University Press (2021). © Anna von der Goltz. DOI: 10.1093/oso/9780198849520.003.0006

Illustration 5.1 RCDS chair Gerd Langguth, speaking at a 'Spartakus Tribunal' at the University of Hamburg on 19 January 1972. The white specks on his right sleeve are curd cheese that left-wing students in the audience had thrown at the student activist. Still from *ZDF Magazin*, 26 January 1972.
(Gerd Langguth Private Papers)

the small white specks on the jacket and face of the RCDS national chair […], who was talking himself hoarse, were curd cheese which was flying towards him from the audience, that his restlessly darting gaze was directed at other missiles that missed him, that the fluctuations in sound and lighting were caused by 'Spartakus' people trying to switch off the stage lights and the microphone, that the swaying of the camera was the result of assaults […].[4]

Other papers were similarly impressed with the young Christian Democrat's stance. He had shown great 'morale' and the ability to 'hold out' against a prolonged onslaught, the *Rheinische Post* noted with tangible admiration for the combative student leader.[5] According to *Die Welt*, the event signalled the end of the phase of relatively open discussion in campus politics that had been

---

[4] Joachim Neander, 'Wer von Bukowskij spricht, wird vom Spartakus ausgebuht', *Die Welt* (5 February 1972).
[5] '"Spartakus" knüppelt andere Meinung nieder', *Rheinische Post* (2 February 1972).

characteristic of the mid- to late 1960s. At best, the Left now responded to arguments in an entirely predictable and one-sided manner, the conservative paper insisted. 'He who mentions the name of the Soviet [dissident, AvdG] writer [Vladimir] Bukovsky, gets booed. He who invokes the Prague Spring and its sudden end is faced with a chorus of voices shouting "Nazis out".'[6] The clear implication was that RCDS activists had no choice but to stand up forcefully to such examples of left-wing intolerance. Their stance soon earned them the adoration of Christian Democratic hardliners, who had previously been far warier of restive young activists in their own ranks. The student association was waging a 'brave, self-sacrificial, and in no way unsuccessful battle for our democracy in the universities', Alfred Dregger, a representative of the CDU's national-conservative wing, noted in approvingly martial language in a Bundestag debate in early 1974.[7]

The spectacle of a composed and lucid Langguth confronting a raucous crowd of left-wing activists at the 'Spartakus Tribunal' (of which more below) indeed hints at an important shift under way in the nature of student activism—and the centre-right's role within it—on West German campuses in the early 1970s. This shift towards a much more combative form of politics than had been common for most of the 1960s is the focus of this chapter.

Hardening Fronts

The 1970s, which have often been described—somewhat misleadingly—as a 'red decade', saw an unprecedented politicization across the political spectrum and a deep polarization in the Federal Republic.[8] This development was fuelled in no small measure by the election of the Social Democrat Willy Brandt as Federal Chancellor and head of the new Social-Liberal coalition government in 1969. To Christian Democratic politicians and conservative West Germans generally, the first passing of the torch from the CDU/CSU to the SPD since the war represented far more than a routine turnover of democratic power. To a party that was convinced it had a natural right to govern, it seemed like nothing short of a historical aberration, an attack on the very foundations of the Federal Republic that Christian Democrats had built. Given that the Social Democrats did not receive an overall majority in the federal elections of 28 September 1969 (42.7 per cent to the CDU/CSU's 46.1 per cent) and were only able to form the government because of the liberal Free Democrats' leftward turn, Christian Democrats

---

[6] Neander, 'Wer von Bukowskij spricht'.
[7] Deutscher Bundestag, 79. Sitzung (14 February 1974).
[8] For the classic formulation of the 1970s as a 'red decade', see Gerd Koenen, *Das Rote Jahrzehnt: Unsere kleine deutsche Kulturrevolution, 1967–1977* (Cologne, 2001); for a critique, see Schildt, '"Die Kräfte der Gegenreform sind auf breiter Front angetreten'; and Livi, Schmidt and Sturm, *Die 70er Jahre als schwarzes Jahrzehnt.*

considered it a 'stolen election'. It sparked a deeply felt crisis of hegemony that many conservatives experienced as extremely traumatic.[9]

The concurrent developments in the universities caused particular alarm. Around 1968, for the first time in the history of the postwar republic, many young intellectuals turned their back on the Christian Democrats and embraced left-wing ideas en masse. The Left's dominance was reflected particularly strongly in student parliamentary elections. In the early 1970s, left-wing groups or coalitions held majorities in more than three-quarters of student councils.[10] The break-up of the extraparliamentary opposition as well as the dissolution of SDS in March 1970 led to the subsequent emergence of a plethora of sectarian left-wing groups, varying between a communist, Marxist, Leninist, Trotskyist or Maoist orientation. While many who had been politicized around 1968 now invested their energy into one of the new social movements or the emerging alternative milieu, university politics were dominated by leftist groups that had turned their backs on the anti-authoritarian disposition that had characterized much of the protest movement in the 1960s. More often than not, a tighter theoretical corset and more rigid organization had replaced spontaneity and a provocative mischievousness.[11]

The relationship between the student Left and the centre-right changed noticeably as a result of this. It became a true clash and sometimes a physical confrontation in which nothing short of the republic's survival seemed to be at stake. Student activists in the 1970s thus operated in a climate that differed markedly from the days of the Grand Coalition government. Centre-right activists increasingly thought of themselves as the last bastion of democratic politics in a world dominated by left-wing radicals. The dividing lines between a transformed and fragmented student Left and the centre-right thus sharpened considerably.

For older Christian Democratic activists who had been students in the 1960s but who kept an eye on what was going on inside the universities, this change from an intense engagement and often-playful competition between Left and centre-right to a much more hard-edged confrontation was particularly palpable. Peter Radunski, who had found considerable common ground with the now-dissolved SDS around 1968, recalled that his positive reminiscences of engaging with the Left later confounded younger Christian Democratic activists. '[T]hey say that

[9] Pridham, *Christian Democracy*, 188–9; Schildt, *Konservatismus in Deutschland*, 244–5; Bösch, 'Die Krise als Chance'; Daniel Schmidt, 'Die geistige Führung verloren'. Antworten der CDU auf die Herausforderung "1968"', in Kersting, Reulecke, and Thamer, *Die zweite Gründung der Bundesrepublik*, 85–107.

[10] Rohstock, *Von der 'Ordinarienuniversität' zur 'Revolutionszentrale'*, 365. By this point, the Student Unions had also moved leftward. The DSU, for one, renamed itself Social-Liberal Higher Education Association to express its affinity with Brandt's government. Bartz, 'Konservative Studenten'.

[11] Andreas Kühn, *Stalins Enkel, Maos Söhne: Die Lebenswelt der K-Gruppen in der Bundesrepublik der 1970er Jahre* (Frankfurt am Main, 2005); on the fragmentation of the radical Left in the 1970s and the importance of the alternative milieu, see Reichardt, *Authentizität und Gemeinschaft*, 11–14.

Radunski glorifies things. They were much more combative with each other.'[12] In his heyday, personal relationships among student activists had often been capable of transcending the political dividing lines between Left and Right. In the eyes of Christian Democratic activists who were a few years younger than him, by contrast, the student Left as a whole seemed inextricably linked to the terror of the Red Army Faction (RAF), he recalled. Although the membership and overall number of supporters of the RAF and related groups was very small, never exceeding more than 1,000–2,000 people, the phenomenon of left-wing terrorism captured the public's imagination and shaped political discourse in the 1970s like few others. As a result, 'political opposition often turned into personal ill will', according to Radunski.[13]

Rather than considering themselves the Left's intellectual sparring partners, engaged in an intense but important debate about how best to remedy the ills of West Germany's postwar democracy, Christian Democratic students began to think of themselves as the Federal Republic's first line of defence. In the 1960s, their predecessors had also been concerned about the growth of the right-wing NPD, but now the extremist threat seemed to emanate solely from the radical Left, with the universities representing the key battleground in the struggle for the survival of West German democracy.[14]

Christian Democratic students directed their fire at two groups in particular: besides MSB Spartakus, the Social Democratic (later renamed Socialist) Higher Education League (SHB) was their main target.[15] The SHB had been founded in 1960 when SDS had split from the Social Democrats. In the wake of the student protests of the late 1960s, it had veered left, openly embracing Marxism and a strategy of cooperation with communist student groups. To the oppositional Christian Democrats, the SHB was a welcome tool with which to attack the Brandt government and to imply that social democracy and socialism were really one and the same thing. According to Christian Democratic activists, SHB and MSB Spartakus were willing to use any means necessary to overthrow West German democracy and to erect a socialist dictatorship—including violence. By

---

[12] Radunski interview. On micro-cohorts within social movements, see Whittier, 'Political Generations, Micro-Cohorts and the Transformation of Social Movements'.

[13] Radunski, *Aus der politischen Kulisse*, 62. Others concurred that cordial relations between activists of the Left and Right were a rarity in the 1970s. Stronk interview; Männle interview; van Schewick interview; Reeder interview; on the numbers of supporters of RAF, Red Cells, and June 2nd Movement, see Klaus Weinhauer, 'Zwischen "Partisanenkampf" und "Kommissar Computer": Polizei und Linksterrorismus in der Bundesrepublik bis Anfang der 1980er Jahre', Klaus Weinhauer, Jörg Requate, and Heinz-Gerhard Haupt (eds.), *Terrorismus in der Bundesrepublik: Medien, Staat und Subkulturen in den 1970er Jahren* (Frankfurt am Main, 2006), 244–70.

[14] ACDP 4/6/44/3, 'Aufruf zum Kampf gegen den Radikalismus', RCDS Pressemitteilung (10 July 1969).

[15] ACDP 04-006-013-2, Gerd Langguth, 'Ständig Konflikte schaffen: DKP-Studenten verdrängen SDS'; also ACDP, 04/006/043/1, lengthy report on the first federal convention of the MSB Spartakus in *RCDS Aktuell*, 6 (1971).

breaking up seminars and lectures and using 'targeted terror against unpopular persons or groups', they had allegedly planted the 'seed of violence'. '[I]t seems the radical Left wants to use force to achieve what it cannot gain by democratic means: power within the university and in society.'[16]

The RCDS was not alone in sounding the alarm; its increasingly confrontational course reflected a broader trend of centre-right and conservative mobilization in the wake of 1968, and the universities were at the eye of the developing storm. Chief among the new clubs and organizations with the shared goal of combatting a resurgent campus Left was a group of prominent academics, who founded the Association for the Protection of Academic Freedom (*Bund Freiheit der Wissenschaft*, BFW), a political pressure group that counted up to 5,000 members at the height of its popularity.[17] Many of its leading members, among them the prominent political scientists Wilhelm Hennis and Richard Löwenthal, had initially been quite supportive of the student movement and favoured reforms in higher education. However, they had grown deeply concerned about the politicization of teaching and research and the radicalization of left-wing activism that had occurred in the wake of Ohnesorg's death. In the early 1970s, they ran a fervent and highly successful political campaign to inform the public about the perceived threat, hoping that external pressure would help to turn the tide in the universities. Despite the presence of a few Social Democrats in the organization, the BFW therefore quickly acquired a reputation as a right-wing cartel.[18] While Christian Democratic student activists often kept their distance from the organization in public for this reason, many nevertheless had close ties to the group. Approximately 10 per cent of its members were students and some of the leading Christian Democratic activists of the late 1960s and early 1970s were among them.[19] Gerd Langguth had begun to liaise with its protagonists before the BFW was even founded, and many activists from the centre-right Student Unions set up in 1967/68 were similarly closely connected to the organization.[20]

In a speech Langguth delivered on a number of occasions in the early 1970s, he charted the confrontation with the radical Left as a struggle between blind ideological conviction and critical reason. Contrary to leftist student groups,

---

[16]   Michael Lingenthal, 'Saat der Gewalt', *Demokratische Blätter*, 1 (1971/72), 1.

[17]   The BFW has been the subject of a number of excellent studies in recent years. Wehrs, *Protest der Professoren*, offers the most thorough treatment of the organization and its membership. See also Dirk Moses, *German Intellectuals and the Nazi Past*; Daniela Münkel, 'Der "Bund Freiheit der Wissenschaft": Die Auseinandersetzung um die Demokratisierung der Hochschule', in Geppert and Hacke, *Streit um den Staat*, 171–86; Hacke, *Philosophie der Bürgerlichkeit*.

[18]   Wehrs, *Protest der Professoren*, 250.

[19]   Among them were the former RCDS national chair Wulf Schönbohm and his deputy Erich Röper, for instance. HIA, Häuser Papers, Box 1.

[20]   Michael Zöller, who had been chair of the Munich Student Union, became the BFW's managing director; and, Jürgen Aretz, one-time chair of the Bonn Student Union, was an Assistant to Hatto Schmitt, the Provost of the University of Bonn, who took over the BFW leadership in 1973. Aretz interview.

which, Langguth proclaimed, had become politically dogmatic, the RCDS rejected all truths of salvation. Invoking a famous verdict by Karl Popper that became *the* RCDS motto in the 1970s, Langguth contended that 'the attempt to create heaven on earth invariably produces hell'.[21] The Austrian-British philosopher was indeed something of a patron saint of centre-right student activists in the 1970s. Their forerunners in the 1960s had found some of their most important intellectual inspiration in the work of one of Popper's students from the London School of Economics, in Ralf Dahrendorf's description of postwar West German democracy as structurally deficient and full of authoritarian residues. Their successors now regarded Popper's ideas as a 'shield against Marxism-Leninism'.[22]

In his *The Open Society and Its Enemies*, first published in 1945, Popper had argued that what he termed the 'open society' was endangered by the claim of totalitarian ideologies, notably communism and fascism, to be in possession of the ultimate truth.[23] But human beings were fallible, Popper insisted, and ultimate truth was a dangerous fallacy. Instead of ideological fixation, he called for a 'critical rationality'. The 'open society' had to protect the freedom of the individual and establish laws and institutions that allowed people with divergent views and interests to live together in peace.

In the 1970s, centre-right groups adopted Popper's ideas as their own, using them to school their members for rhetorical confrontations with the Left. His philosophy left a deep imprint on the RCDS's policy programs, notably the basic program of 1976, which took its name from Popper's famous two-volume tome and cited human fallibility as one of its guiding assumptions.[24] Popper's ideas also captured the imagination of individual activists. 'I read this book twenty times, I devoured it, my whole life long. My whole life!', remembered Detlef Stronk.[25]

Popper was attractive to centre-right activists because of his endorsement of an incrementalistic trial-and-error approach to politics and, perhaps even more importantly, because he helped them to distinguish clearly between friend and foe. The enemies were those who believed in ideological blueprints, above all the Marxist student Left. Armed with Popper's theoretical justification for their rejection of left-wing ideas and methods, and in concert with other groups of the centre-right, Christian Democratic activists saw their primary task as alerting the public to the rising threat allegedly emanating from the country's universities.

---

[21] Gerd Langguth, 'RCDS – die progressive Alternative zur reaktionären Linken'.
[22] Pflüger interview.
[23] Karl R. Popper, *The Open Society and its Enemies*, 2 vols. (London, 1945).
[24] Universitätsarchiv Bonn, AStA 081–235, Thomas-G. Vetterlein (Aktion Demokratische Mitte), 'Thesen zur kritischen Rationalität und praktischen Politik', 19 June 1973; RCDS Grundsatzprogramm 'Plädoyer für eine offene und solidarische Gesellschaft' (March 1976); see also '5 Fragen 5 Antworten zum politischen Grundkonzept des RCDS', *RCDS-Mainz Schriftenreihe*, 4 (1971); ACDP 04/006/13/2, long summary of Popper's ideas in Dorothee Buchhaas, 'Wer ist, was will der SLH' (1974), *RCDS Dokumentation* G 17.
[25] Stronk interview.

In the first half of the 1970s, Langguth, whose tenure as RCDS chair lasted from 1970 to 1974 and thus longer than that of any previous chair, was *the* central figure in this struggle.[26] Born in Wertheim in the southwestern state of Baden-Württemberg in 1946, he entered student politics at the University of Bonn in the late 1960s to study political science, law, and history. Understanding and combatting the Left became his lifelong obsession—so much so that some of his peers were quite uneasy with what they saw as the student association's anti-socialist showmanship during his tenure as chair.[27] For one, Wolfgang Reeder, who was his deputy from 1971, thought that Langguth pursued a confrontational course in large part to collect material for his dissertation on the radical Left.[28] Other reform-minded Christian Democrats felt even more alienated. Volker Hassemer (b. 1944), a Christian Democrat from West Berlin who served as Senator for Urban Development and Environmental Protection in the city in the 1980s, was put off by the chair's martial rhetoric and belligerent disposition:

Gerd Langguth, he [...] was ridiculous to me, because he tried to defend something. He took up the fight there. Brave! But he should have engaged. When he entered a lecture hall, he should have engaged. Just like the other side should have engaged with him [...]. It was always strange to me. [...] When the war begins it is difficult to talk about peace or the rules of engagement. And at that time it was a war and so that was how it was treated.[29]

This 'war' against the Left became the focus of much of Langguth's career as a political scientist, public intellectual, and CDU politician. His first book on the Left, written in the wake of the APO's disintegration, was an exhaustive chronicle of different left-wing splinter groups that focused on the danger of left-wing 'infiltration' of public institutions and portrayed the entire protest movement of the late 1960s as the vanguard of the GDR-sponsored German Communist Party.[30] In 1975, Langguth submitted his doctoral dissertation about the nature of the left-wing protest movement since 1968, and he would continue to publish on the subject for the next thirty years.[31] While his books were academic treatments based on a wealth of contemporary sources he had collected, they were also in no small measure informed by his personal experiences as a Christian

---

[26] Weberling, *Für Freiheit und Menschenrechte*, 261–4.
[27] *Hans Reckers Papers*, Lothar Theodor Lemper, 'Strategiepapier' (February 1973).
[28] Reeder interview.   [29] Hassemer interview.
[30] Gerd Langguth, *Protestbewegung am Ende: Die Neue Linke als Vorhut der DKP* (Mainz, 1971); see also the scathing review of the book in the left-leaning *Frankfurter Rundschau*, Rainer Weber, 'Kommunisten sind gegen Kapitalismus. Die Erkenntnisse des Gerd Langguth', *Frankfurter Rundschau* (2 August 1973); ACDP, 4/6/63/1, memorandum on a conversation with Langguth about his book by the Centrale für Information und Organisation in Studienfragen (CIOS) (10 September 1970).
[31] Gerd Langguth, *Die Protestbewegung der Bundesrepublik Deutschland 1968–1976* (Cologne, 1976); Gerd Langguth, *Protestbewegung: Entwicklung, Niedergang, Renaissance: Die Neue Linke seit 1968* (Cologne, 1983).

Democratic activist. He and his peers had been denounced as 'prostitutes of bourgeois class justice' or 'clerico-fascists', Langguth recalled in a monograph on the myth of 1968 published in 2001, for instance. Student politics in the 1970s had been 'highly emotionalized and polarized', he explained.[32] Although he did not see it that way, as the architect and public face of the RCDS's strategy of confrontation—so clearly on display in the auditorium in Hamburg in January 1972—Langguth contributed much to this febrile climate.

Weimar Re-enactments

The 'Spartakus Tribunal' of January 1972, invoked at the opening of this chapter, was a characteristic, albeit especially effective, example of Langguth's strategy to bring his campaign against the Left—and the MSB Spartakus in particular—into the public eye. In doing so, Langguth was able to build on RCDS efforts that had commenced in the late 1960s, namely, to turn originally left-wing protest repertoires against the group's opponents.

Beginning in the mid-1960s, the anti-authoritarian wing of SDS had baited state authorities with a strategy of provocation aimed at facilitating an overly forceful response that would then provide evidence of the repressive reality beneath the Federal Republic's democratic façade. In the late 1960s, centre-right students began to emulate this method quite successfully by hosting campus events to goad the Left. In early July 1968, for instance, the Cologne RCDS chapter invited the Minister of the Interior, Ernst Benda, to the University of Cologne to discuss the recently passed—and highly controversial—emergency laws. Posters announced simply that 'Benda is coming!', and left-wing student activists took the bait. During his visit, they pelted the Christian Democrat with eggs and tomatoes, and one demonstrator dressed up as an SS guard to denounce the Interior Minister as a fascist in democratic guise. The local RCDS chapter duly used the negative press coverage of the attacks on the Minister in a glossy brochure entitled 'Progress without Terror', which explained that the group was mounting a 'democratic counter-offensive' against SDS.[33] The national leadership of RCDS lauded the simple slogan—one of the first times that the group used the word 'terror' to describe left-wing protests—for its effective combination of a 'positive statement with a clear demarcation'. It then recommended the Cologne strategy to all local chapters in a circular mailer: 'Organize a prominent politician,

---

[32] Gerd Langguth, *Mythos '68: Die Gewaltphilosophie von Rudi Dutschke—Ursachen und Folgen der Studentenbewegung* (Munich, 2001), 10. I met with Gerd Langguth in 2011, two years before his death. We had a long conversation about his memories of student activism, but he did not agree to a formal recorded interview.

[33] ACDP, 4-6-10, brochure 'Fortschritt ohne Terror' (October 1968).

who can survive the crucible. Advertise the event widely and aggressively.'[34] All political student groups ought to receive an invitation, because a packed room would spark confrontations that would then provide evidence of the Left's terror-ist practices, according to similar guidance. Posters with photographs of violent street battles and the slogan 'Not like this!' would do the same trick, Stronk, the deputy national chair of RCDS, who later ran election campaigns for Eberhard Diepgen in West Berlin, explained in detailed campaign guidelines he sent to all local RCDS chapters in 1969.[35]

Langguth followed this strategy very closely in January 1972. The only differ-ence was that he did not bring a prominent politician to campus, instead styling himself as a public prosecutor in a show trial against the Left. For several months prior to the event, the student public had been primed with a set of questions, distributed via an official press release and hundreds of thousands of RCDS leaflets. These leaflets were addressed to MSB Spartakus's national chair Christoph Strawe, a student activist who had previously been involved in SDS in Bonn. They accused him of glorifying the conditions of life in East Germany and the Soviet Union, asked about the relationship between MSB Spartakus's goal of Marxist revolution and the Federal Republic's Basic Law, and taunted the group for attacking Western imperialism while defending the Warsaw Pact's brutal crushing of the Prague Spring in 1968.[36] At a time when grassroots conservative opposition to Chancellor Brandt's efforts to normalize relations with the GDR through *Ostpolitik* was reaching a fever pitch, the RCDS skilfully utilized the Spartakus's close ties to the East German regime to tar the entire West German student Left with the same brush as the socialist dictatorship on the other side of the Wall.[37]

The provocative tone and advance distribution of the questions all but guar-anteed a full house on 19 January 1972, the day the heavily publicized 'Spartakus Tribunal' took place at the University of Hamburg. In front of the ZDF's cameras, many members of the student audience behaved in ways that seemed to confirm the worst stereotypes about the Left's radicalism. Not only did they stamp their feet, throw curd cheese and paper balls, and attempt to shout Langguth down, they also eventually demolished the wooden barricades and stormed the podium.

Gerhard Löwenthal, the editor of the television broadcast *ZDF Magazin* and an early member of the Association for the Protection of Academic Freedom, care-fully edited the material and included seven minutes showing the most tumultu-ous scenes in his program, which aired on 26 January. Without denying that the scenes had been 'frightening' and conceding that many viewers had probably realized for the first time that the existence of 'terrorist student groups was not just

---

[34] ACDP, 4-6-53-2, Detlef Stronk, 'Leitfaden zur Wahlkampfführung', n.d. [1969], 7 and 11.

[35] ACDP, 4-6-53-2, Detlef Stronk, 'Leitfaden zur Wahlkampfführung', n.d. [1969], 16.

[36] Gerd Langguth, 'Zehn Fragen an den Spartakus', RCDS-Info (30 November 1971); RCDS Pressemitteilung (7 December 1971).

[37] Pridham, *Christian Democracy*, 202.

an invention of the CDU/CSU', the liberal weekly *Die Zeit* nevertheless reserved its most critical comments for the reporter's methods. 'The technique is not new [...]: you cut out the quiet scenes and overload the microphones that record the background sound. Sensitive types will then experience the acoustic impression alone as terror.' The following week, in response to such criticism, the ZDF felt compelled to show the full twenty-six minutes of material that its team had recorded in Hamburg. 'The event did not exactly unfold quietly either, and some scenes were almost unbearable', noted *Die Zeit*, but because of Löwenthal's tendentious editing 'something that often approached terror [had] appeared as amplified terror in the ZDF Magazin'.[38]

Much like Langguth, Löwenthal had a clear interest in painting student radicals in the worst possible light. He had hosted the *ZDF Magazin* since it first aired in 1969 and conceived of the show as a contribution to protecting the Federal Republic from dangerous extremists. Löwenthal and his fellow journalists thought of their newsroom as a 'pocket of resistance' against the 'left-wing Zeitgeist' that allegedly dominated public-service broadcasting.[39] The conservative and staunchly anti-communist editor—the younger brother of BFW founding member Richard Löwenthal—was a '45er, and thus part of a generational collective that Dirk A. Moses has aptly described as suffering from a 'Weimar syndrome', meaning that they routinely accused their political opponents of seeking to destroy German democracy.[40]

For Löwenthal, who was Jewish and who had been imprisoned in Sachsenhausen concentration camp in the Nazi years, the memory of Weimar's collapse carried special resonance. It also gave his frequent reporting on political radicalism a visceral sense of urgency. His feature on the 'Spartakus Tribunal' duly compared the contemporary situation at West German universities to the rise of the Nazis and framed the need to respond as part of a resistance struggle to defend West German democracy.[41] This framing gave Langguth's appearance at the tribunal existential meaning and chimed with Christian Democratic activists' understanding of their own efforts as a replay of the early 1930s. 'Will the Federal Republic meet the same fate as Weimar?' the group had begun to ask in the late 1960s. 'Today extremist groups once again foster irrational friend-or-foe modes of thought, deny the values of pluralist democracy, undermine the readiness for compromise and tolerance, and create a climate of emotions that inevitably leads to acts of terror.' In order to calm

---

[38] 'Selbstentlarvung des ZDF-Magazins', *Die Zeit*, 5 (2 February 1972), 20.

[39] 'Ein "Widerstandsnest" im öffentlich-rechtlichen Fernsehen: Das ZDF-Magazin. Gespräch mit Fritz Schenk, Frankfurt, 7.1.2003', in Becker, Dirsch, and Winckler, *Die 68er und ihre Gegner*, 208–27; BAK, B443/9/1/9, Gerhard Löwenthal to Hubert Schrübbers, President of the Federal Office for the Protection of the Constitution, 23 December 1968; Schrübbers to Löwenthal (3 January 1969).

[40] Moses, *German Intellectuals and the Nazi Past*; see also Wehrs, *Protest der Professoren*, 68–147.

[41] HIA, GSC, Box 85, 'ZDF-Löwenthal im Audi-Max. Wahlhelfer der Rechten'.

such dangerous passions, the democratic centre had to take on extremists in a 'rational' manner, they concluded.[42]

The carefully planned 'Spartakus Tribunal' offered the audience a kind of Weimar re-enactment that illustrated the dangers of extremist passion while showing that the centre-right had learned the right lessons from the demise of Germany's first democracy. By remaining calm in the face of the left-wing racket and continuing to read his scripted speech even when curd splashed in his face, Langguth styled himself as the archetypal militant democrat who met left-wing irrationality with cool rationality and reason.[43] MSB Spartakus responded by mocking Langguth as the 'RCDS chair, who valiantly throws himself into the trajectory of the flying tomatoes that his own organization had ordered'.[44] They equally invoked Weimar when accusing Langguth (and Löwenthal) of emulating Alfred Hugenberg, the demagogic right-wing press baron of the 1920s, and argued that Christian Democratic activists had manipulated reality by orchestrating the mayhem in Hamburg. Brazen defamations and raging anti-communism had provoked the estimated 3,000 students present and led them to act out, Spartakus suggested. What the group did not say was that this staging only worked so well because the left-wing protesters performed their assigned roles. For when Langguth attempted to repeat the feat in May 1972 with an 'SHB Tribunal', the audience remained calm and responded to his prosecutorial demeanour with no more than ironic laughter. As a result, the ZDF camera team, which again accompanied the RCDS chair, left without visual evidence of left-wing 'terror'.[45]

In Hamburg, however, Langguth's strategy had worked spectacularly well, not just inside the auditorium. The piece of political theatre chimed with many television viewers, who read the cues provided by Langguth's performance and Löwenthal's framing only too readily. In the days after the scenes had first been broadcast, Federal Minister of the Interior Hans-Dietrich Genscher and Chancellor Brandt were inundated with letters from viewers that invoked Germany's wartime past as well as the contemporary threat posed by the socialist dictatorship on the other side of the Wall. The authors argued that West German democracy was under siege from both a new type of domestic fascism in left-wing guise and from communism externally.[46] These letters, written by housewives, high school teachers,

---

[42] ACDP 4/6/44/3, 'Aufruf zum Kampf gegen den Radikalismus', RCDS Pressemitteilung (10 July 1969).

[43] On political emotions and the fate of Weimar democracy, Ian Beacock, *Heartbroken: Democratic Emotions, Political Subjectivity and the Unravelling of the Weimar Republic, 1918–1933* (Stanford University, PhD Diss., 2018).

[44] IfZ, ED 734-6-7, 'Richtigstellung zur RCDS-Hetzsendung im ZDF', Leaflet.

[45] Dieter Stäcker, 'Da vorn leuchtet mich die Löwenthal-Presse an', *Frankfurter Rundschau* (12 May 1972); BAK, B138, 33,494, Bernhard Braun und Harald Stappmanns, 'Der Ring Christlich-Demokratischer Studenten – weder christlich noch "entschieden demokratisch". RCDS – ein willfähriges Instrument der CDU/CSU'.

[46] About twenty of these letters were archived in the files of the Ministry of Education and Science. An accompanying letter from the Head of the Federal Chancellor's Office noted that the number of

artisans, and blue-collar workers, invoked the spectre of Nazi terror to discredit the Hamburg protesters, but also often couched their observations about student activists in distinctly Nazi vocabulary. They were full of class-based resentments against an allegedly lazy and ungrateful young elite that lived off taxpayer money and referred to left-wing students as 'pigs', 'work-shy rabble', and the 'plague'.[47] Many letters conveyed a revealing sense of German victimhood at the hands of Soviet troops, an enduring sentiment with wartime roots that had been contained easily in the Federal Republic's postwar anti-communist consensus.[48] 'Because of exaggerated tolerance in the Weimar years, we have had to pay the price once before', one woman told Genscher.[49] Another man compared the students to Hitler's SA and SS, but also accused them of damaging the 'people's property' [*Volksvermögen*] and felt compelled to explain that, as a young man, he had 'lost my father, mother and three sisters in Königsberg [postwar Kaliningrad, AvdG], where they starved to death'.[50]

Like Löwenthal, most of the letter writers had been born in the 1920s, and some of them were self-conscious '45ers'. A few even sent a short biography along to explain their reaction and explicitly interpreted the left-wing revolt as a threat to their own generational project, the successful construction of the postwar West German republic after the total defeat of the 'Third Reich' and the healthy disenchantment with ideology that had accompanied it. As one man explained:

> I belong to the generation that still has memories of the war and the Nazi years (born in 1928). One can only say: [there are] striking parallels. We toiled and worked and paid a lot of taxes for a country, for a state, which has been exemplary in many ways thus far. Are we seeing a new elite that wants to destroy all of this in order to play into the hands of the Communist East?[51]

To some, the need to combat the Marxist student Left was directly linked to the Nazi-era struggle against 'Bolshevism'. 'I never was and am not now a Nazi...but, having been born in 1922, I had to suffer through four years on the Russian [sic] front and I don't want fanatics to push us into chaos once again', wrote one man.[52] Describing left-wing students as 'Bolshevist agents' another man argued that 'protesting like this would certainly cost the radicals their lives in Russia [beim

---

petitions regarding student radicalism and internal security had risen sharply in early 1972—a fact that was of great concern to the government in a federal election year. BAK, B138-14834, Head of the Federal Chancellor's Office to Minister of Education and Science (10 March 1972).

[47] BAK, B138-14834, P.N. to Genscher (26 January 1972); A. H. to Genscher (27 January 1972).

[48] Weitz, 'The Ever-Present Other: Communism in the Making of West Germany'; Creuzberger and Hoffmann, *'Geistige Gefahr' und 'Immunisierung der Gesellschaft'*.

[49] BAK, B138-14834, Frau S. to Genscher (26 January 1972).

[50] BAK, B138-14834, G. O. to Brandt (27 January 1972).

[51] BAK, B138-14834, H. S. to Genscher (3 February 1972).

[52] BAK, B138-14834, Illegible name to Genscher, n.d.

Russen]—or [lead to] banishment to Sieberia [sic].'⁵³ Virtually all these letters revealed the close imaginative proximity of Germany's wartime and postwar past and the 1970s Cold War present. They also illustrate the ways in which this Christian Democratic student agitation brought older—and often much uglier—resentments against the Left to the fore.⁵⁴

Langguth's performance not only succeeded in presenting his struggle as part of a wider attempt to combat extremist forces in German public life; he also managed to garner votes for the RCDS in student council elections.⁵⁵ At a time when the Christian Democrats were otherwise struggling to break through against the Social-Liberal coalition with its popular Chancellor, there is even some evidence to suggest that the strategy yielded additional votes for the party in a national election year. 'I have never voted CDU, but I no longer see any other alternative. This development would not have been possible under Adenauer', a stonemason born in 1921 wrote to Genscher after watching the scenes in Hamburg.⁵⁶ A journalist from the city also reported to the Liberal Minister that plenty of people in his circle had 'quietly joined the CDU' after witnessing scenes like those at the 'Spartakus Tribunal'.⁵⁷ The prospect of national elections later that year no doubt magnified the attention paid to the events in Hamburg. But one specific issue that was high on the political agenda in January 1972 heightened their significance: the debate about so-called 'radicals' entering the civil service.

Centre-Right Activists and the 'Radicals Decree'

The timing of the 'Spartakus Tribunal' and the ZDF Magazin's reporting could not have been better. On 27 January 1972, the day after Löwenthal's segment had first aired in prime time, the Standing Council of State Interior Ministers met to discuss a set of guidelines to deal with civil servants deemed 'hostile to the constitution'. The meeting had been scheduled for some time. The issue had been on the political agenda since the previous summer, in large part because, at a time when the Brandt government was in the process of negotiating the

---

⁵³ BAK, B138-14834, Letter from J. W. (30 January 1972).

⁵⁴ Bill Schwarz makes a similar point about letters written to British conservatives Enoch Powell and Mary Whitehouse in the late 1960s and early 1970s. British letter writers often invoked Britain's imperial past to make sense of immigration and cultural change in the present. Bill Schwarz, 'The Silent Majority. How the Private Becomes Political', in von der Goltz and Waldschmidt-Nelson, *Inventing the Silent Majority*, 147–71. Similarly, Stuart Hilwig has shown that, when confronted with left-wing radicals in the 1960s, older Italians often looked back nostalgically at the 'orderly' nature of the fascist period. See his *Italy and 1968: Youthful Unrest and Democratic Culture* (Houndmills, Basingstoke, UK, New York, 2009), 58–79.

⁵⁵ 'RCDS-Bundesvorsitzender zieht positive Bilanz des WS 71/72', RCDS Press Release (1 March 1972); 'Stichwort RCDS', *Die Welt* (11 February 1972).

⁵⁶ M.D. to Genscher (27 January 1972), B138-14834.

⁵⁷ W.E. to Genscher (2 February 1972), B138-14834.

German-German Treaty as part of its new *Ostpolitik*, the Christian Democrats in opposition decided to use the spectre of left-wing infiltration of the civil service to paint the governing Social Democrats as 'soft on communism'.

The following day, on 28 January 1972, the federal and state governments issued the 'Basic Principles on the Question of Anti-constitutional Personnel in the Public Service', better known as the 'Radicals Decree'. According to this controversial ordinance, all applicants for jobs in the civil service would be subjected to a review by the Federal Office for the Protection of the Constitution to determine whether they were loyal to the 'free democratic order'. Due to the high number of civil servants in Germany, this statute of loyalty applied to a host of ordinary individuals, not just judges, university professors, and teachers, but also postal workers, trash collectors, train and bus drivers.[58] Those who had been active in groups that were 'hostile to the constitution' were denied employment. The 'Radicals Decree'—termed 'Occupational Ban' by its left-wing critics—was not a new law per se, but an attempt to update and make more stringent existing legislation first introduced by the Adenauer government in 1950 to prevent the Bonn Republic from becoming 'another Weimar'.[59]

Originally conceived to protect the civil service from all hostile elements, not least those on the extreme right, the 1970s iteration of the decree overwhelmingly targeted left-wing activists. Until the Social-Liberal government stopped the routine loyalty check for new civil servants in 1979, around 2,000 people had been hindered from entering (or remaining in) state employment, the vast majority of them on the Left. Many more had faced extensive political intrusion into their private lives and years of professional uncertainty.[60] The ordinance thus had an effect that was much greater than its professional toll. As its critics pointed out, it created a climate of fear and intimidation against the Left and suggested continuities to Germany's illiberal past with its long history of anti-socialist persecution.[61]

However, for the oppositional Christian Democrats, as well as for those members of the Brandt government who were intent on proving their vigilance in the fight against communism, ensuring the bureaucracy's loyalty was not an authoritarian anti-socialist measure, but part and parcel of West Germany's character as a 'militant democracy'.[62] They saw the ordinance as a vital safeguard against a

---

[58] Gerard Braunthal, *Political Loyalty and Public Service in West Germany: The 1972 Decree against Radicals and Its Consequences* (Amherst, MA, 1990); Rigoll, *Staatsschutz in Westdeutschland*; Mary Nolan, 'Pushing the Defensive Wall of the State Forward: Terrorism and Civil Liberties in Germany', *New German Critique*, 117, 39/3 (2012), 109–33.

[59] Ullrich, *Der Weimar-Komplex*, 348–75.

[60] Rigoll, *Staatsschutz in Westdeutschland*, 408–10, 473.

[61] Braunthal, *Political Loyalty*, ix–x; Rigoll, *Staatsschutz in Westdeutschland*, 473–5.

[62] Hanshew, *Terror and Democracy*, 133; on the postwar, anti-communist origins of the idea of 'military democracy', see further Greenberg, 'Militant Democracy and Human Rights'.

creeping but meticulously planned takeover of government institutions by left-wing extremists. Given the failure of Weimar democracy in the early 1930s, West German democrats had to be especially vigilant, they insisted. Rudi Dutschke's Mao-inspired slogan of left-wing activists' 'long march through the institutions', first brought to the awareness of the general public in a *Der Spiegel* interview in the late 1960s, had begun to raise fears of left-wing entryism and an eventual takeover. By mid-1971, the rise of the DKP and its student wing MSB Spartakus had given the problem a greater sense of urgency.[63] The prospect of a horde of tenured communist teachers, jurists, and professors, loyal to the GDR, now seemed an imminent threat to the democratic order. It was also too good an opportunity for the oppositional Christian Democrats to pass up in their quest to regain their standing as the natural party of government.

From summer 1971 onward, the CDU's federal party board repeatedly discussed the looming 'march through the institutions' in its closed meetings and prepared to 'go to war in this area' if the Social-Liberal government did not agree to issuing a set of assertive principles to ward off the threat.[64] The 'Spartakus Tribunal', so timely shown on television the day before the Interior Ministers met to contemplate the exact language of these guidelines, helped to visualize the gravity of the threat. This fact was not lost on the authors of the letters to Brandt and Genscher, some of whom urged the two politicians to keep communists out of the civil service.[65]

Christian Democratic students had been among the earliest voices warning against the spectre of left-wing 'infiltration' of the civil service, well before the issue was high on the public agenda. After all, they studied alongside activists of the Left, saw them graduate, and were thus well aware that many of them were aspiring teachers or judges and that a large number of young left-wing academics was moving into newly-created university posts at a time of rapid expansion in higher education. At the very least, left-wing graduates posed a serious and long-term threat to Christian Democratic hegemony—something the party had taken for granted until very recently; at worst, they signalled that the left-wing 'seizure of power' was already under way. Wighard Härdtl, who had been something of a hardliner at the Free University in Berlin in the 1960s, was convinced that the latter was the case. In a 1971 essay for the Konrad Adenauer Foundation, he argued that a 'seizure of power' by the New Left was now a serious possibility, especially within the Federal Republic's socializing institutions. Parliamentary democracy was in grave danger, he contended, and a centre-right 'anti-guerrilla

[63] Rigoll, *Staatsschutz in Westdeutschland*, 199, 271.

[64] See the comments by JU Chair Jürgen Echtnernach, cited in the Minutes of the Meeting of 9 December 1971, in Barzel: *'Unsere Alternativen für die Zeit der Opposition': Die Protokolle des CDU-Bundesvorstands 1969–1973*, ed. by Günter Buchstab and Denise Lindsay (Düsseldorf, 2009), 632.

[65] B138-14834, K. W. to Genscher (26 January 1972).

strategy' aimed at 'smashing the guerrillas' fortified positions' was called for, he insisted.[66]

Contrary to the often-maligned Social-Liberal governing coalition, whose members were divided on the issue, the Christian Democratic parties whole-heartedly backed the 'Radicals Decree'.[67] They helped to place the issue on the agenda in 1971/72 and continued to seize on it in the coming years in an effort to push the Brandt government onto the defensive. Pressuring Brandt to be tough on radical leftists became one of the cornerstones of the CDU's new and bolder oppositional strategy under the leadership of the party's new chair, Rainer Barzel, who took office in 1971.[68] RCDS was intimately involved in this endeav-our and, in fact, played a vanguard role. Its leader, Gerd Langguth, who was a member of the CDU's federal board, kept his senior colleagues abreast of the conditions at the universities, regularly providing minute details of alleged transgressions of the SHB and MSB Spartakus.[69] This was the same Gerd Langguth who, in Hamburg, had helped the public to visualize the danger of left-wing 'terror' at the crucial moment of the debate in January 1972.

In the coming months and years, the RCDS chair continued his campaign of seeking public confrontations with the campus Left in the hope that such displays would further unmask his opponents as violent extremists. Langguth carefully chose centres of left-wing activism for such events to demonstrate that the left-wing takeover of public institutions was well underway. For instance, in October 1973 he hosted a public meeting to found a local RCDS chapter at the 'red' University of Bremen, a newly created reform university with a decidedly left-wing bent, housed in a city with an entrenched Social Democratic majority. In the 1970s, the University of Bremen became a powerful symbol to conservatives of everything that was wrong with student activism and higher education policy.[70]

Left-wing activists duly disrupted the meeting and roughed up Langguth in the process. The RCDS chair was pushed off his chair and forcefully removed from the meeting room and driven down a flight of stairs; his jacket was damaged during the commotion.[71] The conservative *Rheinischer Merkur* duly interpreted this display of 'brute force' as evidence of the 'triumph of left-wing terror at

---

[66] Wighard Härdtl, 'Strategie der Neuen Linken zur Machtergreifung', in Wulf Schönbohm (ed.), *Die Studentische Protestbewegung: Analysen und Konzepte* (Mainz, 1971), 95–123, here 118–19.

[67] Hanshew, *Terror and Democracy*, 133.   [68] Braunthal, *Political Loyalty*, 28.

[69] E. g. Minutes of Meeting of 13 March 1972, in Barzel: *'Unsere Alternativen für die Zeit der Opposition'*, 734–8.

[70] When Langguth visited in 1973, SHB, MSB Spartakus, and two other communist student groups were the only ones represented in the Bremen student parliament and council. Westdeutsche Rektorenkonferenz (ed.), 'Übersicht über die Ergebnisse der Wahlen zu den Studentenvertretungen im Sommersemester 1973', *Dokumentation*, 20 (1973), 5.

[71] Staatsarchiv Bremen 4.111/7, 178, 'Urteil (10 Ns 14/75), in der Strafsache gegen Scheer, Schelz, Behm wegen Vergehens gegen das Versammlungsgesetzes'.

German universities'.[72] A few weeks later and with a number of television cameras in tow, Langguth returned for a second attempt to found an RCDS chapter in the city. This time he was successful, generating widespread media coverage, much of it positive.[73] The *Rheinischer Merkur* even urged RCDS's mother party to take note of Langguth's combative strategy. It was pointless, the paper contended, to shirk taking on the radicals and to play the 'compassionate liberal'. 'The CDU, many of whose members still display the exaggerated affected behaviour of dignitaries, could learn something from RCDS [...]', the paper was convinced.[74]

The events in Bremen garnered public attention not least because a tenured academic had taken part in the scuffle of 23 October. The nuclear physicist Jens Scheer helped the left-wing students block the door to the room where the RCDS meeting took place and grabbed a microphone from the Christian Democrats. Langguth complained about the professor's conduct to Bremen's Social Democratic Senator of Education and Science, and the CDU in the Bremen Senate then demanded to know what steps would be taken to discipline the left-wing academic.[75] Langguth also filed charges against Scheer for disturbing the peace, leading to a criminal investigation of the professor and anti-nuclear activist. He was ordered to pay a fine for malfeasance and placed on probation for putting Christian Democratic activists under duress. To many, the case against the left-wing academic—later removed from his post for supporting a communist K-Group—seemed like the perfect illustration of the necessity of the 'Radicals Decree'. 'The fact that this man was able to enter state employment ought to prove once more how a law that ensures that radicals are kept out of the civil service is necessary', a Bremen man wrote in a letter to the editor of the local daily *Weser Kurier*. 'We have to keep an eye on these people, otherwise we will have academics in posts who will destroy our society before we know it', a local woman argued in a similarly worded letter to the paper.[76] Such RCDS events thus helped to illustrate the potential danger of allowing communists to enter the civil service and, in doing so, bolstered public support for the 'Radicals Decree'.[77]

Because the 'Radicals Decree' of 28 January 1972 only established basic principles rather than binding rules on how to vet civil servants' political loyalty, the issue continued to be the subject of fierce debate throughout the 1970s. Much like

---

[72] 'RCDS: Bremer Lehren', *Rheinischer Merkur* (16 November 1973).

[73] Staatsarchiv Bremen 4.111/7, no. 177, 'RCDS-Gründungsveranstaltung in Bremen klappte im zweiten Anlauf', Press Release of the Bremen Senate (7 November 1973); 'RCDS verschafft sich Gehör', *Frankfurter Allgemeine Zeitung* (8 November 1973).

[74] 'RCDS: Bremer Lehren', *Rheinischer Merkur* (16 November 1973).

[75] Staatsarchiv Bremen 4.111/7, no. 177, Langguth to Thape (24 October 1973); Bremische Bürgerschaft, Drucksache 8, 660 (1 November 1973).

[76] ACDP, 4/6/44/1, Letters to the editor from Kurt Wittig and Mia Evers, *Weser Kurier*, 254, 15.

[77] Bonn's centre-right Aktion Demokratische Mitte also wrote to a number of State Ministers in North Rhine-Westphalia to complain about the employment of the DKP member Volker Götz as a judge in the state. ACDP, 1-365-86, ADM Spokesman Clemens von Wendt to State Minister of Justice Posser, n.d.. On Götz's case further Rigoll, *Staatsschutz in Westdeutschland*, 398–400.

the emergency laws of the 1960s, the 'Radicals Decree' signalled to its left-wing critics that authoritarian sentiments still reigned supreme in West Germany and that the 'system' could not be trusted. Many Social Democrats and Liberals had quickly grown uneasy with the disproportionate effects that the ordinance had on activists of the Left and refused to tighten the guidelines at the federal level.[78] This meant that individual states had different benchmarks and followed varying vetting procedures to establish civil servants' loyalty (some required a written declaration of loyalty to the 'free democratic order', for instance, while others did not). This gave the whole endeavour an air of unevenness, arbitrariness, and uncertainty that fuelled public controversy.

Throughout the decade, the fate of individual civil servants or civil service applicants who were denied employment on the grounds of prior political activities served to illustrate the decree's human consequences. Figures such as the popular Hanover Professor of Psychology Peter Brückner, whose Jewish mother had fled from Germany during the Nazi years, became political martyrs in the eyes of the Left. His suspension from his university post in 1972 for having provided shelter to RAF leader Ulrike Meinhof, a long-time acquaintance of Brückner's from her days as a journalist, seemed to illustrate that the 'Radicals Decree' stood in a discomforting line of historical continuity with the Nazi past. That many of the judges tasked with deciding the fate of left-wing 'radicals' had been in office since the Nazi years reinforced this connection.[79]

While much of the general public initially supported the restrictive measures, public opinion began to shift against their staunch implementation in the second half of the 1970s. This was at least in part as a result of international outrage about what many observers abroad perceived as West Germany's resurgent authoritarianism. The French Socialist leader François Mitterrand, for one, criticized the ban publicly. Moreover, in 1978, the Federal Republic became the subject of an International Russell Tribunal on human rights violations as a result of the ban, a questionable honour hitherto bestowed only on the United States because of their conduct in Vietnam and on a number of Latin American dictatorships for killing and torturing dissidents.[80]

RCDS, by contrast, did not waver in its conviction that individuals 'hostile to the constitution' had to be kept out of state employment. Christian Democratic students continued to campaign fervently for the decree. In doing so, they acquired plenty of first-hand experiences that only convinced them further of

---

[78] Braunthal, *Political Loyalty*, 54–7.

[79] HIA, Lewy Papers, Box 3, 'Politischer und krimineller Radikalismus in der Bundesrepublik', dpa Hintergrund, Archiv-und Informationsmaterial (3 December 1973); Hans Mayer, 'Peter Brückner: Leben und Denken. Selbstbefreiung in der normalisierten Welt', *Die Zeit* (23 November 1984).

[80] Internationales Russell Tribunal, *Berufsverbote Condemned: Third Russell Tribunal* (Nottingham, 1978); Michael März, *Linker Protest nach dem Deutschen Herbst* (Bielefeld, 2012), 245–318; Braunthal, *Political Loyalty*, 66–92; Rigoll, *Staatsschutz in Westdeutschland*, 449–54.

the radical Left's malice and anti-constitutionalism. In June 1975, during a discussion on the measure held in Freiburg, for instance, the leader of the local RCDS chapter was knocked unconscious and admitted to a local hospital. Hans Reckers (b. 1953), then RCDS national chair, was attacked physically at the same event, his glasses broken and his clothes torn.[81] At a similar event in Münster in November 1973, a young Georg Milbradt (b. 1945), who would serve as Christian Democratic Governor of Saxony in the early 2000s, and Ruprecht Polenz (b. 1946), a future head of the Bundestag Committee on Foreign Affairs, were both assaulted, and other RCDS activists were also beaten up badly.[82]

Such violent confrontations with activists of the Left—though no doubt personally traumatic at the time—were then readily exploited by Christian Democratic activists to persuade the public that left-wing radicals were plotting a violent takeover of the Federal Republic under legal guise. To this end, the RCDS national board issued documentation that chronicled the worst left-wing attacks on Christian Democratic activists in detailed fashion.[83] A cartoon entitled 'Civil Servant '75 (representing the interests of the state)' published on the front page of a Hessian Christian Democratic student newspaper gave visual expression to the idea that aspiring civil servants were secretly scheming to overthrow liberal democracy. It depicted a figure that was one half suited civil servant with the Basic Law under his arm, while the other half was a long-haired radical wearing flared trousers and a hammer and sickle button, carrying a belted knife and hand grenade, and wielding a machine gun.[84]

In line with the slow shift in public opinion, however, Christian Democratic students began to soften their language somewhat in the second half of the 1970s. They increasingly talked about the need to safeguard both the rule of law *and* civil liberty, argued that 'rabble-rousing' against radicals was counterproductive, and suggested specific ways in which the federal government could streamline the vetting procedures and make them fairer.[85] When Helmut Schmidt's government

---

[81] 'Freiburger RCDS-Vorsitzender Erös von kommunistischen Studenten bewusstlos geschlagen', RCDS Bundesvorstand, Press Release (27 June 1975).

[82] 'Diskussionsveranstaltung gewaltsam gesprengt', *Westfälische Nachrichten* (7 November 1973); ACDP, 4/6/13/2, Georg Milbradt, Letter to Fachschaft Jura (1 December 1973); Hans Reckers, 'Eidesstattliche Versicherung zur Vorlage bei Gericht' (24 July 1974).

[83] See e.g. ACDP, 4/6/13/2, '"Vorsicht! Sie kommen...aus ihren Löchern". Gewaltsame Sprengungen von RCDS-Veranstaltungen im Zeichen der linksradikalen Presse'. Wehrs makes a similar point regarding the public information campaign of the BFW, which consisted primarily of documenting student attacks on its members, see his *Protest der Professoren*, 267.

[84] 'Beamter '75 (staatstragend)', *Campus* (1975), ACDP, 4/46/3/2. RCDS used similar depictions of left-wing subversion to raise donations from the private sector. HIA, GSC, Box 85, Bundesvereinigung Freundes- und Foerderkreis e. V. des RCDS to B. Z., n.d.; Letter by Gerd Langguth and Hans Reckers, 7 July 1976, in the name of the RCDS Bundesvereinigung Freundes- und Förderkreis e. V.

[85] 'RCDS-Bundesvorsitzender bekräftigt: Verfassungsfeinde nicht in den öffentlichen Dienst aufnehmen', *Demokratische Blätter*, 3 (June/July 1975), 18; ACDP, 4/6/54/2, 'Sechs Punkte zur Sicherung rechtsstaatlicher Liberalität beim Schutz des demokratischen Rechtsstaates' (4 November 1976); BAK, B138/57523, RCDS national chair Hans Reckers to Minister of Education and Science, n.d.; 'Plädoyer für ein "liberales Klima"', *Frankfurter Allgemeine Zeitung* (6 June 1976); 'Der RCDS fordert liberalen

Illustration 5.2 'Civil Servant '75 (representing the interests of the state)'.

Cartoon from the cover of the Hessian RCDS publication *Campus.*

(RCDS Frankfurt am Main, ACDP 04-046). Unnamed artist.

decided to forgo routine political background checks on new civil service applicants in 1979—hitherto the cornerstone of the controversial decree—Christian Democratic students were nevertheless highly critical, insisting that the FRG still required protection from extremist infiltration.[86]

Throughout the 1970s, the politics of the past remained central to the fierce debate surrounding the decree. Christian Democratic students regarded ensuring the bureaucracy's loyalty as a life-or-death matter for the democratic order and strongly rejected the portrayal of the 'Radicals Decree' as a dangerous hangover from Germany's history of authoritarianism. When a discussion on the subject featuring the RCDS and none other than Gerhard Löwenthal—by now notorious in left-wing circles for his one-sided reporting on student activism—was broken up by students sympathetic to the MSB Spartakus at the University of Cologne in 1978, Christian Democratic activists were convinced that the bullying of a journalist who had been persecuted by the Nazis only proved that the Left was blind to

---

Umgang mit den Radikalen', *Frankfurter Rundschau* (5 November 1976); Friedbert Pflüger, 'Für eine rechtsstaatliche Einstellungspraxis, aber: Von "Berufsverboten" keine Rede!', *Demokratische Blätter* 3 (November 1976), 10.

[86] 'Regelanfrage beibehalten', RCDS Press Release, no. 94 (15 February 1979).

the real historical continuities at play.[87] Vehemently denying any resemblance to Bismarck's anti-Socialist laws of the 1870s and 1880s, and to the persecution of Social Democrats and Communists under the Nazis, Christian Democratic students instead invoked the fragility of German democracy in the Weimar years to underline the Federal Republic's need to remain especially vigilant. West Germany's uncompromising stance towards extremists was a sign of democracy's strength, maturity, and stability, not proof of its shallow roots, RCDS insisted.[88] Clearly, activists did not have to be born in the 1920s to think that the 'lessons of Weimar' were crucial to the West German polity. However, much as it was for the '45ers, the exact meaning of these lessons remained heavily contested among student activists.[89]

Protecting the Constitution

Given their embrace of West Germany's assertive brand of 'militant democracy', it should come as no surprise that Christian Democratic student activists had quite an intimate relationship with the Federal Office for the Protection of the Constitution (*Bundesamt für Verfassungsschutz*, BfV), West Germany's domestic security agency. After all, they regarded the Federal Republic's 'free democratic order' as worth protecting and were therefore deeply comfortable with an institution whose explicit task this was.[90] RCDS leaders already corresponded and met with senior officials of the *Verfassungsschutz* in the late 1960s, exchanging material about the political goals of the SDS.[91] After being in touch with RCDS leaders in April 1968, the President of the Federal Office for the Protection of the Constitution reported to Chancellor Kiesinger's Office that Christian Democratic student leaders were very much 'willing to contribute' to the government's efforts to contain SDS.[92]

While this cooperation was not made public, the student Left always took for granted that young Christian Democrats were in bed with the security agency. One Christian Democratic activist remembered feeling quite threatened because it

---

[87] 'RCDS-Veranstaltung gewaltsam gestört', RCDS Press Release, no. 70 (17 November 1978).

[88] Hans Reckers, 'Für eine rechtsstaatliche Einstellungsregelung', *Demokratische Blätter*, no. 4 (September/October 1975), 8; see also the extensive chapter on the Weimar precedent published in a collection of essays edited by former RCDS chair Wulf Schönbohm: Hans-Helmuth Knütter, 'Verfassungsfeindliche Beamte in der Weimarer Republik', in *Verfassungsfeinde als Beamte? Die Kontroverse um die streitbare Demokratie*, edited by Wulf Schönbohm (Munich and Vienna, 1979), 13–38.

[89] For the contrasting manifestations of the 'Weimar syndrome' among the '45ers, see Moses, *German Intellectuals and the Nazi Past*.

[90] Bender interview.

[91] ACDP, 04/006/045/3, RCDS national chair Wulf Schönbohm to the Federal Office for the Protection of the Constitution (3 November 1967).

[92] BAK, B136/5035, President of the Federal Office for the Protection of the Constitution to the State Secretary in the Federal Chancellor's Office (23 April 1968).

seemed as though anyone who even vaguely looked the part was suspected of being a covert agent. He recalled hearing rumours of a left-wing slogan 'People who wear ties are from the *Verfassungsschutz* and we have to hunt them'.[93] An infamous issue of the MSB Spartakus's newspaper *Rote Blätter*, which became the subject of a court case in 1974, indeed painted all members of the RCDS as 'police agents and collaborators with fascists'.[94] A leaflet distributed in Bremen went even further in labelling the RCDS an 'organization of snitches and denunciators'. Christian Democratic student activists were 'fascistic' and nothing but 'hustlers of the Verfassungsschutz', it went on.[95] MSB Spartakus was also convinced that Christian Democratic activists had colluded with the Cologne-based agency when planning the 'Spartakus Tribunal' in 1972.[96]

In spite of the fact that accusations about Christian Democratic activists 'snitching' for the security agency had circulated throughout the 1970s, it caused quite a stir when a newspaper article finally revealed that RCDS had indeed been on the agency's payroll since 1969. On 4 January 1979, this explosive news item made the front page of the left-leaning daily *Frankfurter Rundschau*, which first reported that the centre-right student group had received up to 160,000 Deutsche Mark (DM)—the equivalent of approximately 300,000 Euros today—annually from a covert *Verfassungsschutz* fund controlled by the Interior Ministry. The money was designated for endeavours that would lead to the 'advancement of the intellectual-political confrontation with political extremism'.[97] These were substantial sums for a student group and far exceeded what other government agencies provided.[98] Other student groups of the centre-right, such as the DSU (and its successor, the SLH) received the same amount; the Christian Labor Association also received money. All in all, the agency dished out more than two million marks annually.

---

[93] Reeder interview.

[94] 'RCDS: Polizeiagenten und Faschisten-Kollaborateure', *Rote Blätter*, 18 (1974), 21–6; ACDP, 4/6/13/2, Beschluss des Landgerichts Bonn, Einstweilige Verfügung, 22 May 1974; ACDP, 4/6/13/2, RCDS national chair Ulrich Schröder, RCDS-Rundbrief, 15 (26 August 1974); see also 'Gutes Verhältnis zu Faschisten', *Deutsche Volkszeitung*, 22 (15 August 1974).

[95] Staatsarchiv Bremen 4.111/7, no. 177, 'RCDS—Raus aus der Uni!' Leaflet (6 November 1973).

[96] IfZ, ED 734-6-7, 'Richtigstellung zur RCDS-Hetzsendung im ZDF', MSB Spartakus leaflet; HIA, GSC, Box 85, 'ZDF-Löwenthal im Audi-Max. Wahlhelfer der Rechten', Leaflet by the Uni-Basisgruppen Freiburg, While there is scant archival evidence to suggest such joint planning, the agency's involvement on 19 January nevertheless seems clear. The ZDF's camera footage of the day shows a man in civilian clothes next to Langguth on the stage of the Hamburg auditorium—likely a *Verfassungsschutz* agent—taking photographs of the most vocal members in the audience. Twenty-six-minute film in the author's possession.

[97] 'Geld für Studenten aus Geheimetat: Seminare für Studenten mit Verfassungsschutz-Mitteln', *Frankfurter Rundschau* (4 January 1979), 1–2.

[98] In 1971, the Ministry for Science and Education provided just over 25,000 DM for RCDS events. The previous year, the RCDS's entire staff costs had been less than 70,000 DM, and the group only received 81,000 DM from the National Youth Plan, the government's main funding source for political and cultural activities of West German youth. These figures are taken from a brief on the RCDS compiled for the Federal Minister of Education and Science to prepare him for a speech he was scheduled to give at the RCDS annual meeting in Koblenz on 5 July 1972, BAK, B138, 10,326. The RCDS also received funding from the federal board of the CDU and from other CDU organization.

While the numbers alone certainly raised eyebrows, the secrecy with which the payments were made was even more controversial. The covert disbursements to centre-right students had first started in the final year of the Grand Coalition government, a time of growing concern about the phenomenon of 'youth unrest'. On 21 June 1967, shortly after Benno Ohnesorg's death, a high-level inter-ministerial working group on 'youth radicalism' was founded. Chaired by Christian Democratic Minister of Family and Youth Bruno Heck, this committee was especially concerned with the growing radicalism inside the universities. The working group recommended in-depth academic study of the phenomenon and the dissemination of suitable scholarly works to enlighten the public in the hope that such literature would dissuade students from embracing radical ideas en masse.[99] Literary instruments were not deemed sufficient, however. Nurturing moderate student groups who opposed the left-wing radicals was another import-ant measure that the committee recommended: 'It is [. . .] necessary at all places of higher education to support the students who embrace our state system and to enable them to confront established extremists.'[100]

Given the federalized structure of West German higher education and the relatively strict rules governing official civic education programming, financing such groups through conventional channels—such as the Ministry of Family and Youth or the Federal Agency for Civic Education (*Bundeszentrale für politische Bildung*)—was difficult to accomplish. In addition, the committee feared that open government funding would tarnish 'sober-minded forces' within the student body as representatives of the 'the so-called establishment'.[101] Therefore 'a solution that aided the positive protection of the constitution' was needed.[102] The idea of nurturing active democrats and battling political extremism through civic education—termed 'positive protection of the constitution'—was an older concept championed by the Federal Republic's security organs.[103] Since it could not be done easily through open channels, the bureaucrats in the Interior Ministry had to get creative. To mobilize 'counterforces against groups hostile to the constitution', suitable youth organizations should receive funds 'indirectly through patrons', a

---

[99] BAK, B 106/63585, vol. 1, 'Empfehlungen für praktische Maßnahmen zur Überwindung extremistischer Bestrebungen im Hochschulbereich', compiled by Interior Ministry Department K7, 12 December 1968; among the studies deemed suitable for such a task and distributed by the Federal Agency for Civic Education were René Ahlberg, *Die politische Konzeption des Sozialistischen Deutschen Studentenbundes* (Bonn, 1968) and Giselherr Schmidt, *Die Weltanschauung der Neuen Linken* (Bonn, 1968). Ahlberg was a member of the *Notgemeinschaft für eine Freie Universität* (NoFU), a predecessor of the BFW.

[100] BAK, B 106/63585, vol. 2, Memorandum by Interior Ministry Department K7 (4 January 1969).

[101] BAK, B 106/63585, vol. 3, 'Aufrechterhaltung von Sicherheit und Ordnung: Ein Katalog von Maßnahmen gegen Ausschreitungen radikaler Elemente der Jugend', First Draft (13 January 1969).

[102] BAK, B 106/63585, vol. 1, 'Empfehlungen für praktische Maßnahmen zur Überwindung extremistischer Bestrebungen im Hochschulbereich', compiled by Interior Ministry Department K7 (12 December 1968).

[103] 'Diskrete Gelder vom Verfassungsschutz', *Der Spiegel*, 2 (1979), 10; Hanshew, *Terror and Democracy*, 124–5.

memorandum drafted for the Christian Democratic Interior Minister Ernst Benda suggested in December 1968.[104]

The solution that his Ministry eventually came up with was to hide the money for politically moderate student activists in the budget of the Federal Office for the Protection of the Constitution. The agency had seen a massive increase in its budget in previous years, its finances were not made public, and it had used a similar covert funding mechanism to pay for anti-extremist measures since the early 1950s.[105] Throughout the 1970s, then, Christian Democratic student leaders submitted receipts for events and publications to the Interior Ministry and regularly received a suitcase full of cash in return—a strikingly conspiratorial practice for financing the endeavours of a student group affiliated with one of West Germany's main political parties.[106] While RCDS was usually only too happy to flaunt its efforts to combat political extremism, the revelations were quite embarrassing. A terse press release issued the day after the *Frankfurter Rundschau* article was published did its best to downplay the covert nature of the payments.[107]

What was perhaps even more remarkable than the secrecy was the fact that this practice continued for ten years under the Social-Liberal coalition government. The idea that Christian Democratic politicians were happy to entrust their own student organization and other centre-right groups with battling political extremism in the late 1960s is hardly surprising. Chancellor Kiesinger had pointed out the need to nurture student 'combat groups, [...] with people who are determined' in an internal party meeting in June 1968, for instance.[108] However, it bears explaining why the Brandt and Schmidt governments continued the practice even when Christian Democratic students stoked public fears of the student Left and helped to paint Social Democrats as 'soft on communism'. After all, the Social Democratic party youth organization, the Young Socialists (*Jungsozialisten*, Jusos), only began to receive funds from the same secret pot belatedly in 1976.[109] At the very least, this cooperation suggests that the SPD mistrusted its

---

[104] BAK, B 106/63585, vol. 1, Arbeitsgruppe politische Grundsatzfragen, 'Repressive Maßnahmen im Zusammenhang mit den Ausschreitungen der unruhigen Jugend' (December 1968).

[105] Rigoll, *Staatsschutz in Westdeutschland*, 188; 'Diskrete Gelder vom Verfassungsschutz', *Der Spiegel*, 2 (1979), 10.

[106] Gunter Hofmann, 'Richter über Gut und Böse', *Die Zeit*, 3 (1979), 4.

[107] 'RCDS bestätigt Förderung aus öffentlichen Mitteln. Keine Beteiligung an "Geheimoperation"', RCDS Press Release, no. 85 (5 January 1979). None of my interviewees discussed the funding practice during our formal interview. However, one interviewee mentioned it once the tape was switched off.

[108] See his remarks in a meeting of the CDU's federal board on 21 June 1968. *Kiesinger: 'Wir leben in einer veränderten Welt' (1965–1969), Die Protokolle des CDU-Bundesvorstandes*, vol. 5, ed. by Günter Buchstab (Düsseldorf, 2005), 993.

[109] Contrary to Christian Democratic students, JuSo leaders never picked the cash up from the Interior Ministry, but received payments from the SPD-affiliated Friedrich-Ebert Foundation instead. Payments to the JuSos only started after Jürgen Schmude, the Social Democratic State Secretary in the Interior Ministry, began to apply political pressure. Gunter Hofmann, 'Richter über Gut und Böse', *Die Zeit*, 3 (1979), 4.

own—famously rebellious—youth organization and deemed Christian Democratic students (and other anti-Socialist groups) as better placed to uphold the 'free democratic order' at the universities.[110]

The Spectre of Left-Wing Terrorism

The increasingly heated clashes of the 1970s meant that Christian Democratic student leaders thought of activists of the Left first and foremost as their political enemies. This was not just true of the ever-combative Langguth, who made battling leftist student radicals one of his life's missions; it also applied to his successors, who entered student politics some time after 1968. They lacked first-hand experiences of the student movement's more playful beginnings. The defining concern of their tenures was combatting 'left-wing extremism' and what they perceived as widespread support for terrorism by students at large. According to Friedbert Pflüger, who served as national chair of RCDS from 1977 until 1978:

> This was probably the worst phase of the confrontational intolerance of the Left, which erupted with the terrorism of the RAF and the sympathy for it. All that frustration about the failed anti-authoritarian revolution! And then a part of the Left became radical and didn't want to accept it, and a very small number became terrorists. And that was formative and fascinating [for an activist of the centre-right].[111]

Coming of age around the turn of the decade, at a time when left-wing ideas dominated political debates in many West German schools, Pflüger and his peers had felt even more like outsiders than their slightly older predecessors among the other '68ers. Pflüger, who was a prominent member of the Bundestag for much of the 1990s and 2000s, styled himself as an outcast from a young age in both the interview for this book and in his memoirs. Rather than defying the authoritarian remnants of the postwar republic, as some of the older other '68ers had done, he had rubbed up against signs of a new left-wing hegemony.

Growing up in Hanover in the wake of 1968, he recalled, 'it was the age of the late student revolts. At school there was a "Red Cell", "being on the Left" was your fashionable duty. As I wanted to protest, I took a different path.'[112] Instead of

---

[110] For other reports of this surprising rapprochement between the Social-Liberal coalition and RCDS in the 1970s, see Rudolf Walter Leonhardt, 'Generationensprung: Der Ring Christlich-Demokratischer Studenten geht sozialliberale Wege', *Die Zeit* (5 April 1974); 'Brandt würdigt Haltung des RCDS', in *Süddeutsche Zeitung* (24 March 1972).

[111] Pflüger interview. Pflüger described this period similarly in his memoir: Pflüger, *Ehrenwort*, 21–2.

[112] Pflüger, *Ehrenwort*, 135.

Marx's *Capital*, he had read the Basic Law and joined the Christian Democrats, he explained.[113] He was elected leader of the Göttingen RCDS chapter soon after taking up his studies and also served as the editor of the student association's journal, a publication tellingly named *Rational*.[114] Pflüger drew a sharp contrast between the left-wing activists of the late 1960s and those he encountered in Göttingen in the mid-1970s.

> Well, the 68ers were still very anti-authoritarian. And here we encountered an authoritarian left-wing extremism. And I was in the social sciences! [...] During my studies I experienced this everyday: ostracism! You sat more or less alone. And you were considered right-wing, and if you were right-wing you were tarnished in the department. It was not *en vogue*.[115]

Illustration 5.3 Friedbert Pflüger, then the RCDS deputy national chair, speaking at the CDU's annual party convention on 26 May 1976.
(Bundesarchiv-Bildarchiv, Photograph by Ulrich Wienke)

[113] Pflüger interview.   [114] Pflüger interview; Pflüger, *Ehrenwort*, 135.
[115] Pflüger interview.

Contrary to some of his older peers, he was not interested in contemplating alternative utopias, not even in limited form. He thought that West German democracy was already a major accomplishment worth protecting. 'Defending the Basic Law, defending the free democratic order, militant democracy against the enemies of Right and Left, that was the key idea', as he put it.[116]

Much like their campaign against human rights abuses in socialist and right-wing dictatorships, invoking the spectre of left-wing terrorism and admonishing the Left for its alleged support for the armed struggle—intellectual or otherwise—offered Christian Democratic activists the chance to reclaim the moral high ground they had lost since the 1960s. If the Left supported political violence, so their argument ran, its earlier critiques of liberal democracy in the name of a better and more peaceful world rang hollow.[117] As a number of studies have shown, the allegedly pervasive support of left-wing 'sympathizers' for terrorist groups was a major theme of West German public discourse about terrorism in the second half of the 1970s.[118] What is far less well known is that this was in large part because of Christian Democratic agitation, not least by student activists like Pflüger.

As we have seen, Christian Democrats had equated the conduct of left-wing activists at West German universities with 'terror' for some time. This was defamatory, to be sure, but left-wing political violence was a real feature of the 1970s. There were even some direct personal links between left-wing student groups of the late 1960s and the terrorist groups of the 1970s, notably to the RAF and the June 2nd Movement. While the vast majority of former left-wing activists threw their support behind the mainstream political parties in the 1970s or got involved in one of the nascent new social movements, a small number of left-wing activists became convinced that the system could only be altered through violent means. Although they represented no more than a tiny fraction of students on the Left, it nevertheless gave Christian Democrats the opportunity to suggest that left-wing student activists and left-wing terrorists were generally cut from the same cloth.

From 1970 onward, RAF and the June 2nd Movement committed attacks against targets viewed as outposts of imperialist power in West Germany, starting with symbolic centres such as the headquarters of the 5th US army corps in Frankfurt, which the RAF bombed in 1972. Both groups soon began to target representatives of the West German state as well—a state they deemed complicit

---

[116] Pflüger interview.

[117] On discourses about terrorism and political morality, see further Jörg Requate, 'Gefährliche Intellektuelle? Staat und Gewalt in der Debatte um die RAF', in Hacke and Geppert, *Streit um den Staat*, 251–69, here 266.

[118] On public discourses about left-wing terrorism in general, see Hanno Balz, *Von Terroristen, Sympathisanten und dem starken Staat: Die öffentliche Debatte über die RAF in den 70er Jahren* (Frankfurt/Main, 2008) on the role of Christian Democrats in stoking the public hysteria, see Petra Terhoeven, *Deutscher Herbst in Europa: Der Linksterrorismus der siebziger Jahre als transnationales Phänomen* (Munich, 2014); also Biess, *Republik der Angst*, 346–58.

in the crimes of global imperialism. They kidnapped and killed a number of high-profile victims, among them the West Berlin judge Günter von Drenkmann, the banker Jürgen Ponto, and Hanns Martin Schleyer, a leading business and industry representative. Christian Democratic politicians were also targets. Of these, the most famous was the case of the West Berlin CDU chair and mayoral candidate Peter Lorenz, whom the June 2nd Movement kidnapped a few days before the 1975 elections in West Berlin. While Lorenz was later let go after the government agreed to release a number of terrorists from prison in exchange, the fact that Christian Democratic politicians were among the terrorists' targets gave centre-right warnings against the violent threat a particular sense of urgency.[119]

The issue was personal in other ways as well. Given their participation in student politics and some of the key protest events around 1968, centre-right activists were sometimes acquainted with those on the Left who would later be radicalized. This point was emphasized when somebody they knew suddenly resurfaced on a wanted poster. Former Bonn Student Union leader Jürgen Aretz, for one, recalled that he had known Reiner Hochstein, who later had ties to the June 2nd Movement. He had also met Margrit Schiller, the daughter of a CDU politician, who studied in Bonn and later joined the RAF. Detlef Stronk recalled that he once met an attractive young woman who was later killed in Hamburg in the company of an RAF member with whom she was in a relationship. He was also well acquainted with Rolf Pohle, who was head of the Munich student council when Stronk served as head of the student parliament. Pohle later joined the RAF and was one of the prisoners released in exchange for Peter Lorenz.[120] Christian Democratic activists could therefore legitimately claim a personal investment in the matter.

Such personal ties notwithstanding, they also exploited any sign of broader left-wing support for terrorism to further their political agenda. In particular, the huge public uproar surrounding students' reaction to the RAF's murder of Federal Attorney General Siegfried Buback, a key figure in the government's fight against left-wing terrorism, cannot be fully understood without taking the role of Christian Democratic students into account. An RAF assassin sitting on the back of a motorcycle shot Buback on 7 April 1977. The Attorney General had been on his way to work in Karlsruhe, and his Mercedes had stopped at a traffic light. He was shot and killed while sitting in the back seat; the bullets also took the lives of the two drivers accompanying him.

The brutal murder was the opening salvo in a string of terrorist attacks—later termed the 'German Autumn'—that would culminate in the kidnapping and murder of Schleyer, the related hijacking of a Lufthansa plane, and the suicide

---

[119] Matthias Dahlke, '"Nur eingeschränkte Krisenbereitschaft": Die staatliche Reaktion auf die Entführung des CDU-Politikers Peter Lorenz 1975', *VfZ* 4 (2007), 641–78.
[120] Aretz interview. Stronk interview.

of several imprisoned RAF leaders in October 1977. The Buback assassination not only heralded the carnage that was still to come and led to a long and complex criminal investigation; but it also sparked an intense public conversation about the Left's 'sympathy' for terrorism and about what, if any, limits should be placed on the freedom of expression in a militant democracy.

The events that would soon come to be known as the 'Mescalero Affair' began with a rather obscure article. On 25 April 1977, an anonymous student, a self-declared 'urban Indian' writing under the pseudonym 'Göttingen Mescalero', published an 'obituary' to Buback in the *Göttinger Nachrichten*, the newspaper of the University of Göttingen's student council. While the author warned that leftists should not become 'killers' and cautioned that 'our way to socialism [...] cannot be paved with corpses', he confessed that he could also not easily distance himself from the murder of the Attorney General, who had been a member of the Nazi Party. 'My immediate reaction, my "shock" after the execution of Buback, is quickly described: I couldn't, didn't want to (and still don't want to) deny a clandestine joy.'[121]

This anonymous admission of 'clandestine joy' at the slaying of a leading public servant caused a huge outcry, suggesting, as it did, that the student Left condoned acts of terror, including political murder. The 'Mescalero Affair' saw over 100 individuals charged for distributing the text and several academics reproached and disciplined after they had reprinted the 'obituary' to defend its content and protest their freedom of expression. The Hanover Professor of Psychology Peter Brückner, who, in the wake of the Radicals Decree, had already become a symbol of the Left's persecution, was one of the academics suspended from his post. The fact that one of the young lawyers who defended Brückner in court was none other than Gerhard Schröder, future Federal Chancellor of the first 'red-green' coalition government between Social Democrats and Greens, illustrates how deeply inter-twined this episode was with the trajectory of the West German Left.[122]

As a result, most scholars have interpreted the 'Mescalero Affair'—much like the controversy surrounding the 'Radicals Decree'—first and foremost as a symbol of the Left's complex relationship to state power, as an intra-Left dispute driven by the governing SPD's hardline stance towards left-wing dissent and the party's illiberal turn, particularly in the Schmidt era.[123] In criticizing the Schmidt government for its—admittedly—repressive posture and in homing in on debates on

---

[121] 'Buback: Ein Nachruf', *Göttinger Nachrichten (GN)*, 25 April 1977, 10–12; available at: http://www.graswurzel.net/news/mescalero.shtml (accessed on 7 October 2013). English translation cited from Hanshew, *Terror and Democracy*, 198. Two decades later, one Klaus Hülbrock revealed that he had been the author: 'Ich bleibe ein Indianer', *tageszeitung* (10 February 2001).

[122] Peter Brückner and Axel R. Oestmann, *'Über die Pflicht des Gelehrten auch als Bürger tätig zu sein': Zum Disziplinarverfahren des Niedersächsischen Ministers für Wissenschaft und Kunst* (Hanover, 1982); on Schröder's career as a lawyer for left-wing radicals, see Gregor Schöllgen, *Gerhard Schröder: Die Biographie* (Munich, 2015), 66–7.

[123] Brown, *West Germany and the Global 1960s*, 330–1; Rigoll, *Staatsschutz in Westdeutschland*.

Illustration 5.4 Cover page of Christian Democratic student magazine *Demokratische Blätter* no. 14 (June/July 1977). The photographs shows the crime scene with the covered corpses of Siegfried Buback (back) and his driver Wolfgang Göbel (front), as well as the official car, in which both were shot. The caption reads 'Left-wing radicals: "Joy about Buback murder"'.

(RCDS-Bundesvorstand; photographer Heinz Wieseler, dpa/picture-alliance)

the Left, however, historians have for the most part overlooked the role of Christian Democratic students. With a significant presence in Göttingen student politics at the time, it was centre-right students who had intentionally set the whole affair in motion when they alerted a wider public to the obscure article.[124] 'I helped to uncover it. [...] [W]e were the first to make this public and to show that it was clearly a scandal', recalled former RCDS national chair Pflüger, an alumnus of the local university.[125]

On 28 April 1977, a few days after the 'obituary' first appeared, Michael Schulte, a former chair of the RCDS in Lower Saxony, filed charges against the anonymous author for 'rewarding and condoning a crime', a punishable offence under paragraph 140 of the German criminal code. He also penned an open letter to the university chancellor, explicitly stating his hopes that the accompanying publicity would alert a wider audience to the events in Göttingen.[126] It was these acts that set a full-blown campaign in motion: the conservative dailies Die Welt and Frankfurter Allgemeine Zeitung picked up the story on 30 April, citing only the 'obituary's' most incriminatory passages. On 2 May, the Christian Democratic faction in the state parliament of Lower Saxony issued an urgent parliamentary request demanding a full explanation of the circumstances surrounding the publication.[127] The conservative press coverage then led Hans-Jochen Vogel, the Social Democratic Federal Minister of Justice, to file charges against the author on 3 May.[128] As a result, the national press began to fan the flames of the nascent scandal, the judicial fallout of which would command the public's attention for months, if not years, to come. RCDS kept adding fuel to the fire, doing its utmost to keep the public abreast of similarly worded leaflets that surfaced on other campuses.[129] CDU chair Helmut Kohl played his part by suggesting that the sentiments expressed in Göttingen were actually emblematic

---

[124] Westdeutsche Rektorenkonferenz (ed.), 'Übersicht über die Ergebnisse der Wahlen zu den Studentenvertretungen im Sommersemester 1977', Dokumentation, 26 (1977), 8; 'Jagdszenen aus Niedersachsen. Dokumentation der Kampagne gegen den Göttinger AStA', GN, 20 May 1977; 'Staatsfeind Nr. 2', Der Spiegel, 10 (1980), 63; Balz, Von Terroristen, Sympathisanten und dem starken Staat, 100–8.

[125] Pflüger interview.

[126] Michael Schulte to Professor Beug, 28 April 1977, printed in Output, 3 (6 May 1977), ACDP, 4/6/142/1.

[127] 'Göttinger AStA billigt den Mord an Buback', Die Welt (30 April 1977); 'Gewaltverherrlichung in Göttinger AStA-Zeitung', Frankfurter Allgemeine Zeitung (30 April 1977); Report by the Press and Public Relations Department of the Lower Saxon Minister for Science and Art, 4 May 1977, Staatsarchiv Bremen, 4.111/7, no. 205; 'Buback-Artikel des Göttinger AStA-Organs zieht Kreise', dpa, 3 May 1977.

[128] 'Göttinger AStA billigt den Mord an Buback', Die Welt (30 April 1977); 'Gewaltverherrlichung in Göttinger AStA-Zeitung', Frankfurter Allgemeine Zeitung (30 April 1977); Report by the Press and Public Relations Department of the Lower Saxon Minister for Science and Art, 4 May 1977, Staatsarchiv Bremen, 4.111/7, no. 205; 'Buback-Artikel des Göttinger AStA-Organs zieht Kreise', dpa, 3 May 1977.

[129] 'Dokumentation des Linksfaschismus. Der Buback-Nachruf', Demokratische Blätter, 15 (1977), 13–14; '"Menschenverachtender, grausamer Zynismus', in RCDS-Magazin, 2 (1977), 8–9; 'Neue Beleidigungen gegen Buback—Vogel stellt Strafanträge', dpa, 11 May 1977; Ernst Martin, 'Skandal

of a much wider malaise, which the Schmidt government had allegedly failed to avert:

> These facts shine a spotlight on a situation that exists at many universities in our country. Unbeknown to the public, a subculture has evolved, the chief trait of which is that many students, as well as a number of academics, are so openly hostile to our state that it often culminates in blindness towards the rule of law. Often there is only a short distance from this intellectual environment to the sympathizers of terrorism.[130]

The RCDS took great pride in the role it had played in uncovering what it called 'the most horrific incident that the university scene has produced in recent years'.[131] They had good reasons for emphasizing their part. Without their organized campaign of communal outrage, the wider German public would almost certainly not have taken notice of opinions voiced by an anonymous student in a little-known local student paper. After RCDS had set the ball rolling, however, the most controversial sections of the Buback 'obituary' reached publication figures bested only by the Bible or the phone book, as the *Spiegel* later commented sardonically.[132] In the late spring and summer of 1977, prompted by Christian Democratic agitation, public anxiety about student support for terrorism reached its first climax.

Analogies to the end of the Weimar Republic and the Nazi years abounded in this febrile climate, never more so than in the aftermath of Schleyer's murder a few months later. The well-known President of the Confederation of German Employers' Associations and of the Federation of German Industries had been abducted by members of the RAF on 5 September, sparking a massive manhunt. The RAF had kidnapped Schleyer to force the Schmidt government to release members of the group imprisoned in Stammheim, among them two of the RAF's founders, Andreas Baader and Gudrun Ensslin. Given that Schleyer's driver and three policemen had been murdered during the kidnapping, and since some of the prisoners released in exchange for Lorenz in 1975 had returned to violence, Schmidt refused to negotiate.

An already tense situation escalated when members of the Popular Front for the Liberation of Palestine, a Palestinian Marxist-Leninist group allied with the RAF, hijacked a Lufthansa plane en route from the Spanish island of Mallorca to Frankfurt, with the aim of upping the pressure on the West German government.

---

um Buback-Schmähschrift', ZDF Magazin, 17 August 1977, copy of script in ACDP Press Archive, Siegfried Buback, Rundfunk-Fernsehen, Box 32.

[130] Helmut Kohl, Deutschland-Union-Dienst, no. 93 (16 May 1977).

[131] Christian Lauritzen, Letter from the editor, *RCDS Magazin* (Zeitschrift der RCDS-Bundesvereinigung Freundes- und Förderkreis), 2 (1977), 3.

[132] 'Staatsfeind Nr. 2', *Der Spiegel*, 10 (1980), 63.

When news of the successful rescue of the hostages by West German special operations unit GSG 9 at the airport at which the plane had landed in the Somali capital, Mogadishu, reached the RAF inmates in Stammheim on 18 October, they committed mass suicide. The kidnappers shot and killed Schleyer the same day. His body was found in the boot of a green Audi in the Alsatian town of Mulhouse on 19 October 1977.[133]

Schleyer was no accidental victim. To his captors, the industrialist was not only an embodiment of capitalist oppression in the present; he had also been a leading member of the Nazi student movement in the 1930s and an officer in Hitler's SS, the Nazi organization chiefly responsible for the genocide of Europe's Jews. Schleyer had served in Czechoslovakia under the notoriously brutal Chief of the Security Service (SD), Reinhard Heydrich, one of the main architects of the Holocaust. Schleyer's seamless reintegration into postwar West German society and its flourishing business world—he had been imprisoned by the French after the war, but was able to launch a successful career at Daimler Benz soon after his release—made him a living symbol of the continuities between Nazi-era fascism and the 'fascist' Federal Republic.[134] In a rare personal interview he granted to the magazine *Stern* in 1974, Schleyer refused to repent for his past, which signalled to the paper's largely left-leaning readership that the process of denazification after 1945 had indeed been at best incomplete.[135]

At the same time, the industry representative took a forceful stance on contemporary political issues. An early ally of Helmut Kohl's, he was a staunch critic of labour union power, joined the CDU in 1970, and, according to reports by the MSB Spartakus, helped to raise money for RCDS.[136] Schleyer also offered his opinions on the student movement of 1968 and its legacy. The year before his murder, for instance, the former SS officer gave a wide-ranging speech on 'Youth and the State' to a gathering of fraternity students in Würzburg, which criticized the utopian thinking and 'promises of salvation' offered by the radical Left. The emancipatory impulses of the Left had gone too far, he contended, undermining the achievement principle in the education sector and the traditional role of the mother, who he claimed had been a previous guarantor of a well-integrated youth.[137] His Nazi past, for which he refused to express regret, the business interests he represented so unapologetically, and ideas like these made the

---

[133] Jeremy Varon, *Bringing the War Home: The Weather Underground, the Red Army Faction, and Revolutionary Violence in the Sixties and Seventies* (Berkeley, CA, 2004).

[134] Lutz Hachmeister, *Schleyer: Eine deutsche Geschichte* (Munich, 2004); Varon, *Bringing the War Home*, 197.

[135] Hachmeister, *Schleyer*, 314–15.

[136] Hachmeister, *Schleyer*, 278–90, 297; *Rote Blätter* (May/June 1974).

[137] Hanns Martin Schleyer, 'Jugend und Staat', *Akademische Blätter*, 5 (1976), 158–64; for Schleyer's views on 1968 and its aftermath see further Hachmeister, *Schleyer*, 299–307.

conservative Schleyer seem like an especially appropriate target to the RAF. 'After 43 days, we have ended Hanns Martin Schleyer's miserable and corrupt existence', the terrorist group announced on 19 October 1977.[138]

Christian Democratic student activists also saw continuities between the Nazi past and the case of Schleyer, but in a manner very much distinct from the RAF's logic. Not Schleyer's career trajectory, but his murder and the reactions to it suggested unmistakable parallels to the Third Reich, Pflüger insisted in an op-ed.

So much is reminiscent of the period around 1933. [...] Red flags are flying today instead of the brown ones back then. But one sees the same hateful eyes, the same fanatical types, the same strained gaze. Once again no regard is shown for human life. We are dealing with a leftist fascism.[139]

Like Hitler before them, left-wing radicals portrayed the bourgeois state as the enemy, Pflüger pointed out. Whereas Hitler had singled out Jews and Communists, in the 1970s the persecuted were the representatives of this bourgeois state, the RCDS chair contended. 'It is the mentality of intolerance, of inhumanity, of elitist thinking, of violence, of terror, the mentality of a hateful emotionality.'[140]

Moreover, the murderers of the RAF merely displayed the most extreme version of a mindset that was far more widespread, he suggested. Reminding his readers of the Göttingen Mescalero, Pflüger presented a number of quotations from left-wing student publications to underline his claim that 'morally almost the entire Maoist Left [...] back[ed] the assassination of Buback'. Once again concentrating on the theme of students as 'sympathizers', Pflüger pronounced that the failure of the wider Left to uncover and protest such sentiments was almost more dangerous than the existence of a relatively small number of left-wing terrorists.[141]

It is worth noting that neither Schleyer's Nazi past nor the broader continuities in personnel between Nazi Germany and the Federal Republic featured in the statements from Christian Democratic students. Much as it had been in the 1960s, their understanding of fascism was filtered through an anti-totalitarian lens, which meant that Auschwitz and the Soviet Gulag appeared as twin evils. For them, fascism's legacy was represented less by the existence of ex-Nazis in public life

---

[138] RAF Communiqué sent to the French paper *Libération*, cited in Stefan Aust, *The Baader-Meinhof Complex: The Inside Story of the R.A.F.* (London, 2008), 418.
[139] Friedbert Pflüger, 'Kampf dem Linksfaschismus: 1933 darf sich nicht wiederholen', *Demokratische Blätter*, 15 (1977), 8–9. The phrase 'left fascism' was attributed to Jürgen Habermas, who had coined it to warn against the dangers of left-wing violence in the wake of Ohnesorg's death in 1967. Jürgen Habermas, 'Meine Damen und Herren, ich hoffe, dass Herr Dutschke noch hier ist...', 9 June 1967, in *Frankfurter Schule und Studentenbewegung: Von der Flaschenpost bis zum Molotowcocktail 1946 bis 1995, vol. 2: Dokumente*, edited by Wolfgang Kraushaar (Hamburg, 1998), 254–5.
[140] Pflüger, 'Kampf dem Linksfaschismus'.   [141] Pflüger, 'Kampf dem Linksfaschismus'.

than by the continued pull of extremist ideology in the present, especially of the Marxist variety. Schleyer, who had proven himself a loyal servant of the Federal Republic, on the other hand, posed no danger in their eyes. They were therefore free to imagine the business leader as a virtuous representative of the postwar liberal democratic order, who had fallen victim to a senseless criminal attack. 'We are saddened and outraged by the cruel crime committed by bandits without a conscience against Hanns-Martin [sic] Schleyer. Hanns-Martin [sic] Schleyer *was a convinced democrat, who always stood passionately on the side of freedom and partnership*', the RCDS federal board announced after his death.[142] If Schleyer's killing carried any political message for Christian Democratic student activists, it was the need to continue the struggle against the extreme Left, particularly inside the universities. The fact that he had 'sacrificed' his life in the battle for the preservation of the Federal Republic was a calling to 'defend our social order, for which he fought and for which he died, against all those who are attacking it out of blind hate and based on criminal motives'.[143]

Invoking the spectre of left-wing terrorism, then, was about far more than condemning the violent acts of a handful of radicals. It was a moral crusade that branded the alleged 'sympathizers'—a label that potentially encompassed large parts of the West German Left—as a grave danger to the liberal democratic order. It was an attempt to exorcize the ghosts of Germany's Nazi past in ways fundamentally different from those proposed by the Left. It was an attack on all (left-wing) ideological commitment in the aftermath of the Third Reich. And, it was a strategy that increasingly bonded Christian Democratic students to their mother party.

Returning to the Fold

In the second half of the 1970s, the CDU was the RCDS's closest ally in its struggle against the radical Left on campus. In some ways, this was not surprising; after all, the student association was one of the party's auxiliary organizations. As we saw in the first two chapters of this book, however, student activists had had a more conflicted relationship with the party in the late 1960s. This changed in the 1970s.

---

[142] RCDS-Bundesvorstand, 'Wir trauern um Hanns-Martin Schleyer', *Demokratische Blätter*, 15 (1977), 8. Emphasis added.

[143] RCDS-Bundesvorstand, 'Wir trauern um Hanns-Martin Schleyer'. The fraternities endorsed the notion that Schleyer had 'sacrificed' himself to the nation even more explicitly, see Rolf Clauß, 'Ein Opfer für Deutschland', *Akademische Blätter*, 2 (1978), 37–40. At his funeral, Federal President Walter Scheel had also portrayed Schleyer as a sacrificial object and model democrat. See Varon, *Bringing the War Home*, 279–82.

'While the relationship between RCDS and CDU was often tense in the mid- to late 1960s, the relationship has loosened and normalized', the association's national chair Hans Reckers reported in 1977.[144]

Reckers had taken over leadership of the RCDS after cutting his teeth as the speaker of the Schüler Union, an association of Christian Democratic pupils set up in 1972 to counter the perceived left-wing hegemony in the country's classrooms.[145] By the time he entered student politics in the mid-1970s, the CDU had overcome its worst electoral defeat to that day: its loss in the national elections of 1972, which marked the first time in the history of the Federal Republic that the SPD gained more votes than the CDU/CSU. This administered another profound shock to the Christian Democrats and finally forced them to really come to terms with their oppositional role.[146] Over the course of the 1970s, the Christian Democrats underwent a process of far-reaching internal reform and modernization, leading to greater intellectual and programmatic efforts, greater participation by ordinary members, and an unprecedented growth in party membership.[147] Its membership figures rose from just over 303,000 in 1969 to 693,000 in 1980, doubling in the party's first eight years in opposition alone. Members also became much younger on average; 40 per cent of the new party members who joined in 1975 had been born after 1941.[148] The CDU of the 1970s was thus a much bigger and more youthful party.

To the activist micro-cohort of Hans Reckers and Friedbert Pflüger, the Christian Democrats were no longer the sclerotic party of the post-Adenauer period dominated by what Radunski had termed the 'late harvest of Weimar', nor an opposition in denial. They were an increasingly agile party that was in the process of reinventing itself as a determined opposition force under the new leader Helmut Kohl, who had been elected in 1973.[149] When the two young students met Kohl for the first time in May 1975, they were 'utterly enthused', as Pflüger recalled in his memoir.[150] Kohl, who was then in his early forties, indeed oversaw a rejuvenation of the party's apparatus, promoting a new generation of Christian Democrats to leadership roles. Among them were his peers Heiner Geißler, Kurt

---

[144] Hans Reckers, '25 Jahre RCDS', *Demokratische Blätter*, 4 (1976/77), 2; see also Helmut Kohl's remarks about RCDS to the CDU's federal board, 29 November 1976, printed in *Kohl: Stetigkeit, Klugheit, Geduld und Zähigkeit, Die Protokolle des CDU-Bundesvorstands 1980–1983*, edited by Günther Buchstab (Düsseldorf, 2018), 136–7.

[145] Joseph Stenger, *La Schüler-Union: étude d'un mouvement politique de jeunes lycéens en République fédérale allemande de 1972 à 1980* (Frankfurt am Main, 1982); Linde Apel, 'Die Opposition der Opposition: Politische Mobilisierung an Oberschulen jenseits der Protestgeneration', Livi, Schmidt, and Sturm, *Die siebziger Jahre als schwarzes Jahrzehnt*, 57–72.

[146] Pridham, *Christian Democracy*, 207.

[147] Bösch, *Macht und Machtverlust*; Pridham, *Christian Democracy*.

[148] Pridham, *Christian Democracy*, 285, 279; Schönbohm, *Die CDU wird moderne Volkspartei*, 167; the CSU's membership also rose by 240 per cent in this period.

[149] Bösch, *Macht und Machtverlust*, 108; Pridham, *Christian Democracy*, 201.

[150] Pflüger, *Ehrenwort*, 15.

Biedenkopf, Bernhard Vogel, and Norbert Blüm, all of whom had been born in the 1930s.[151]

In the aftermath of Schleyer's murder, the new party leadership and Christian Democratic student activists cooperated ever more closely, and, in the process, the party increasingly began to adopt campaign methods that student activists had championed for years. The CDU had been involved in the crisis meetings during Schleyer's kidnapping and the related hijacking of the Lufthansa plane, but it wasted little time in exploiting the episode to extract political capital and to attack the SPD as weak on 'internal security'—a key theme of Christian Democratic messaging in the late 1970s. A few weeks after Schleyer's murder, the party issued a controversial report on the Left's allegedly extensive support for terrorism. This 'terror documentation', was the brainchild of the party's new and notoriously provocative Secretary General Heiner Geißler. It was also strongly reminiscent of earlier RCDS reports, which had quoted the Left's own words to suggest that students widely backed violent acts committed in the name of the anti-imperialist struggle.[152] Geißler's documentation now extended the critique to left-wing intellectuals and politicians by presenting quotations from figures like Willy Brandt and the novelist Günter Grass that suggested that they promoted or condoned left-wing terrorism, at least implicitly. As Petra Terhoeven has argued, this 'terror documentation', which critics abroad interpreted as an unmistakable sign of the Federal Republic's illiberal turn, was evidence of the Christian Democrat's frequent and increasingly hyperbolic attempts to exploit the public fear of terrorism to discredit their left-wing opponents.[153]

---

[151] Bösch, *Macht und Machtverlust*, 111; Pridham, *Christian Democracy*, 214.

[152] After the Palestinian group Black September attacked and killed eleven Israeli athletes and a West German police officer at the Munich Summer Olympics in 1972, for instance, the RCDS issued a press release accusing West German radical student groups of offering ideological support, however indirectly, to those responsible for the massacre. ACDP Press Archive, 'Terror "ein Mittel der Revolution". Linskradikale Studenten unterstützen Terror-Gruppen', RCDS press release, 14 September 1972. Furthermore, the association's federal board issued a documentary report that chronicled the alleged cooperation between West German left-wing radical student groups and other foreign terrorists. The document quoted from a number of leaflets issued by West German student groups, including the MSB Spartakus and SHB, which described the armed struggle as ideologically justifiable or expressed solidarity with foreign groups committed to violent tactics, particularly Palestinian groups fighting Israel. ACDP Press Archive, 'Der Antizionismus der Neuen Linken: Zur Kooperation zwischen Linksradikalen in der BRD und ausländischen Extremisten', September 1972. RCDS thereby anticipated a theme—left-wing anti-Zionism—that has become a strong focus of scholarship on the West German far left in recent years. Reimann, 'Letters from Amman: Dieter Kunzelmann and the Origins of German Anti-Zionism during the late 1960s'; Jeffrey Herf, *Undeclared Wars with Israel: East Germany and the West German Far Left, 1967–1989* (New York, 2016). For another example of these early RCDS tactics, see ACDP, 4/6/13/2, '"Vorsicht! Sie kommen . . . aus ihren Löchern". Gewaltsame Sprengungen von RCDS-Veranstaltungen im Zeichen der linksradikalen Presse'.

[153] CDU-Bundesgeschäftsstelle (ed.), *Terrorismus in der Bundesrepublik Deutschland: Eine Auswahl von Zitaten* (Bonn, 1977); see further Terhoeven, *Deutscher Herbst in Europa*, 453–4; 522–3.

From November 1977 onward, the CDU and RCDS also jointly staged a number of performances of highly successful political theatre that pursued a similar aim. In an effort to create public awareness of the climate of intolerance and violence in the universities, these events were choreographed to link left-wing students directly to the terror of the RAF. Kohl had long argued that Christian Democratic politicians had to take a principled stand on West German campuses in order to break the 'absolute terror' that was prevalent there. They also had to develop the rhetorical skills necessary to prevail even against raucous opponents— skills he considered essential in 'modern politics'.[154] As party chair he had encouraged student leaders to continue their 'work on the front line against left-wing extremists and offered his support', as Pflüger recalled in his memoir.[155]

Illustration 5.5 Tumultuous scenes during an RCDS-run event with Helmut Kohl at the University of Freiburg on 19 January 1976. Kohl's speech was disrupted by left-wing demonstrators. The police used tear gas and batons to escort the CDU chair from the auditorium.

(Lutz Rauschnick, dpa/picture-alliance)

[154] Kohl, cited in the minutes of the CDU's federal board meeting of 13 March 1972, printed in *Barzel: 'Unsere Alternativen für die Zeit der Opposition'*, 741; Kohl, cited in the minutes of the CDU's federal board meeting of 10 June 1974, in *Kohl: 'Wir haben alle Chancen': Die Protokolle des CDU-Bundesvorstands 1973–1976*, 2 vols., edited by Günter Buchstab (Düsseldorf, 2015), 729–30.

[155] Pflüger, *Ehrenwort*, 15; see also Kohl's remarks in the CDU's federal board meeting of 25 April 1977, in *Kohl: 'Stetigkeit, Klugheit, Geduld und Zähigkeit'*, 536–7.

The most visible sign of this cooperation, however, was a series of over a dozen RCDS events with leading Christian Democratic politicians that took place on different West German campuses in the autumn and winter of 1977/78, advertised as a 'Democratic Dialogue' between university and society.[156] Much like the previous RCDS chair Langguth, who had skilfully picked the epicentres of left-wing protest for many of his events, Kohl and RCDS chair Pflüger chose some of the hotbeds of left-wing activity as venues for their events. In doing so, they were fully aware that the visiting Christian Democrats would encounter considerable hostility and that this would generate publicity—after all, violent scenes had accompanied a visit by Kohl to Freiburg university the previous year. The aim was to present Christian Democratic politicians as upright taboo-breakers who bravely entered the lion's den, while the Social Democrats wilfully ignored the true conditions and anti-democratic spirit of West German campus politics. Kohl's stated goal was 'the total polarization [of the debate about terrorism and security] inside the universities'.[157]

The CDU chair took the lead. On 29 November 1977, Kohl arrived at one of the centres of left-wing student activism since 1968, the Technical University (TU) of Berlin, to give a public lecture. In a press conference that preceded the event, Pflüger explained that the location had been chosen to kick off the series to send the 'definitive signal' that Christian Democrats did not shy away from difficult encounters and that they sought to 'plant a flag' on West German campuses.[158] A difficult encounter it was indeed. There was a heavy police presence when Kohl arrived outside the university's main auditorium, which was already occupied by around 2,000 student protesters. In a slight against the CDU leader's last name, which means 'cabbage' in German, two heads of cabbage had been placed prominently on the lectern. At the entrance, protesters had painted the slogan 'Helmut – the swamp of sympathizers greets you'—a reference to a controversial statement that the Christian Democratic Governor of Baden-Württemberg, Hans Filbinger, had made a few weeks earlier about the connections between students and terrorists.[159] Because of the auditorium's occupation, Kohl's speech was moved to a different venue down the street; on his way over there, he was hit by a tomato.[160] Despite an even heavier police presence at the new venue, a few hundred left-wing protesters were able to disrupt Kohl's speech, which spoke of left-wing 'terror' in the universities and called for an end to the government's 'false tolerance'. According to a report in the liberal daily Der Tagesspiegel, he received much applause from some

---

[156] RCDS (ed.), Demokratischer Dialog zwischen Hochschule und Gesellschaft: CDU-Spitzenpolitiker auf RCDS-Veranstaltungen im Wintersemester 1977/78 an deutschen Hochschulen (Bonn, 1978); Kohl: 'Stetigkeit, Klugheit, Geduld und Zähigkeit', 536–7.

[157] Kohl, cited in the minutes of the meeting of the CDU's federal party board on 12 September 1977, in Kohl: 'Stetigkeit, Klugheit, Geduld und Zähigkeit', 677.

[158] 'Diskussion mit Kohl verlegt', Der Tagesspiegel (30 November 1977).

[159] 'Diskussion mit Kohl verlegt', Der Tagesspiegel (30 November 1977).

[160] 'RCDS-Veranstaltung mit Kohl kurzfristig verlegt', dpa, 29 November 1977; Pflüger, Ehrenwort, 22.

of the older West Berliners in the audience.[161] To the young activist Pflüger, Kohl had seemed like a 'bastion of calm'.[162] Together they had dinner that night with Kohl's close friend Peter Lorenz, the West Berlin CDU leader who had been kidnapped by left-wing radicals of the June 2nd Movement and held hostage two years earlier. This no doubt amplified their sense that standing up to left-wing 'terror', in the universities and elsewhere, was potentially a matter of life and death.

Kohl's West Berlin speech was only the beginning. Other party leaders would follow his example over the next few months. Richard von Weizsäcker and Kurt Biedenkopf had a fairly easy time in Münster, a city with a strongly Catholic and conservative bent where the RCDS was the strongest group, as did Rainer Barzel in Bonn and Gerd Langguth in Paderborn. However, protesters disrupted similar events with Baden-Württemberg's Interior Minister Lothar Späth in Heidelberg, with Biedenkopf in Bielefeld and with the Lower Saxon Finance Minister Walter Leisler Kiep in Osnabrück and Kiel.[163] In Bielefeld, protesters even threw containers with foul-smelling liquid at Biedenkopf and eggs hit Leisler Kiep in Kiel.[164] In January 1978 in Aachen, noisy protesters once again confronted Kohl, this time equipped with several sacks of brussels sprouts (*Rosenkohl* in German).[165]

Some of the most tumultuous scenes during the 'Democratic Dialogue' occurred at the University of Bremen, where Geißler attempted to speak about 'progress and freedom' at the invitation of RCDS on 12 December 1977. Given that RCDS only held a single seat in the Bremen student parliament at this time, and, as we saw earlier, members of the group had previously clashed forcefully with protesters in the city, it was all but certain ahead of time that left-wing groups would attempt to scuttle the event.[166] Leaflets and open letters that circulated at the university prior to Geißler's appearance denounced RCDS as an organization 'of a reactionary type', called Christian Democratic students 'snitches' and 'denunciators', and argued that Geißler, 'the author of the CDU's terror documentation', should not be allowed on campus under any circumstances.[167]

Aware of the tumultuous scenes surrounding Kohl in West Berlin a few weeks earlier and keen to protect the city and university's image, the governing Social

---

[161] 'Studenten-Proteste gegen Rede Kohls in Berlin', dpa, 29 November 1977; 'Diskussion mit Kohl verlegt', *Der Tagesspiegel*, 30 November 1977.

[162] Pflüger, *Ehrenwort*, 23.

[163] 'Christdemokraten in der Offensive', in *CDU-Extra*, 9 March 1978, 4, available online at http://www.kas.de/wf/doc/kas_25858-544-1-30.pdf?110,826,092,417 (accessed on 18 August 2015). For the composition of the Münster student parliament, see Westdeutsche Rektorenkonferenz (ed.), 'Übersicht über die Ergebnisse der Wahlen zu den Studentenvertretungen im Sommersemester 1977', *Dokumentation* no. 26 (1977), 12.

[164] 'Im Auditorium Maximum herrschte zeitweise ein Höllenlärm', *Neue Westfälische Zeitung*, 18 January 1978; 'Kieps Rede gestört', *Frankfurter Rundschau* (3 February 1978).

[165] Dieter Putz, 'Starker Kohl bei Sponti-Krach', *Aachener Volkszeitung* (19 January 1980).

[166] Westdeutsche Rektorenkonferenz (ed.), 'Übersicht über die Ergebnisse der Wahlen zu den Studentenvertretungen im Sommersemester 1977', *Dokumentation*, 26 (1977), 5.

[167] Open letter of different 'Basisgruppen' to University Provost Alexander Wittkowsky, n.d.; Staatsarchiv Bremen, 4.111/7, no. 763, 'RCDS und Geißler raus aus der Uni!', Leaflet.

Democrats tried their utmost to prevent violent disruptions. Nevertheless, a few hundred protesters managed to break up the event, and the CDU's Secretary General never even made it inside the building. Instead, he gave a short speech from a loudspeaker car in the university's parking lot.[168] Students who attempted to attend the original event witnessed chaotic scenes, which led to legal proceedings against a number of protesters. Pflüger, who had accompanied Geißler, recalled having felt physically threatened.[169] Bremen's public prosecutor described the scenes thus: protesters had put

> participants under duress [...] by using force to block the entrance to the event, then themselves occupying the room, and finally moving the furniture and bellowing slogans through a megaphone, so that the event could not be held. In connection with this, physical assaults were committed. [...] Individual participants were beaten and sprayed with butyric acid. Firecrackers were thrown into a group of RCDS supporters who found themselves on the podium. Others were sprayed with foam from the fire extinguishers mounted throughout the university. [...] Paint bombs and butyric acid damaged the clothing of many participants and other members of the university.[170]

Leaflets by left-wing student groups hailed the disruption as an unqualified success. The 'red-black-gold reaction' had suffered an embarrassing defeat and been prevented from building a 'counter-revolutionary centre' inside the university, because the auditorium had been 'cleansed', as one such leaflet put it.[171] RCDS, by contrast, pointed out that it was an 'unbelievable incident that a German politician no longer has the possibility to speak at a German university without being disrupted and that a handful of extremists and gangs of thugs determine events'.[172]

Of course, such events were no everyday occurrence, not even at the 'red' University of Bremen. Nevertheless, when Bernhard Vogel, Governor of the Rhineland-Palatinate, fled from the Göttingen campus where he received a similarly hostile reception and sustained minor injuries to his hand a month later, even the liberal and left-leaning press had to concede that RCDS might have a point. In

---

[168] Handwritten memorandum by Bremen Senator of Science and the Arts Horst Werner Franke, n.d.; Staatsarchiv Bremen, 4.111/7, no. 763, 'Dokumentation des RCDS Bremen anlässlich der Geißler-Veranstaltung am 12. Dezember 1977 in der Universität Bremen'.

[169] Pflüger interview.

[170] Staatsarchiv Bremen, 4.111/7, no. 161, Draft letter of the Bremen public prosecutor's office to the Provost of the University of Bremen, n.d. [January 1979]. Twenty-two witnesses were questioned in connection with the incident, but the perpetrators of the assaults could not be identified, and the case was closed without charges filed in March 1979. Staatsarchiv Bremen, 4.111/7, no. 161, Senator für Rechtspflege und Strafvollzug to the Senatskanzlei, 29 March 1979.

[171] Staatsarchiv Bremen, 4.111/7, no. 763, 'Ein erfolgreicher Schlag gegen die Reaktion', Leaflet.

[172] Günther Heckelmann, 'Stinkbomben und Säuren in Bremen', Deutschland-Union Dienst, no. 237, 13 December 1977.

its coverage, the *Süddeutsche Zeitung* invoked the by now familiar parallel to the collapse of Weimar democracy:

> Had television existed in 1931/32, one could study the striking similarity of the scenes at the universities. Shouting down professors, not wanting to listen to arguments, driving out democratic politicians by force, finally the brutal act of violence, alas, all this has a long tradition in German universities. This is where political irrationality had its stomping ground. The only new aspect is that, as opposed to before, for the past ten years or so it has been sustained by leftist ideologies and in the hope of salvation.[173]

The paper was strongly critical of commentators who blamed the Christian Democratic politicians for the hostility and violence they experienced. 'It sometimes sounds as though CDU politicians like Kohl, Geißler, Kiep, and Vogel had themselves to blame when their appearances in academic lecture halls were broken up amid shouting, bombardment with tomatoes and eggs, and acts of violence.'[174] Not those beaten, but the ones who did the beating were responsible, the paper insisted. When Kohl was again shouted down by left-wing protesters in Marburg in July 1978, even the left-wing *Frankfurter Rundschau* found the protesters' 'deficit of tolerance shocking'—although the paper was fully aware that the clashes played into the CDU's political strategy.[175]

It is indeed worth noting that, much like Gerd Langguth's 'Spartakus Tribunal' held six years earlier, the Christian Democratic strategy of exposing the violent nature of left-wing students worked only because the Left conformed to (stereo) type and responded to the party's provocative cues in a manner so hostile and predictable that it was difficult to maintain that the CDU was not indeed onto something. It was therefore no surprise that Pflüger and Geißler judged their 'Democratic Dialogue' to have been a tremendous success. At a joint press conference held in March 1978, they gloated that the campaign had generated considerable media coverage and that the public had finally been made aware of the conditions in the universities. It was now clear, they concluded, 'that the CDU's warning about the strong communist influence on the campuses had not simply been plucked out of the air'.[176]

A few months later, their alarmist portrayal of campus politics was further bolstered by the publication of the results of a controversial opinion poll,

---

[173] 'Im radikalen Abseits', *Süddeutsche Zeitung* (20 January 1978); see also Wolfgang Meyer, 'Bernhard Vogel aus Göttinger Uni vertrieben', *Die Welt* (1 January 1978).
[174] 'Im radikalen Abseits', *Süddeutsche Zeitung* (20 January 1978).
[175] 'Pfiffe für Kohl', *Frankfurter Rundschau* (7 July 1978).
[176] 'Christdemokraten in der Offensive', in *CDU-Extra* (9 March 1978), 4, available at http://www.kas.de/wf/doc/kas_25858-544-1-30.pdf?110826092417 (accessed on 18 August 2015); see also Pflüger's report to the CDU's federal party board on 27 February 1978, in *Kohl: 'Stetigkeit, Klugheit, Geduld und Zähigkeit'*, 881–2.

commissioned by the conservative *Frankfurter Allgemeine Zeitung* and conducted by Elisabeth Noelle-Neumann's Allensbach polling institute. It purported to show that 61 per cent of students thought communism was a good idea, that around one third supported violence against things or people, and that a large number had an ambiguous attitude towards parliamentary democracy.[177] Ever since the Allies had used extensive polling to gauge Germans' democratic potential after the war, polling had been considered a reliable instrument to study the viability of democracy in the Federal Republic. Noelle-Neumann, a campaign adviser to the Christian Democrats, now painted a horrifying 'scientific' portrait of a young elite that threatened to undermine democracy's foundations and warned that the governing Social-Liberal coalition had been complacent in the face of the threat. The Brandt and Schmidt governments had fostered the left-wing march through the institutions and propagated the 'spirit of 1968', Fritz Ullrich Flack, one of the editors of the *FAZ*, charged in response.[178] Noelle-Neumann's findings were heavily (and rightfully) criticized, not least for the study's small sample size and its one-sided interpretation of the numbers. In spite of its questionable findings, however, the 1978 *Allensbach* poll caused quite a public stir, suggesting, as it did, that the violent scenes that had accompanied the speeches of Christian Democratic politicians on West German campuses earlier that year were evidence of a much greater malaise.[179]

In the second half of the decade, then, anxieties about student 'intolerance' and 'terror' fully entered mainstream political discourse in the Federal Republic. In the wake of the 'German Autumn', the climate of mistrust against left-wing activists and the student population at large reached its fever pitch. This was thanks, in no small measure, to campaigns that centre-right students had championed since the beginning of the decade.

*   *   *

The 1970s pitted centre-right students firmly and decisively against their peers on the Left. When fears about leftist infiltration of state institutions and student support for terrorism focused the public's attention on threats to internal security—some real, others imagined—the more playful beginnings of the student movement in the 1960s, which had seen Christian Democratic and socialist students ponder similar questions and even stage the occasional joint sit-in,

---

[177] Elisabeth Noelle-Neumann, 'Wie demokratisch sind unsere Studenten?', *FAZ*, 2 October 1978, copy in HIA, NOFU, Box 820; Kruke, *Demoskopie*, 511–12.

[178] Fritz Ullrich Fack, 'Links schlägt das Herz der Studenten', *FAZ* (2 October 1978), copy in HIA, NOFU, Box 820.

[179] BAK, B138/33393, Hoschulinformationsystem to Ministerialdirektor Böning in the Ministry for Education and Science, 23 November 1978; 'Wie demokratisch ist Frau Noelle-Neumann', *Der Spiegel*, 41 (1978), 81–5; 'Ein Horrorgemälde der deutschen Hochschullandschaft', *Frankfurter Rundschau*, 14 October 1978; Kurt Reumann, 'Allensbacher Orakel', *FU Info*, 13 (1978); E. v. Loewenstern, 'Die Angst vor den Studenten', *Die Welt* (9 October 1978), 6.

became at best a distant memory. The different camps now adopted a much more combative stance. Looking back on this period in his autobiography, Peter Radunski noted how relieved he had been 'when we were able to argue positively again once we were back in government in 1982'. 'In the oppositional 1970s', he admitted, 'the anti-position was often better articulated than the pro-position.'[180]

Centre-right students and their 'anti-position' have rarely been the focus of historical scholarship on what is still commonly described as a 'red decade'. The heated debates and clashes of these years—surrounding the 'Radicals Decree' and 'Mescalero Affair', for instance—have usually been interpreted as a series of intra-Left disputes about the power of the state, the legitimacy of political violence, surveillance, about what, if any, limits to place on free expression in a pluralist society, and the political obligations that come with public service in a liberal democracy. The role that the oppositional Christian Democrats played in pushing the Social-Liberal government towards adopting a hard-line stance towards left-wing dissent has been highlighted far less often, but it was a crucial element of the story.[181] Rattled by the experience of being in opposition for the first time since the war, Christian Democrats stoked public hysteria about a left-wing radical threat to paint the governing Social Democrats as weak on security and soft on communism.

Christian Democratic student activists were the vanguard. They first directed the public's attention to the worst features of West German campus politics. Seemingly disregarding the fact that, by doing so, they helped to cast suspicions on the Left per se, the Social-Liberal coalition government nevertheless treated centre-right activists as useful collaborators in their effort to contain left-wing radicals, as the long-term secret payments to centre-right groups from the Federal Office for the Protection of the Constitution, of which the RCDS was a chief recipient, so clearly illustrated. The public obsession with stopping a left-wing 'march through the institutions'—by repressive means, if needed—and the anxiety about student 'sympathizers of terrorism' were fuelled in no small measure by RCDS-orchestrated displays of leftist 'terror' inside the universities. In contrast, Christian Democratic students cast themselves as passionate militant democrats. These were carefully calculated pieces of political theatre, later successfully replicated at joint events with a newly agile CDU.

The radicalization of significant parts of the student Left in the 1970s was not just the stuff of right-wing propaganda, however. These theatrical productions worked only because enough left-wing students in the audience did their opponents the favour of behaving as intolerably as predicted. However, in seeking out the centres of left-wing activism for their events and by adopting prosecutorial rhetoric clearly designed to provoke, Christian Democratic activists helped to

---

[180] Radunski, *Aus der politischen Kulisse*, 49.
[181] I build on Petra Terhoeven and Karrin Hanshew's arguments here, who are both mindful of the important ways in which the CDU/CSU shaped the state's response to left-wing terrorism. Terhoeven, *Deutscher Herbst in Europa*; Hanshew, *Terror and Democracy*.

create—or at least escalate—situations they were supposedly committed to fighting.[182] What is more, while this public agitation shone a spotlight on the actually growing radicalization of some West German students, it also stoked up distinctly ugly resentments against the Left as a whole, with some letter writers using unmistakable Nazi vocabulary to describe the students. Campaigns conducted in the name of anti-totalitarianism and protecting the 'free democratic order' could thus have effects that were rather detrimental to the liberal democratic spirit. This was especially true in a state that, at this point, had only been a liberal democracy for just over two decades. The perception that the very viability of democracy hung in the balance gave the political exchanges of the 1970s in the Federal Republic an unusually hard edge. In this period, other Western liberal democracies also faced a radical Left, instances of political violence, and growing polarization, but in few other countries were these interpreted as existential threats to the very foundations of the established order in quite the same way.[183]

Although they did much to orchestrate them in the first place, the clashes with left-wing activists also provided Christian Democratic activists with a real experiential basis for their conviction that the stakes in their struggle were high. This lived experience helps to explain the bitterness of the subsequent memory wars about 1968. With hindsight, especially during the early years of Chancellor Gerhard Schröder's 'red-green' coalition government, former centre-right student activists frequently highlighted the Left's embrace of political violence, which, they insisted, had negated much of 1968's emancipatory impulses. They portrayed their role around 1968 and its aftermath as one of standing up against the excesses of these years, of having protected liberal democracy from an extremist overthrow. Like most collectively honed stories, theirs contained a kernel of truth. Like most, however, it also smoothed over some of the rougher parts of this history and offered a sanitized account of their own roles within it. As this chapter has shown, centre-right activists contributed to the febrile climate of the 1970s themselves. They stoked public hysteria and helped to create a climate of distrust that alienated many left-wing activists from democratic institutions and made left-wing dissent politically suspect. In this light, it was not just the radical student Left or the heavy-handedness of the Social-Liberal government that displayed an illiberal streak in the 1970s. The conduct of centre-right activists similarly underlines that the process of political liberalization in the wake of 1968 was not a linear but at best a winding one. Why the liberalization narrative nevertheless took centre stage in the 1980s—including among the other '68ers who now portrayed themselves as key agents in this process—is the subject of the next and final chapter of this book.

---

[182] Nikolai Wehrs makes a similar argument concerning activists of the BFW. See his *Protest der Professoren*, 266.
[183] Rigoll, *Staatsschutz in Westdeutschland*, 17.

6

The (Ir)Resistible Rise of the Other '68ers

For all their efforts to reinvent themselves, the 1970s were challenging years for the Christian Democrats. They were, after all, the party's first time in opposition since the Federal Republic had been founded. The 1980s, by contrast, were marked by triumph as the political strategies honed over the previous decade finally paid off at the ballot box.

In the national elections of 1980, Franz Josef Strauss, the CSU's authoritarian populist leader and Governor of Bavaria who ran as the Christian Democratic candidate for Chancellor that year, tried but failed to defeat Schmidt on a hard-line platform. Winning just 44.9 per cent of the national vote, this was the Christian Democrats' worst result since 1949. But this turned out to be a temporary setback. Two years later, the party's fortunes changed rapidly. Because of disputes over economic policy, the Free Democrats abandoned their coalition with Schmidt's SPD and, in September 1982, entered negotiations with the Christian Democrats. The Bundestag approved a constructive vote of no confidence on 1 October, ousting Schmidt and electing CDU leader Helmut Kohl as the new Chancellor. He would hold this office for an astonishing sixteen years, longer than any occupant before or since.

In national elections held the following March, voters gave their emphatic backing to the earlier vote in the Bundestag. On 6 March 1983, the Christian Democrats achieved their second-best result in the history of the Federal Republic, gaining 48.8 per cent of the national vote. Only in 1957, at the height of Adenauer's popularity, had they fared better. It was also the first time since the 1960s that the rejuvenated Christian Democrats did better among young voters—those aged between 18 and 34—than the Social Democrats.[1] Clear majorities in many state elections held at the same time rounded out the Christian Democratic win. In the words of *Der Spiegel*: 'That was a resounding victory for the Right.'[2]

The Christian Democrats' return to power was a major moment for the other '68ers, who suddenly became something of a public phenomenon. Their ideas, political trajectories, and style were dissected endlessly by journalists and public intellectuals, who were convinced that studying these centre-right activists of 1968 was key to understanding—and potentially combatting—the Christian Democrats' surprising new strength. Many commentators were confident that it

---

[1] Wirsching, *Abschied vom Provisorium*, 46.
[2] 'Die Wende ist perfekt', *Der Spiegel*, 10 (7 March 1983), 6–23.

The Other '68ers: Student Protest and Christian Democracy in West Germany. Anna von der Goltz,
Oxford University Press (2021). © Anna von der Goltz. DOI: 10.1093/oso/9780198849520.003.0007

was these former student activists who had fashioned Kohl and the party with a modern image and made it appealing to voters once again. As the left-liberal weekly *Die Zeit* put it a year after Kohl's 1983 victory:

> [The CDU] has built itself a sleek apparatus which prepared election campaigns and events perfectly, assisted the eternally overburdened politicians with their thinking, and which has done a huge amount of public relations work— internally an enormously productive an externally an unassuming court for the CDU's king. [...]

The CDU's 'reform generation', made up of individuals who had been students around 1968, now cast the new Chancellor in the best possible light, the paper observed. They

> took naturally to power, [were] liberal to the extent that they found it fun to chat with others who thought differently, but were beholden enough to tradition that they would not transgress fundamental conservative values, and always flexible enough to accept new developments in society.[3]

These 'bearded pipe smokers in rumpled jackets who know the right jargon' had learned the art of theorizing and dialectics from their opponents and now represented 'the most effective *brain trust* that the Christian Democrats have possessed since the party's founding', as the political scientist (and left-wing '68er) Claus Leggewie put it in another piece.[4] Having placed them into positions of influence within the party was the 'secret of Helmut Kohl's success', he opined.[5]

Peter J. Grafe, one of the founders of the left-wing alternative daily *taz* and the author of one of the first books to scrutinize the newly agile CDU, made a similar argument. The Christian Democrats of the 1980s no longer lived up to traditional left-wing clichés about an imminent return to the 'fustiness of the Adenauer era'; instead, they controlled a dynamic political machine that was surprisingly in sync with the *Zeitgeist*.[6] If the Left did not catch up to what he termed the "68ers of the CDU', the centre-right would remain dominant for the foreseeable future, Grafe warned.

While analyses such as these offered an overly personalized interpretation of the Christian Democrats' modernization, they were also onto something. In the 1970s, the other '68ers had indeed helped the CDU to recapture the discursive dominance the centre-right had lost around 1968, and some had played tangible

---

[3] Gerhard Sport, 'Der Maskenbildner der Union', *Die Zeit*, 19 (4 May 1984).
[4] Leggewie, *Der Geist steht rechts*, 116. Leggewie was in some ways critical of what he termed 'the myth of the 'other "68ers"', but he actually did more than most to identify and elevate them as a group.
[5] Leggewie, *Der Geist steht rechts*, 116 and 111.
[6] Peter J. Grafe, *Schwarze Visionen: Die Modernisierung der CDU* (Hamburg, 1986), 8.

roles in bringing Kohl to power. They may not have actually led the party in the 1980s; most of the leading government and party posts were still occupied by members of the preceding generation, by men like Kohl and Geißler. However, as we shall see, they played influential roles behind the scenes and were central to how Kohl's government was perceived at the time.

This chapter examines how and why the other '68ers became a major public phenomenon in the 1980s. It charts the rise of several individuals to positions of considerable political prominence and their programmatic, strategic, and cultural impact on Christian Democracy from the 1970s into the 1980s. Second, it analyses the role that commemorations of 1968 and generational claims played in their rise. It shows that the other '68ers helped to shape memories of the student movement in important ways and, from the 1980s into the early 2000s, were key players in the memory wars about how 1968 had transformed West German politics and society.

The Short March Through the Institutions

The 'long march through the institutions' by the '68ers has been a consistent theme in the scholarship and in popular accounts of 1968. Discussed mostly in relation to fears over the left-wing infiltration of state institutions in the 1970s, the idea was reinterpreted over the course of the next decade and received a more positive slant. That many former student radicals eventually filled leading posts— especially in the media, in academia, the education and cultural sector, and in politics—was now often pointed to as evidence of the long-term and largely positive impact of 1968 on West German society. The '68ers had 'grown up'.[7]

Centre-right students went on their own march in the wake of 1968. Without first having to come to terms with a failure to bring about political revolution, or to find their way out of often bruising personal and political experiments, theirs was usually less twisted and far shorter than that experienced on the Left. In the words of Peter Radunski, who pursued one of the most remarkable careers of the other '68ers, 'it was a great intellectual movement, but it was also a dream-like career move, this whole student revolution'.[8] 'Knowing the student revolution from within, there was a vocational quality to it, which made me hopeful of landing a good job, with good pay.' His hopes quickly became reality: 'Our

---

[7] One of the earliest German works to focus on the trajectories of former activists was Mosler, *Was wir waren, was wir wurden*. For an influential US treatment of sixties activists 'growing up', see Jack Whalen and Richard Flacks, *Beyond the Barricades: The Sixties Generation Grows Up* (Hanover, 1990); see also Mark, von der Goltz, and Warring, 'Reflections'.

[8] Radunski interview.

march through the CDU led directly to the offices of the party apparatus', as he noted in his autobiography.[9]

Time was certainly on their side. The fact that the wave of student revolt crested shortly before the Christian Democrats experienced their shock of opposition in 1969 opened up considerable professional opportunities for former student activists. They had honed their rhetorical, programmatic, and organizational skills in confrontation with the Left at the height of the student movement. Such skills were in great demand as Christian Democrats sought to reinvent themselves. The CDU changed fundamentally during its time in opposition. It did not just expand its membership exponentially; it also underwent profound organizational changes, developing a highly effective party apparatus with modern management, political planning, and improved intra-party and external communication.

The CDU's federal party headquarters was the new centre of gravity of the revitalized party. The number of employees in the party headquarters, which moved into the newly built Konrad Adenauer Haus in Sankt Augustin in 1972, rose by 50 per cent between 1969 and 1972 alone.[10] A significant portion of these newly created posts was filled by recent university graduates, many of whom had been active in student politics. As a result, former centre-right activists now staffed the party's policy planning and strategy divisions. This signalled a marked change from the dignitaries who had previously been in charge. It also went hand in hand with a considerable democratization of internal decision-making processes, one of the key changes for which former RCDS activists had advocated continuously since the late 1960s.[11]

The glowing journalistic portraits of Kohl's 'brain trust' written after 1982/83 often focused on a number of individuals who had been student activists in the late 1960s and then become party apparatchiks in the 1970s. Such accounts often singled out Radunski, by now the CDU's managing director (and thus the party's number three); Wulf Schönbohm, who led the CDU's planning and strategy unit from 1983 onward; and Horst Teltschik, who advised Kohl on foreign policy.[12] Though unusually conspicuous, the trajectory of each of these three men indeed tells us something meaningful about the different ways in which some of the other

[9] Radunski, *Hinter der Kulisse*, 65–6, 64. On Radunski's career trajectory, see also Leggewie, *Der Geist steht rechts*, 117–19.
[10] Schönbohm, *Die CDU wird moderne Volkspartei*, 267; Grafe, *Schwarze Visionen*, 46–7; Hemmelmann, *Der Kompass der CDU*, 151.
[11] Helmuth Pütz, Peter Radunksi, Wulf Schönbohm, '34 Thesen zur Reform der CDU', *Sonde*, 4 (1969), 4–22; Wulf Schönbohm, 'Wo sind sie geblieben? Die Union und ihre Reformen', *Sonde*, 4 (1970), 7–20; Helmuth Pütz, Peter Radunksi, Wulf Schönbohm, and Uwe Rainer Simon, '18 Thesen zur Reorganisation der CDU', *Sonde*, 3, 4 (1973), 15–30; Wulf Schönbohm, 'Mehr Demokratie in der CDU', *Sonde*, 2 (1975), 29–35; see further Pridham, *Christian Democracy*, 224; Bösch, *Macht und Machtverlust*, 102.
[12] Sport, 'Maskenbildner der Union'. Leggewie's book also singled out Schönbohm and Radunski and provided biographical sketches of both. See Leggewie, *Der Geist steht rechts*, 117–19.

'68ers left their mark on Christian Democratic politics—and West German political culture more generally.

Radunski's name, perhaps more than anybody else's, became synonymous with the CDU's transformation, not least with the party's revamped election campaigns and political communication, which increasingly relied on methods developed by advertising experts. The CDU's 'legendary campaign manager', the party's 'make-up artist', West Germany's 'first spin doctor', and the 'most successful campaign manager that the CDU ever had' were just some of the ways in which leading newspapers summed up the career trajectory of the former centre-right student activist over time.[13]

In the 1970s, Radunski, who cited Rudi Dutschke as the most important role model of his youth and had closely observed New Left tactics as a student, began

Illustration 6.1 Former RCDS activist and CDU campaign strategist Peter Radunski (left) with CDU Secretary General Heiner Geißler at the 1986 party convention.
(Bundesarchiv-Bildarchiv, Photograph by Lothar Schaack)

[13] Werner van Bebber, 'Peter Radunski – der erste Spindoctor der Republik', *Der Tagesspiegel*, 26 January 2015; Anett Seidler, 'Der Macher der Mächtigen: Peter Radunski gilt als der beste Wahlkampf-Manager Deutschlands', *Welt am Sonntag* (15 April 2001). Hajo Schumacher, 'Eine Schlacht um Gefühle', *Der Spiegel*, 11 (9 March 1998), 92–5; Sport, 'Maskenbildner der Union'. Mildly hagiographic though some of these portrayals were, they echo verdicts in the literature on the history of West German election campaigns. Radunski is a central character in Mergel's history of propaganda after Hitler, for instance. Thomas Mergel, *Propaganda nach Hitler: Eine Kulturgeschichte des Wahlkampfs in der Bundesrepublik 1949–1990* (Göttingen, 2010), 30, 65, 78, 190, 200; on Radunski and Dutschke, see further 56–7.

to channel his expertise into the CDU's campaigns. He was part of a new party working group on language and politics, for instance, set up to help Christian Democrats to 'occupy terms' and thereby spark a 'social revolution through language'. This was a favourite subject of then Secretary General Biedenkopf and a direct response to the New Left's broadening of what was considered political.[14]

Radunski quickly emerged as one of the party's chief campaign strategists. In 1976, he managed the CDU's highly successful, though not victorious, national election campaign, which was designed to overcome the so-called 'spiral of silence', a theory of public opinion developed by Elisabeth Noelle-Neumann. The influential Christian Democratic pollster had proposed that conservative-leaning voters were marginalized publicly because the Left dominated the conversation and shaped the *Zeitgeist*. Since people in general 'feared isolation', voters therefore tended to side with the Social Democrats.[15] In the introduction to the book that formulated the theory, Noelle-Neumann claimed that she had first developed it after witnessing the marginalization and intimidation of a student who openly identified as a Christian Democrat on a university campus at the height of 1968.[16] The CDU's media strategy in 1976 was based directly on her central tenets. In an effort to create greater visibility, the party distributed campaign buttons to encourage voters to publicly identify themselves as Christian Democrats and thereby break the 'spiral of silence'.[17]

Many of the campaign's other key themes also sounded as though they had been lifted straight from the experiences and slogans of centre-right students a decade earlier. This was true of the party's official self-description as the 'Alternative '76', which clearly contrasted Christian Democratic values with those of the SPD and harked back to the late 1960s, when Christian Democratic students had often referred to themselves as the only political 'alternative' to the radical Left.[18] Moreover, two of the 1976 campaign's most memorable election posters featured the same seductive blonde: in one, she wore boxing gloves and asked voters to 'Come out of your left corner'; in the other, she donned a referee outfit and gave 'A red card now for the lefties'. Both were reminiscent of earlier centre-right student campaign materials that had featured seductive 'election girls' next to punny slogans that contrasted centre-right student groups with those of the Left.[19]

---

[14] Anja Kruke, *Demoskopie in der Bundesrepublik Deutschland: Meinungsforschung und Medien 1949–1990* (Düsseldorf, 2007), 158; Martin Geyer 'War over Words', in Willibald Steinmetz (ed.), *Political Languages in the Age of Extremes* (Oxford, 2011), 293–330; Mergel, *Propaganda nach Hitler*, 266–7; Steber, *Hüter der Begriffe*.

[15] Elisabeth Noelle Neumann, *Die Schweigespirale: Öffentliche Meinung—Unsere soziale Haut* (Munich, 1980); Elisabeth Noelle Neumann, *Öffentliche Meinung: Die Entdeckung der Schweigespirale* (Berlin, 1989), 20.

[16] Noelle Neumann, *Entdeckung der Schweigespirale*, 17.

[17] Noelle Neumann, *Entdeckung der Schweigespirale*, 242–3. Pictures of such buttons are in HIA, GSC, Box 85.

[18] HIA, Koenigs Papers, Box 1, *Alternativ: Studentenzeitung Berliner Hochschulen*, 1 (1969).

[19] HIA, GSC, Box 85, 'Komm aus Deiner linken Ecke', *Es geht um jede Stimme. Die Werbemittel für den Wahlkampf*, ed. by the CDU (1976), 10; also Mergel, *Propaganda nach Hitler*, 78.

Illustration 6.2 'Come out of your left corner', Christian Democratic campaign poster for the 1976 national elections.
(ACDP, Plakatsammlung, 10-001-1862)

Radunski also looked to American politics for inspiration. From the early 1970s onward, he regularly observed US election campaigns and sought to import the techniques he witnessed to West Germany. Convinced of the ever-growing import-ance of visuals in an age of television, he became an ardent proponent of the need to professionalize and 'Americanize' West German campaigns. His 1980 book on election campaigns as a form of modern political communication became a 'bible' for people in his industry.[20] Kohl's 1983 campaign, which Radunski again managed, exerted particularly tight control over Kohl's visual image—down to planning the right camera angle in television interviews with the candidate. Under Radunski's auspices, the party ran a perpetual media campaign intended to secure Kohl's image and power. He also stage-managed all of the party's conventions, which became true public spectacles and symbolic displays of the party's new dynamism, and ran every one of the Chancellor's victorious campaigns until 1990.[21]

After he left the federal party headquarters in 1991 to serve as a Senator in Berlin under Eberhard Diepgen, whom he had known since his student days at the Free University, he continued his electoral wizardry in the reunited city, managing both Diepgen's successful 1995 and 1999 campaigns for Governing Mayor.[22] In 1998, after sixteen years in office, Kohl finally struggled to gain traction against his Social Democratic opponent, the media-savvy Gerhard Schröder. Der Spiegel speculated that the Chancellor's difficulties were the result of not having replaced Radunski with a similarly talented and experienced campaign manager after his departure in the early 1990s. At the time, Schröder's campaign manager Bodo Hombach indeed told an interviewer that Radunski was the only rival he feared.[23]

While Radunski managed the party's external image from the 1970s onward, Schönbohm oversaw much of its policy work and strategy. The former RCDS national chair took over the party headquarters' influential Policy and Planning Division after Kohl's victory. Like that of his old friend Radunski, Schönbohm's trajectory had been a linear one—and one that was propelled in no small measure by his student activist credentials. Under his leadership in 1967/68, RCDS had begun its own intellectual work. When the CDU finally took a distinct programmatic turn while in opposition, Schönbohm was ideally positioned to contribute. In 1971, the party board appointed him to a new commission, chaired by future West Berlin Governing Mayor and Federal President Richard von Weizsäcker, which was tasked with laying the groundwork for a basic party programme. In an internal meeting of the party board in July of that year, both Kohl and Langguth pushed Schönbohm's appointment and cited his intellectual profile and effective opposition to the student Left in the late 1960s as the reason for his suitability for the role.[24]

[20] Peter Radunski, Wahlkämpfe: Moderne Wahlkampfführung als politische Kommunikation (Munich, 1980); Grafe, Schwarze Visionen, 57–69; Mergel, Propaganda nach Hitler, 30, 78 and 190.

[21] Carl-Christian Kaiser, 'Nichts dem Zufall überlassen', Die Zeit no. 6 (4 February 1983); Mergel, Propaganda nach Hitler, 190; Heinrich Oberreuter, 'The CDU and Social Change', German Politics and Society, 14 (June 1988), 9.

[22] Seidler, 'Macher der Mächtigen'.

[23] Hajo Schumacher, 'Eine Schlacht um Gefühle', Der Spiegel, 11 (9 March 1998), 92–5; Seidler, 'Macher der Mächtigen'.

[24] Minutes of meeting of 5 July 1971, in: Barzel: 'Unsere Alternativen für die Zeit der Opposition', 654.

Wulf Schönbohm,
47, gilt als »Lenin der
CDU«. Während
der Studentenrevolte
(kleines Bild) war
er Vorsitzender des
Berliner RCDS.
Heute ist er Leiter der
Planungs- und
Entwicklungsabteilung
der CDU: einer der
Strategen des
Generalsekretärs
Heiner Geißler

»1968 mußten
wir an zwei Fronten
kämpfen. Die Linken
hielten uns für
Reaktionäre, die
Älteren in der Partei
für links infiltriert«

10 ZEITmagazin

Illustration 6.3 Former RCDS chair and CDU strategist Wulf Schönbohm featured in *Die Zeit* as the 'Lenin of the CDU' in 1988.

(Matthias Horx und Marie Weinberger, 'Die 68er der CDU', *Zeit Magazin* no. 33 (1988), 12. Photograph by Paul Schirnhofer)

Looking back, Schönbohm was similarly convinced that the skills he had obtained through his struggle with SDS had made him stand out within a CDU that was largely unaccustomed to internal deliberation:

> [In 1968] I became pretty good at political argument. And also pretty resilient. And that helped me later, after my degree. Almost no one was a patch on me

when it came to political conversations. [. . .] The period of debate with the SDS brought me a long way, and I learnt a lot in the process.[25]

The work of the Weizsäcker commission, on which Schönbohm served as one of fourteen members, represented the party's most consistent intellectual efforts since the early postwar years. It was accompanied by lively debate and eventually led to the adoption of the CDU's first basic programme in Ludwigshafen in October 1978. The document identified 'freedom, solidarity, and justice' as the CDU's three interlocking basic values and sought to position the party firmly in the political centre. There were clear traces of Dahrendorf and Popper's formative works that had so fascinated student activists around 1968: the programme envisaged an open society that would resolve social and political conflicts through healthy and respectful debate and explained that the principle of human fallibility made political ideology a dangerous fallacy.[26] Much like the RCDS's conceptual musings of a decade earlier, it also took an explicitly secular turn. In an attempt to speak to its new members for many of whom religious faith was not the main source of their political identity, it insisted that Christianity no longer served as the party's main programmatic basis. At the same time, it still offered the 'Christian idea of man' as a general guiding principle to appeal to older religious voters, particularly the party's Catholic faithful.

Although members of the '45er generation were in charge of the party's programmatic efforts, Schönbohm later interpreted the process of party renewal as the generational project of the other '68ers. Since 1968, the former RCDS leader had been editor-in-chief and co-publisher of the *Sonde*, the party's most important new forum for debating its organization and tenuous conceptual profile. Interviewed in 2008, Schönbohm explained that the *Sonde*—and, by extension, the entire project of party reform—had been driven by a sense of generational mission:

So this magazine tried, especially in the 70s, [. . .] to influence [the] reform process in the CDU. [. . .] Always after elections, and on occasion in between, we published the *Sonde*-Theses. For this, three or four friends got together—I was always there and coordinated it, and we [framed] theses on the political situation, and on what the CDU should do now. [. . .] Both in terms of policy and in terms

---

[25] Schönbohm interview.
[26] Grundsatzprogramm 'Freiheit, Solidarität, Gerechtigkeit' (1978), available at https://www.kas.de/c/document_library/get_file?uuid=c44fbaf4-a603-d097-6898-e72e6fae6f39&groupId=252038 (accessed on 24 February 2020); Wulf Schönbohm, 'Das CDU-Grundsatzprogramm: Dokument politischer Erneuerung', *Aus Politik und Zeitgeschichte*, 29 (1979), B 51–52, 27–39; Schönbohm, *Die CDU wird moderne Volkspartei*, 143; also Grafe, *Schwarze Visionen*, 71–5.

of party organization, the CDU as a party was in a wretched state. And the party headquarters was just full of has-beens, who had no idea. The party itself was totally unprofessional right down to the core. We made very many concrete suggestions as to how the party organization could be changed, the decision-making process in the party and how the party could become more dynamic. These were all people who had been involved during [...] my time as a student. Or who were involved three or four years later in RCDS. So there you didn't need to talk too much about it, it was a collective approach.[27]

He had already argued along these lines in the 1980s, in his doctoral dissertation supervised by Karl Dietrich Bracher, which examined the CDU's transformation into a modern people's party. The work is still cited frequently in the literature on Christian Democracy, and it gave major credit to Schönbohm's own student generation in explaining the party's transformation. RCDS had set up a political strategy unit that began to think in systemic terms in 1968 because it had been confronted by an extraparliamentary opposition enamoured with theory. This impetus, in turn, had eventually found its way into the CDU, he argued. Its more clearly delineated party profile had then made it much more appealing to voters.[28] It was none other than the former RCDS national chair of 1967/8, then, who first put forward the idea that the other '68ers had almost single-handedly reformed the CDU—a generational interpretation that journalists and scholars picked up and disseminated.[29]

Of course, Schönbohm did not just study and interpret the party's transform-ation. He also continued to shape its profile in direct ways. From the late 1970s until 1989, he was one of the closest confidants of CDU Secretary General Heiner Geißler, who was second only to Kohl in terms of influencing the party's direction and who relied heavily on his younger aide's concepts.[30] In the 1970s, Geißler had worked closely with RCDS activists like Pflüger to make a scandal of left-wing dissent and link students and left-wing intellectuals to the terror of the RAF. Through joint events with RCDS like the one held in Bremen in December 1977 and publications like his infamous 'terror documentation', he developed a public profile as a particularly combative advocate of Christian Democratic positions and scourge of the Left. Schönbohm later recalled with pride that he and Radunski had always helped the feared polemicist and renowned provocateur prepare for major events, especially the big party conventions of the 1980s. As

---

[27] Schönbohm interview; also Schönbohm, *Die CDU wird moderne Volkspartei*, 103 and 124.
[28] Schönbohm, *Die CDU wird moderne Volkspartei*, 124, 132, 142, 301–2; also Schönbohm interview.
[29] Grafe, *Schwarze Visionen*, 71; Leggewie, *Der Geist steht rechts*; Oberreuter, 'The CDU and Social Change', 3–12; Hemmelmann, *Der Kompass der CDU*, 150.
[30] Oberreuter, 'The CDU and Social Change', 7.

he remembered in 2008: '[H]is speeches at party conferences were always the high point of the conference. And I prepared them. And that was always—you cannot even imagine—we sat there night after night [...] pushing drafts back and forth.'[31]

Whereas Schönbohm's standing within the CDU rested at least in part on his proximity to Geißler, Horst Teltschik had unfettered access to Helmut Kohl himself. Much like the careers of Radunski and Schönbohm, his two old acquaintances from the Free University in West Berlin, Teltschik's professional career took off very soon after graduating with a degree in political science. In fact, he hardly 'marched' at all. After finishing his studies, Teltschik taught at the Free University for a couple of years as an assistant to Richard Löwenthal, but quickly landed a senior role within the growing CDU apparatus. There, he ran the group on foreign and inner-German policy from 1970 until 1972. The RCDS network had helped, he later reported.[32]

Kohl, then still Governor of Rhineland-Palatinate, took note of the young political scientist and, in 1972, persuaded him to move to the State Chancellery in Mainz as his assistant and speechwriter. Teltschik quickly became one of Kohl's most important political advisors. After the 1976 election, Kohl appointed him as his Chief of Staff as Leader of the Opposition in the *Bundestag* and, after Kohl's election in 1982, Teltschik followed him to the Chancellery in Bonn. At the age of forty-three, he became the first non-career diplomat to chair its department on Foreign and Inner-German Relations, Development Policy, and External Security. One year later, Kohl also made him Deputy Leader of the Chancellery.[33]

Impressive though these job titles no doubt were, they fail to capture the remarkable extent of Teltschik's influence. In his memoirs, Kohl described him as one of his 'most important political collaborators' and the conservative *Frankfurter Allgemeine Zeitung* called him the 'load-bearing stone in the foundations of Kohl's government'.[34] Many scholars agree that Teltschik was an exceptionally powerful figure in the 1980s and that he held far more sway than an ordinary civil servant.[35]

Teltschik was a long-standing member of Kohl's infamous 'kitchen cabinet', a small, tightly knit circle of advisors in the Chancellery, which represented the true power centre of the Kohl government. Kohl met with this small group of favourites daily first thing in the morning—often before he even got properly dressed for the work day—to go over the major political developments on the agenda. As

---

[31] Schönbohm interview.   [32] Teltschik interview.
[33] Simon Forster, 'Teltschik, Horst' https://www.kas.de/statische-inhalte-detail/-/content/teltschik-horst (accessed on 15 September 2019).
[34] Helmut Kohl, *Erinnerungen: 1930–1982* (Munich, 2004), 346; Claus Gennrich, 'Nach loyaler Arbeit macht Teltschik von seiner Freiheit Gebrauch', *FAZ* (6 December 1990).
[35] Wirsching, *Abschied vom Provisorium*, 182; Sarotte, *1989*, 159.

Illustration 6.4 Former RCDS activist and 'Kohl's Kissinger' Horst Teltschik (left) with the newly elected Federal Chancellor on a flight to Rome on 18 November 1982. (Bundesarchiv-Bildarchiv, Photograph by Ulrich Wienke)

such, Teltschik was involved in virtually all major political decisions taken by the Chancellor, who generally championed a highly personalized leadership style.[36]

Given his long-standing interests and portfolio in the Chancellery, the former student leader was especially influential in the realm of foreign policy. This was a particularly important policy area given that Kohl, in contrast to his predecessor, the 'global Chancellor' Schmidt, did not have much of an international profile or foreign policy experience when arriving in office.[37] What is more, he was hardly cosmopolitan, and was well-known for being deeply rooted culturally in the Palatinate. Although *Der Spiegel* had a famously contentious relationship with Kohl, a year after his election, the paper nevertheless noted that the new Chancellor had managed to navigate the international stage with surprising ease—and it credited none other than Teltschik with making this happen:

---

[36] 'Die Souffleure der Kanzler', *Die Zeit* no. 28 (8 July 1983); '"Der Kanzler wünscht das so": Wie Helmut Kohls Küchenkabinett die Bundesrepublik regiert', *Der Spiegel*, 24 (9 June 1986); Werner Filmer and Heribert Schwan, *Helmut Kohl* (Econ Verlag, 1985); Teltschik, *329 Tage*, 25; Wirsching, *Abschied vom Provisorium*, 182–3.

[37] Kristina Spohr, *The Global Chancellor: Helmut Schmidt and the Reshaping of the International Order* (New York, 2016); Wirsching, *Abschied vom Provisorium*, 182.

That Kohl has until now not done any harm in German or foreign policy [. . .], indeed that on visits abroad he has made a good impression against expectations, is largely due to his adviser Teltschik."[38]

A few years later, at the height of East Germany's November revolution, *Die Zeit* argued in a similar vein that the very fact that Kohl had acquired major foreign policy credentials was the result of Teltschik's coaching. 'It is thanks to Teltschik's influence on him that Kohl found the foreign policy practitioner in himself.' He was nothing less than the 'Chancellor's brain', the paper's Bonn correspondent opined in a memorable turn of phrase.[39]

Under Teltschik's influence, Kohl continued key elements of the Social-Liberal coalition's foreign policy, including much of its *Ostpolitik*. In contrast to what the Christian Democrats had initially signalled in opposition, there was no new freeze in relations with the GDR. Kohl's government gave millions in loans to the East Germans, and, in September 1987, the Chancellor welcomed Erich Honecker to Bonn on an official state visit. This was the first and, ultimately, only time that the leader of East Germany was received in the west during Germany's division.[40] At the same time, however, Teltschik, who had not just advocated for a pragmatic approach to the GDR as a student but also supported the American intervention in Vietnam, steered Kohl toward a much closer relationship to the United States. He interpreted this move as continuing the tradition of Christian Democratic foreign policy that had existed since Adenauer, namely one defined by the primacy of Western integration.[41]

In doing so, the ambitious Teltschik frequently clashed with the Liberal Foreign Minister and Vice Chancellor Hans-Dietrich Genscher. Genscher, who had been in post since 1974, openly resented Teltschik's intrusion into his policy realm—to no avail. Teltschik routinely shunned conventional diplomatic channels and cultivated his own personal relationships in other western capitals, not least with senior staff in Ronald Reagan's White House. Newspapers reported regularly that Genscher was left out of the loop on sensitive discussions with the Americans, especially on missile defence.[42]

The former Christian Democratic student leader also choreographed all of Kohl's moves on the international stage. Like Radunski, he had a penchant for symbolic displays. For instance, Teltschik engineered Kohl and Reagan's visit to a military cemetery near Bitburg in May 1985 to commemorate the end of the

---

[38] 'Die lange Schonzeit ist zu Ende', *Der Spiegel*, 40 (3 October 1983).

[39] Gerhard Spörl, 'Der Kopf des Kanzlers', *Die Zeit*, 46 (10 November 1989).

[40] Andreas Rödder, *Deutschland einig Vaterland: Die Geschichte der Wiedervereinigung* (Munich, 2009).

[41] 'Vom Englischen sofort ins Russische', *Der Spiegel*, 43 (2 October 1986), 19–24.

[42] 'Bizeps zeigen', *Der Spiegel*, 49 (3 December 1984); 'Vom Englischen sofort ins Russische', *Der Spiegel*, 43 (2 October 1986), 19–24; 'Der Kanzler wünscht das so', *Der Spiegel*, 24 (1986).

Second World War and showcase the strength of the German-American bond forty years after. However, the ceremonial visit backfired spectacularly after it emerged that members of the Waffen-SS were buried on the grounds alongside regular *Wehrmacht* soldiers. Instead of symbolizing German-American reconciliation, as Teltschik had chiefly intended, the ceremony seemed designed to rehabilitate Nazi perpetrators. Weeks of protests in Germany and the United States were the result.[43]

Though ill-judged at best, the episode highlights Teltschik's close involvement in shaping Kohl's growing international profile. Though formally no more than an ordinary civil servant, his role was in effect closer to that of the American National Security Advisor—and to a particularly powerful one at that. American officials and West German journalists indeed began to refer to the high-profile aide as 'Kohl's Kissinger'.[44]

Teltschik's portfolio and profile only grew over the course of the 1980s. When things began to stir in the Polish People's Republic in 1989, spelling the gradual end of Communist rule in the country, Kohl sidelined the *Auswärtiges Amt* and put Teltschik in charge of West German policy toward Poland.[45] The former West Berlin student leader reached the apex of his influence after the Berlin Wall fell suddenly on 9 November 1989. Over the course of the next year, he was intimately involved in crafting the West German government's response, pushing early on for the Chancellor to call publicly for a reunification of the two Germanies.

In his memoirs, in which he recounted these heady days in minute detail, Teltschik outlined how, after receiving encouraging signs from the Soviets via a back channel, he had urged Kohl to lead public opinion on the matter.[46] In a late-night meeting on 23 November, Teltschik first suggested the idea of developing a plan toward ways of German unity embedded in a pan-European architecture. The preparations and drafting of this document, which Teltschik oversaw, remained a closely guarded secret. Not even Genscher knew of its existence. The result was Kohl's Ten-Point Plan for German Unity, which he unveiled to the public in the Bundestag on 28 November 1989—a moment that is widely recognized as a major milestone on the road to 3 October 1990.[47]

Teltschik's memoir concluded with what he considered the crowning moment of his career, the celebration of German reunification in front of the Berlin Reichstag. The book's final scene depicted Kohl, Teltschik, and a handful of the

---

[43] 'Keine Silbe', *Der Spiegel*, 51 (16 December 1985); Charles Maier, *The Unmasterable Past: History, Holocaust, and German National Identity* (Cambridge, MA: Harvard University Press, 1988), 9–16; Bill Niven, *Facing the Nazi Past: United Germany and the Legacy of the Third Reich* (London and New York, 2002), 105–6.

[44] Jürgen Leinemann, 'Ich wirke oft farblos und nüchtern', *Der Spiegel*, 47 (18 November 1985).

[45] 'Wann kommt "die Zeit nach Genscher"'?, *Der Spiegel*, 31 (31 July 1989), 19.

[46] Teltschik, *329 Tage*, 49.

[47] Teltschik, *329 Tage*, 44–58, particularly 44, 49–51; Hans-Peter Schwarz, *Helmut Kohl: Eine politische Biographie* (Munich, 2012), 531–2.

Chancellor's other confidants sitting in the Reichstag building in the early hours of 3 October while tens of thousands of people stood outside and shouted Kohl's name. With his help, Teltschik thereby conveyed, Germany had been united and Kohl had arrived at the height of his popularity.[48]

Even if we stripped this portrayal of the self-aggrandizement that is characteristic of the political memoir genre, it would be difficult to deny that Teltschik played a central role in crafting West German foreign policy in the early Kohl era. Especially during the crucial moment that was 1989/90, Teltschik helped to shape what is commonly considered to be Helmut Kohl's single most important political achievement.[49] 'Kohl's Kissinger' enabled the Christian Democratic Chancellor, who had often been ridiculed for his parochialism after arriving in office in 1982 and whose domestic record was decidedly mixed, to build a lasting reputation as a German statesman and great European.[50]

As we can see, Teltschik, Schönbohm, and Radunski, the three former Christian Democratic student leaders from West Berlin, followed remarkable trajectories after 1968. Each of them left a discernible mark on the CDU and the early Kohl era in a different way, shaping the party's image, programmatic profile, and policies. Each one of them was also convinced that 1968 had been a training ground that had propelled his career in important ways. These three men clearly stood out among the other '68ers, and their prominent presence in the party apparatus and the Chancellery helps to explain the public attention the broader group received. However, their journeys were not unique. Other former student activists also marched through the institutions in record time, and they often displayed a similar knack for party strategy, programmatic work, and political communication. It was in these areas above all, it seems, that an engagement with the 1968 Left provided an edge.

Schönbohm, for one, was not the only former student activist who was deeply involved in the CDU's programmatic renewal. Meinhard Ade, who had helped to engineer the open-air Dutschke-Dahrendorf debate in Freiburg in January 1968, served alongside Schönbohm on the Weizsäcker commission. One of his professors in Freiburg, the political scientist Wilhelm Hennis, had recommended him to Weizsäcker, who sought input from the party's restive and more theory-savvy younger generation and asked around among politically like-minded intellectuals for recommendations. Ade remembered that Weizsäcker had called him

---

[48] Teltschik, *329 Tage*, 375.   [49] Wirsching, *Abschied vom Provisorium*, 183.

[50] These themes were omnipresent in the many obituaries published after his death in June 2017. See e.g. Peter Sturm, 'Trauer um den Kanzler der Einheit', *FAZ* (16 June 2017) https://www.faz.net/aktuell/politik/inland/helmut-kohl-ist-tot-trauer-um-den-kanzler-der-einheit-14041427.html (accessed on 20 November 2020); Werner A. Perger, 'Staatsmann und Machtmensch', *Die Zeit* (16 June 2017), https://www.zeit.de/politik/deutschland/2017-06/helmut-kohl-nachruf (accessed on 20 November 2020); Wolfram Bickerich, 'Der schwarze Riese', *Der Spiegel* (16 June 2017), https://www.spiegel.de/politik/deutschland/helmut-kohl-der-schwarze-riese-nachruf-a-1152576.html (accessed on 20 November 2020); also Schwarz, *Helmut Kohl*.

personally to recruit him for the post of Secretary to the Commission.[51] He would serve as a close aide to Weizsäcker throughout the latter's time as West Berlin's Mayor and Federal President. Such were the doors that a visible engagement with the Left around 1968 could, and did, open for many.

Nor was Teltschik the only other '68er in Kohl's close orbit or Radunski the only one who developed expertise in political marketing and campaigns. Wolfgang Bergsdorf combined both. He had been active in the Bonn RCDS in the 1960s, joined the party headquarters in the 1970s, and was another key aide to Helmut Kohl who remained at his side throughout the 1980s. Bergsdorf's formal job description, that of head of the Domestic Press Division of the Government's Press and Information Office, failed to capture the full weight of his role. Another key member of Kohl's 'kitchen cabinet', he counselled the Chancellor on matters far beyond his official portfolio and helped to craft his public image.[52] He shared with Radunski a keen interest in political rhetoric and semantics. He wrote his second dissertation (his *Habilitationsschrift*) about the nexus between power and language in the Federal Republic and published widely on how words could be wielded as political weapons. He put this expertise to good use as Kohl's press guru.[53]

Moreover, Warnfried Dettling, who had studied political science in Freiburg in the 1960s and been a leading figure in RCDS in the city, similarly crafted a career as a coveted political consultant and Christian Democratic campaign manager. According to Thomas Mergel, both Dettling and Radunski represented a new type of campaign manager in the history of West German electioneering—one with actual academic expertise.[54] Dettling helped to shape the party's electoral strategy until well into the 1980s. As Schönbohm's predecessor as head of the party headquarters' Policy and Planning Division, he was also a major driving force behind the CDU's programmatic renewal. Later, he exerted considerable influence as State Secretary under Geißler, when the latter was Minister of Youth, Family Affairs, and Health and sought to push the party toward a more socially liberal profile.[55]

The list of the other '68ers who left their mark on the early Kohl era could be extended further. One might point to Jürgen Aretz, who had chaired the Bonn Student Union in the late 1960s, and who was later closely involved in the

---

[51] Ade interview.

[52] See Bergsdorf's biography at http://www.kas.de/wf/doc/kas_9990-544-1-30.pdf?070124113949 (accessed on 5 May 2016); also Leggewie, *Der Geist steht rechts*, 108–14; Wirsching, *Abschied vom Provisorium*, 181–2.

[53] Wolfgang Bergsdorf, *Herrschaft und Sprache: Studie zur politischen Terminologie der Bundesrepublik* (Pfullingen, 1983); Wolfgang Bergsdorf, *Politik und Sprache* (Munich and Vienna, 1978); Wolfgang Bergsdorf (ed.), *Wörter als Waffen: Sprache als Mittel der Politik* (Stuttgart, 1979).

[54] Mergel, *Propaganda nach Hitler*, 37, 101, 269 and 279.

[55] Warnfried Dettling, *Das Erbe Kohls: Bilanz einer Ära* (Eichborn, 1994), 139–42; Grafe, *Schwarze Visionen*, 33.

negotiations over German reunification in his capacity as a senior civil servant in the Federal Ministry for Inner-German Relations.[56] Or one could follow the path of Detlef Stronk, who had helped to run the Munich Student Union's victorious 1967 campaign and served as RCDS's deputy national chair. In 1985, he ran Eberhard Diepgen's first victorious campaign for Governing Mayor of West Berlin and later served as Chief of Staff in Diepgen's State Chancellery.[57] He was one of several former student activists who occupied leading roles under Diepgen, be it in his administration or as Senators in his cabinet.

Other former centre-right student activists pursued careers outside party politics and the civil service, but often no less distinguished ones. After finishing his Filbinger-commissioned study of the student movement, Ignaz Bender, for one, became a senior academic administrator. He served as Assistant to the Provost of the University of Konstanz, and, as early as 1970, was appointed to lead the newly founded Trier University. From 1979 until his retirement in 2001, he served as the university's chancellor. Klaus Laepple, the erstwhile 'Provo of the CDU', meanwhile, became a key figure in the (West) German tourism industry, founding his own travel agency and later serving as a high-ranking functionary in various major trade associations, all the while remaining an influential figure in Christian Democratic politics in Cologne.

For all these impressive accolades, however, it clearly was the men who fared best on the short 'march through the institutions'. The leading Christian Democratic apparatchiks with roots in the student movement were all male. Looking back, female centre-right activists were equally convinced that they had benefitted intellectually from their engagement with the Left, but they rarely recalled that it had represented a 'dream-like career move'. Ingrid Reichart-Dreyer, who had worked closely with Schönbohm in West Berlin's RCDS in the late 1960s, rejected outright the notion that her student activism had furthered her career in any direct way. It was very different for the men, she noted. 'They went to Bonn and I got stuck in Berlin. [...] I didn't make it into that network.'[58] She partly attributed this to falling into what she called the 'family trap' (Reichart-Dreyer had two children in the 1970s) and partly to the continued male chauvinism of her generation of Christian Democrats—a factor she had become more attuned to over time, she explained. '[T]hese obstacles were not visible as such before. I was useful. They became visible in due course, and noticeable in the fact

---

[56] From 1992 onward, he also led the working group on the new (East German) states in the Chancellery. Aretz interview; Bothien, *Protest und Provokation*, 123. At the time of writing this book, Aretz was featured frequently in the German media as legal representative of the House of Hohenzollern, the heirs of Germany's last Kaiser, Wilhelm II, who recently stepped up their controversial efforts to reclaim family property expropriated after 1945.

[57] Before then, he had already been appointed as the youngest State Secretary of Economics in a West German Ministry under Elmar Pieroth, West Berlin's Economics Senator. Stronk, *Berlin in den Achtziger Jahren.*

[58] Reichart-Dreyer interview.

that I wasn't brought along with them.'[59] Reichart-Dreyer continued to be active in local Christian Democratic politics in West Berlin and later pursued an academic career but never obtained a tenured position.[60]

Dorothee Buchhaas-Birkholz, who had served as deputy national chair of RCDS in the 1970s, shared similar impressions. Although she was far less explicitly feminist than Reichart-Dreyer, she also observed that RCDS networks had primarily benefitted the men. When I interviewed her in Berlin in 2012, she was a mid-level career civil servant in the Education Ministry, where she had served since the mid-1980s. She recalled that she had attended a few RCDS reunions after her student days, but increasingly felt as though she did not belong. Such gatherings were often held over a weekend during the season of Advent, she remembered, which she had found difficult to fit into life with a family—an obstacle the men seemingly had not faced. 'There was also the sense that: "If you are not a State Secretary, then you are nothing!" And then I thought: "This is clearly stupid." From there I somehow didn't want it anymore.'[61]

Ursula Männle's path represented a clearer success story in some ways. She had already been the only woman to chair RCDS at the state level in the 1960s—she was Bavarian state chair from 1966–67—and was later elected as a Christian Democratic delegate to the Bundestag as well as the Bavarian state parliament where she held a seat until 2013. One year later, she was appointed as the first woman to chair the Hanns-Seidel Foundation, the CSU's think tank, a post she held until 2019. Unlike many of her male peers, however, especially in the 1980s and 1990s, even she never gained the same proximity to real political power and influence that a more equitable peer network might have facilitated.

It is indeed telling that the women who occupied more visible roles during the early Kohl era and who came to symbolize the party's reformist image had not begun their political careers in RCDS or other student groups of the centre-right. Rita Süßmuth, who was appointed as Federal Minister of Family Affairs, Senior Citizens, Women and Youth in 1985, for instance, had been a professor of pedagogy in Hanover prior to her appointment. Having only joined the Christian Democrats in 1981, she was a political outsider and an unexpected choice for the role.[62] While her appointment and policies thus clearly reflected the party's changing profile and the reach of the women's movement into the CDU,

---

[59] Reichart-Dreyer interview.

[60] Ingrid Reichart-Dreyer, Werte -Systeme—Programme: Modell, Praxis und Alternativen politischer Willensbildung und Programmatik entwickelt am Beispiel der CDU (Bonn, 1977); Ingrid Reichart-Dreyer, Macht und Demokratie in der CDU, dargestellt an Prozess und Ergebnis der Meinungsbildung zum Grundsatzprogramm 1994 (Wiesbaden, 2000).

[61] Buchhaas-Birkholz interview.

[62] Rita Süßmuth, 'In der Politik brauchen sie Grundsätze', in Neuss and Neubert, Mut zur Verantwortung, 196 ff.; Süßmuth, Das Gift des Politischen, 70–4; Ina vom Hofe, Die Frauenpolitik der CDU: Traditionen, Entwicklungen, Einflüsse 1945–2013 (Sankt Augustin and Berlin, 2017), 126. Ursula Lehr, her successor as Federal Minister, was appointed after a similar lateral move. She had also been an academic. See also Bösch, Macht und Machtverlust, 251–3.

her trajectory simultaneously illustrated the barriers that women activists still faced within the party. All in all, the other '68ers' short 'march through the institutions' remained an overwhelmingly male affair.

The Other '68ers and the Political Culture of the Late Federal Republic

Its male dominance notwithstanding, the other '68ers' short march shaped the political culture of the early Kohl era in specific ways. For one, these former student activists helped the CDU to clearly delineate its political identity—not just through shaping its programmatic profile but also through affective resistance against and continuous verbal attacks on the party's opponents.

In the 1970s, the other '68ers had already helped to harness fears of left-wing terrorism and its alleged mass of student sympathizers to elevate the CDU's profile. In the 1980s, the Greens, a newly founded alternative party with roots in the student movement and which gained seats in the Bundestag for the first time in March 1983, became Secretary General Geißler's favourite new target. Geißler's apparatchiks closely studied the new party, which they portrayed as eco-Marxists hostile to the constitution.[63] A few months after the 1983 elections, in the midst of protests and heated debates about the stationing of Pershing II missiles in West Germany, the CDU's Secretary General even linked the pacifist Greens to the Holocaust by stating in a *Bundestag* speech that 'The pacifism of the 1930s was what first made Auschwitz possible'.[64] Two years later, after Geißler had equated the Nazi dictatorship with the GDR regime and accused the Social Democrats of whitewashing the latter, SPD leader Willy Brandt called him 'the worst rabble-rouser in this country since Goebbels'.[65] Schönbohm, by contrast, offered a positive spin on Geißler's rhetorical and political talents—talents the former student leader was proud to have helped to hone in nightly speechwriting sessions:

---

[63] CDU-Bundesgeschäftsstelle (ed.), *Die Grünen: Eine Analyse der öko-marxistischen Radikalopposition* (Bonn, 1984); Heiner Geißler and Peter Radunski, Bericht der Bundesgeschäftsstelle. Anlage zum Bericht des Generalsekretärs 33. Bundesparteitag 19.-22. März 1985 Essen, 27–8, available at https://www.kas.de/c/document_library/get_file?uuid=fa54e766-f7b9-1da3-adaa-55286e4a56fd& groupId=252038 (accessed on 28 February 2020); Grafe, *Schwarze Visionen*, 67–8, 95–103; Schönbohm, cited in Jochen Blind, *Heimspiel der 'Europa-Parteien'?: Die Europawahlkämpfe der Union von 1979 bis 2009* (Wiesbaden, 2012), 112–13; on the history of the early Greens, Silke Mende, *'Nicht rechts, nicht links, sondern vorn': Eine Geschichte der Gründungsgrünen* (Munich, 2011).

[64] Geißler, cited in 'Egal wie', *Der Spiegel*, 25 (20 June 1983), 27. His argument was that Appeasement had been a pacifist policy and that it had emboldened Hitler to start the war and the Holocaust. See further Christoph Weckenbrock, *Schwarz-Grün für Deutschland?: Wie aus politischen Erzfeinden Bündnispartner wurden* (Bielefeld, 2017), 79–84.

[65] 'Der schlimmste Hetzer in diesem Land', *Der Spiegel*, 21 (20 May 1985), 28–30.

He did it in the way that a polemicist must. Kohl simply read something out. [...]
And Geißler was able to grab people's attention through the content and form
[of his speeches], political opponents too. And that work took night after night.[66]

Nurturing this combativeness was only one side of the coin, however. At the same
time that the other '68ers in the party apparatus helped to arm Christian
Democrats to the hilt rhetorically, they carefully projected progressivism on social
issues to appeal to a changing electorate—just as the 'children of Adenauer and
Coca-Cola' had done in the late 1960s. In fact, this double-sided approach of
combative politics on the one hand and social liberalism on the other helps us to
grapple with one of the key questions surrounding Kohl's Chancellorship,
namely why his government did not mark a clearer break with the Social-
Liberal coalition. In other words, why, contrary to what Kohl had initially
proclaimed, there was no comprehensive 'spiritual-moral change' [geistig-
moralische Wende] in West Germany under his leadership.

After Kohl was elected, observers were initially certain that his victory was a
defining moment for West German society. In an interview that he gave a month
after the 1983 vote, the philosopher Jürgen Habermas famously warned 'that the
swing to the neo-conservatives, which the March elections confirmed, could mean
a caesura that goes deeper than a mere change of government'.[67] Five years later,
however, Habermas offered a very different analysis of where Kohl had taken the
country. The Christian Democrats had not been able to reverse the social and
cultural changes of the past two decades, the philosopher now argued. On the
contrary, the party had been forced to adapt to a modern society and adjust its
platform accordingly.[68] True conservatives had been disappointment by the
direction of Kohl's policies. Instead of a real turn—an actual Wende—to the
right, the Chancellor often chose to continue the course charted by his Social
Democratic predecessors and championed an assertive centrism rather than a
truly conservative politics.[69]

---

[66] Schönbohm interview.

[67] Habermas, quoted in Peter Hoeres, 'Von der "Tendenzwende" zur "geistig-moralischen Wende".
Konstruktion und Kritik konservativer Signaturen in den 1970er und 1980er Jahren', VfZ, 61, 1 (2013),
93–119, here 93.

[68] 'Der Marsch durch die Institutionen hat auch die CDU erreicht', Frankfurter Rundschau,
11 March 1988; an English translation of the interview was published as Jürgen Habermas, 'Political
Culture in Germany since 1968: An Interview with Dr. Rainer Erd for the Frankfurter Rundschau', in
Jürgen Habermas, The New Conservatism: Cultural Criticism and the Historians' Debate, edited and
translated by Shierry Weber Nicholsen (Cambridge, 1989).

[69] See e.g. Günther Rohrmoser, Das Debakel: Wo bleibt die Wende? Fragen an die CDU (Krefeld,
1985); for analysis see Williarty, The CDU and the Politics of Gender in Germany, 108–33; Wirsching,
Abschied vom Provisorium; Andreas Wirsching, 'Eine "Ära Kohl"? Die widersprüchliche Signatur
deutscher Regierungspolitik 1982–1998', Archiv für Sozialgeschichte, 52 (2012), 667–84; Hoeres, 'Von
der ,Tendenzwende' zur 'geistig-moralischen Wende"'; on Kohl's centrism and penchant for the
'Mitte', Grafe, Schwarze Visionen, 76–8.

That 1982/83 was a turning point that failed to turn (to loosely quote G.M. Trevelyan's famous dictum about the 1848 revolutions)—or at the very least a turning point that produced outcomes very different from those anticipated at the time—has been an underlying theme in recent works on the 1980s and West German conservatives' often uneasy relationship with Christian Democracy.[70] The fact that the presence of the Free Democrats in the governing coalition acted as a hinge between the era of Brandt and Schmidt and that of Kohl no doubt goes some way toward explaining why a more radical turn failed to materialize. The other '68ers and their particular brand of politics are other pieces of this puzzle.

Tellingly, the rise of the other '68ers to positions of influence was not just central to how contemporary observers understood the sources of Kohl's electoral success but also to how they made sense of his government's seemingly contradictory impulses. To underline his point about what he called the 'fundamental liberalization' that West German society had undergone since the 1960s, Habermas pointed to the presence in Kohl's administration of individuals with biographical ties to 1968 and to second-wave feminism. He singled out the socially liberal former student activist Warnfried Dettling, who had shaped the CDU's programmatic and public profile since the 1970s, as well as Federal Minister Süßmuth, who identified publicly with the women's movement.[71] Critically minded, socially liberal, and yet politically influential Christian Democrats like them reflected how comprehensively West Germany's political culture had changed since the 1960s when such figures would have been found exclusively on the Left, he argued. Conversely, it was precisely the rise of individuals like these that especially irked conservative commentators who had pushed for a real *Wende.*[72]

Such verdicts about the link between the other '68ers and the CDU's more socially liberal turn were based on the trajectories of those former student activists, who clustered on the CDU's progressive wing and who had entered the party apparatus.[73] It is worth noting, however, that not all former centre-right students from the 1960s were champions of social liberalism in the 1980s. Some adopted an overwhelmingly combative posture, including on social issues. Peter Gauweiler, who had led the Munich RCDS around 1968 and was then state secretary in the Bavarian Interior Ministry, for one, gained notoriety for crafting the state's hard-line response to the developing HIV crisis in the mid-1980s. He called for the quarantining of HIV-positive individuals, the forced testing of prostitutes and

---

[70] Wirsching, *Abschied vom Provisorium;* Biebricher, *Geistig-moralische Wende,* 12, 81, 145–6, 181.
[71] 'Simone de Beauvoir ist mein großes Vorbild', *Die Zeit,* 37 (1985); Margit Gerste, 'Knochenarbeit für die Männer-Partei', *Die Zeit,* 1 (1986); Süßmuth, *Das Gift des Politischen,* 72, 102–3; see also the critical take on Süßmuth's 'conservative feminism' in Mechthild Jansen, '"Konservativer Feminismus" mit Rita Süßmuth?, in *Blätter für deutsche und internationale Politik,* 2 (1986), 184–201.
[72] Rohrmoser, *Das Debakel;* see further Wirsching, *Abschied vom Provisorium,* 55.
[73] For a similar focus, see Oberreuther, 'The CDU and Social Change', 6–7; Grafe, *Schwarze Visionen,* 46.

non-European immigrants, and for banning HIV-positive applicants from entering the civil service.[74] Despite this, and even though Gauweiler also participated in commemorations of the centre-right's 1968 in this period, it was not his hard-line stance that came to be understood as rooted in 1968. Instead, in line with the narrative of 1968 as 'cultural revolution' that was taking shape at this time, it was the socially reformist profile of those who populated the CDU's apparatus that journalists and public intellectuals viewed as owing the most to 1968.

Since the late 1960s, some of the other '68ers had indeed shown a keen and enduring interest in understanding social and cultural change in an effort to stay politically relevant. In the 1970s, social scientists had begun to capture and analyse a widespread shift in individual and collective attitudes across western societies, a shift away from 'materialist' to 'postmaterial' values, such as self-realization, personal autonomy, and quality of life. Most famously, the American sociologist Ronald Inglehart had postulated that modern industrial societies had undergone a 'silent revolution' since the 1960s. The other '68ers around Geißler and the Secretary General himself paid close attention to these diagnoses.

Changing gender roles and growing demands for women's emancipation were especially visible signs of this transformation, according to Inglehart.[75] This had major political consequences, not least for the Christian Democrats in the Federal Republic. While women had been a reliable voting bloc for the Christian Democrats throughout the entire postwar era, their preferences had changed in the 1970s. In the national elections held between 1972 and 1980, women—especially younger women—had leaned toward the Social Democrats whose reformist profile better accommodated their rising demands and emancipatory spirit. In the words of Wulf Schönbohm: 'Those are warning signs that a large catch-all party cannot overlook.'[76] The CDU apparatus sought to adjust the party's profile accordingly.

The party had already begun to engage with the 'woman question' in its 1978 basic program, which had posited that women should be able to choose between focusing on their family or professional lives.[77] At the same time, however, it had argued that children needed their mothers as their sole caregivers in the first years of life—a normative take on parenting that was difficult to square with supporting women's professional development. However, by the mid-1980s, the party sang a far more progressive tune. In March 1985, the CDU even made women's issues the central theme of its annual party convention—its biggest up to that

---

[74] Peter Gauweiler, *AIDS: Die Zeit drängt* (Munich, 1985); 'Jetzt muaß i allmählich bremsen', *Der Spiegel*, 22 (25 May 1987), 21–4; also Herzog, *Sex after Fascism*, 252.

[75] Inglehart, *The Silent Revolution*; the book was published in German as *Die Stille Revolution* (1979).

[76] Wulf Schönbohm, 'Wie die Essener Leitsätze entstanden sind und was sie bewirkt haben', in Heiner Geißler (ed.), *Abschied von der Männergesellschaft* (Berlin, 1986), 178–89, here 180; also Biebricher, *Geistig-moralische Wende*, 189–90.

[77] CDU Grundsatzprogramm 'Freiheit, Solidarität, Gerechtigkeit' (1978).

point—held under the heading 'For a New Partnership Between the Sexes'. In addition to the roughly 800 delegates who attended this gathering, chief organizer Radunski and his staff had invited 500 women from different sectors to debate a wide variety of issues facing contemporary West German women.

Radunski had invented this new format, one he termed 'party conference of dialogue', which was designed to showcase the CDU's participatory spirit, new culture of debate, and all-round vitality and modernity.[78] No fewer than 1,200 journalists covered the convention, which was held in Essen that year, and all major television channels reported extensively on the Christian Democratic discussions in their evening programs.[79] The delegates debated and ultimately agreed on a set of guidelines for future party policy on women's issues that dealt with topics as diverse as women's professional lives, marriage and family, issues facing single women, sexist depictions in the media and advertising, and combating violence against women.[80] On the eve of the convention, Geißler even participated in a televised discussion with the well-known feminist Alice Schwarzer. Although critical of the Secretary General, she acknowledged that the Christian Democrats had come a long way.[81] Left-wing journalists Peter J. Grafe noted how much strategic effort it had taken the party apparatchiks to cultivate and project this new progressivism: 'A party conference, choreographed in such a way that the male delegates listened to the women instead of playing Skat in the bar, conveys the impression of a professional entity in the Adenauer Haus. These are fruits of ten years' labour', he concluded.[82]

These efforts did not end there. The following year, Geißler published an edited collection with contributions from many of the convention's leading female participants under the title *Farewell to the Male-dominated Society*. The volume threw a bone to conservative readers in that it opened with a chapter examining the 'dark side' of women's emancipation: children allegedly neglected by their working mothers.[83] However, most of the contributions had a progressive bent. Süßmuth, for one, surveyed the important role that fathers had to play in child-rearing. In an early foreshadowing of 'black-green' rapprochement, the book also

---

[78] Grafe, *Schwarze Visionen*, 54. The first such 'party conference of dialogue' had taken place in 1981 and dealt with youth. As with the women invitees in 1985, Radunski invited 500 young people as participants. See the transcript of the proceedings: CDU, 'Mit der Jugend: Unser Land braucht einen neuen Anfang', 2–5 November 1981, available at https://www.kas.de/c/document_library/get_file? uuid=56c81f98-a709-a9ed-40f8-7a12e8ff74c4&groupId=252038 (accessed on 11 October 2019).

[79] Peter Radunski, 'Der CDU-Frauenparteitag als Modell der politischen Willensbildung', in Geißler, *Abschied von der Männergesellschaft*, 170–7, here 173.

[80] 'Leitsätze der CDU für eine neue Partnerschaft zwischen Mann und Frau', printed in Geißler, *Abschied von der Männergesellschaft*, 191–214.

[81] Bösch, *Macht und Machtverlust*, 250; Bernhard Gotto, *Enttäuschung in der Demokratie* (Berlin and Boston, 2018), 184–5.

[82] Grafe, *Schwarze Visionen*, 69.

[83] Elisabeth Motschmann, 'Die Schattenseiten der Emanzipation: Kinder ohne Mutter', in Geißler, *Abschied von der Männergesellschaft*, 21–32.

included a chapter by two left-wing social scientists with close ties to the Green Party, who called for a new culture of motherhood that was compatible with women's professional lives.[84]

Schönbohm's own contribution was among the most interesting ones, combining, as it did, analysis of women's changing political attitudes with personal observations about the work of the party commission that had prepared the 1985 convention. The former RCDS national chair confessed that leading a commission staffed with both men and women had been a novel experience, despite his prior programmatic work. He had read a lot about women's issues in preparation, Schönbohm explained, but had only begun to truly understand the obstacles women faced in their daily lives when listening to the stories of the women present. In what read like a deliberate nod to the feminist practice of consciousness raising, he noted that this was a 'learning process that did not pass me by without trace, but rather led me to question my own opinions and ways of behaving'. As a result, he no longer automatically delegated problems at home or at his children's school to his wife, he claimed. '[W]hat had seemed obvious became less than self-evident. I became similarly allergic to lord-of-the-manor affectations, as I had earlier to excessive women's libber rhetoric.'[85]

Left-wing commentators often mocked this Christian Democratic feminist makeover. Writing in Der Spiegel, Cora Stephan, a journalist (then) on the Left, attributed the shift to naked electoral calculations and noted wryly 'Women's liberation stops for no one—not even for the CDU'.[86] A cartoon that showed Chancellor Kohl donning an ill-fitting bra over his suit accompanied her acerbic review of Geißler's book.

Conservative critics, on the other hand, were outraged by what they saw as a genuine display of social progressivism. The conservative journal Criticón, for instance, scolded the CDU for its 'brutal adoption of radical feminist demands, which neither friend nor foe had thought was possible'.[87] Many rank-and-file

[84] Gisela Anna Erler and Monika Jaeckel, 'Die Grenzen der Partnerschaft—von der Notwendigkeit einer Frauenkultur', in Geißler, Abschied von der Männergesellschaft, 56–66. Erler was a member of the Green Party and, like Jaeckel, one of the signatories to a Green 'mother manifesto' published in 1987—deemed 'revisionist' by its left-wing critics who argued that, by calling on the Greens to speak for mothers, it advocated a conception of women that the women's liberation movement had long fought to overcome. See Dorothee Pass-Weingartz and Gisela Erler (eds.), Mütter an die Macht: Die neue Frauen-Bewegung (Hamburg, 1989). Former SDS activist Erler is married to other '68er Warnfried Dettling.

[85] Schönbohm, 'Wie die Essener Leitsätze entstanden sind', 181–2. These self-reflections in the mid-1980s did not stop Schönbohm from recalling in the 2008 interview for this book that, around 1968, he had been repelled by the 'hysterical broads [...] [who] were the worst, these fanatic ones'. Schönbohm interview. See further Chapter 3.

[86] Cora Stephan, 'Die Männer müssen Defizite abbauen', Der Spiegel, 27 (30 June 1986), 80. Stephan later became something of a renegade. On these feminist reactions see further Gotto, Enttäuschung in der Demokratie, 184.

[87] Cited in Schönbohm, 'Wie die Essener Leitsätze entstanden sind', 187. That Schönbohm included the quote in his chapter nevertheless highlights that these were carefully calculated 'transgressions', done both to project a progressive image publicly and to push the party forward internally.

members were also sceptical. Instead of a change in societal values to which the party had to adapt to remain electable, they detected a dangerous erosion of values, values Christian Democrats should have been upholding. The socially liberal course pushed by the other '68ers in Geißler's orbit may have been central to the party's public image and strategy in the mid-1980s, but it always remained quite controversial. Throughout the 1980s, the other '68ers, who pushed it, competed with far more traditionalist factions within the party, who viewed their modernizing impulses with great suspicion.[88]

Commemorating 1968

For much of the 1980s, commemorations of 1968 played a key role in promoting the other '68ers' distinctive political program of social liberalism on the one hand and a strong anti-left affect on the other. As we saw at the beginning of this book, it was in the late 1980s that former centre-right student activists most emphatic-ally invoked 1968 and claimed that they were different kinds of '68ers. In doing so, they were spurred on by left-wing journalists and intellectuals of the same age— notably Grafe and Leggewie—who were endlessly fascinated by their Christian Democratic counterparts now in power in Bonn and who published frequently on their endeavours.[89] The number of articles written about the other '68ers by journalist Werner A. Perger, who was a political correspondent in Bonn for a number of major left-wing papers at the time, was also quite remarkable.[90] This abundance of coverage highlights the role that members of the press played in facilitating the 'generationalizing' of centre-right experiences in this period. As a result, the other '68ers were ubiquitous by the time the twentieth anniversary of the student movement came around in 1988—so much so that the left-leaning *Frankfurter Rundschau*, in an ironic nod to Bertolt Brecht's Arturo Ui, expressed astonishment at their 'irresistible rise'.[91]

The most vocal among the other '68ers emerged as true memory entrepreneurs, who, by virtue of their social and political position, had access to television and

---

[88] Oberreuter, 'The CDU and Social Change', 12; Biebricher, *Geistig-moralische Wende*, 190.

[89] Grafe, *Schwarze Visionen*; Leggewie, *Der Geist steht rechts*, 116.

[90] Werner A. Perger, 'Die Linke, der Zeitgeist und das Krokodil', *Deutsches Allgemeines Sonntagsblatt* (30 November 1986); 'Wir 68er waren alle ganz anders', interview with Tilman Fichter and Wulf Schönbohm, conducted by Werner A. Perger, *Deutsches Allgemeines Sonntagsblatt* (10 April 1988). Perger (b. 1942), who originally hailed from Austria, was on the Left, but he often attended a small salon that Teltschik hosted in Bonn. He wrote for the *Deutsches Allgemeines Sonntagsblatt* and, later, for *Die Zeit*. In 1988, Perger also made a television documentary about the other '68ers. Heinz Hemming/Werner A. Perger, *Die anderen 68er: Dutschkes Gegenspieler und was aus ihnen wurde*, Dokumentation, BRD 1988, 43', first shown on ZDF, 4 August 1988, 10.15 p.m.; Teltschik interview; conversation with Werner A. Perger, Berlin (16 June 2011).

[91] Helmut Lölhöffel, 'Unaufhaltsamer Aufstieg der Alternativ-68er', *Frankfurter Rundschau* (17 May 1988).

print media, gave numerous interviews about their experiences, and seemed determined to shape public narratives about 1968 and its legacies.[92] Schönbohm, whom *Die Zeit* termed 'the Lenin of the CDU', gave numerous interviews around this time. In the weekly's multi-page spread on the '68ers of the CDU', he appropriated an old SDS slogan to suggest that he and his centre-right student peers had represented the 'true radical minority' in the late 1960s.[93]

As this direct appropriation and self-fashioning suggests, this memory work was closely intertwined with left-wing commemorations of the student movement, which had begun in the late 1970s and intensified in the mid-1980s. In November 1986, former left-wing activists organized the so-called 'Prima-Klima-Congress' in Frankfurt. The convention brought together several thousand erstwhile members of the extraparliamentary opposition to reminisce about their pasts and debate the state of left-wing politics in the era of Kohl, Reagan, and Margaret Thatcher.[94] The gathering of the other '68ers held in Bonn in May 1988 was a direct reaction to this upsurge in left-wing remembrances and organized reunions.[95] As such, it underlines the relational character of the memory work of Left and Right, which is often lost in accounts that focus exclusively on left-wing narratives and commemorations. Just as student activism of the Left and Right was closely intertwined in the late 1960s, so the very notion that 1968 had shaped a political generation—the '68ers—encompassed activists from different parts of the political spectrum from its inception.

Jürgen Rosorius, who, in 1967, had spearheaded the Bonn campaign to make the contraceptive pill available to unmarried students, initiated the other 68ers' Bonn reunion.[96] Schönbohm, Radunski, and Teltschik spoke at the event, and many of the other activists who have featured prominently in this book attended: Meinhard Ade, Ignaz Bender, Jürgen Aretz, Gerd Langguth, Wighard Härdtl, Klaus Laepple, Peter Gauweiler, Wolfgang Bergsdorf, Wolfgang Reeder, Warnfried Dettling, and Friedbert Pflüger were there.[97] The tone at this overwhelmingly male gathering was triumphant and celebratory. Teltschik expressed particular pride in his foresight in the realm of foreign policy. In the late 1960s, he and his centre-right student peers had 'already thought [. . .] what today is

---

[92] On the 'memory entrepreneurs' of the Left, see Behre, *Bewegte Erinnerung*, 369.

[93] 'Die 68er der CDU', *Zeit-Magazin*, 33 (12 August 1988), 10.

[94] Behre, *Bewegte Erinnerung*, 216–18; Albrecht von Lucke, *68 oder neues Biedermeier: Der Kampf um die Deutungsmacht* (Berlin, 2008), 34. Schönbohm was among the most vocal of these memory entrepreneurs. He has continued to publish on 1968 on the occasion of every major anniversary of the revolt since. See e.g. Wulf Schönbohm, 'Die 68er: Politische Verirrungen und gesellschaftliche Veränderungen', *Aus Politik und Zeitgeschichte* (2008), B 14–15, 16–30.

[95] Schönbohm, for one, had closely observed the Prima Klima Congress. See Wulf Schönbohm, 'Von den Bannerträgern zu den Klageweibern des Fortschritts', *Frankfurter Rundschau* (11 November 1986). On the May 1988 event also von der Goltz, 'Eine Gegen-Generation von, 1968'?

[96] '"Klassentreffen" einmal anders', *RCDS Magazin*, no. 5 (1988), 8–10. See further 126–28.

[97] Lölhöffel, 'Unaufhaltsamer Aufstieg der Alternativ-68er'; AdsD, Jupp Darchinger photographic collection.

common knowledge in the Union: you have to recognize the reality of the GDR and not do what Kiesinger did and pretend it is a mere phenomenon'.[98] Their stance should command respect, he told his peers. 'We did good work then and can be satisfied with what came of it.'[99]

The lone dissenting voice on the day was that of 'renegade' Jürgen-Bernd Runge (not yet exposed as an informal collaborator of the Stasi), whom Schönbohm had invited for old times' sake despite strong protestations from other attendees who resented his leftward turn.[100] Rather than backslapping the other '68ers for their accomplishments, Runge confessed that he felt partially responsible for the right-wing assassination attempt on Dutschke in April 1968. RCDS agitation had fed into media stories demonizing the SDS activist, he suggested. Other attendees objected vehemently to this assertion. Gauweiler, for one, countered bitterly that the Left had first broken the state's monopoly on violence and was therefore solely to blame for the consequences.[101]

The 1988 reunion was even more strongly male-dominated than centre-right activism around 1968 itself. Maria-Theresia van Schewick, the former deputy national chair of RCDS, was one of only two women present.[102] Nor did women activists feature much in the media coverage. It focused on the experiences of the famous men, who told deeply masculinist 'veterans'' stories of agency and conquest about how they had done 'battle' with the Left on campus, 'resisted' and 'held out' against great odds.[103] In a nod to Ernst Jünger's famous front novel, one participant, former West Berlin activist Christian Hacke, then professor of political science in Bonn, even went as far as describing 1968 as his personal 'storm-of-steel-experience'.[104] Such martial depictions of the political struggle inside the universities helped to cast the other '68ers as heroic resisters against a left-wing insurgency. The 'alternative '68ers'—as the other '68ers preferred to call

---

[98] Teltschik, cited in Rüdiger Durth, 'Ein wenig Nostalgie bei den 68ern der CDU', Bonner Rundschau (16 May 1988).

[99] Sabine Etzold, 'Reformtrompete tapfer geblasen', Kölner Stadt-Anzeiger (16 May 1988).

[100] Härdtl interview; Runge interview.

[101] Runge and Gauweiler cited in Sabine Etzold, 'Reformtrompete tapfer geblasen', Kölner Stadt-Anzeiger (16 May 1988); also Heiko Gebhardt, 'Wir waren Demokraten', Stern (19 May 1988).

[102] Gebhardt, 'Wir waren Demokraten'. The official photograph taken by Jupp Darchinger on the day showed only one woman. Such overwhelming male dominance was also a feature of other commemorative gatherings like this. In 1998, for instance, former RCDS national chair Hans Reckers invited 55 former student activists to a similar gathering. Only six of the invitees were women. Hans Reckers Private Papers, Einladungsliste der Konrad Adenauer Stiftung, Bereich Forschung und Beratung, 30 Jahre '1968': Grundsatzauseinandersetzung heute, 17–18 October 1998; such 'veterans' meetings' continued into the 2000s. See Jürgen Rosorius Private Papers, Invitation from Jürgen Rosorius to a meeting held from 12–14 March 2004 in Königswinter addressed to the 'Dear 68ers'.

[103] Schönbohm Private Papers, 'Die alternativen "68er" – was bleibt von der APO-Zeit?', MS (15 May 1988). Such masculinist tales are typical features of generational narratives. George et al., 'AHR Conversation: Each Generation Writes Its Own History of Generations'; see further von der Goltz, 'Von alten Kämpfern'.

[104] '"Klassentreffen' einmal anders, RCDS Magazin, 5 (1988), 8–10; Ernst Jünger, Storm of Steel (London, 1929).

themselves on this occasion—had been 'warriors against the radical Left', the invitation letter noted.[105]

Such combat stories were not the only narratives advanced that day, however. In his keynote speech, Schönbohm unabashedly embraced the idea that 1968 had set in motion a 'cultural revolution'. This story of social liberalization and cultural democratization had begun to dominate popular and scholarly narratives about 1968 in the 1980s.[106] It was what Habermas had meant two months earlier when he had spoken of the 'fundamental liberalization' of West German society since 1968. The former RCDS chair explained that activists from across the political spectrum had agreed at the time that the 'dreadful social paralysis of the end of the 1960s had to come to an end. That through commitment it was possible to change something.'[107] The student movement had been like a surge of adrenaline to the whole of society, he asserted. In an interview he had given a month before the Bonn event, he had also conceded that 1968 had brought major benefits: 'Without a doubt this onslaught, perhaps unconsciously, cracked ways of thinking and certain mentalities, which brought fresh air into society and with it a positive effect to this day.'[108]

Schönbohm did not stop at appropriating the 'cultural revolution'; he also suggested that his side were the victors. While they were now 'well-established', their former opponents were in crisis, he asserted, out of power in Bonn and overtaken by the Zeitgeist.[109] 'From the perspective of power politics, we accomplished more of our ideas of reform from that time than they did of their revolutionary ones.'[110] The retroactive separation of culture from politics that was at the heart of the paradigm of 'cultural revolution'—and that is often criticized by scholars who rightly stress that 1968 had been about broadening the very definition of the political—helped him to claim victory.[111] After all, centre-right activists had always embraced a narrower and more traditionalist definition of politics. For them, it was about organization, posts, and, above all, about power—and, seen from the vantage point of the 1980s, it was clear that they had won in this realm.

All of this was no doubt motivated, at least in part, by a desire to outdo their political opponents, whose superior public profile they had often envied twenty years earlier. By the late 1980s, "68er' had become a public designation with

---

[105] *Jürgen Rosorius Private Papers*, Invitation Letter, 'Die alternativen '68er: Was blieb von der APO Zeit?'.

[106] Behre, *Bewegte Erinnerung*; Ross, *May '68 and its Afterlives*.

[107] *Schönbohm Private Papers*, 'Die alternativen "68er" – was bleibt von der APO-Zeit?', MS (15 May 1988); 'Die 68er der CDU', *Zeit Magazin*, 33 (12 August 1988), 10.

[108] 'Wir 68er waren alle ganz anders', Interview with Tilman Fichter and Wulf Schönbohm, conducted by Werner A. Perger, *Deutsches Allgemeines Sonntagsblatt* (10 April 1988).

[109] *Schönbohm Private Papers*, 'Die alternativen "68er" – was bleibt von der APO-Zeit?', MS (15 May 1988).

[110] 'Wir 68er waren alle ganz anders'.   [111] Behre, *Bewegte Erinnerung*, 364–5.

immense symbolic capital—a kind of 'alternative aristocratic title', as Silja Behre has aptly put it.[112] Understandably, the other '68ers, who had often felt marginalized around 1968, wanted in on this.

However, contrary to what some of their critics claimed at the time or with hindsight, the stories they told in 1988 were neither total inventions of tradition nor just a cheap publicity stunt.[113] As we have seen throughout this book, they had concrete experiences of student activism and encounters with the Left that provided the experiential basis for their generational claims. The stories the other '68ers told, be it that of having contributed to the liberalization of the Federal Republic by modernizing Christian Democracy or of having waged a 'resistance' struggle against radical leftists, though highly selective, were always tied to actual encounters and experiences around 1968. Over the course of the 1960s and 1970s, they had acquired enough of these to tell varied stories, different elements of which they could choose to accentuate depending on political expediency. In the late 1980s, it was particularly advantageous for the party apparatchiks to emphasize the extent to which they had shared the desire for cultural democratization that had found expression in the revolt of the late 1960s. Of course, this meant glossing over the fact that these self-declared Christian Democratic liberal reformers had contributed much to the febrile climate and polarization of the 1970s by stoking public hysteria about left-wing violence.

These competing generational self-projections served a number of different political purposes in the present, just as particular outside pressures shaped them. For the Left, in a period of right-wing political hegemony and fears about 'spiritual-moral change', interpreting the 'cultural revolution' as a generational achievement offered one way of renewing one's sense of political purpose. Meanwhile, former activists of the centre-right insisted that they had been the true champions of liberalization and defended West German democracy against left-wing extremists.

Activists from each side were thus writing themselves into the narrative of the Federal Republic's 'success' that was taking shape in the 1980s. This was the decade in which the West German state abandoned its sense of itself as provisional and scholars began to write official histories of the Federal Republic.[114] The

---

[112] Behre, *Bewegte Erinnerung*, 158.

[113] E. g. 'Freche Umdeutung', *epd (Evangelischer Pressdienst) Kirche und Rundfunk*, no. 63 (10 August 1988); von Lucke, *68 oder neues Biedermeier*, 37.

[114] Between 1981 and 1987, the five-volume official history of the Federal Republic appeared, for instance, and museums began to exhibit this history. Eberhard Jäckel, Karl Dietrich Bracher, and Theodor Eschenburg (eds.), *Geschichte der Bundesrepublik Deutschland* 5 vols (Leipzig, 1992); see further Wirsching, *Abschied vom Provisorium*, 11; Andreas Rödder, *Die Bundesrepublik Deutschland 1969–1989* (Munich, 2004), 94; Biess and Eckert, 'Why Do We Need New Narratives'. Emphasizing the success of the generational collective is a classic feature of generational storytelling. Thomas Ahbe and Rainer Gries, 'Gesellschaftsgeschichte als Generationengeschichte: Theoretische und methodische Überlegungen', in *Die DDR aus generationengeschichtlicher Perspektive: Eine Inventur*, edited by Annegret Schüle, Thomas Ahbe, and Rainer Gries (Leipzig, 2006), 485.

'cultural revolution' paradigm made it possible to integrate 1968—a major moment of political contestation that actually involved questioning what kind of democracy West Germany had become—into this story. In the late 1980s, the '68ers of the Left and Right agreed that 1968 had been an important caesura on a par with 1945 or 1949, but they disagreed exactly over how these years had helped to democratize West German society, with each side stressing its own heroic agency.

Moreover, commemorating 1968 in 1988 allowed the other '68ers to position themselves forcefully within a debate over strategy that had been raging among Christian Democrats since the disappointing results in the national elections held the previous year. In January 1987, the CDU/CSU lost 4.5 per cent of its national vote share compared to 1983. The Christian Democrats also lost votes in many state elections held the same year, sparking an intense internal debate over the party's future course. Geißler advocated shifting even more explicitly to the centre on social issues; conservatives within the party, on the other hand, blamed his centrist course and called for a move to the right instead.[115]

The years around 1968 featured prominently in these debates about whether future Christian Democratic voters were to be found on the right or in the centre; the date was often treated as a synonym for changing societal values. To conservatives within and beyond the party, the spirit of 1968 simply had to be purged from West German society to restore order and morality. As Bruno Heck, who had been Secretary General of the CDU in the late 1960s, put it in memorably polemical terms: 'The rebellion of 1968 had destroyed more values than the era of National Socialism. [...] To overcome it is therefore more important than overcoming Hitler a second time.'[116]

By embracing 1968 and projecting themselves as 'alternative '68ers', these former student activists offered a competing reading of what these years meant to Christian Democrats. When Hacke described 1968 as his 'storm of steel', for instance, he was not just fashioning himself as a Christian Democratic warrior at the campus 'front'. He was no doubt also invoking Kohl's infamous meeting with Ernst Jünger on the occasion of the controversial author's ninetieth birthday in 1985—a meeting widely interpreted at the time as pandering to conservatives within and outside the party who were growing restive in the absence of true 'spiritual-moral change'.[117] By pointing toward 1968 as a character-defining

---

[115] Hemmelmann, Der Kompass der CDU, 154. Advocates of a shift to the right argued that the party's new centrism would lead to the emergence of a right-wing alternative party, a fear that was not wholly unwarranted. 1989 would mark the electoral breakthrough of Die Republikaner at the European and state level. Bavarian Christian Democrats disillusioned with the Kohl government's caving in on Ostpolitik and lack of a real Wende had founded this right-wing party in 1983.

[116] Hermann Ludolf, 'Hitler, Bonn und die Wende: Wie die Bundesrepublik ihre Lebenskraft zurück gewinnen kann', Die Politische Meinung, 28, 209 (1983), 13–28; see also 'Wäre ich Deutscher, würde ich schreien', Der Spiegel, 2 (5 January 1987).

[117] Biebricher, Geistig-moralische Wende, 150.

moment, Hacke implied that the modern CDU had been shaped by a different set of battles than those fought by older conservatives whose reference points were the Weimar era and the immediate postwar. Schönbohm's keynote made a similar point. Rather than an external force to be combatted, the modernizing and liberalizing impulses of 1968 had become part of the party's own genetic code, he suggested. The party could not win by turning back the clock; rather, it had to fully embrace the changing times.[118]

That many of those who spoke at the May 1988 event in Bonn were influential representatives of the CDU's liberal wing goes a long way toward explaining why the West German media covered the proceedings so comprehensively and why there was even a television documentary about the other '68ers that aired a few months later. Besides taking well-known figures like Radunski and Teltschik back to their former haunts at the Free University to show how they had experienced the 1960s, the film—directed by Heinz Hemming and Werner A. Perger—dealt in considerable detail with the political impact they had had since. It included an interview with Geißler in which he connected his own political project of a more socially liberal CDU directly to the biographies of these student activists. The 'political and intellectual renewal of the CDU would have been unthinkable without the '68er generation', he stated on camera.[119] The film also featured a short interview with Kohl, in which he praised the other '68ers for having carried fresh ideas into the CDU. Given that the two leading figures of the governing party appeared in this film, it is no surprise that journalists in the capital read this generational portrait correctly as part and parcel of a debate over Christian Democratic strategy.[120]

Things came to a head a little over a year after the Bonn reunion. In September 1989, in an effort to push through his socially liberal course, Geißler, whose personal relationship with Kohl had become increasingly contentious over the years, attempted a 'coup' against the party leader at the CDU's annual convention in Bremen. However, the Secretary General failed to mobilize the necessary support for his plan to replace Kohl as party leader with Lothar Späth, the politically moderate Governor of Baden-Württemberg. His plot failed, and the Chancellor sacked Geißler instead. Geißler confidants such as

---

[118] For a similar argument to Schönbohm's, see Ulf Fink, '1968—Die Antwort der CDU: Programmpartei', *Aus Politik und Zeitgeschichte* B 20 (1988), 27–35. Fink was a liberal West Berlin Christian Democrat who had worked for Geißler and von Weizsäcker.

[119] Geißler, quoted in Stephan Richter, 'Was die "anderen 68er" heute machen', *Flensburger Tageblatt* (2 August 1988); Heinz Hemming/Werner A. Perger, *Die anderen 68er: Dutschkes Gegenspieler und was aus ihnen wurde*, Dokumentation, BRD 1988, 43', first shown on ZDF, 4 August 1988, 10.15 p.m.

[120] See e. g. Jürgen Wahl, 'Impressionen von einer Revolution in verträglicher Dosis', *Christ und Welt/Rheinischer Merkur* (20 May 1988).

Schönbohm were then purged en masse from the party headquarters.[121] Others, like Radunski and Teltschik left the Chancellor's side of their own accord over the next two years.

In 1991, Schönbohm summed up the effects of the purge thus: 'We have only Helmut Kohl left. The party doesn't play a role any more. That is dangerous.'[122] A notable anti-programmatic turn indeed followed in the 1990s. Rescued politically by unification, Kohl was able to remain in post until 1998, but he did so while presiding over a far less influential and vibrant party apparatus. 'Lethargy, blind faith in the Chancellor, and an internal lack of ideas' was how one recent study characterized the CDU in this period.[123]

In the 1990s, some of the most prominent other '68ers, who had done so much to shape the early Kohl era, were scathing about the Chancellor's leadership and the turn the party had taken since their ouster. Schönbohm chose a rather unusual format to vent his frustrations. He published a novel, later also turned into a television film, that offered a deeply unflattering portrayal of a certain ruthless Chancellor 'Klumper'. The thinly veiled plot was based on the inner workings of the party apparatus in the run up to the attempted coup against Kohl. Schönbohm modelled the protagonists directly on Geißler, Radunski, and himself: he turned Geißler into the unnamed conservative party's executive director Hermann Rais. Like Geißler, 'Rais' was a slim man with ascetic features, olive skin, and a strong nose. Radunski was immortalized as one Gerhard Leister, the party's visionary communication director, whose job was made near-impossible by the Chancellor's ignorance of modern media and visual communication. Like the former student activist, Leister believed in American-style campaigns and the power of emotions in politics, which had earned him the nickname 'Emo-Jerry'. The novel's main character and tragic hero was a smart, bearded political scientist called Wolfgang Klaasen, who ran the political department of the unnamed government party. Like Schönbohm, Klaasen had studied in West Berlin and was known as a leftie within the party. He thus not only looked like the book's author, he also held the same job and had a near-identical political profile.[124] Rarely has the desire to cast oneself as the star in one's own story—a standard feature of generational narratives—been expressed in purer form.

Warnfried Dettling chose a more traditional venue for his critique. In 1994, he published a non-fiction book on Kohl's legacy that lamented the anti-theoretical turn the party had taken since the 1980s. Kohl had paved his path to power as a

---

[121] 'Säuberungswelle', Der Spiegel, 43 (23 October 1989). Kohl had already toyed with the idea to sack Geißler for a while. See 'Wird Geißler kaltgestellt?', Der Spiegel, 27 (3 July 1989).

[122] Cited in Werner A. Perger, 'Ein diskreter Beobachter', Die Zeit (22 February 1991).

[123] Hemmelmann, Der Kompass der CDU, 155; Biebricher, Geistig-moralische Wende, 151–2.

[124] Wulf Schönbohm, Parteifreunde (Düsseldorf, 1990), 8–9 and 31–2; the book was used as the basis for a 1993 film called Stunde der Füchse, which was aired during prime time on Germany's first television channel ARD on 22 December 1993. Stunde der Füchse, dir. Detlef Rönfeldt (1993); see also the review by Werner A. Perger, 'Zeit der Füchse', Die Zeit, 50 (10 December 1993).

spirited party reformer but had decided to govern in the spirit of Adenauer's slogan 'No experiments', the former Freiburg student activist asserted.[125] No other postwar Chancellor had been less ambitious intellectually, Dettling charged; the party had become paralysed under Kohl's leadership.[126] The former student activist contended that Kohl had aborted the party's modernization—a project that had been principally driven by the other '68ers in Dettling's telling. Kohl had therefore sold out the very generation that had helped to put him in power in the first place, he suggested.

> As long as Helmut Kohl remains in office and in everyone's good graces, the future of the reformers in the CDU is behind them [...] Helmut Kohl consumed not just one—his—generation of the CDU, but also the next one. The Class of 1955 onwards will accomplish the rebuilding of the CDU—or they won't. All that the reformers from that era, (who are getting long in the tooth) can still do is keep the memory and hope for another type of CDU alive.[127]

Its grandiosity aside, Dettling's analysis was prescient in many ways. For one, it correctly predicted that the next party leader with a decidedly reformist and centrist bent would be significantly younger than his own student peers. In fact, the former student activist's projection was off by just one year. Angela Merkel, who, as party leader in the 2000s, oversaw a programmatic and organizational overhaul of the CDU comparable to the reform process the party had undergone in the 1970s, was born in 1954.[128] Moreover, Dettling's analysis correctly identified one of the main reasons why the other '68ers never rose to the top of the party. Ultimately, Kohl's personal leadership style, which meant that proximity to the Chancellor was the most important political currency in Christian Democratic politics, was their undoing once he ceased to see their social liberalism and modernizing project as political assets. Ultimately, their proclamations of political victory in 1988 thus turned out to be short-lived.

Mescalero Returns

Situating the commemorations of the late 1980s in context—both in terms of who the leading voices were at the time and what outside pressures shaped how they narrated their activist past—helps to explain why centre-right commemorations of 1968 in the 1990s and early 2000s often sounded very different.[129] Not only had

---

[125] Dettling, *Das Erbe Kohls*, 29–32.   [126] Dettling, *Das Erbe Kohls*, 47–57.
[127] Dettling, *Das Erbe Kohls*, 132–3.   [128] Hemmelmann, *Der Kompass der CDU*, 157.
[129] This shift has occasionally been noted, but not fully explained. See e.g. Lucke, *68 oder neues Biedermeier*, 40.

many of the other '68ers left the national stage; the larger political context also made the kind of triumphalism that had been on display in 1988 more difficult. The collapse of state socialist regimes in 1989 and the reunification of the two German states in 1990 were of course developments that the centre-right welcomed. However, the loss of the spectre of communism next door also deprived Christian Democrats of one of the most important sources of their political identity, namely anti-communism. In addition, the Greens, which Christian Democrats had increasingly defined themselves against in the 1980s, lost their representation in the Bundestag in the December 1990 elections after receiving less than 5 per cent of the national vote share. In the early 1990s, the spectre of 1968 radicalism increasingly had to fill the void left by the disappearance of two of the Christian Democrats' favourite foes.[130]

Even Schönbohm, who had embraced a largely positive reading of 1968 as 'cultural revolution' in 1988, changed his tune after his ouster. Remembering the emancipatory aspects of the student movement no longer served the purpose of shoring up his own modernizing credentials within the CDU. Moreover, any largesse that he might have felt toward his opponents had probably dissipated after his demotion. Nor was 1968 still as useful, in the far more politically challenging post-unification era, to highlight the democratic achievements and stability of the old Federal Republic.

On the occasion of the revolt's twenty-fifth anniversary in 1993, therefore, Schönbohm portrayed himself as an unequivocal opponent of the '68ers. 'The dogmatism of the Left, their faux-revolutionary behaviour and their pushy sense of mission turned me against them', he recounted in an article for a major conservative daily.[131] In some ways, he was as triumphalist as he had been in the late 1980s. But, instead of celebrating their modernization of the CDU, he now insisted that it had been the other '68ers' focus on German division and East German repression that had landed them on the right side of history—before history ended in 1989. 'I experienced with joyful satisfaction the collapse of totalitarian communism in Eastern Europe, in the Soviet Union, and finally in the GDR, and with it all illusions the new and old Left held about really existing socialism.' He and his centre-right peers had constantly clashed with the Left on these issues, the former RCDS national chair recalled. 'And we who argued against equating the Soviet Union with the USA, against pacifism,

---

[130] Lau, *Die letzte Volkspartei*, 196; Biebricher, *Geistig-moralische Wende*, 153–4. Biebricher calls the CDU's 1994 'red-sock campaign', which summoned the spectre of a red-red-green coalition, the party's 'last anti-communist fireworks' after the end of the Cold War. Tellingly, it was conceived and executed by a former centre-right student activist of the 1970s, the CDU's new Secretary General Peter Hintze.

[131] Wulf Schönbohm, 'Hier linke Spinner, dort Faschisten', *Christ und Welt/Rheinischer Merkur* (16 April 1993).

and advocated for NATO and the German military; we were right. That felt good.'[132]

Schönbohm was far from the only one who attacked the left-wing '68ers around the time of the twenty-fifth anniversary. Such attacks often still built on the basic premises of the 'cultural revolution' paradigm but now viewed it as a negative stigma.[133] In the wake of several high-profile instances of anti-immigrant violence in towns such as Hoyerswerda, Rostock, and Mölln, and in the midst of a moral panic about an overly hedonistic youth, the social and cultural changes 1968 had wrought had lost much of their positive connotation—even for some on the Left. More often than not, 1968 was now equated with the destruction of values, the decline of social morality, and the loss of respect for authority.[134]

One of the greatest broadsides around this time came from Christian Democratic Minister of the Interior Wolfgang Schäuble. In a *Bundestag* speech of 10 December 1992, Schäuble argued that it was time to finally overcome the legacies of 1968, linking the revolt directly to the brutal anti-immigrant violence that had rocked the country since the previous year:

> Perhaps we should add to this list of causes the fact that we have not yet adequately processed the upheaval of the 1960s. [...] [T]he incision ran deep. [...] Perhaps, in truth, the dismantling of [...] values succeeded, but the construction of new values to take their place has not yet happened. Perhaps we lost too much of an authority, perhaps young people need an authoritative figure, a guiding principle. [W]e allowed too many developments to occur through which all taboos were consciously broken. Now we are dealing with the fact that even the last taboo, the condemnation of Nazi barbarism, is being openly dismantled. He who allows all taboos to be damaged, will not be able to stop himself at the last.[135]

Schäuble (b. 1942), who, by this point, had emerged as Kohl's most likely successor as CDU leader, had been active in RCDS in Freiburg in the 1960s, but at no point had he identified as one of the other '68ers. Instead, he came out to

---

[132] Wulf Schönbohm, 'Hier linke Spinner, dort Faschisten'. Conversely, there was plenty of self-flagellation on the Left for having turned a blind eye to repression in Eastern Europe. E.g. see Cora Stephan (ed.), *Wir Kollaborateure: Der Westen und die deutschen Vergangenheiten* (Hamburg, 1992).

[133] Gunter Hofmann, 'Kulturkampf gegen die Kulturrevolutionäre', *Die Zeit*, 1 (1 January 1993); Kurt Sontheimer, 'Eine Generation der Gescheiterten', *Die Zeit* (9 April 1993); Eckhard Fuhr, 'Alles Achtundsechziger', *FAZ* (27 March 1993). The more positive reading of 1968 did not disappear entirely, though, not even among former activists of the centre-right. See e.g. the film 'Ich hab noch einen Koffer in Berlin', dir. Werner Doyé, ZDF, 1 September 1993, 22.15 p.m.

[134] Claus Leggewie, 'Plädoyer eines Antiautoritären für Autorität', *Die Zeit*, 10 (5 March 1993).

[135] Schäuble, Deutscher Bundestag, 12. Wahlperiode, 128. Sitzung, Bonn, 10 December 1992, 11,046. Available at http://dipbt.bundestag.de/doc/btp/12/12128.pdf (accessed on 20 November 2020).

embrace a view of the revolt that seemed to be very much in line with those of (older) conservatives within the party.

His former Freiburg student peer Dettling was furious about Schäuble's memory politics, which he read as an expression of the CDU's rightward reorientation after the exit of many more socially liberal figures a few years earlier. He remembered Schäuble from RCDS meetings in the late 1960s but recalled that young Wolfgang had never participated in the intellectual discussions about the need for reform that had intensified after Ohnesorg's death in 1967. Instead, Schäuble had always been single-mindedly focused on advancing his political career, Dettling charged. While he and others had worked tirelessly on the party's programmatic profile in the 1970s, Schäuble had been the parliamentary spokesman on sports policy, he contrasted mockingly. The Minister of the Interior's attacks on 1968 were not based on political conviction or, even more importantly, on personal experience but on naked political calculations, Dettling contended:

> When Kohl's heir today, twenty-five years later, invokes the anti-68er trauma, then he knows what he is doing: he is presenting this, cool and calculated, as a means to an end. He needs an image of the enemy, in order to prepare a new CDU of the right-wing centre.[136]

As we can see, then, centre-right remembrances of 1968 were always at least in part a debate about Christian Democratic politics in the present, and, just as in debates on the Left, biographical experiences often featured prominently within them.

Biographical readings of 1968 came even more clearly to the fore after 1998, the revolt's thirtieth anniversary. It was also the year when Kohl was voted out of office and the 'red-green' coalition government between Social Democrats and Greens took power for the first time. The focus now shifted to the political biographies of key members of Gerhard Schröder's cabinet. This was a shift that the new Chancellor emphatically embraced. In his first government statement, Schröder, who had defended left-wing academic Peter Brückner in court at the height of the 'Mescalero affair', explicitly portrayed the red-green coalition as the generational project of the '68ers:

> These are the biographies of democracy in living form. We have experienced and shaped the cultural awakening from this time of reconstruction. [...] This generation stands in the tradition of civic mindedness and civil courage. It grew up in revolt against authoritarian structures and in an experiment in new social and political models.[137]

---

[136] Dettling, *Das Erbe Kohls*, 158.
[137] 'Regierungserklärung 1998', in Karl-Rudolf Korte (ed.), *'Das Wort hat der Herr Bundeskanzler': Eine Analyse der grossen Regierungserklärungen von Adenauer bis Schröder* (Berlin, 2013), 437; see also 210.

Christian Democratic politicians and other commentators soon began to turn their opponents' pasts against them, arguing that state power could not be entrusted to erstwhile left-wing radicals. The most memorable episode in this debate was the 2001 'Fischer affair', a scandal surrounding the activist past of Green Foreign Minister and Vice Chancellor Joseph ('Joschka') Fischer, who had been a major figure on the radical Left in Frankfurt after 1968. Fischer was forced to apologize when old photographs of him beating up a policeman in 1973 surfaced at the same time as he was linked to the terrorist crimes of a former acquaintance from his street fighting days.[138] He was even rumoured to have supported the Venezuelan terrorist 'Carlos the Jackal', one of the 1970s' most wanted fugitives.[139] Soon after, the Maoist past of Green Environment Minister Jürgen Trittin and his alleged condoning of the RAF's murder of Attorney General Buback also made headlines. 'Mescalero', as the anonymous author of the notorious 'Buback obituary' had called himself in 1977, seemed to have returned to the centre of public debate.[140] For the first time since the late 1970s, these events put the issue of left-wing violence and the connections between the student movement and the left-wing terrorism of the 1970s centre stage in debates about 1968—where they would remain for years thanks to the sensibilities of the post-9/11 world.[141]

However, as hyperbolic and unfounded as many of the claims put forward by Fischer and Trittin's critics certainly were, it would be flawed to understand them solely as calculated political point scoring. Fischer was the most popular politician of the red-green era, to be sure, and, as such, a favourite target. Focusing on his moral transgressions also allowed Christian Democrats to deflect attention from their own party donations scandal, which had done so much to undermine their public image and political standing since 1999.[142] But these were more than retroactive attacks on liberalism and tolerance, as some commentators argued at the time.[143] Nor were they simply attacks on 1968 as such, as many on the Left

---

[138] 'Joschkas wilde Jahre', *Der Spiegel*, 2 (8 January 2001).

[139] See Eckart von Klaeden's question during a Bundestag debate on Fischer's past, Deutscher Bundestag, 14. Wahperiode-142. Sitzung, Berlin, Mittwoch, den 17. Januar 2001, 13,909 (available at http://dip21.bundestag.de/dip21/btp/14/14142.pdf; accessed on 20 November 2020); also Edgar Wolfrum, *Rot-Grün an der Macht: Deutschland 1998–2005* (Munich, 2013), 648.

[140] Around this time, Trittin encountered Buback's son Michael during a train ride, and the latter asked Trittin, a former Göttingen student, to distance himself from the Buback obituary. Trittin refused and Michael Buback went to the press. See further Wolfram, *Rot-Grün an der Macht*, 651; for evidence of the renewed interest in the Mescalero affair at this time, see Thomas Leif, Erich Neumann, 'Mescalero—die 68er und die Gewalt', Report (Mainz), ARD, 29 January 2001. It was in this context that Klaus Hülbrock revealed that he had been 'Mescalero'. Klaus Hülbrock, 'Ich bleibe ein Indianer', *tageszeitung*, 10 February 2001.

[141] Koenen, *Rotes Jahrzehnt*; Paul Berman, 'The Passions of Joschka Fischer', *New Republic* (27 August 2001); Paul Hockenos, *Joschka Fischer and the Making of the Berlin Republic* (Oxford, 2008), 446–9; Wolfrum, *Rot-Grün an der Macht*, 646–54.

[142] Cornils, *Writing the Revolution*, 4.

[143] Heribert Prantl, cited in Wolfrum, *Rot-Grün an der Macht*, 652–3.

contended: 'You want to put an entire political generation on trial', as Rezzo Schlauch, the head of the Green Party's parliamentary faction, suggested in a *Bundestag* debate on Fischer's past, held on 17 January 2001.[144]

Rather, this was a memory contest about which members of the extended 1968 generation had behaved with greater moral integrity. In attacking Fischer, and, alongside him, all those activists who had joined one of the radical left-wing groups of the 1970s, former centre-right activists were also reliving their own personal and political history.

Centre-right memory entrepreneurs still played key roles in these debates. Gerd Langguth, who had been RCDS national chair in the early 1970s, for instance, was one of the loudest voices that drove the national conversation in the red-green era about the legacies of 1968 and left-wing violence. He did not suddenly highlight the Left's violence out of sheer expediency, however. Since the 1970s, Langguth had continuously argued that violence had lain at the heart of 1968, but he had often been drowned out by the voices of the other '68ers in the CDU apparatus who had found it more advantageous to highlight the era's liberalizing impulses. With Christian Democrats out of office and the likes of Fischer as foes in the early 2000s, however, the time was ripe for the Langguth version of 1968 to move to the fore.[145]

Langguth was not alone. One of the people who spoke up repeatedly in the heated and highly emotional *Bundestag* debate on Fischer's trajectory was Friedbert Pflüger. He had been RCDS national chair in 1977/78, served as Federal President von Weizsäcker's spokesman in the 1980s, and had held a seat in the *Bundestag* since 1990. As we saw in Chapter 5, he had done much to fan the flames of public outrage about student sympathizers of terrorism during the 'German autumn', not least in Göttingen, the birthplace of the 'Mescalero Affair'. In attacking Fischer in 2001 for having used and condoned political violence, he thus returned to a script he had helped to write in the 1970s.

At the same time, he was also making a forceful point about his own past. Standing in the *Bundestag* chamber, Pflüger questioned the authenticity of Fischer's mea culpa and accused the Foreign Minister of still nurturing a secret sense of pride in his street fighting days. The transcript of the debate gives a vivid sense of how, facing repeated mocking interruptions from Green politician Schlauch, he directly contrasted Fischer's biography with his own:

---

[144] Schlauch in Deutscher Bundestag, 14. Wahperiode-142. Sitzung, Berlin, Mittwoch, den 17. Januar 2001, 13,906 (available at http://dip21.bundestag.de/dip21/btp/14/14142.pdf; accessed on 20 November 2020); Peter Schumacher, 'Fischer verteidigt seine Vergangenheit', *FAZ* (17 January 2001); Berman, 'The Passions of Joschka Fischer'.

[145] Gerd Langguth, 'Die Leuchtkraft der Demagogen', *Christ und Welt/Rheinischer Merkur* (20 May 1988); Langguth, *Mythos '68; Streitfall: 'Die 68er—Eine Generation im Streit'*, televised debate between Gerd Langguth and Green politician Rupert von Plottnitz, moderated by Bodo Hauser, 3 *Sat*, 26 April 2001; Langguth, *Mythos '68: Die Gewaltphilosophie von Rudi Dutschke*.

In 1973, I joined RCDS [aside, Rezzo Schlauch, Alliance 90/The Greens: Congratulations! A success story!], so at the time when Fischer began to get radical and violent alongside his 'cleaning squad'. At that time we were excluded, isolated, and sometimes also beaten up [Schlauch: the RCDS was excluded?]. We suffered under the manifest violence of the student movement, or rather offshoots of the student movement [Schlauch: Mr Pflüger, the victim!]. At that time they voted on whether we from the RCDS were even allowed to talk, my colleague Mr. Schlauch. I was hauled out of Bremen University with the justification: fascists have no business here! I would like to say to you, Mr. Schlauch: In this period, those of us in RCDS recognized that fascism cannot just come from the right, but also from the left [applause from the CDU and the FDP]. If you now present Mr. Fischer as an asset to the Republic—it really is lovely, when someone has fractures in his biography; because that shows that he has developed, that he has devoted himself to democracy after a long process of self-torment— then I say to you: I am happy and am proud of the fact that on my way to the *Bundestag* and to a position of political responsibility, I never beat up police officers.[146]

As we can see, these debates were deeply personal. It was not just the history and validity of left-wing dissent that they litigated, but the other 68ers' trajectories, too.

Edgar Wolfrum has termed the Fischer debate a kind of 'third period of [Germans] coming to terms with the past' after those that dealt with Nazi crimes in the late 1950s and 1960s and the East German past in the 1990s. At stake, he suggested, was not just the political morality of the '68ers but the 'self-concept of the Republic'.[147] While that may be true, what such assessments often miss is that it was not random conservative politicians and commentators—people who had no stake in the subject other than point scoring in the present—who attacked 1968 in the 1990s and 2000s. Instead, it was often former centre-right activists—the other '68ers—who had themselves been intimately involved in the events they narrated.

As this book has shown, the political clashes of the late 1960s and 1970s are at best only partially understood without taking into account centre-right students' presence. Similarly, we fail to fully grasp the memory wars about 1968 that raged in the 1980s, 1990s, and 2000s without being mindful of centre-right involvement. They shaped public representations of 1968 in significant and lasting ways—just as they left a strong imprint on Christian Democracy and the late Federal Republic's political culture. The years around 1968 were their history, too, and they helped to make sense of them from the outset.

---

[146] See Pflüger's speech in Deutscher Bundestag, 14. Wahperiode-142. Sitzung, Berlin, Mittwoch, den 17. Januar 2001, 13,914–13,915, (available at http://dip21.bundestag.de/dip21/btp/14/14142.pdf; accessed on 20 November 2019). For a more detailed discussion of the overall debate see Wolfrum, *Rot-Grün an der Macht*, 648–51. On Pflüger's role in the 1970s, see 206–8; 710–12; 215; 220–23.

[147] Wolfrum, *Rot-Grün an der Macht*, 648.

Conclusion

The Other '68ers in German History

In what ways, then, do the findings of this book change how we understand the history of 1968 and of the late Federal Republic? By way of conclusion, I want to suggest three main takeaways from *The Other '68ers*.

First, 1968 involved the centre-right. One basic aim of this book has been to show that centre-right students were present around 1968, and not just as passive observers or staunch opponents of protest. Writing them back into the history of 1968 and its afterlives, as this study has done, reveals that student activism in these years was a broader, more versatile, and, ultimately, more consequential phenomenon than the traditionally narrower focus on left-wing radicals allows. It also reminds us that the Left did not operate in a vacuum at this time but in an environment that was shaped by the centre-right in significant ways.

The centre-right presence around 1968 took different forms, ranging from participation to forceful resistance. Activists from RCDS and the Student Unions participated in, and sometimes organized, teach-ins and demonstrations. Some were tried for their actions in West German courts. They engaged with social and political theory and criticized older Christian Democrats for their sclerotic politics and rigid mindsets. Their protest repertoires included events designed to goad their opponents and attract press coverage. They organized rock concerts and ran campaigns to make the contraceptive pill available to more students. Women activists engaged with the ideas of second-wave feminists and sometimes decried sexism and misogyny in their ranks. Like that of their left-wing peers, centre-right students' political imagination was increasingly global, even if the Cold War and anti-totalitarian thinking remained at the core of how they viewed the world. Their presence was equally central to the far more combative campus politics of the 1970s, when their carefully calculated pieces of political theatre stoked fears of students' support for terrorism and left-wing infiltration of state institutions. And their interpretations and commemorations of 1968 influenced how the student movement was understood from early on.

All of this highlights that there was a relational character to student activism around 1968 that is lost in studies that deal solely with the Left and its relationship to social institutions and the state. Activists from different sides of the political spectrum interacted directly with each other in numerous ways—be it on the roof

The Other '68ers: Student Protest and Christian Democracy in West Germany. Anna von der Goltz, Oxford University Press (2021). © Anna von der Goltz. DOI: 10.1093/oso/9780198849520.003.0008

of a car in Freiburg in January 1968 (the scene depicted on this book's cover) or at teach-ins where centre-right activists stimulated the discussion, as Dutschke's widow observed.

Similarly, there was a relational dimension to the ways in which political identities, memories of activism, and generational narratives took shape and evolved. In the late 1960s, the other '68ers began to develop a collective sense of self as a result of their encounters with left-wing students and turned to the concept of generation to give their political programme and aspirations narrative shape. In the late 1970s, after initially resisting this framework, convinced that it belittled their revolutionary aspirations, left-wing activists began to embrace generation as a mode of making sense of their collective accomplishments.[1] This was in no small part because their political goals had been tarnished by association with the terror of the RAF and related groups, a link Christian Democratic student agitation had helped to draw in the mind of the public.

The generational commemorations of the 1980s also fed off each other. Left-wing reunions were meant to instil hope during a period of Christian Democratic hegemony by highlighting the many ways in which the '68ers of the Left had succeeded regardless of who now held power in Bonn. Centre-right activists, spurred on by left-wing authors and journalists, answered the Left's commemorative efforts by insisting that they were the true victors of 1968 and that their 'march through the institutions' had been the more consequential one. These competing generational narratives remained tied to each other for the next two decades, as the heated debates about the moral integrity of different biographical trajectories showed during the early years of the red-green coalition government.

Just as we cannot fully understand many debates and events of 1968 without considering centre-right students' presence, so we cannot fully grasp the specific forms that the memory of 1968 took in the 1980s, 1990s, and 2000s without being mindful of their involvement. What is more, centre-right activists helped to make sense of the revolt from the beginning, be it by publishing analyses of student protest in the late 1960s and advising Christian Democratic politicians on how to respond; by shifting the focus of public debate to left-wing violence in the 1970s; or by commemorating 1968 and their own role within it from the 1980s onwards.

Second, this book has shown that we need a more nuanced history of the role that generation played around 1968. In contrast to how they have often been portrayed in the literature, the '68ers were no uniform collective. This generation of student activists comprised individuals from across the political spectrum, who often had very different ideas about what kind of a society they envisaged and how to address the shortcomings of West German democracy. The years around 1968

---

[1] von Lucke, *68 oder neues Biedermeier*, 31–3; Behre, *Bewegte Erinnerung*, 141–3.

were indeed an era of intense political contestation, but it also played out within the student body and nurtured contrasting identities.

At the same time, there was plenty that united the different generation units of '68ers, not least similar life experiences from which they nevertheless fashioned different identities. Most of them had been born during or just after the Second World War. They lived through bombing raids, flight and resettlement, had family members who had been killed or were held in captivity, had relatives that had been complicit in the Nazi regime, and grew up in a divided country that was a product of the Cold War. Members of both units experienced the 'economic miracle', West Germany's transformation into a consumer society, and the resulting erosion of traditional social milieus—experiences that set them apart from their parents and older generations in many ways. They embraced a largely liberalized sexuality; young women from across the political spectrum donned mini-skirts, and the hair of centre-right men gradually grew longer and more dishevelled—so much so that commentators in the 1980s still noted the surprising stylistic similarities between some of the '68ers of the Left and centre-right. Even if the other '68ers liked to emphasize their sobriety and moderation, they also shared with their left-wing peers an intense passion for politics and a belief in the power of debate, critique, and political action.

Given how much the concept has been critiqued in recent years, it is, of course, worth asking if we should still be relying on generation at all to write histories of 1968—or perhaps any histories at all, for that matter. The concept's critics have rightly pointed out that generational takes on 1968 tend to oversimplify a complex political and cultural moment that had multiple causes and involved far broader sections of society than students or even youth. Moreover, generational histories of 1968—and of Germany's twentieth century as a whole—tend to focus on particularly visible and vocal groups of activists, who often feature as stars in their own stories. Consequently, histories of generation tend to ascribe more agency to their protagonists than they really had—evident, for instance, in the frequent portrayals of the '68ers as the first ones to break the silence about the Nazi past or to democratize West German society from below.[2]

While such critiques are important and convincing and have informed the analysis here in numerous ways, generation is also impossible to avoid in a history of 1968 and its legacies. Talking about (my) generation was a key feature of this era. It framed how observers made sense of the tumultuous events and their causes. Social scientists and the media were quick to interpret the protests as symptoms of a generational conflict. More importantly, these interpretations also structured how activists thought of themselves. Like the '45ers, the other '68ers

---

[2] For critiques of this trope, see Nehring, '"Generation" as Political Argument'; Siegfried, 'Don't Trust Anyone Older Than 30?'; Bracke, 'One-dimensional conflict?'; Jureit, 'Generation, Generationalität, Generationenforschung'.

began to conceive of themselves as an age-specific community with distinct characteristics while the protests were under way. They did not simply invent their generation ex post to attract attention and further later political agendas, which makes their claims difficult to ignore.

The approach of this book has therefore been to adopt a reflexive use of generation, one that is mindful of both the concept's explanatory potential and its limitations and distortions. This is, of course, a delicate balancing act. The book is based on the premise that writing a history of the other '68ers may well be one of the better ways to critique interpretations of 1968 that rest on simple generational explanations. Including individuals with divergent political profiles and trajectories into our analysis of 1968 allows us, for instance, to question overly deterministic portrayals that simply trace the left-wing rebellion back to activists' traumatic wartime or postwar childhoods. Moreover, a gendered analysis that includes the experiences of centre-right women highlights that the Mannheimian model of political generations, with its male-centredness and emphasis on political binaries, does not always capture the fluidities of activist identities and experiences around 1968. Nor do the life paths of the Christian Democratic renegades suggest that events affected and shaped everybody in the same way. Such an approach also enables us to see clearly that the generational memory of the other '68ers was quite selective—and that it was closely intertwined with the narratives that took shape on the Left. Using generation in this way thus yields considerable new insights and may have the potential to do the same for other periods of history, in Germany and beyond.

Finally, the centre-right involvement in 1968 that this book lays bare had real consequences. It mattered, and not just because centre-right activists shaped events and debates as they unfolded. Their involvement also left its mark on (West) German political culture, especially on Christian Democracy. Saying this does not simply reproduce the other '68ers' own tales of their heroic agency. In their own version of their history, most clearly on display at the 1988 event in Bonn that this book opened with, they almost single-handedly modernized and liberalized the CDU while protecting the Federal Republic from a left-wing extremist overthrow.

Like most collectively honed stories, theirs contained some truths: these children of Adenauer and Coca-Cola had indeed already been more liberal on social issues around 1968 than most older Christian Democrats. They had even embraced Ralf Dahrendorf's call for the democratization of German society from below—and thus the key text that would later come to underpin the entire liberalization narrative in German historiography.[3] Furthermore, some of them did indeed contribute to the transformation of the CDU in very meaningful ways, staffing the party's policy planning and communications apparatus and shaping

---

[3] Herbert, 'Liberalisierung als Lernprozess'.

its programmatic work and public image from the 1970s onward. They had also campaigned against a left-wing radicalization that was at least partly real and, in doing so, acquired first-hand experiences with left-wing militancy that only fed their perception that democratic resistance was critical. Nevertheless, theirs was also a partial and sanitized story, one that neglected the manifold ways in which their own combative politics had contributed to the political climate they were supposedly committed to fighting. This raises some serious doubts about the narrative of Christian Democratic liberalization in the wake of 1968. Much like the tale that the 1968 Left only brought about the cultural democratization of the Federal Republic, it is one-sided and far too linear.

The other '68ers also overemphasized their own generation unit's agency, downplaying, as they did, the extent to which they had been beneficiaries of an inner-party opening and programmatic turn that was beginning to get under way in the late 1960s. Likewise, the other '68ers' generational narrative tended to understate the extent to which older party leaders, such as Kohl, Geißler or von Weizsäcker, had nurtured their rise to prominence in the first place and ultimately called the shots. And it left out almost entirely the experiences of their female peers.

Notwithstanding these omissions, the other '68ers who ended up in high-ranking government or party posts in the 1980s had the most discernible influence on the CDU and the political culture of the early Kohl era. Their embrace of social liberalism goes some way toward explaining why the return to Christian Democratic rule in the 1980s did not transform West German society as thoroughly as many observers had predicted—or indeed feared. These former student activists championed a winning political formula of relative liberalism on social issues to capture the values of a changing electorate combined with affective resistance against the party's left-wing opponents that delineated a robust political identity and mobilized core voters. This helped the CDU/CSU win in 1982/3 and recapture political hegemony after more than a decade in opposition, giving rise to a new Christian Democratic era in (West) German politics that endured until the final years of the twentieth century. Even then, the party's time in opposition lasted only seven years, until Angela Merkel's election in 2005.

Contrary to what astute observers of German politics may expect, however, this does not mean that all of the other '68ers inevitably embraced Merkel's course of party reform and emphatically centrist governance as their legacy. Some did, to be sure. Christian Democratic campaign guru Peter Radunski, for one, argued that Merkel would never have become Chancellor without the transformative effects of 1968—including the modernizing effects he attributed to centre-right student activists.[4] However, at least one of the other '68ers has been one of Merkel's

---

[4] 'Ohne die 68er wäre Merkel nicht Kanzlerin geworden', Marek Dutschke and Peter Radunski interviewed by Korbinian Frenzel, *Deutschlandfunk Kultur* (11 April 2018), available at https://www.

most vocal critics. Writing in the conservative *Die Welt* in 2007, former RCDS chair Wulf Schönbohm denounced Merkel's policies as a 'pseudo-liberal centrist stew' and faulted her for giving up the CDU's core conservative values—a statement that made major waves at the time.[5] Schönbohm admitted being surprised himself that he of all people—somebody who had been known as a party reformer for much of his career—was the one to make this point about a leader who, at least at first glance, seemed to be continuing where he and his peers had left off in the 1980s. However, it is only counter-intuitive if we forget that the other '68ers' political project had never been defined by party modernization and social liberalism alone. The project was always a dual one. A combative political style was just as important to them. It was this latter part that Schönbohm faulted the far less habitually combative Merkel for forgetting. Moreover, he was convinced that her alleged political deficits were the result of her socialization in East Germany. This implied that she lacked the formative experience of political combat that had shaped his own generation unit in West Germany.[6] Interviewed for this book a few months after his first public attack on Merkel, the former RCDS leader explained:

And on that many say: 'But Merkel is progressive. Why are you throwing her under the bus?' And I say to that: 'She doesn't understand certain things. That relates to her socialization. She is a CDU chair, who repeatedly snubs and neglects the party faithful [. . .] She is scared of emotions. And she can't mobilize people. But you need that on the campaign trail. She is scared of going on the attack.'[7]

By contrast, going on the attack against their opponents was a technique Schönbohm and his activist peers in West Germany were proud to have practised and perfected continuously since their student days—and it is one of the ways in which 1968 left its imprint on German political culture.

---

deutschlandfunkkultur.de/studentenproteste-ohne-die-68er-waere-merkel-nicht.2950.de.html?dram: article_id=415293 (accessed on 9 July 2020); see also Peter Radunski, 'Angela Merkel bleibt das Trumpf-Ass der CDU', *Der Tagesspiegel* (29 March 2017); also Radunksi interview.

[5] Wulf Schönbohm, 'Scheinliberale Mitte-Soße', *Die Welt* (16 August 2007); see also Lau, *Die letzte Volkspartei*, 180–1, although Lau categorized Schönbohm simply as one of Merkel's 'conservative critics'. For similar critiques of Merkel by commentators who were much further to the right, see Weiß, *Die autoritäre Revolte*, 76–7.

[6] Merkel responded a few months later, albeit indirectly. In early 2008, she recounted her own memories of 1968 in East Germany to the left-liberal *Süddeutsche Zeitung*. The violent crushing of the Prague Spring in August of that year had cemented her instinctive rejection of socialism, she claimed. 'Und es war Sommer', *Süddeutsche Zeitung Magazin*, 9 (2008); see further Anna von der Goltz, 'Generations Of 68ers'. *Cultural And Social History*, 8, 4 (2011), 473–91.

[7] Schönbohm interview.

Bibliography

Archives

Akademie der Künste, Berlin

Kunstsammlung; Ruetz, Michael

Archiv der deutschen Frauenbewegung, Kassel

Gabriele Strecker Papers
Newspapers and periodicals

Archiv der sozialen Demokratie, Bonn

Josef Heinrich Darchinger photographic collection

Archiv für Christlich-Demokratische Politik, Sankt Augustin

CDU-Bundesgeschäftsstelle (Konrad-Adenauer-Haus)
European Democrat Students (EDS)
Junge Union Deutschlands (JU)
Gerd Langguth Papers
Medienarchiv: Film, Ton, Plakate Pressearchiv
Newspapers and Periodicals
Ring Christlich-Demokratischer Studenten der CDU Deutschlands (RCDS)
Jürgen Wohlrabe Papers

Archiv für Christlich-Soziale Politik, Munich

Poster collection

Archiv APO und soziale Bewegungen (APO-Archiv), Berlin

Sozialistischer Deutscher Studentenbund (SDS)
Ring Christlich-Demokratischer Studenten, Berliner Landesverband
Newspapers and periodicals

Bundesarchiv, Koblenz

Bundesamt für Verfassungsschutz
Bundeskanzleramt
Bundesministerium des Innern
Bundesministerium für Bildung und Wissenschaft
Bundesministerium für Familie und Jugend
Institut für Demoskopie, Allensbach
Karl Schiller Papers
Ring Politischer Jugend
Ständige Konferenz der Kultusminister der Länder der Bundesrepublik Deutschland
Verband der Vereine Deutscher Studenten (VVDSt)

Evangelisches Zentralarchiv, Berlin

Aktion Sorge um Deutschland

Hoover Institution Library and Archives, Stanford, CA

Bund Freiheit der Wissenschaft
Notgemeinschaft für eine freie Universität (NofU)
Folkmar Koenigs Collection
Georg Nicolaus Knauer Papers
Guenter Lewy Collection
Karl Häuser Papers
German Subject Collection

Hamburger Institut für Sozialforschung

Zeitschriften Protestbewegungen
Studentenbewegung, Studentische Verbände, RCDS
Rudi Dutschke Papers

Institut für Zeitgeschichte, Munich

Rijk Hilferink Collection
Eberhard Zorn Collection

Landesarchiv Berlin

Senatsverwaltung für Inneres
Senatsverwaltung für Wissenschaft und Forschung

Landesarchiv Baden-Württemberg

Fotosammlung Willy Pragher

Staatsarchiv Bremen

Bund Freiheit der Wissenschaft, Bremen
Senator für das Bildungswesen
Senator für Wissenschaft und Kunst

Universitätsarchiv Bonn

Allgemeiner Studenten-Ausschuss

Universitätsarchiv Münster

Semester-Spiegel

Private Collections

Ignaz Bender Private Papers
Jürgen Klemann Private Paper
Gerd Langguth Private Papers
Hans Reckers Private Papers
Wolfgang Reeder Private Papers
Jürgen Rosorius Private Papers
Jürgen-Bernd Runge Private Papers
Wulf Schönbohm Private Papers

Interviews

Ade, Meinhard, Bonn, 3 June 2014
Aretz, Jürgen, Bad Godesberg, 2 June 2014
Bender, Ignaz, Trier, 27 May 2014
Bergsdorf, Wolfgang, Bad Godesberg, 2 June 2014
Buchhaas-Birkholz, Dorothee, Berlin, 6 July 2012
Diepgen, Eberhard, Berlin, 26 April 2010
Haberl, Othmar Nikola, Essen, 30 May 2014
Härdtl, Wighard, Bonn, May 28, 2014
Hassemer, Volker, Berlin, 6 June 2014
Kempe, Martin, Hamburg, 18 June 2013
Klemann, Jürgen, Berlin, 12 June 2014

Laepple, Klaus, Cologne, 6 June 2013
Langguth, Gerd, Königswinter-Oberdollendorf, 22 June 2011
Männle, Ursula, Munich, 4 June 2013
Perger, Werner A., Berlin, 16 June 2011
Pflüger, Friedbert, Berlin, 13 June 2013
Radunski, Peter, Berlin, 26 October 2009
Reckers, Hans, Berlin, 6 July and 17 December 2012
Reeder, Wolfgang, Unkel, 29 May 2014
Reichart-Dreyer, Ingrid, Berlin, 10 June 2014
Röper, Erich, Bremen, 21 December 2009
Rosorius, Jürgen, Bonn, 30 June 2011
Runge, Jürgen-Bernd, Bonn, 6 June 2013
Schönbohm, Wulf, Berlin, 20 February 2008
Stronk, Detlef, Berlin, 11 June 2014
Teltschik, Horst, Munich, 3 June 2013
van Schewick, Maria-Theresia ('Musch'), Bonn, 3 June 2014

Newspapers

Aachener Volkszeitung, Akademische Blätter, Akut, Badische Zeitung, Berliner Rundschau, Bonner Rundschau, Burschenschaftliche Blätter, B.Z., Christ und Welt/Rheinischer Merkur, Cicero, Civis, Colloquium, Demokratische Blätter, Der Spiegel, Die Welt, Welt am Sonntag, Die Zeit, Deutsche Volkszeitung, Deutsches Allgemeines Sonntagsblatt, Facts, Frankfurter Allgemeine Zeitung, Frankfurter Rundschau, FU Spiegel, Göttinger Nachrichten, The Guardian, Kölner Stadt-Anzeiger, Münchner Merkur, Neue Westfälische Zeitung, Rheinische Post, Rote Blätter, Sonde, Stern, Stuttgarter Zeitung, Süddeutsche Zeitung, Der Tagesspiegel, tageszeitung (taz), The Times, Weser Kurier, Westfälische Nachrichten

Audiovisual Sources

Bönnen, Ute and Gerald Endres, *Die Stasi in West-Berlin*, RBB, 5 August 2010.Bonn direkt, ZDF, 15 May 1988.
Doyé, Werner, dir., *Ich hab noch einen Koffer in Berlin*, ZDF, 1 September 1993.
Hemming, Heinz and Werner A. Perger, *Die anderen 68er: Dutschkes Gegenspieler und was aus ihnen wurde*, Documentary (West Germany, 1988).
Leif, Thomas and Erich Neumann, *Mescalero—die 68er und die Gewalt*, Report (Mainz), ARD, 29 January 2001.
Rönfeldt Detlef, dir., *Stunde der Füchse* (Germany, 1993).
Spartakus-Tribunal, ZDF Magazin, 26 January 1972, footage in the author's possession.
Streitfall: 'Die 68er—Eine Generation im Streit', Gerd Langguth, Rupert von Plottnitz, and Bodo Hauser, 3 Sat, 26 April 2001.

Published Primary Sources

Ahlberg, René, 'Die politische Konzeption des Sozialistischen Deutschen Studentenbundes', *Beilage zur Wochenzeitung Das Parlament* B20/68 (15 May 1968).

Ahlberg, René, *Akademische Lehrmeinungen und Studentenunruhen in der Bundesrepublik: Linker Irrationalismus in politologischen und soziologischen Theorien* (Freiburg, 1970).

Alleg, Henri, *La question* (Lausanne, 1958).

Baumann, Bommi, *How it All Began: The Personal Account of a West German Urban Guerilla* (Vancouver, 2006).

Bender, Ignaz, *Weltordnung: Der Weg zu einer besser geordneten Welt* (Baden-Baden, 2017).

Bender, Ignaz, *Erlebtes und Bewegtes—in Hochschule, Europe und Welt* (Baden-Baden, 2020).

Bergsdorf, Wolfgang, *Politik und Sprache* (Munich and Vienna, 1978).

Bergsdorf Wolfgang, ed, *Wörter als Waffen: Sprache als Mittel der Politik* (Stuttgart, 1979).

Bergsdorf, Wolfgang, *Herrschaft und Sprache: Studie zur politischen Terminologie der Bundesrepublik* (Pfullingen, 1983).

Bloch, Ernst, *Geist der Utopie* (1918).

Bloch, Ernst, *Das Prinzip Hoffnung*, 3 vols (1938–1947).

Bothien, Horst-Pierre, *Protest und Provokation: Bonner Studenten 1967/1968* (Essen, 2007).

Brückner, Peter and Axel R. Oestmann, '*Über die Pflicht des Gelehrten auch als Bürger tätig zu sein*': Zum Disziplinarverfahren des Niedersächsischen Ministers für Wissenschaft und Kunst (Hanover, 1982).

Buchstab, Günter, ed., *Kiesinger: 'Wir leben in einer veränderten Welt' (1965–1969), Die Protokolle des CDU-Bundesvorstandes* (Düsseldorf, 2005).

Buchstab, Günter and Denise Lindsay, eds, *Barzel:'Unsere Alternativen für die Zeit der Opposition': Die Protokolle des CDU-Bundesvorstands 1969–1973* (Düsseldorf, 2009).

Buchstab, Günter, ed., *Kohl: 'Wir haben alle Chancen': Die Protokolle des CDU-Bundesvorstands 1973–1976* (Düsseldorf, 2015).

Buchstab, Günther, ed., *Kohl: 'Stetigkeit, Klugheit, Geduld und Zähigkeit': Die Protokolle des CDU-Bundesvorstands 1976–1980* (Düsseldorf, 2018).

Buchstab, Günter, ed., *Kohl: 'Gelassenheit und Zuversicht': Die Protokolle des CDU-Bundesvorstands 1980–1983* (Düsseldorf, 2018).

CDU-Bundesgeschäftsstelle, ed., *Terrorismus in der Bundesrepublik Deutschland: Eine Auswahl von Zitaten* (Bonn, 1977).

CDU-Bundesgeschäftsstelle, ed., *Die Grünen: Eine Analyse der öko-marxistischen Radikalopposition* (Bonn, 1984).

Cohn-Bendit, Daniel and Claus Leggewie, '1968: Power to the Imagination', *The New York Review of Books*, 10 May 2018, 6.

Comité résistance, spirituelle, *Des rappelés témoignent* (Clichy, Seine, 1957).

Dahrendorf, Ralf, *Gesellschaft und Demokratie in Deutschland* (Munich, 1965).

de Beauvoir, Simone, *Das andere Geschlecht: Sitte und Sexus der Frau* (Hamburg, 1951).

Debord, Guy, *The Society of the Spectacle* (St Petersburg, FL, 1970).

Der Bundesbeauftragte für die Unterlagen des Staatssicherheitsdienstes der ehemaligen Deutschen Demokratischen Republik, ed., *Der Deutsche Bundestag 1949 bis 1989 in den Akten des Ministeriums für Staatssicherheit (MfS) der DDR* (Berlin, 2013).

Der Spiegel, ed., *Der deutsche Student: Situation, Einstellungen und Verhaltensweisen: Ergebnisse einer Repräsentativerhebung an 26 deutschen Universitäten und Hochschulen. Durchgeführt vom Institut für Demoskopie, Allensbach 1966–67* (Hamburg, 1967).

Dettling, Warnfried, *Das Erbe Kohls: Bilanz einer Ära* (Eichborn, 1994).

Deutsche Studenten Union, 'Wer ist, was will die DSU?' (Bonn, 1970).

Domes, Jürgen, *Politik und Herrschaft in Rotchina* (Stuttgart, Berlin, Cologne, and Mainz, 1965).

Dutschke, Rudi, 'Die geschichtlichen Bedingungen für den internationalen Emanzipationskampf', in *1968: Eine Enzyklopädie*, edited by Rudolf Sievers (Frankfurt am Main, 2004), 259.

Dutschke-Klotz, Gretchen, *Wir hatten ein barbarisches, schönes Leben: Rudi Dutschke: Eine Biographie* (Cologne, 2007).

Erler, Gisela Anna and Monika Jaeckel, 'Die Grenzen der Partnerschaft—von der Notwendigkeit einer Frauenkultur', in *Abschied von der Männergesellschaft*, edited by Heiner Geißler (Berlin, 1986), 56–66.

Faltlhauser, Kurt, 'Die 68er-Bewegung: Persönliche und gesellschaftliche Wirkungen'. *Politische Studien*, 59, 422 (2008), 27–8.

Fink, Ulf, '1968—Die Antwort der CDU: Programmpartei'. *Aus Politik und Zeitgeschichte* B 20 (1988), 27–35.

Friedan, Betty, *Der Weiblichkeitswahn: Ein vehementer Protest gegen das Wunschbild von der Frau* (Reinbek near Hamburg, 1966).

Gauweiler, Peter, *AIDS: Die Zeit drängt* (Munich, 1985).

Geißler, Heiner, ed., *Abschied von der Männergesellschaft* (Berlin, 1986).

Geißler, Heiner, *Im Gespräch mit Gunter Hofmann und Werner A. Perger* (Eichborn, 1993).

Giese, Hans and Gunter Schmidt, *Studenten-Sexualiät: Verhalten und Einstellung: Eine Umfrage an 12 westdeutschen Universitäten* (Reinbek near Hamburg, 1968).

Gundelach, Herlind, 'Mein Weg in die Politik – Erfahrungen und Erkenntnisse', in *Mut zur Verantwortung, Mut zur Verantwortung: Frauen gestalten die Politik der CDU*, edited by Beate Neuss and Hildigund Neubert (Cologne, Weimar, Vienna, 2015), 441–60.

Habermas, Jürgen, 'Political Culture in Germany since 1968: An Interview with Dr. Rainer Erd for the Frankfurter Rundschau', in idem, *The New Conservatism: Cultural Criticism and the Historians' Debate*, translated by Shierry Weber Nicholsen (Cambridge, 1989), 183–95.

Habermas, Jürgen, '"Meine Damen und Herren, ich hoffe, dass Herr Dutschke noch hier ist...", 9 June 1967', in *Frankfurter Schule und Studentenbewegung: Von der Flaschenpost bis zum Molotowcocktail 1946 bis 1995, vol. 2: Dokumente*, edited by Wolfgang Kraushaar (Hamburg, 1998), 254–5.

Härdtl, Wighard, 'Strategie der Neuen Linken zur Machtergreifung', in *Die Studentische Protestbewegung: Analysen und Konzepte*, edited by Wulf Schönbohm (Mainz, 1971), 95–123.

Internationales Russell Tribunal, *Berufsverbote Condemned: Third Russell Tribunal* (Nottingham, 1978).

Jansen, Mechthild, '"Konservativer Feminismus" mit Rita Süßmuth?'. *Blätter für deutsche und internationale Politik*, 2 (1986), 184–201.

Jünger, Ernst, *Storm of Steel* (London, 1929).

Kaul, Friedrich Karl, *Ich klage an: Der berühmte DDR-Anwalt berichtet als Nebenkläger und Verteidiger in westdeutschen Strafprozessen* (Hamburg, 1971).

Kaul, Friedrich Karl, *Auschwitz trial in Frankfurt-on-Main: summing up and reply of Friedrich Karl Kaul, legal representative of the co-plaintiffs resident in the German Democratic Republic in the criminal proceedings against Mulka and others before the criminal court at the Provincial Court in Frankfurt-on-Main* (Dresden, 1965).

Kellner, Douglas, ed., *Herbert Marcuse: Technology, War, and Fascism: Collected Papers of Herbert Marcuse*, Vol. 1 (Routledge, 1998).

Knütter, Hans-Helmuth, 'Verfassungsfeindliche Beamte in der Weimarer Republik', in *Verfassungsfeinde als Beamte? Die Kontroverse um die streitbare Demokratie*, edited by Wulf Schönbohm (Munich and Vienna, 1979), 13–38.

Kohl, Helmut, *Erinnerungen: 1930–1982* (Munich, 2004).

Kommune 2, *Versuch der Revolutionierung des bürgerlichen Individuums* (Berlin, 1969).

Kraushaar, Wolfgang, ed., *Frankfurter Schule und Studentenbewegung: Von der Flaschenpost bis zum Molotowcocktail 1946 bis 1995*, 3 vols (Hamburg, 1998).

Langguth, Gerd, *Protestbewegung am Ende: Die Neue Linke als Vorhut der DKP* (Mainz, 1971).

Langguth, Gerd, *Die Protestbewegung der Bundesrepublik Deutschland 1968–1976* (Cologne, 1976).

Langguth, Gerd, *Protestbewegung: Entwicklung, Niedergang, Renaissance: Die Neue Linke seit 1968* (Cologne, 1983).

Langguth, Gerd, *Mythos '68: Die Gewaltphilosophie von Rudi Dutschke—Ursachen und Folgen der Studentenbewegung* (Munich, 2001).

Leggewie, Claus, *Der Geist steht rechts: Ausflüge in die Denkfabriken der Wende* (Berlin, 1987).

Leonhard, Wolfgang, *Die Revolution entlässt ihre Kinder* (Cologne, 1955).

Leonhard, Wolfgang, *Child of the Revolution* (London, 1957).

Lönnendonker, Siegward and Tilman Fichter, eds, *Hochschule im Umbruch: Teil IV: Die Krise (1964–1967)* (Berlin, 1975).

Lönnendonker, Siegward, Tilman Fichter, and Jochen Staadt, eds, *Hochschule im Umbruch: Teil V: Gewalt und Gegengewalt (1967–1969)* (Berlin, 1983).

Löwenthal, Richard, *Romantischer Rückfall: Wege und Irrwege einer rückwärts gewendeten Revolution* (Stuttgart, 1970).

Ludolf, Hermann, 'Hitler, Bonn und die Wende: Wie die Bundesrepublik ihre Lebenskraft zurück gewinnen kann'. *Die Politische Meinung*, 28, 209 (1983), 13–28.

Männle, Ursula, 'Unkonventionelle Anmerkungen'. *Politische Studien*, 59, 422 (2008), 33–5.

Männle, Ursula, 'Weibchen oder Feigenblatt. Die Frau in der Politik', in *Für eine humane Gesellschaft: Beiträge zum Programmdenken der jungen Generation*, edited by Wulf Schönbohm and Matthias Wissmann (Frankfurt am Main, 1976), 97.

Marcuse, Herbert, *One-dimensional Man: Studies in the Ideology of Advanced Industrial Society* (Boston, MA, 1964).

Mosler, Peter, *Was wir wollten, was wir wurden* (Reinbek near Hamburg, 1988).

Motschmann, Elisabeth, 'Die Schattenseiten der Emanzipation: Kinder ohne Mutter', in *Abschied von der Männergesellschaft*, edited by Heiner Geißler (Berlin, 1986), 21–32.

Mündemann, Tobias, *Die 68er... und was aus ihnen geworden ist* (Munich, 1988).

Neuss, Beate and Hildigung Neubert, eds, *Mut zur Verantwortung: Frauen gestalten Politik in der CDU* (Cologne, Weimar, and Vienna, 2013).

Noelle Neumann, Elisabeth, *Die Schweigespirale: Öffentliche Meinung—Unsere soziale Haut* (Munich, 1980).

Noelle Neumann, Elisabeth, *Öffentliche Meinung: Die Entdeckung der Schweigespirale* (Berlin, 1989).

Pass-Weingartz, Dorothee and Gisela Erler, eds, *Mütter an die Macht: Die neue Frauen-Bewegung* (Hamburg, 1989).

Pflüger, Friedbert, *Ehrenwort: Das System Kohl und der Neubeginn* (Munich, 2000).

Philipp, Beatrix, 'Ich bin eine 1968erin!', in *Mut zur Verantwortung: Frauen gestalten Politik in der CDU*, edited by Beate Neuss and Hildigung Neubert (Cologne, Weimar, and Vienna, 2013), 347–54.

Picht, Georg, *Die deutsche Bildungskatastrophe: Analyse und Dokumentation* (Freiburg im Breisgau, 1964).

Popper, Karl R., *The Open Society and its Enemies*, 2 vols (London, 1945).

Radunski, Peter, *Wahlkämpfe: Moderne Wahlkampfführung als politische Kommunikation* (Munich, 1980).

Radunski, Peter, 'Der CDU-Frauenparteitag als Modell der politischen Willensbildung', in *Abschied von der Männergesellschaft*, edited by Heiner Geißler (Berlin, 1986), 170–7.

Radunski, Peter, *Aus der politischen Kulisse: Mein Beruf zur Politik* (Berlin, 2014).

RCDS Grundsatzprogramm (1969), available at https://www.kas.de/documents/252038/253252/7_file_storage_file_18226_1.pdf/d550a2e9-0af2-f69d-6a46-6c41c8fc3658?version=1.0&t=1539637748989 (accessed on 12 November 2019).

RCDS, ed., *Demokratischer Dialog zwischen Hochschule und Gesellschaft: CDU-Spitzenpolitiker auf RCDS-Veranstaltungen im Wintersemester 1977/78 an deutschen Hochschulen* (Bonn, 1978).

Reichart-Dreyer, Ingrid, *Werte -Systeme—Programme: Modell, Praxis und Alternativen politischer Willensbildung und Programmatik entwickelt am Beispiel der CDU* (Bonn, 1977).

Reichart-Dreyer, Ingrid, 'Relevanz vorherrschender Geschlechtsleitbilder in der Programmarbeit der CDU', in *Die politische Steuerung des Geschlechterregimes: Beiträge zur Theorie politischer Institutionen*, edited by Annette Henninger and Helga Ostendorf (Wiesbaden, 2005), 57–73.

Reichart-Dreyer, Ingrid, 'Partizipation von Frauen in der CDU', in *Gefährtinnen der Macht: Politische Partizipation von Frauen im vereinigten Deutschland: Eine Zwischenbilanz*, edited by Eva Malecky-Lewy and Virginia Penrose (Berlin, 1995), 37–63.

Reichart-Dreyer, Ingrid, *Macht und Demokratie in der CDU, dargestellt an Prozess und Ergebnis der Meinungsbildung zum Grundsatzprogramm 1994* (Wiesbaden, 2000).

Reichart-Dreyer, Ingrid, 'War die K-Frage in den C-Parteien eine F-G-V-Frage?'. *Femina Politica*, 1 (2002), 97–101.

Rohrmoser, Günther, *Das Debakel: Wo bleibt die Wende? Fragen an die CDU* (Krefeld, 1985).

Rowbotham, Sheila, *Promise of a Dream* (London, 2000).

Ruetz, Michael, *'Ihr müsst diesen Typen nur ins Gesicht sehen' (Klaus Schütz, SPD): APO Berlin, 1966–1969* (Frankfurt am Main, 1980).

Schelsky, Helmut, *Die skeptische Generation: Eine Soziologie der deutschen Jugend* (Düsseldorf and Cologne, 1957).

Scheuch, Erwin K., 'Soziologische Aspekte der Unruhe unter den Studenten'. *Aus Politik und Zeitgeschichte: Beilage zur Wochenzeitung Das Parlament*, 36 (1968), 3–25.

Scheuch, Erwin K., ed., *Die Widertäufer der Wohlstandsgesellschaft: Eine kritische Untersuchung der 'Neuen Linken' und ihrer Dogmen* (Cologne, 1968).

Schmidt, Giselherr, *Die Weltanschauung der Neuen Linken* (Bonn, 1968).

Schmidt, Gunter, ed., *Kinder der sexuellen Revolution: Kontinuität und Wandel studentischer Sexualität 1966–1996* (Gießen, 2000).

Schneider, Peter, *Rebellion und Wahn: Mein '68* (Cologne, 2008).

Schönbohm, Jörg, *Wilde Schermut: Erinnerungen eines Unpolitischen* (Berlin, 2010).

Schönbohm, Wulf, Peter Radunski, and Jürgen-Bernd Runge, *Die herausgeforderte Demokratie: Deutsche Studenten zwischen Reform und Revolution* (Mainz, 1968).

Schönbohm, Wulf, *Die Thesen der APO: Argumente gegen die radikale Linke* (Mainz, 1969).

Schönbohm, Wulf, ed., *Die Studentische Protestbewegung: Analysen und Konzepte* (Mainz, 1971).

Schönbohm, Wulf and Matthias Wissmann, eds, *Für eine humane Gesellschaft: Beiträge zum Programmdenken der jungen Generation* (Frankfurt am Main, 1976).

Schönbohm, Wulf, 'Das CDU-Grundsatzprogramm: Dokument politischer Erneuerung'. *Aus Politik und Zeitgeschichte*, 29 (1979), B 51–52, 27–39.

Schönbohm, Wulf, ed., *Verfassungsfeinde als Beamte? Die Kontroverse um die streitbare Demokratie* (Munich and Vienna, 1979).

Schönbohm, Wulf, 'Wie die Essener Leitsätze entstanden sind und was sie bewirkt haben', in *Abschied von der Männergesellschaft*, edited by Heiner Geißler (Berlin, 1986), 178–89.

Schönbohm, Wulf, *Parteifreunde: Ein Roman aus der Provinz* (Düsseldorf, Vienna, and New York, 1990).

Schönbohm, Wulf, 'Die 68er: politische Verirrungen und gesellschaftliche Veränderungen'. *APuZ*, 14–15 (2008).

Schröder, Gerhard, 'Regierungserklärung 1998', in *'Das Wort hat der Herr Bundeskanzler': Eine Analyse der grossen Regierungserklärungen von Adenauer bis Schröder*, edited by Karl-Rudolf Korte (Berlin, 2013), 435–67.

Semler, Christian, '1968 im Westen—was ging uns die DDR an?'. *Aus Politik und Zeitgeschichte*, B 45 (2003), 3–5.

Sozialwissenschaftliches Forschungsinstitut der Konrad-Adenauer Stiftung, *Empirische Daten im Zusammenhang der Diskussion um eine Tendenzwende in der Bundesrepublik* (Sankt Augustin, 1978).

Steinbach, Erika, 'Recht und Ordnung sind Substanz eines pfleglichen Miteinanders', in *Mut zur Verantwortung, Mut zur Verantwortung: Frauen gestalten die Politik der CDU*, edited by Beate Neuss and Hildigund Neubert (Cologne, Weimar, Vienna, 2015), 281–302.

Stephan, Cora, ed., *Wir Kollaborateure: Der Westen und die deutschen Vergangenheiten* (Hamburg, 1992).

Stronk, Detlef, *Berlin in den Achtziger Jahren: Im Brennpunkt der Deutsch-Deutschen Geschichte* (Berlin, 2009).

Süßmuth, Rita and Birgit Breuel, 'In der Politik brauchen sie Grundsätze und Kompromissbereitschaft. Mit Überzeugung muss man anfangn', in *Mut zur Verantwortung, Mut zur Verantwortung: Frauen gestalten die Politik der CDU*, edited by Beate Neuss and Hildigund Neubert (Cologne, Weimar, Vienna, 2015), 195–214.

Süßmuth, Rita, *Das Gift des Politischen: Gedanken und Erinnerungen* (Munich, 2015).

Teltschik, Horst, *329 Tage: Innenansichten der Einigung* (Berlin, 1991).

Westdeutsche Rektorenkonferenz, ed., *Übersicht über die Ergebnisse der Wahlen zu den Studentenvertretungen* (Bonn, 1968–1984).

Westley, William A. and Nathan B. Epstein, *The Silent Majority: Families of Emotionally Healthy College Students* (San Francisco, CA, 1969).

Wildenmann Rudolf and Max Kaase, *'Die unruhige Generation': Eine Untersuchung zu Politik und Demokratie in der Bundesrepublik* (Mannheim, 1968).

Secondary Sources

Abrams, Lynn, *Oral History Theory*, 2nd ed. (Abingdon, 2016).

Ahbe, Thomas and Rainer Gries, 'Gesellschaftsgeschichte als Generationengeschichte: Theoretische und methodische Überlegungen', in *Die DDR aus generationengeschichtlicher Perspektive: Eine Inventur*, edited by Annegret Schüle, Thomas Ahbe, and Rainer Gries (Leipzig, 2006), 475–571.

Ahonen, Pertti 'The Berlin Wall and the Battle for Legitimacy in Divided Germany.' *German Politics and Society*, 29, 2 (2011), 40–56.

Albrecht, Clemens, Günter C. Behrmann, and Michael Bock, eds, *Die intellektuelle Gründung der Bundesrepublik: Eine Wirkungsgeschichte der Frankfurter Schule* (Frankfurt am Main, 1999).

Albrecht, Willy, *Der Sozialistische Deutsche Studentenbund (SDS). Vom parteikonformen Studentenverband zum Repräsentanten der Neuen Linken* (Bonn, 1994).

Allerbeck, Klaus, *Soziologie radikaler Studentenbewegungen: Eine vergleichende Untersuchung in der Bundesrepublik Deutschland und den Vereinigten Staaten* (Munich and Vienna, 1973).

Altbach, Philip G., 'The International Student Movement'. *Journal of Contemporary History*, 5, 1 (1970), 156–74.

Aly, Götz, *Unser Kampf. 1968—Ein irritierter Blick zurück* (Frankfurt am Main, 2015).

Andresen, Knud, Linde Apel, and Kirsten Heinsohn, eds, *Es gilt das gesprochene Wort: Oral History und Zeitgeschichte heute* (Göttingen, 2015).

Andresen, Knud, *Gebremste Radikalisierung: Die IG Metall und ihre Jugend 1968 bis in die 1980er Jahre* (Göttingen, 2016).

Andrew, John A., *The Other Side of the Sixties: Young Americans for Freedom and the Rise of Conservative Politics* (New Brunswick, NJ, 1997).

Apel, Linde, 'Die Opposition der Opposition. Politische Mobilisierung an Oberschulen jenseits der Protestgeneration', in *Die 1970er Jahre als schwarzes Jahrzehnt: Politisierung und Mobilisierung zwischen christlicher Demokratie und extremer Rechter*, edited by Massimiliano Livi, Daniel Schmidt, and Michael Sturm (Frankfurt am Main, 2010), 57–72.

Apel, Linde, 'Jenseits von "1968". Politische Mobilisierung im Schwarzen Jahrzehnt', in *Zeitgeschichte in Hamburg: Nachrichten aus der Forschungsstelle für Zeitgeschichte in Hamburg 2018* (Hamburg, 2019), 52–70.

Artières, Philippe and Michelle Zancarini-Forunel, eds, *68: Une Histoire Collective (1962–1981)* (Paris, 2008).

Audier, Serge, *La pensée anti-68: Essai sur les origines d'une restauration intellectuelle* (Paris, 2009).

Audigier, François, *Histoire Du SAC: La Part D'ombre Du Gaullisme* (Paris, 2003).

Aust, Stefan, *The Baader-Meinhof Complex: The Inside Story of the R.A.F.* (London, 2008).

Bajohr, Frank, Anselm Doering-Manteuffel, Claudia Kemper, and Detlef Siegfried, eds, *Mehr als eine Erzählung: Zeitgeschichtliche Perspektiven auf die Bundesrepublik* (Göttingen, 2016).

Balz, Hanno, *Von Terroristen, Sympathisanten und dem starken Staat: Die öffentliche Debatte über die RAF in den 70er Jahren* (Frankfurt am Main, 2008).

Bar-On, Tamir, *Where Have All the Fascists Gone?* (Ashgate, 2007).

Bartz, Olaf, 'Konservative Studenten und die Studentenbewegung: Die "Kölner Studenten-Union"'. *Westfälische Forschung*, 48 (1998), 241–56.

Bavaj, Riccardo, 'Turning "Liberal Critics" into "Liberal-Conservatives": Kurt Sontheimer and the Re-Coding of the Political Culture in the Wake of the Student Revolt of "1968"'. *German Politics and Society*, 27, 1 (2009), 39–59.

Bavaj, Riccardo, 'Young, Old, and In-Between. Liberal Scholars and "Generation Building" at the Time of West Germany's Student Revolt', in *Talkin' 'Bout My Generation: Conflicts of Generation Building and Europe's '1968'*, edited by Anna von der Goltz (Göttingen, 2011), 177–94.

Bavaj, Riccardo and Martina Steber, eds, *Germany and the 'West': The History of a Modern Concept* (New York and Oxford, 2015).

Beck, Paul Allen and M. Kent Jennings, 'Family Traditions, Political Periods, and the Development of Partisan Orientations'. *The Journal of Politics*, 53, 3 (1991), 742–63.

Behre, Silja, *Bewegte Erinnerung: Deutungskämpfe um „1968' in deutsch-französischer Perspektive* (Tübingen, 2016).

Benninghaus, Christina, 'Das Geschlecht der Generation. Zum Zusammenhang von Generationalität und Männlichkeit um 1930', in *Generationen: Zur Relevanz eines wissenschaftlichen Grundbegriffs*, edited by Ulrike Jureit and Michael Wildt (Hamburg, 2005), 127–58.

Berghoff, Hartmut, Bernd Weisbrod, Uffa Jensen, and Christina Lubinski, eds, *History by Generations: Generational Dynamics in Modern History* (Göttingen, 2013).

Berman, Paul, 'The Passions of Joschka Fischer'. *New Republic* (27 August 2001).

Bernhard, Patrick, *Zivildienst zwischen Reform und Revolte: Eine bundesdeutsche Institution im gesellschaftlichen Wandel 1961–1982* (Munich, 2005).

Bessel, Richard and Dirk Schumann, 'Introduction: Violence, Normality and the Construction of Postwar Europe', in *Life after Death: Approaches to a Cultural and Social History of Europe during the 1940s and 1950s*, edited by Richard Bessel and Dirk Schumann (Cambridge, 2003), 1–14.

Bessel, Richard and Dirk Schumann, eds, *Life after Death: Approaches to a Cultural and Social History of Europe during the 1940s and 1950s* (Cambridge, 2003).

Bessel, Richard, *Germany 1945: From War to Peace* (New York, 2009).

Biebricher, Thomas, *Geistig-moralische Wende: Die Erschöpfung des deutschen Konservatismus* (Berlin, 2018).

Biermann, Ingrid, *Von Differenz zur Gleichheit: Frauenbewegung und Inklusionspolitiken im 19. und 20. Jahrhundert* (Bielefeld, 2009).

Biess, Frank, *Homecomings: Returning POWs and the Legacies of Defeat in Postwar Germany* (Princeton, NJ, 2006).

Biess, Frank, *Republik der Angst: Eine andere Geschichte der Bundesrepublik* (Hamburg, 2019).

Biess, Frank and Astrid Eckert, 'Why Do We Need New Narratives for the History of the Federal Republic?'. *Central European History*, 52, 1 (2019), 1–18.

Biess, Frank and Robert Moeller, eds, *Histories of the Aftermath: The Legacies of the Second World War in Europe* (Oxford, 2010).

Bilstein, Helmut et al., *Organisierter Kommunismus in der Bundesrepublik Deutschland: DKP-SDAJ-MSB Spartakus-KPD/KPDml/KBW/KB*, 4th ed. (Opladen, 1977).

Black, Lawrence, '1968 and all That(cher). Cultures of Conservatism and the New Right in Britain', in *Inventing the Silent Majority in Western Europe and the United States: Conservatism in the 1960s and 1970s*, edited by Anna von der Goltz and Britta Waldschmidt-Nelson (Cambridge, 2017), 356–76.

Blee, Kathleen, 'Evidence, Empathy and Ethics: Lessons from Oral Histories of the Klan'. *Journal of American History*, 80, 2 (1993), 596–606.

Blind, Jochen, *Heimspiel der 'Europa-Parteien'?: Die Europawahlkämpfe der Union von 1979 bis 2009* (Wiesbaden, 2012).

Blücher, Viggo Graf, *Die Generation der Unbefangenen* (Düsseldorf, 1964).

Böhme, Kurt, 'Zum Schicksal der weiblichen Kriegsgefangenen', in *Die deutschen Kriegsgefangenen*, edited by Erich Maschke (Bielefeld, 1974), 317–45.

Bohnenkamp, Björn, Till Manning, and Eva-Maria Silies, eds, *Generation als Erzählung: Neue Perspektiven auf ein kulturelles Deutungsmuster* (Göttingen, 2009).

Borstelmann, Thomas, *The 1970s: A New Global History From Civil Rights to Economic Inequality* (Princeton, NJ, 2012).

Bösch, Frank, *Die Adenauer-CDU: Gründung, Aufstieg und Krise einer Erfolgspartei 1945–1969* (Stuttgart, 2001).

Bösch, Frank, *Macht und Machtverlust: Die Geschichte der CDU* (Munich, 2002).

Bösch, Frank, 'Die Krise als Chance. Die Neuformierung der Christdemokraten in den siebziger Jahren', in *Das Ende der Zuversicht? Die siebziger Jahre als Geschichte*, edited by Konrad Jarausch (Göttingen, 2008), 296–309.

Bösch, Frank and Lucian Hölscher, eds, *Jenseits der Kirche: Die Öffnung religiöser Räume seit 1945* (Göttingen, 2013), 256–87.

Bösch, Frank, 'Engagement für Flüchtlinge: Die Aufnahme vietnamesischer "Boat People" in der Bundesrepublik'. *Zeithistorische Forschungen/Studies in Contemporary History*, 14 (2017), 13–40.

Bösch, Frank, ed., *A History Shared and Divided: East and West Germany since the 1970s* (New York, 2018).

Bösch, Frank, *Zeitenwende 1979: Als die Welt von heute begann* (Munich, 2019).

Bourdieu, Pierre, *Distinction: A Social Critique of the Judgement of Taste* (Cambridge, MA, 1984).

Bracke, Maud Anne, 'One-dimensional Conflict? Recent Scholarship on 1968 and the Limitations of the Generation Concept'. *Journal of Contemporary History*, 47, 3 (2012), 638–46.

Braunthal, Gerard, *Political Loyalty and Public Service in West Germany: The 1972 Decree against Radicals and Its Consequences* (Amherst, MA, 1990).

Bren, Paulina, '1968 in East and West: Visions of Political Change and Student Protest from across the Iron Curtain', in *Transnational Moments of Change: Europe 1945, 1968, 1989*, edited by Gerd-Rainer Horn and Padraic Kenney (Oxford, 2004), 119–36.

Brodie, Thomas, *German Catholicism at War, 1939–1945* (Oxford, 2018).

Brown, Timothy S., '1968. Transnational and Global Perspectives', Version: 1.0. *Docupedia-Zeitgeschichte*, 11.06.2012, available at http://docupedia.de/zg/1968?oldid=84582 (accessed on 24 November 2020).

Brown, Timothy S., *West Germany and the Global Sixties: The Antiauthoritarian Revolt, 1962–1978* (New York, 2013).

Brown, Timothy S. and Andrew Lison, eds, *The Global Sixties in Sound and Vision: Media, Counterculture, Revolt* (London, 2014).

Brubaker, Rogers and Frederick Cooper, 'Beyond "Identity"'. *Theory and Society*, 29, 1 (2000), 1–47.

Buchanan, Tom and Martin Conway, eds, *Political Catholicism in Europe 1918–1965* (Oxford, 1996).

Buchanan, Tom '"The Truth Will Set You Free": The Making of Amnesty International', *Journal of Contemporary History*, 37, 4 (2002), 575–97.

Bude, Heinz, *Das Altern einer Generation: Die Jahrgänge 1938 bis 1948* (Frankfurt am Main, 1995).

Bude, Heinz, 'The German Kriegskinder: Origins and Impact of the Generation of 1968', in *Generations in Conflict*, edited by Mark Roseman (Cambridge, 1995), 290–305.

Bude, Heinz, '"Die 50er Jahre im Spiegel der Flakhelfer- und der 68er-Generationä, in *Generationalität und Lebensgeschichte im 20. Jahrhundert*, edited by Jürgen Reulecke and Elisabeth Müller-Luckner (Munich, 2003), 145–58.

Bude, Heinz, *Adorno für Ruinenkinder: Eine Geschichte von 1968* (Munich, 2018).

Busche, Jürgen, *Die 68er: Eine Biografie* (Berlin, 2003).

Chappel, James, *Catholic Modern: The Challenge of Totalitarianism and the Remaking of the Church* (Cambrige, MA, 2018), 182–226.

Christinaens, Kim, Idesbald Godderis, and Magaly Rodríguez García, eds, *European Solidarity with Chile 1970s–1980s* (Frankfurt am Main, 2014).

Clemens, Clay, *Reluctant Realists: The CDU/CSU and West German Ostpolitik* (Durham and London, 1989).

Conway, Martin, 'The Rise and Fall of Western Europe's Democratic Age, 1945–1973'. *Contemporary European History*, 13, 1 (2004), 67–88.

Conway, Martin, 'The Age of Christian Democracy', in *European Christian Democracy: Historical Legacies and Comparative Perspectives*, edited by Thomas Kselman and Joseph A. Buttigieg (Notre Dame, IN, 2003), 43–67.

Conze, Eckart, *Die Suche nach Sicherheit: Eine Geschichte der Bundesrepublik von 1949 bis in die Gegenwart* (Munich, 2009).

Cornelißen, Christoph, ed., *Geschichtswissenschaft im Geist der Demokratie: Wolfgang J. Mommsen und seine Generation* (Berlin, 2010).

Cornils, Ingo, *Writing the Revolution: The Construction of '1968' in Germany* (Rochester, NY, 2016).

Creuzberger Stefan and Dierk Hoffmann, eds, *'Geistige Gefahr' und 'Immunisierung der Gesellschaft': Antikommunismus und politische Kultur in der frühen Bundesrepublik* (Berlin, Munich and Boston, MA, 2014).

Dahlke, Matthias, '"Nur eingeschränkte Krisenbereitschaft": Die staatliche Reaktion auf die Entführung des CDU-Politikers Peter Lorenz 1975'. *VfZ*, 4 (2007), 641–78.

Danyel, Jürgen, ed., *Die geteilte Vergangenheit: Zum Umgang mit Nationalsozialismus und Widerstand in beiden deutschen Staaten* (Berlin, 1995).

Davis, Belinda, 'The Personal Is Political: Gender, Politics, and Political Activism in Modern German History', in *Gendering Modern German History: Rewriting Historiography*, edited by Karen Hagemann and Jean H. Quataert (New York, 2007), 107–27.

Davis, Belinda, 'A Whole World Opening Up: Transcultural Contact, Difference, and the Politicization of "New Left" Activists', in *Changing the World, Changing Oneself: Political Protest and Collective Identities in the 1960s/70s West Germany and US*, edited by Belinda Davis, Wilfried Mausbach, Martin Klimke, and Carla MacDougall (New York and Oxford, 2010), 255–73.

Davis, Belinda, *The Internal Life of Politics: Extraparliamentary Opposition in West Germany, 1962–1983* (Cambridge, forthcoming).

Davis, John and Juliane Fürst, 'Drop-outs', In *Europe's 1968: Voices of Revolt*, edited by Robert Gildea, James Mark, and Anette Warring (Oxford, 2013), 193–210.

Davis, John, 'Silent Minority? British Conservative Students in the Age of Campus Protest', in *Inventing the 'Silent Majority' in Western Europe and the United States: Conservatism in the 1960s and 1970s*, edited by Anna von der Goltz and Britta Waldschmidt-Nelson (Cambridge, 2017), 63–80.

Depkat, Volker, 'Autobiographie und die soziale Konstruktion von Wirklichkeit'. *Geschichte und Gesellschaft*, 29, 3 (2003), 441–76.

Depkat, Volker, *Lebenswenden und Zeitenwenden: Deutsche Politiker und die Erfahrungen des 20. Jahrhundert* (Munich, 2007).

Dietz, Bernhard, Christopher Neumaier, and Andreas Rödder, eds, *Gab es den Wertewandel? Neue Forschungen zum gesellschaftlich-kulturellen Wandel seit den 1960er Jahren* (Munich, 2014).

Doering-Manteuffel, Anselm, *Wie westlich sind die Deutschen: Amerikanisierung und Westernisierung im 20. Jahrhundert* (Göttingen, 1999).

Dostal, Caroline, *Demonstranten vor Gericht: Ein Beitrag zur Justizgeschichte der Bundesrepublik* (Frankfurt am Main, 2006).

Dow, Bonnie J., 'Feminism, Miss America, and Media Mythology', *Rhetoric & Public Affairs*. 6, 1 (2003), 127–49.

Dufner, Georg, 'West Germany: Professions of Political Faith, the Solidarity Movement and New Left Imaginaries', in *European Solidarity with Chile 1970s-1980s*, edited by Kim Christinaens, Idesbald Godderis, and Magaly Rodríguez García (Frankfurt am Main, 2014), 163–86.

Dufner, Georg, 'Chile as a Litmus Test: East and West German Foreign Policy and Cold War Rivalry in Latin America', in *West Germany, the Global South and the Cold War*, edited by Agnes Bresselau von Bressensdorf, Christian Ostermann, and Elke Seefried (Munich, 2017), 77–118.

Duranti, Marco, *The Conservative Human Rights Revolution: European Identity, Transnational Politics, and the Origins of the European Convention* (Oxford, 2017).

Durham, Martin and Margaret Power, eds, *New Perspectives on the Transnational Right* (London, 2010).

Ebeling, Jana, 'Religiöser Straßenprotest? Medien und Kirchen im Streit um den § 218 in den 1970er Jahren', in *Jenseits der Kirche: Die Öffnung religiöser Räume seit 1945*, edited by Frank Bösch and Lucian Hölscher (Göttingen, 2013), 256–87.

Eckel, Jan, '"Under a Magnifying Glass": The International Human Rights Campaign against Chile in the Seventies', in *Human Rights in the Twentieth Century*, edited by Stefan-Ludwig Hoffmann (Cambridge, 2011), 321–42.

Eckel, Jan, 'The International League for the Rights of Man, Amnesty International, and the Changing Fate of Human Rights Activism from the 1940s through the 1970s'. *Humanity* 4, 2 (2013), 183–214.

Eckel, Jan and Samuel Moyn, eds, *The Breakthrough: Human Rights in the 1970s* (Philadelphia, PA, 2014).

Eckel, Jan, 'The Rebirth of Politics from the Spirit of Morality: Explaining the Human Rights Revolution of the 1970s', in *The Breakthrough: Human Rights in the 1970s*, edited by Jan Eckel and Samuel Moyn (Philadelphia, 2014), 226–60.

Eckel, Jan, *The Ambivalence of Good: Human Rights in International Politics since the 1940s* (Oxford, 2019).

Edmunds, June and Bryan S. Turner, *Generations, Culture and Society* (Buckingham and Philadelphia, PA, 2002).

Eilers, Silke, '"Sie kommen". Selbst- und Fremdbilder der Neuen Frauenbewegung'. In *Das Jahrhundert der Bilder*, vol. 2: *1949 bis heute*, edited by Gerhard Paul (Bonn, 2008), 458–65.

Eisel, Stephan, ed., *50 Jahre Bildungszentrum Schloss Eichholz: Die Geburtsstätte der Konrad-Adenauer-Stiftung* (Eichholz, 2006).

Eley, Geoff, *Forging Democracy: The History of the Left in Europe 1850–2000* (Oxford, 2002).

Epstein, Catherine, *The Last Revolutionaries: German Communists and Their Century* (Cambridge, MA, 2003).

Evans, Sara M., 'Sons, Daughters, and Patriarchy: Gender and the 1968 Generation'. *The American Historical Review*, 114, 2 (2009), 331–47.

Fahlenbrach, Katrin, *Protest-Inszenierungen: Visuelle Kommunikation und kollektive Identitäten in Protestbewegungen* (Wiesbaden, 2002).

Farber, David and Jeff Roche, eds, *The Conservative Sixties* (New York, 2003).

Ferguson, Niall, Charles Maier, Erez Manela, and Daniel Sargent, eds, *The Shock of the Global: The 1970s in Perspective* (Cambridge, MA, 2011).

Fichter, Tilman and Siegward Lönnendonker, 'Berlin: Hauptstadt der Revolte' (March 1980), http://web.fu-berlin.de/APO-archiv/Online/BlnHauptRev.htm (accessed 15 June 2015).

Fichter, Tilman, *SDS und SPD: Parteilichkeit jenseits der Partei* (Opladen, 1988).

Fichter, Tilman and Siegward Lönnendonker, *Kleine Geschichte des SDS: Der Sozialistische Deutsche Studentenbund von Helmut Schmidt bis Rudi Dutschke* (Bonn, 2008).

Fietze, Beate, '1968 als Symbol der ersten globalen Generation'. *Berliner Journal für Soziologie*, 3 (1997), 365–86.

Fietze, Beate, *Historische Generationen: Über einen sozialen Mechanismus kulturellen Wandels und kollektiver Kreativität* (Bielefeld, 2009).

Filmer, Werner and Heribert Schwan, *Helmut Kohl* (Düsseldorf, 1985).

Fink, Carole, Philipp Gassert, and Detlef Junker, eds, *1968: The World Transformed* (Cambridge, 1998).

Fraser, Ronald, *1968: A Student Generation in Revolt* (New York, 1988).

Frei, Norbert, *1968: Jugendrevolte und globaler Protest* (Munich, 2008).

Frese, Matthias, Julia Paulus, and Karl Teppe, eds, Demokratisierung und gesellschaftlicher Aufbruch: Die sechziger Jahre als Wendezeit der Bundesrepublik (Paderborn, 2003).

Frevert, Ute, 'Umbruch der Geschlechterverhältnisse? Die 60er Jahre als geschlechterpolitischer Experimentierraum', in *Dynamische Zeiten. Die 60er Jahre in den beiden deutschen Gesellschaften*, edited by Axel Schildt, Detlef Siegfried, and Karl Christian Lammers (Hamburg, 2000), 642–60.

Fulbrook, Mary, *Dissonant Lives: Generations and Violence Through the German Dictatorships* (Oxford, 2011).

Gabriel, Karl, 'Zwischen Aufbruch und Absturz in die Moderne. Die katholische Kirche in den 60er Jahren', in *Dynamische Zeiten. Die 60er Jahre in den beiden deutschen Gesellschaften*, edited by Axel Schildt, Detlef Siegfried, and Karl Christian Lammers (Hamburg, 2000), 528–43.

Gassert, Philipp, *Kurt Georg Kiesinger 1904–1988: Kanzler zwischen den Zeiten* (Munich, 2006).

Gassert, Philipp and Alan E. Steinweis, eds, *Coping with the Nazi Past: West German Debates on Nazism and Generational Conflict, 1955–1975* (New York, 2006).

George, Abosede, Clive Glaser, Margaret D. Jacobs, Chitra Joshi, Emily Marker, Alexandra Walsham, Wang Zheng, and Bernd Weisbrod, 'AHR Conversation: Each Generation Writes Its Own History of Generations'. *The American Historical Review*, 123, 5 (2018), 1505–46.

Geppert, Dominik and Jens Hacke, eds, *Streit um den Staat: Intellektuelle Debatten in der Bundesrepublik 1960–1980* (Göttingen, 2008).

Geyer, Martin, 'War over Words: The Search for a Public Language in West Germany', in *Political Languages in the Age of Extremes*, edited by Willibald Steinmetz (Oxford, 2011), 293–330.

Geyer, Martin, 'Elisabeth Noelle-Neumann's "Spiral of Silence", the Silent Majority, and the Conservative Moment of the 1970s', in *Inventing the Silent Majority in Western Europe and the United States: Conservatism in the 1960s and 1970s*, edited by Anna von der Goltz and Britta Waldschmidt-Nelson (Cambridge, 2017), 251–74.

Giesecke, Jens, *The History of the Stasi: East Germany's Secret Police, 1945–1990*, trans. David Burnett (Oxford, 2014).

Gilcher-Holtey, Ingrid, ed., *A Revolution of Perception?: Consequences and Echoes of 1968* (Oxford, 2014).

Gildea, Robert, James Mark and Anette Warring, eds, *Europe's 1968: Voices of Revolt* (Oxford, 2013).

Gleason, Abbott, *Totalitarianism: The Inner History of the Cold War* (New York and Oxford, 1995).

Glienke, Stephan Alexander, *Die Ausstellung „Ungesühnte Nazijustiz' (1959–1962): Zur Geschichte der Aufarbeitung nationalsozialistischer Justizverbrechen* (Baden-Baden, 2008).

Gordon, Daniel, 'Liquidating May '68. Generational Trajectories of the 2007 Presidential Elections'. *Modern and Contemporary France*, 16, 2 (2008), 143–59.

Görtemaker, Manfred, *Geschichte der Bundesrepublik Deutschland: Von der Gründung bis zur Gegenwart* (Frankfurt, 2004).

Gotto, Bernhard, *Enttäuschung in der Demokratie* (Berlin and Boston, MA, 2018).

Graf, Rüdiger and Kim Christian Priemel, 'Zeitgeschichte in der Welt der Sozialwissenschaften. Legitimität und Originalität einer Disziplin'. *VfZ*, 59, 4 (2011), 479–508.

Grafe, Peter J., *Schwarze Visionen: Die Modernisierung der CDU* (Hamburg, 1986).

Granieri, Ronald J., 'Politics in C Minor: The CDU/CSU between Germany and Europe since the Secular Sixties'. *Central European History*, 42 (2009), 1–32.

Greenberg, Udi, 'Militant Democracy and Human Rights'. *New German Critique*, 42, 3 (2015), 169–95.

Greiner, Bernd, *War Without Fronts: The USA in Vietnam* (New Haven, CT, 2009).

Großbölting, Thomas, *Losing Heaven: Religion in Germany since 1945* (New York and Oxford, 2017).

Großmann, Johannes, *Die Internationale der Konservativen: Transnationale Elitenzirkel und private Außenpolitik in Westeuropa seit 1945* (Munich, 2014).

Grube, Norbert, 'Seines Glückes Schmied? Entstehungs- und Verwendungskontexte von Allensbacher Umfragen zum Wertewandel 1947–2001', in *Gab es den Wertewandel? Neue Forschungen zum gesellschaftlich-kulturellen Wandel seit den 1960er Jahren*, edited by Bernhard Dietz, Christopher Neumaier, and Andreas Rödder (Munich, 2014), 95–120.

Häberlen, Joachim, *The Emotional Politics of the Alternative Left: West Germany 1968–1984* (Cambridge, 2018).

Hachmeister, Lutz, *Schleyer: Eine deutsche Geschichte* (Munich, 2004).

Hacke, Christian, *Weltmacht wider Willen: Die Außenpolitik der Bundesrepublik Deutschland* (Frankfurt am Main and Berlin, 1993).

Hacke, Jens, *Philosophie der Bürgerlichkeit: Die liberalkonservative Begründung der Bundesrepublik* (Göttingen, 2006).

Hanisch, Carol, 'The Personal is Political', in *Notes from the Second Year: Women's Liberation: Major Writings of the Radical Feminists*, edited by Shulamith Firestone and Anne Koedt (New York, 1970).

Hanshew, Karrin, *Terror and Democracy in West Germany* (New York, 2012).

Hastings, Derek, *Catholicism and the Roots of Nazism: Religious Identity and National Socialism* (Oxford, 2010).

Hausen, Karin, *Geschlechtergeschichte als Gesellschaftsgeschichte* (Göttingen, 2012).

Heer, Hannes and Klaus Naumann, eds, *Vernichtungskrieg: Verbrechen der Wehrmacht 1941–1944* (Hamburg, 1995).

Heither, Dietrich, *Verbündete Männer: Die Deutsche Burschenschaft: Weltanschauung, Politik und Brauchtum* (Cologne, 2001).

Hemmelmann, Petra, *Der Kompass der CDU: Analyse der Grundsatz- und Wahlprogramme von Adenauer bis Merkel* (Wiesbaden, 2017).

Heinrich-Böll-Stiftung and Feministisches Institut, eds, *Wie weit flog die Tomate? Eine 68erinnen-Gala der Reflexion* (Berlin, 1999).

Herbert, Ulrich, ed., *Wandlungsprozesse in Westdeutschland: Belastung, Integration, Liberalisierung 1945–1980* (Göttingen, 2002).

Herbert, Ulrich, *Best: Biographische Studien über Radikalismus, Weltanschauung und Vernunft, 1903–1989* (Bonn, 1996).

Herbert, Ulrich, 'Drei politische Generationen im 20. Jahrhundert', in *Generationalität und Lebensgeschichte im 20. Jahrhundert*, edited by Jürgen Reulecke and Elisabeth Müller-Luckner (Munich, 2003), 95–114.

Herbstritt, Georg, *Bundesbürger im Dienst der DDR-Spionage: Eine analytische Studie* (Göttingen, 2007).

Herf, Jeffrey, *Undeclared Wars with Israel: East Germany and the West German Far Left, 1967–1989* (New York, 2016).

Herzog, Dagmar, *Sex after Fascism: Memory and Morality in Twentieth-century Germany* (Princeton, NJ, 2005).

Hilwig, Stuart, 'The Revolt Against the Establishment: Students Versus the Press in West Germany and Italy', in *1968: The World Transformed*, edited by Carole Fink, Philipp Gassert, and Detlef Junker (Cambridge, 1998), 321–50.

Hilwig, Stuart, *Italy and 1968: Youthful Unrest and Democratic Culture* (Basingstoke, UK, and New York, 2009).

Hockenos, Paul, *Joschka Fischer and the Making of the Berlin Republic* (Oxford, 2008).

Hoeres, Peter, 'Von der "Tendenzwende" zur "geistig-moralischen Wende". Konstruktion und Kritik konservativer Signaturen in den 1970er und 1980er Jahren'. *VfZ*, 61, 1 (2013), 93–119.

Hoffmann, Stefan-Ludwig, ed., *Human Rights in the Twentieth Century* (Cambridge, 2011).

Holl, Kurt and Claudia Glunz, eds, *1968 am Rhein: Satisfaction und Ruhender Verkehr* (Cologne, 1998).

Horn, Gerd-Rainer and Padraic Kenney, eds, *Transnational Moments of Change: Europe 1945, 1968, 1989* (Oxford, 2004).

Horn, Gerd-Rainer, *The Spirit of '68: Rebellion in Western Europe and North America, 1956–1976* (Oxford, 2007).

Hosek, Jennifer Ruth, *Sun, Sex and Socialism: Cuba in the German Imaginary* (Toronto, 2012).

Hughes, Celia, *Young Lives on the Left: Sixties Activism and the Liberation of the Self* (Manchester, 2015).

Huntington, Samuel P., 'Conservatism as an Ideology'. *The American Political Science Review*, 51, 2 (1957), 454–73.

Inglehart, Ronald, *The Silent Revolution: Changing Values and Political Styles Among Western Publics* (Princeton, NJ, 1977).

Jäckel, Eberhard, Karl Dietrich Bracher, Theodor Eschenburg, and Joachim C. Fest, eds, *Geschichte der Bundesrepublik Deutschland* 5 vols (Leipzig, 1992).

Kelly, Patrick William, 'The 1973 Chilean Coup and the Origins of Transnational Human Rights Activism'. *Journal of Global History*, 8 (2013), 165–86.

Kersting, Franz-Werner, 'Helmut Schelskys "Skeptische Generation" von 1957: Zur Publikations- und Wirkungsgeschichte eines Standardwerkes'.*VfZ*, 50, 3 (2002), 465–95.

Kersting, Franz-Werner, Jürgen Reulecke, and Hans-Ulrich Thamer, eds, *Die zweite Gründung der Bundesrepublik: Generationswechsel und intellektuelle Wortergreifungen 1955 bis 1975* (Stuttgart, 2010).

Koenen, Gerd, *Das Rote Jahrzehnt: Unsere kleine deutsche Kulturrevolution, 1967–1977* (Cologne, 2001).

Kreis, Reinhild, *Orte für Amerika. Die deutsch-amerikanischen Institute und Amerikahäuser in der Bundesrepublik seit den 1960er Jahren* (Stuttgart, 2012).

Kroll, Thomas, 'Generationenverhältnisse und politischer Konflikt während der Studentenrevolte von 1968 in der Bundesrepublik Deutschland', in *Übergänge und Schnittmengen: Arbeit, Migration, Bevölkerung und Wissenschaftsgeschichte in Diskussion*, edited by Annemarie Steidl (Cologne, Weimar, Vienna, 2008), 319–46.

Kühn, Andreas, *Stalins Enkel, Maos Söhne: Die Lebenswelt der K-Gruppen in der Bundesrepublik der 1970er Jahre* (Frankfurt am Main, 2005).

Kundnani, Hans, *Utopia or Auschwitz: Germany's 1968 Generation and the Holocaust* (London, 2009).

Jackson, Julian, James S. Williams, and Anna-Louise Milne, eds, *May 68: Rethinking France's Last Revolution* (London, 2011).

Jarausch, Konrad, *Deutsche Studenten 1800–1970* (Frankfurt am Main, 1984).

Jarausch, Konrad, 'Critical Memory and Civil Society: The Impact of the 1960s on German Debates about the Past', in *Coping with the Nazi Past: West German Debates on Nazism and Generational Conflict, 1955–1975*, edited by Philipp Gassert and Alan E. Steinweis (New York, 2006), 11–30.

Jarausch, Konrad, *After Hitler: Recivilizing Germans, 1945–1955* (New York, 2006).

Jarausch, Konrad, *Broken Lives: How Ordinary Germans Experienced the 20th Century* (Princeton, NJ, 2018).

Jobs, Richard Ivan, 'Youth Movements: Travel, Protest, and Europe in 1968'. *The American Historical Review*, 114, 2 (2009), 376–404.

Jobs, Richard Ivan, 'The Grand Tour of Daniel Cohn-Bendit and the Europeanism of 1968', in *May 68: Rethinking France's Last Revolution*, edited by Julian Jackson, James S. Williams, and Anna-Louise Milne (London, 2011), 231–44.

Jobs, Richard Ivan, *Backpack Ambassadors: How Youth Travel Integrated Europe* (Chicago, IL, and London, 2017).

Judt, Tony, *Postwar: A History of Europe Since 1945* (New York, 2005).

Jureit, Ulrike, *Generationenforschung* (Göttingen, 2006).

Jureit, Ulrike, 'Generation, Generationalität, Generationenforschung, Version: 2.0', in *Docupedia-Zeitgeschichte*, 03.08.2017, http://dx.doi.org/10.14765/zzf.dok.2.1117.v2

Jureit, Ulrike und Michael Wildt, eds, *Generationen: Zur Relevanz eines wissenschaftlichen Grundbegriffs* (Hamburg, 2005).

Kaiser, Wolfram, *Christian Democracy and the Origins of European Union* (Cambridge, 2007).

Kandora, Michael, 'Homosexualität und Sittengesetz', in *Wandlungsprozesse in Westdeutschland: Belastung, Integration, Liberalisierung 1945–1980*, edited by Ulrich Herbert (Göttingen, 2002), 379–401.

Karl, Michaela, *Rudi Dutschke: Revolutionär ohne Revolution* (Frankfurt am Main, 2003).

Kätzel, Ute, *Die 68erinnen: Porträt einer rebellischen Frauengeneration* (Berlin, 2002).

Kershaw, Ian, *The End: The Defiance and Destruction of Hitler's Germany, 1944–1945* (London, 2011).

Kershaw, Ian, *To Hell and Back: Europe 1914–1949* (London, 2016).

Klages, Helmut, *Wertorientierungen im Wandel: Rückblick, Gegenwartsanalyse, Prognosen* (Frankfurt am Main, 1984).

Klatch, Rebecca E., *A Generation Divided: The New Left, the New Right, and the 1960s* (Berkeley, CA, 1997).

Klimke, Martin, *The Other Alliance: Student Protest in West Germany and the United States in the Global Sixties* (Princeton, NJ, 2009).

Kohut, Thomas A., *A German Generation: An Experiential History of the Twentieth Century* (New Haven, CT, 2012).

Kossert, Andreas, *Kalte Heimat: Die Geschichte der deutschen Vertriebenen nach 1945* (Berlin, 2008).

Krabbe, Wolfgang R., *Kritische Anhänger unbequeme Störer: Studien zur Politisierung deutscher Jugendlicher im 20. Jahrhundert* (Berlin, 2010).

Kraushaar, Wolfgang, 'Denkmodelle der 68er'. *Aus Politik und Zeitgeschichte* B 22–23 (2001), 14–27.

Kraushaar, Wolfgang, *Achtundsechzig: Eine Bilanz* (Berlin, 2008).

Kraushaar, Wolfgang, *Die blinden Flecken der 68er Bewegung* (Stuttgart, 2018).

Kruke, Anja, *Demoskopie in der Bundesrepublik Deutschland: Meinungsforschung, Parteien und Medien 1949–1990* (Düsseldorf, 2007).

Kselman, Thomas and Joseph A. Buttigieg, eds, *European Christian Democracy: Historical Legacies and Comparative Perspectives* (Notre Dame, IN, 2003).

Kutschke, Beate and Barley Norton, eds, *Music and Protest in 1968* (Cambridge, 2013).

Large, David Clay, *Berlin: A Modern History* (New York, 2000).

Lau, Mariam, *Die letzte Volkspartei: Angela Merkel und die Modernisierung der CDU* (Munich, 2009).

Leggewie, Claus, *'Kofferträger': Das Algerien-Projekt der Linken im Adenauer-Deutschland* (Berlin, 1984).

Levsen, Sonja, Cornelius Torp, eds, *Wo liegt die Bundesrepublik? Vergleichende Perspektiven auf die westdeutsche Geschichte* (Göttingen, 2016).

Livi, Massimiliano, Daniel Schmidt and Michael Sturm, eds, *Die 70er Jahre als schwarzes Jahrzehnt: Politisierungs- und Mobilisierungsprozesse zwischen rechter Mitte und extremer Rechter in Italien und der Bundesrepublik 1967–1982* (Bielefeld, 2010).

Lovell, Stephen, ed, *Generations in Twentieth-Century Europe* (Basingstoke, 2007).

Lowe, Keith, *Savage Continent: Europe in the Aftermath of WWII* (London, 2012).

Macmillan, Margaret, *Nixon & Mao: The Week that Changed the World* (New York: Random House, 2007).

Madsen, Mikael Rask, '"Legal Diplomacy"—Law, Politics and the Genesis of Postwar European Human Rights', in *Human Rights in the Twentieth Century*, edited by, Stefan-Ludwig Hoffmann (Cambridge, 2011), 62–84.

Maier, Charles, *The Unmasterable Past: History, Holocaust, and German National Identity* (Cambridge, CA, 1988).

Maier, Charles S., '1968, Did It Matter?', in *Promises of 1968: Crisis, Illusion, and Utopia*, edited by Vladimir Tismaneanu (Budapest and New York, 2011), 403–23.

Major, Patrick, *Behind the Berlin Wall: East Germany and the Frontiers of Power* (Oxford, 2009).

Mammone, Andrea, *Transnational Neofascism in France and Italy* (New York, 2015).

Mark, James and Anna von der Goltz, 'Encounters', in *Europe's 1968: Voices of Revolt*, edited by Robert Gildea, James Mark, and Anette Warring (Oxford, 2013), 131–63.

Mark, James, Anna von der Goltz, and Anette Warring, 'Reflections', in *Europe's 1968: Voices of Revolt*, edited by Robert Gildea, James Mark, and Anette Warring (Oxford, 2013), 283–325.

März, Michael, *Linker Protest nach dem Deutschen Herbst* (Bielefeld, 2012).

Mausbach, Wilfried, 'Auschwitz and Vietnam: West German Protest against America's War in the 1960s', in *America, the Vietnam War, and the World: Comparative and International Perspectives*, edited by Wilfried Mausbach, Andreas W. Daum, and Lloyd C. Gardner (New York, 2003), 279–98.

Mausbach, Wilfried, Andreas W. Daum, and Lloyd C. Gardner, eds, *America, the Vietnam War, and the World: Comparative and International Perspectives* (New York, 2003).

Mazower, Mark, *Dark Continent: Europe's Twentieth Century* (London, 1998).

Meifort, Franziska, *Ralf Dahrendorf: Eine Biographie* (Munich, 2017).

Mende, Silke, *'Nicht rechts, nicht links, sondern vorn': Eine Geschichte der Gründungsgrünen* (Munich, 2011).

Mergel, Thomas, *Propaganda nach Hitler: Eine Kulturgeschichte des Wahlkampfs in der Bundesrepublik 1949–1990* (Göttingen, 2010).

Meyer, Christoph, *Die deutschlandpolitische Doppelstrategie: Wilhelm Wolfgang Schütz und das Kuratorium Unteilbares Deutschland 1954–1972* (Landsberg am Lech, 1997).

Michels, Eckart, *Schahbesuch 1967: Fanal für die Studentenbewegung* (Berlin, 2017).

Miermeister, Jürgen, *Ernst Bloch, Rudi Dutschke* (Hamburg, 1996).

Moeller, Robert G., *Protecting Motherhood: Women and the Family in the Politics of Postwar West Germany* (Berkeley and Los Angeles, CA, 1993).

Moeller, Robert G., *War Stories: The Search for a Usable Past in the Federal Republic of Germany* (Berkeley, CA, 2001).

Mohr, Arno, *Politikwissenschaft als Alternative: Stationen einer wissenschaftlichen Disziplin auf dem Wege zu ihrer Selbständigkeit in der Bundesrepublik Deutschland 1945–1965* (Bochum, 1988).

Moyn, Samuel, 'The Return of the Prodigal: The 1970s as a Turning Point in Human Rights History', in *The Breakthrough: Human Rights in the 1970s*, edited by Jan Eckel and Samuel Moyn (Philadelphia, PA, 2014), 1–14.

Moyn, Samuel, *Christian Human Rights* (Philadelphia, PA, 2015).

Morris, Will, 'Spiel Appeal: Play, Drug Use and the Culture of 1968 in West Germany', *Journal of Contemporary History*, 49, 4 (2014), 770–93.

Moses, Dirk A., *German Intellectuals and the Nazi Past* (Cambridge, 2006).

Mrozek, Bodo, *Jugend—Pop—Kultur: Eine transnationale Geschichte* (Frankfurt am Main, 2019).

Müller, Jan-Werner, *Contesting Democracy: Political Ideas in Twentieth Century Europe* (New Haven, CT and London, 2011).

Muller, Jerry Z., 'German Neoconservatism and the History of the Bonn Republic, 1968 to 1985', *German Politics & Society*, 18/1 (2000), 1–32.

Münkel, Daniela, 'Der "Bund Freiheit der Wissenschaft": Die Auseinandersetzung um die Demokratisierung der Hochschule', in *Streit um den Staat: Intellektuelle Debatten in der Bundesrepublik 1960–1980*, edited by Dominik Geppert and Jens Hacke (Göttingen, 2008), 171–86.

Mushaben, Joyce Marie, *Becoming Madam Chancellor: Angela Merkel and the Berlin Republic* (Cambridge, 2017).

Nagle, John D., *The National Democratic Party: Right Radicalism in the Federal Republic of Germany* (Berkeley, Los Angeles, London, 1970).

Nehring, Holger, 'The British and West German Protests against Nuclear Weapons and the Cultures of the Cold War, 1957–64'. *Contemporary British History*, 19, 2 (2005), 223–41.

Nehring, Holger, '"Generation" as Political Argument in the West European Protest Movements in the 1960s', in *Generations in Twentieth-Century Europe*, edited by Stephen Lovell (Basingstoke, 2007), 57–78.

Nehring, Holger, *Politics of Security: British and West German Protest Movements and the Early Cold War, 1945–1970* (Oxford, 2013).

Niethammer, Lutz, *Angepasster Faschismus: Politische Praxis der NPD* (Frankfurt am Main, 1969).

Niethammer, Lutz, ed., *„Die Jahre weiß man nicht, wo man die heute hinsetzen soll.' Faschismuserfahrungen im Ruhrgebiet* (Berlin/Bonn 1983).

Niethammer, Lutz, ed., „Hinterher merkt man, daß es richtig war, daß es schiefgegangen ist.' Nachkriegserfahrungen im Ruhrgebiet (Berlin/Bonn 1983).

Niethammer, Lutz and Alexander von Plato, eds, 'Wir kriegen jetzt andere Zeiten'. Auf der Suche nach der Erfahrung des Volkes in nachfaschistischen Ländern (Bonn, 1989).

Niethammer, Lutz, 'Die letzte Gemeinschaft: Über die Konstruierbarkeit von Generationen und ihre Grenzen', in Historische Beiträge zur Generationsforschung, edited by Bernd Weisbrod (Göttingen, 2009), 13–38.

Niven, Bill, Facing the Nazi Past: United Germany and the Legacy of the Third Reich (London and New York: Routledge, 2002).

Niven, Bill, ed., Germans as Victims: Remembering the Past in Contemporary Germany (London, 2006).

Nolan, Mary, 'Pushing the Defensive Wall of the State Forward: Terrorism and Civil Liberties in Germany', New German Critique, 117 (2012), 109–33.

Nollmann, Gerd, 'Ralf Dahrendorf: Grenzgänger und zwischen Wissenschaft und Politik'. Soziologie heute, 3, 11 (2010), 32–5.

Norwig, Christina, Die erste europäische Generation: Europakonstruktionen in der Europäischen Jugendkampagne 1951–1958 (Göttingen, 2016).

Oberreuter, Heinrich, 'The CDU and Social Change'. German Politics & Society, 14 (June 1988), 3–12.

Oseka, Piotr, Polymeris Voglis, and Anna von der Goltz, 'Families', in Europe's 1968: Voices of Revolt, edited by Robert Gildea, James Mark, and Anette Warring (Oxford, 2013), 46–71.

Overmans, Rüdiger Deutsche militärische Verluste im Zweiten Weltkrieg (Munich, 1999).

Pas, Niek, Provo! Mediafenomeen 1965–1967 (Amsterdam, 2015).

Passerini, Luisa, Autobiography of a Generation: Italy, 1968 (Hanover, 1996).

Paulus, Julia, Eva-Maria Silies, and Kerstin Wolff, eds, Zeitgeschichte als Geschlechtergeschichte: Neue Perspektiven auf die Bundesrepublik (Frankfurt am Main, 2012).

Petersen, Andreas, Radikale Jugend: Die sozialistische Jugendbewegung in der Schweiz 1900–1930: Radikalisierungsanalyse und Generationentheorie (Zurich, 2001).

Portelli, Alessandro, The Death of Luigi Trastulli and Other Stories: Form and Meaning in Oral History (Albany, NY, 1991).

Portelli, Alessandro, The Battle of Valle Giulia: Oral History and the Art of Dialogue (Madison, WI, 1997).

Pridham, Geoffrey, Christian Democracy in Western Germany: The CDU/CSU in Government and Opposition, 1945–1976 (London, 1977).

Reichardt, Sven, Authentizität und Gemeinschaft: Linksalternatives Leben in den siebziger und frühen achtziger Jahren (Berlin, 2014).

Reimann, Aribert, Dieter Kunzelmann: Avantgardist, Protestler, Radikaler (Göttingen, 2009).

Reimann, Aribert, 'Letters from Amman: Dieter Kunzelmann and the Origins of German Anti-Zionism during the Late 1960s', in A Revolution of Perception?: Consequences and Echoes of 1968, edited by Ingrid Gilcher-Holtey (Oxford, 2014), 69–88.

Requate, Jörg, 'Gefährliche Intellektuelle? Staat und Gewalt in der Debatte um die RAF', in Streit um den Staat: Intellektuelle Debatten in der Bundesrepublik 1960–1980, edited by Dominik Geppert and Jens Hacke (Göttingen, 2008), 251–69.

Reulecke, Jürgen and Elisabeth Müller-Luckner, eds, Generationalität und Lebensgeschichte im 20. Jahrhundert (Munich, 2003).

Richie, Alexandra, Faust's Metropolis: A History of Berlin (London, 1999).

Rigoll, Dominik, Staatsschutz in Westdeutschland: Von der Entnazifizierung zur Extremistenabwehr (Göttingen, 2013).

Rödder, Andreas, *Die Bundesrepublik Deutschland 1969–1989* (Munich, 2004).

Rödder, Andreas, *Deutschland einig Vaterland: Die Geschichte der Wiedervereinigung* (Munich, 2009).

Rohstock, Anne, *Von der 'Ordinarienuniversität" zur „Revolutionszentrale': Hochschulreform und Hochschulrevolte in Bayern und Hessen 1957–1976* (Munich, 2010).

Roseman, Mark, ed., *Generations in Conflict* (Cambridge, 1995).

Rosenthal, Gabriele, 'Zur interaktionellen Konstitution von Generationen: Generationenabfolgen in Familien von 1890 bis 1970 in Deutschland', in *Generationen-Beziehungen, Austausch und Tradierung*, edited by Jürgen Mansel, Gabriele Rosenthal, and Angelika Tölke (Opladen,1997), 57–73.

Ross, Kristin, *May '68 and its Afterlives* (Chicago, IL, 2002).

Ruff, Mark Edward, *The Wayward Flock: Catholic Youth in Postwar West Germany* (Chapel Hill, NC and London, 2005).

Rusinek, Bernd-A., 'Von der Entdeckung der NS-Vergangenheit zum generellen Faschismusverdacht—akademische Diskurse in der Bundesrepublik der 60er Jahre', in *Dynamische Zeiten. Die 60er Jahre in den beiden deutschen Gesellschaften*, edited by Axel Schildt, Detlef Siegfried, and Karl Christian Lammers (Hamburg, 2000), 114–47.

Sarotte, Mary, *1989: The Struggle to Create Post-Cold War Europe* (Princeton, NJ, 2009).

Scanlon, Sandra, *The Pro-War Movement: Domestic Support for the Vietnam War and the Making of Modern American Conservatism* (Amherst, MA, 2013).

Schaefer, Bernd, 'Sino-West German Relations during the Mao Era'. *CWIHP e-Dossier*, 56 (3 November 2014), available at https://www.wilsoncenter.org/publication/sino-west-german-relations-during-the-mao-era (accessed on 23 November 2020).

Scharloth, Joachim, *1968: Eine Kommunikationsgeschichte* (Munich, 2011).

Schildt, Axel, *Moderne Zeiten: Freizeit, Massenmedien und Zeitgeist in der Bundesrepublik der 50er Jahre* (Hamburg, 1995).

Schildt, Axel, *Konservatismus in Deutschland: Von den Anfängen im 18. Jahrhundert bis zur Gegenwart* (Munich, 1998).

Schildt, Axel, *Ankunft im Westen. Ein Essay zur Erfolgsgeschichte der Bundesrepublik* (Frankfurt am Main, 1999).

Schildt, Axel, 'Materieller Wohlstand—pragmatische Politik—kulturelle Umbrüche. Die 60er Jahre der Bundesrepublik', in *Dynamische Zeiten. Die 60er Jahre in den beiden deutschen Gesellschaften*, edited by Axel Schildt, Detlef Siegfried, and Karl Christian Lammers (Hamburg, 2000), 21–53.

Schildt, Axel, Detlef Siegfried, and Karl-Christian Lammers, eds, *Dynamische Zeiten: Die 60er Jahre in den beiden deutschen Gesellschaften* (Hamburg, 2000).

Schildt, Axel, 'Nachwuchs fuer die Rebellion. Die Schülerbewegung der späten sechziger Jahre', in *Generationalität und Lebensgeschichte im 20. Jahrhundert*, edited by Jürgen Reulecke and Elisabeth Müller-Luckner (Munich, 2003), 229–51.

Schildt, Axel, '"Die Kräfte der Gegenreform sind auf breiter Front angetreten." Zur konservativen Tendenzwende in den Siebzigerjahren'. *Archiv für Sozialgeschichte* 44 (2004), 449–7.

Schildt, Axel, *Die Sozialgeschichte der Bundesrepublik Deutschland bis 1989/90* (Munich, 2007).

Schissler, Hanna, ed., *The Miracle Years: A Cultural History of West Germany, 1949–1968* (Princeton NJ, 2001).

Schletter, Christian, *Grabgesang der Demokratie: Die Debatten über das Scheitern der bundesdeutschen Demokratie von 1965 bis 1985* (Göttingen, 2015).

Schmidt, Daniel, '"Die geistige Führung verloren'. Antworten der CDU auf die Herausforderung '1968'", in *Die zweite Gründung der Bundesrepublik. Generationswechsel und intellektuelle*

Wortergreifungen 1955–1975, edited by Franz-Werner Kersting, Jürgen Reulecke, and Hans-Ulrich Thamer (Stuttgart, 2010), 85–107.

Schmidtke, Michael, 'The German New Left and National Socialism', in *Coping with the Nazi Past: West German Debates on Nazism and Generational Conflict, 1955–1975*, edited by Philipp Gassert and Alan E. Steinweis (New York, 2006), 176–93.

Schneider, Gregory L., *Cadres for Conservatism: Young Americans for Freedom and the Rise of the Contemporary Right* (New York, 1999).

Schöllgen, Gregor, *Gerhard Schröder: Die Biographie* (Munich, 2015).

Schönbohm, Wulf, *Die CDU wird moderne Volkspartei* (Stuttgart, 1985).

Schüle, Annegret, Thomas Ahbe, and Rainer Gries, eds, *Die DDR aus generationengeschichtlicher Perspektive: Eine Inventur* (Leipzig, 2006).

Schulz, Hermann, Hartmut Radebold and Jürgen Reulecke, *Söhne ohne Väter: Erfahrungen der Kriegsgeneration* (Berlin, 2003).

Schulz, Kristina, *Der lange Atem der Provokation: Die Frauenbewegung in der Bundesrepublik und in Frankreich 1968–1976* (Frankfurt and New York, 2002).

Schwarz, Bill, 'The Silent Majority. How the Private Becomes Political', in *Inventing the Silent Majority in Western Europe and the United States: Conservatism in the 1960s and 1970s*, edited by Anna von der Goltz and Britta Waldschmidt-Nelson (Cambridge, 2017), 147–71.

Schwarz, Hans-Peter, *Helmut Kohl: Eine politische Biographie* (Munich, 2012).

Schweppe, Peter, 'The Politics of Removal: Kursbuch and the West German Protest Movement'. *The Sixties*, 7, 2 (2014), 138–54.

Sedlmaier, Alexander and Stephan Malinowski, '"1968" -A Catalyst of Consumer Society'. *Cultural and Social History*, 8, 2 (2011), 255–74.

Sedlmaier, Alexander, *Consumption and Violence: Radical Protest in Cold-War West Germany* (Ann Arbor, MI, 2014).

Seegers, Lu, *'Vati blieb im Krieg': Vaterlosigkeit als generationelle Erfahrung im 20. Jahrhundert–Deutschland und Polen* (Göttingen, 2013).

Seegers, Lu, '"Dead Dads": Memory Narratives of War-related Fatherlessness in Germany'. *European Review of History*, 22, 2 (2015), 259–76.

Seitenbecher, Manuel, 'Die Reform als Revolution in verträglicher Dosis: Der Ring Christlich-Demokratischer Studenten (RCDS) während der 68er-Jahre an der FU Berlin'. *Zeitschrift für Geschichtswissenschaft*, 6 (2010), 505–26.

Seitenbecher, Manuel, *Mahler, Maschke und Co: Rechtes Denken in der 68er-Bewegung?* (Paderborn, 2013).

Sheehan, James, *Where Have All the Soldiers Gone? The Transformation of Modern Europe* (Boston, MA and New York, 2009).

Siegfried, Detlef, 'Zwischen Aufarbeitung und Schlussstrich. Der Umgang mit der NS-Vergangenheit in den beiden deutschen Staaten 1958 bis 1969', in *Dynamische Zeiten. Die 60er Jahre in den beiden deutschen Gesellschaften*, edited by Axel Schildt, Detlef Siegfried, and Karl Christian Lammers (Hamburg, 2000), 77–113.

Siegfried, Detlef, '"Don't Trust Anyone Older Than 30?" Voices of Conflict and Consensus between Generations in 1960s West Germany'. *Journal of Contemporary History*, 40, 4 (2005), 727–44.

Siegfried, Detlef, *Time is on My Side: Konsum und Politik in der westdeutschen Jugendkultur der 60er Jahre* (Göttingen, 2006).

Siegfried, Detlef, 'Stars der Revolte: Die Kommune 1', *Medien und Imagepolitik im 20. Jahrhundert: Deutschland, Europa, USA*, edited by Daniela Münkel and Lu Seegers (Frankfurt am Main, 2008), 229–45.

Siegfried, Detlef, *1968: Protest, Revolte, Gegenkultur* (Ditzingen, 2018).

Silies, Eva-Maria, 'Ein, zwei, viele Bewegungen? Die Diversität der Neuen Frauenbewegung in den 1970er Jahren in der Bundesrepublik', in *Linksalternatives Milieu und Neue Soziale Bewegungen in den 1970er Jahren*, edited by Cordia Baumann, Sebastian Gehrig, and Nicholas Büchse (Heidelberg, 2011), 87–106.

Silies, Eva-Maria, *Liebe, Lust und Last: Die Pille als weibliche Generationserfahrung in der Bundesrepublik 1960–1980* (Göttingen, 2010).

Slobodian, Quinn, *Foreign Front: Third World Politics in Sixties West Germany* (Durham, NC, 2012).

Slobodian, Quinn, 'Germany's 1968 and Its Enemies'. *The American Historical Review*, 123, 3, (2018), 749–52.

Sluga, Glenda, *Internationalism in the Age of Nationalism* (Philadelphia, PA, 2013).

Spohr, Kristina, *The Global Chancellor: Helmut Schmidt and the Reshaping of the International Order* (New York, 2016).

Stallmann, Martin, *Die Erfindung von '1968': Der studentische Protest im bundesdeutschen Fernsehen 1977–1998* (Göttingen, 2017).

Stargardt, Nicholas, *Witnesses of War: Children's Lives Under the Nazis* (London, 2004).

Stargardt, Nicholas, *The German War: A Nation Under Arms, 1939–1945: Citizens and Soldiers* (New York, 2015).

Steber, Martina, *Die Hüter der Begriffe: Politische Sprachen des Konservativen in Großbritannien und der Bundesrepublik Deutschland 1945–1980* (Berlin, 2017).

Steinbacher, Sibylle, *Wie der Sex nach Deutschland kam: Der Kampf um Sittlichkeit und Anstand in der frühen Bundesrepublik* (Munich, 2011).

Steinmetz, Willibald, ed., *Political Languages in the Age of Extremes* (Oxford, 2011).

Stenger, Joseph, *La Schüler-Union: Etude d'un mouvement politique de jeunes lycéens en République Fédérale allemande de 1972 à 1980* (Frankfurt am Main, Bern, 1981).

Stoff, Heiko, '"Ungeheuer schlaff". Der Film "Zur Sache, Schätzchen" (1968)—Über Leistungsdenken und Gedankenspiele'. *Zeithistorische Forschungen*, 11, 3 (2014), 500–7.

Stolle, Michael, 'Inbegriff des Unrechtsstaates. Zur Wahrnehmung der chilenischen Diktatur in der deutschsprachigen Presse zwischen 1973 und 1989'. *Zeitschrift für Geschichtswissenschaft*, 51, 9 (2003), 793–813.

Sturges, Paul, 'Collective Biography in the 1980s'. *Biography*, 6, 4 (1983), 316–32.

Suri, Jeremi, *Power and Protest: Global Revolution and the Rise of Detente* (Cambridge, MA, 2003).

Sziedat, Konrad, *Erwartungen im Umbruch: Die westdeutsche Linke und das Ende des 'real existierenden Sozialismus'* (Munich, 2019).

Tent, James F., *The Free University of Berlin: A Political History* (Bloomington, IN, 1988).

Terhoeven, Petra, *Deutscher Herbst in Europa: Der Linksterrorismus der siebziger Jahre als transnationales Phänomen* (Munich, 2014).

Teune, Simon, 'Humour as a Guerrilla Tactic: The West German Student Movement's Mockery of the Establishment'. *International Review of Social History*, 52 (2007), 115–32.

Thamer, Hans-Ulrich, 'Die NS-Vergangenheit im politischen Diskurs der 68er-Bewegung'. *Westfälische Forschungen*, 48, edited by Karl Teppe (1998), 39–53.

Ther, Philipp, *Europe Since 1989* (Princeton, NJ, 2016).

Thomas, Nick, *Protest Movements in 1960s West Germany: A Social History of Dissent and Democracy* (New York, 2003).

Thome, Helmut, 'Wandel gesellschaftlicher Wertvorstellungen aus der Sicht der empirischen Sozialforschung', in *Gab es den Wertewandel? Neue Forschungen zum gesellschaftlich-kulturellen Wandel seit den 1960er Jahren*, edited by Bernhard Dietz, Christopher Neumaier, and Andreas Rödder (Munich, 2014), 41–68.

Thuss, Holger and Bence Bauer, *Students on the Right Way: European Democrat Students 1961–2011* (Brussels, 2012).

Tichenor, Kimba Allie, 'Protecting Unborn Life in the Secular Age: The Catholic Church and the West German Abortion Debate, 1969-1989'. *Central European History*, 47, 3 (2014), 612–45.

Tilly, Charles, *Stories, Identities and Political Change* (Oxford, 2002).

Troche, Alexander, *'Berlin wird am Mekong verteidigt': Die Ostasienpolitik der Bundesrepublik in China, Taiwan und Süd-Vietnam, 1954–1966* (Düsseldorf, 2000).

Ullrich, Sebastian, *Der Weimar-Komplex: Das Scheitern der ersten deutschen Demokratie und die politische Kultur der Bundesrepublik 1945–1959* (Göttingen, 2009).

Varon, Jeremy, *Bringing the War Home: The Weather Underground, the Red Army Faction, and Revolutionary Violence in the Sixties and Seventies* (Berkeley, CA, 2004).

Verheyen, Nina, *Diskussionslust: Eine Kulturgeschichte des 'besseren Arguments' in Westdeutschland* (Göttingen, 2010).

Vinen, Richard, *Bourgeois Politics in France, 1945–1951* (Cambridge, 1995).

Vinen, Richard, *The Long '68: Radical Protest and Its Enemies* (London, 2018).

vom Hofe, Ina, *Die Frauenpolitik der CDU: Traditionen, Entwicklungen, Einflüsse 1945–2013* (Sankt Augustin and Berlin, 2017).

von Bülow, Mathilde, *West Germany, Cold War Europe and the Algerian War* (Cambridge, 2016).

von Dannenberg, Julia, *The Foundations of Ostpolitik: The Making of the Moscow Treaty Between West Germany and the USSR* (Oxford, 2008).

von der Goltz, Anna, 'Eine Gegen-Generation von "1968"? Politische Polarisierung und konservative Mobilisierung an westdeutschen Universitäten', in *Die 70er Jahre als schwarzes Jahrzehnt: Politisierungs- und Mobilisierungsprozesse zwischen rechter Mitte und extremer Rechter in Italien und der Bundesrepublik 1967–1982*, edited by Massimiliano Livi, Daniel Schmidt and Michael Sturm (Frankfurt am Main, 2010), 73–90.

von der Goltz, Anna, ed., *Talkin' 'Bout My Generation: Conflicts of Generation Building and Europe's "1968"* (Göttingen, 2011).

von der Goltz, Anna, 'A Polarized Generation? Conservative Students and West Germany's "1968"', in *Talkin' 'Bout My Generation: Conflicts of Generation Building and Europe's '1968'*, edited by Anna von der Goltz (Göttingen, 2011), 195–215.

von der Goltz, Anna, 'Generations Of 68ers'. *Cultural And Social History*, 8, 4 (2011), 473–91.

von der Goltz, Anna, 'Von alten Kämpfern, sexy Wahlgirls und zornigen jungen Frauen. Überlegungen zur Beziehung von Generationalität, Geschlecht und Populärkultur im gemäßigt-rechten Lager um 1968', in *Hot Stuff: Gender, Popkultur und Generationalität in West- und Osteuropa nach 1945*, edited by Lu Seegers (Göttingen, 2015), 29–51.

von der Goltz, Anna, 'Other '68ers in West Berlin: Christian Democratic Students and the Cold War City'. *Central European History*, 50, 1 (2017), 86–112.

von der Goltz, Anna, 'A Vocal Minority: Student Activism of the Center-Right and West Germany's 1968', in *Inventing the Silent Majority in Western Europe and the United States: Conservatism in the 1960s and 1970s*, edited by Anna von der Goltz and Britta Waldschmidt-Nelson (Cambridge, 2017), 82–104.

von der Goltz, Anna and Britta Waldschmidt-Nelson, eds, *Inventing the Silent Majority in Western Europe and the United States: Conservatism in the 1960s and 1970s* (Cambridge, 2017).

von Lucke, Albrecht, *68 oder neues Biedermeier: Der Kampf um die Deutungsmacht* (Berlin, 2008).

von Hodenberg, Christina, *Das andere Achtundsechzig: Gesellschaftsgeschichte einer Revolte* (Munich, 2018).

von Hodenberg, Christina, *Konsens und Krise: Eine Geschichte der westdeutschen Medienöffentlichkeit, 1945 bis 1973* (Göttingen, 2006).

von Hodenberg, Christina and Detlef Siegfried, eds, *Wo „1968' liegt: Reform und Revolte in der Geschichte der Bundesrepublik* (Göttingen, 2006).

von Miquel, Marc, *Ahnden oder amnestieren? Westdeutsche Justiz und Vergangenheitsbewältigung in den sechziger Jahren* (Göttingen, 2004).

Walter, Franz and Frank Bösch, 'Das Ende des christdemokratischen Zeitalters? Zur Zukunft eines Erfolgsmodells', in *Die CDU nach Kohl*, edited by Tobias Dürr and Rüdiger Soldt (Frankfurt am Main, 1998), 46–58.

Weberling, Johannes, *Für Freiheit und Menschenrechte: Der Ring Christlich-Demokratischer Studenten (RCDS), 1945–1986* (Düsseldorf, 1990).

Weckenbrock, Christoph, *Schwarz-Grün für Deutschland? Wie aus politischen Erzfeinden Bündnispartner wurden* (Bielefeld, 2017).

Wehler, Hans Ulrich, *Deutsche Gesellschaftsgeschichte:* vol. 5: *Bundesrepublik und DDR 1949–1990* (Munich, 2008).

Wehrs, Nikolai, *Der Protest der Professoren: Der 'Bund der Freiheit der Wissenschaft' in den 1970er Jahren* (Göttingen, 2014).

Weinhauer, Klaus, *Schutzpolizei in der Bundesrepublik: Zwischen Bürgerkrieg und Innerer Sicherheit: Die turbulenten sechziger Jahre* (Paderborn, 2003).

Weinhauer, Klaus, 'Zwischen "Partisanenkampf" und "Kommissar Computer": Polizei und Linksterrorismus in der Bundesrepublik bis Anfang der 1980er Jahre', in *Terrorismus in der Bundesrepublik: Medien, Staat und Subkulturen in den 1970er Jahren*, edited by Klaus Weinhauer, Jörg Requate, and Heinz-Gerhard Haupt (Frankfurt am Main, 2006), 244–70.

Weinke, Anette, *Die Verfolgung von NS-Tätern im geteilten Deutschland: Vergangenheitsbewältigungen 1949–1969, oder: eine deutsch-deutsche Beziehungsgeschichte im Kalten Krieg* (Paderborn, 2002).

Weisbrod, Bernd, 'Generation und Generationalität in der Neueren Geschichte'. *Aus Politik und Zeitgeschichte* (2005), B8, 3–9.

Weisbrod, Bernd, ed., *Historische Beiträge zur Generationsforschung* (Göttingen, 2009).

Weiß, Volker, *Die autoritäre Revolte: Die Neue Rechte und der Untergang des Abendlandes* (Stuttgart, 2017).

Weiss, Michael, 'Bildt in a Day'. *Foreign Policy*, 8 May 2014.

Weitbrecht, Dorothee, *Aufbruch in die Dritte Welt: Der Internationalismus der Studentenbewegung von 1968 in der Bundesrepublik* (Göttingen, 2012).

Weitz, Eric D., 'The Ever-Present Other: Communism in the Making of West Germany', in *The Miracle Years: A Cultural History of West Germany, 1949–1968*, edited by Hanna Schissler (Princeton, NJ, 2001), 219–32.

Wetterau, Karin, *68—Täterkinder und Rebellen: Familienroman einer Revolte* (Bielefeld, 2017).

Whalen, Jack and Richard Flacks, *Beyond the Barricades: The Sixties Generation Grows Up* (Chicago, IL, 1990).

Whittier, Nancy, 'Political Generations, Micro-Cohorts and the Transformation of Social Movements'. *American Sociological Review*, 62 (1997), 760–78.

Wienhaus, Andrea, *Bildungswege zu '1968': Eine Kollektivbiografie des Sozialistischen Deutschen Studentenbundes* (Bielefeld, 2014).

Wierling, Dorothee, *Geboren im Jahr Eins: Der Jahrgang 1949 in der DDR: Versuch einer Kollektivbiographie* (Berlin, 2002).

Wierling, Dorothee, '"Kriegskinder": westdeutsch, bürgerlich, männlich?', in *Die „Generation der Kriegskinder". Historische Hintergründe und Deutungen*, edited by Lu Seegers and Jürgen Reulecke (Gießen, 2009), 141–55.

Wildenthal, Lora, *The Language of Human Rights in West Germany* (Philadelphia, PA, 2013).

Wildt, Michael, *Generation of the Unbound: The Leadership Corps of the Reich Security Main Office* (Jerusalem, 2002).

Wildt, Michael, 'Die Angst vor dem Volk. Ernst Fraenkel in der deutschen Nachkriegsgesellschaft', in *„Ich staune, dass Sie in dieser Luft atmen können": Jüdische Intellektuelle in Deutschland nach 1945*, edited by Monika Boll and Raphael Gross (Frankfurt am Main, 2013), 317–44.

Wiliarty, Sarah Elise, *The CDU and the Politics of Gender in Germany: Bringing Women to the Party* (Cambridge, 2010).

Winckler, Stefan, 'Die Welt—Ein Sprachrohr der schweigenden Mehrheit? Die Gegnerschaft zu den politischen Demonstrationen der Studenten 1967/68 aus publizistikwissenschaftlicher Sicht', in *Die 68er und ihre Gegner: Der Widerstand gegen die Kulturrevolution*, edited by Stefan Winckler, Felix Dirsch, and Hartmuth Becker (Graz and Stuttgart, 2004), 183–207.

Winckler, Stefan, Felix Dirsch, and Hartmuth Becker, eds, *Die 68er und ihre Gegner: Der Widerstand gegen die Kulturrevolution*, edited by (Graz and Stuttgart, 2004).

Winkler, Heinrich August, *Der lange Weg nach Westen*, vol. 2: *Deutsche Geschichte vom 'Dritten Reich' bis zur Wiedervereinigung* (Munich, 2000).

Winkler, Willi, 'Adolf Eichmann und seine Verteidiger: Ein kleiner Nachtrag zur Rechtsgeschichte', *Einsicht: Bulletin des Fritz-Bauer-Instituts*, 5 (2011), 33–41.

Wirsching, Andreas. *Abschied vom Provisorium: Geschichte der Bundesrepublik Deutschland 1982–1990* (Munich, 2006).

Wirsching, Andreas, 'Eine "Ära Kohl"? Die widersprüchliche Signatur deutscher Regierungspolitik 1982–1998'. *Archiv für Sozialgeschichte*, 52 (2012), 667–84.

Wolfrum, Edgar, Die *geglückte Demokratie: Geschichte der Bundesrepublik und ihren Anfängen* (Stuttgart, 2006).

Wolfrum, Edgar, *Rot-Grün an der Macht: Deutschland 1998–2005* (Munich, 2013).

Wüst, Jürgen, *Menschenrechtsarbeit im Zwielicht: Zwischen Staatssicherheit und Antifaschismus* (Bonn, 1999).

Yow, Valerie R., *Recording Oral History: A Guide for the Humanities and Social Sciences* (Walnut Creek, CA, 2005).

Zellmer, Elisabeth, 'Protestieren und Polarisieren. Frauenbewegung und Feminismus der 1970er Jahre in München', in *Zeitgeschichte als Geschlechtergeschichte: Neue Perspektiven auf die Bundesrepublik*, edited by Julia Paulus, Eva-Maria Silies, and Kerstin Wolff (Frankfurt am Main, 2012), 284–96.

Ziemann, Benjamin, *Encounters with Modernity: The Catholic Church in West Germany 1945–1975* (Oxford, 2014).

Zinnecker, Jürgen, '"Das Problem der Generationen": Überlegungen zu Karl Mannheims kanonischem Text', in *Generationalität unβd Lebensgeschichte im 20. Jahrhundert*, edited by Jürgen Reulecke and Elisabeth Müller-Luckner (Munich, 2003), 33–58.

Unpublished PhD theses

Beacock, Ian, *Heartbroken: Democratic Emotions, Political Subject and the Unravelling of the Weimar Republic, 1918–1933* (PhD dissertation, Stanford University, 2018).

Brandt, Sebastian *Universität und Öffentlichkeit: Das Beispiel der Albert-Ludwigs-Universität Freiburg, 1945–1975* (Dr Phil dissertation, Albert-Ludwigs-Universität Freiburg, 2014).

Macartney, Alexander Finn, *War in the Postwar: Japan and West Germany Protest the Vietnam War and the Global Strategy of Imperialism* (PhD dissertation, Georgetown University, 2019).

Spreen, David, *Cold War Imaginaries: Mao's China and the Making of a Postcolonial Far Left in Divided Germany* (PhD dissertation, University of Michigan, 2019).

Index

Note: Figures are indicated by an italic '*f*', respectively, following the page number.

For the benefit of digital users, indexed terms that span two pages (e.g., 52–53) may, on occasion, appear on only one of those pages.